# THE RULE OF LAW

NOMOS

## XXXVI

# NOMOS

**Harvard University Press**
I          *Authority* 1958, reissued in 1982 by Greenwood
           Press

**The Liberal Arts Press**
II         *Community* 1959
III        *Responsibility* 1960

**Atherton Press**
IV         *Liberty* 1962
V          *The Public Interest* 1962
VI         *Justice* 1963, reissued in 1974
VII        *Rational Decision* 1964
VIII       *Revolution* 1966
IX         *Equality* 1967
X          *Representation* 1968
XI         *Voluntary Associations* 1969
XII        *Political and Legal Obligation* 1970
XIII       *Privacy* 1971

**Aldine-Atherton Press**
XIV        *Coercion* 1972

**Lieber-Atherton Press**
XV         *The Limits of Law* 1974
XVI        *Participation in Politics* 1975

**New York University Press**
XVII       *Human Nature in Politics* 1977
XVIII      *Due Process* 1977
XIX        *Anarchism* 1978
XX         *Constitutionalism* 1979
XXI        *Compromise in Ethics, Law, and Politics* 1979
XXII       *Property* 1980
XXIII      *Human Rights* 1981
XXIV       *Ethics, Economics, and the Law* 1982

# NOMOS XXXVI

Yearbook of The American Society for Political and Legal Philosophy

# THE RULE OF LAW

Edited by

**Ian Shapiro,** *Yale University*

NEW YORK UNIVERSITY PRESS *New York and London*

NEW YORK UNIVERSITY PRESS
New York and London

*The Rule of Law: NOMOS XXXVI*
edited by Ian Shapiro
Copyright © 1994 by New York University
Manufactured in the United States of America

Library of Congress Cataloging-in-Publication Data
The Rule of law / edited by Ian Shapiro.
p.   cm.—(Nomos ; 36)
Based on presentations and commentaries from the annual meeting of
the American Society for Political and Legal Philosophy, held in
conjunction with the Association of American Law Schools in San
Antonio, January 1992.
Includes bibliographical references and index.
ISBN 0-8147-7983-2 (acid-free paper)
1. Rule of law—United States.   2. Rule of law.   I. Shapiro, Ian.
II. American Society for Political and Legal Philosophy, Meeting
(1992 : San Antonio, Tex.)   III. Association of American Law
Schools.   IV. Series.
KF382.R85   1994
340'.11—dc20          93-30298
                    CIP

10   9   8   7   6   5   4   3   2   1

*For John Chapman*

# CONTENTS

# PREFACE

This, the thirty-sixth volume of NOMOS, grew out of presentations and commentaries at the annual meeting of the American Society for Political and Legal Philosophy that was held in conjunction with the Association of American Law Schools in San Antonio in January 1992. The subject discussed at that meeting, selected by the vote of the society's members, was "The Rule of Law." I am grateful to Randy Barnett for organizing the program.

I would like to thank all the contributors for meeting tight production deadlines with uncommon efficiency and good humor; without them there would have been no volume. Thanks are also due to our tireless managing editor Kathryn McDermott for keeping the various appropriate wheels turning in the right directions, and to Despina Papazoglou Gimbel and Niko Pfund of NYU Press for guiding the manuscript skillfully into print.

I.S.

# CONTRIBUTORS

ROBERT A. BURT
*Law, Yale University*

STEVEN J. BURTON
*Law, University of Iowa*

WILLIAM N. ESKRIDGE, Jr.
*Law, Georgetown University*

JOHN FEREJOHN
*Political Science, Stanford University*

RICHARD FLATHMAN
*Political Science, Johns Hopkins University*

GERALD F. GAUS
*Political Science, University of Minnesota—Duluth*

JEAN HAMPTON
*Philosophy, University of Arizona*

RUSSELL HARDIN
*Political Science and Philosophy, University of Chicago*

JAMES JOHNSON
*Political Science, University of Rochester*

*Contributors*

# INTRODUCTION

## IAN SHAPIRO

From the sprawling remnants of the Soviet empire to the southern tip of Africa, attempts are underway to replace arbitrary political regimes with governments constrained by the rule of law. This ideal, which subordinates the wills of individuals, social movements, and even, sometimes, democratically elected majorities, to the requirements of law, has always had its critics. Yet in parts of the world where the rule of law is lacking, its benefits are manifested by their absence; small wonder that the ideal persists in the modern intellectual consciousness.

The rule of law promises predictability in social life by placing constitutional limits on the kinds of powers that governments may legitimately exercise, as well as on the extent of those governmental powers. Historically, it evolved out of the seventeenth-century idea of limited government and was buttressed by the eighteenth-century republican commitment to the separation of powers among different governmental agencies. Advocated in its modern form first by Montesquieu and the authors of *The Federalist Papers,* it was enshrined in the American Constitution and subsequently embedded in the political order by the Supreme Court in *Marbury v. Madison* in 1803. In his opinion for the Court in that case, Chief Justice Marshall insisted that "it is, emphatically, the province of the judicial department to say what the law is," thereby assuring the Court's power to review the constitutional validity of actions

1

taken by other branches of the national government.[1] These developments ensured that, in the American context at least, arguments about the rule of law would henceforth be dominated by debates about the proper place of courts in a democratic constitutional order.

Those seeking relief from the arbitrary exercise of power in the contemporary world appeal to democracy at least as often as they appeal to the rule of law. Yet there are tensions between the two ideals. Whereas democracy revolves around infusing the law with the will of the majority, the appeal of the rule of law is an appeal to its supremacy over the wills of persons, however measured or aggregated. The authors in part 1 of this volume are centrally concerned with this tension, which turns out to be considerably more complex than the preceding summary statement might imply. For Jean Hampton contemporary democracy is distinctive in being based on the rule of law. In the opening chapter she argues that democracy's viability rests on the existence of metarules, built into the political process, that are designed to allow people to reconcile their differing points of view. Accordingly, she rejects the Hobbesian contention that a workable political order must be founded on political will as opposed to legal rules. On the contrary, she argues that Hobbes's contractarian method implies commitments both to the supremacy of the rule of law and to the idea that the law should have a certain democratic content. Ironically, this saddles Hobbes with a legacy that he would doubtless have resisted: that of being the father of modern democracy.

For Catherine Valcke, Hampton's reconciliation of democracy with the rule of law via a theory of metarules that are implicit in the social contract does not go sufficiently far. Whereas Hampton's account confines citizens' input to the political process, on Valcke's Lockean view it should also shape the product of political activity. This more expansive view of citizen action leads Valcke to defend the right to civil disobedience as essential to reconciling democracy with the rule of law via a social contract theory. She proposes that we think of civil disobedience as having been agreed upon by all parties to the social contract as the mechanism by which citizens manifest to officials their disapproval of enacted laws. Since the disobeying citizens readily undergo the sanctions provided by officials for the violation of the laws, such disobedience constitutes no challenge to the officials' legislative authority. On Valcke's theory, therefore, civil disobedience does not amount to a failure to perform the social contract; rather, it follows from the contract's very terms.

In chapter 3, Michael Zuckert stands back and evaluates the contest between Hobbesian and Lockean conceptions of the rule of law in which Hampton and Valcke are engaged. He demurs from the contentions of both sides that the other violates the spirit if not the letter of the rule of law ideal. He argues that consideration of the contemporary debate in light of the historical Hobbes and Locke suggests that neither side has a corner on commitment to the rule of law. Insofar as contemporary theorists do reproduce the debate between Hobbes and Locke (which they do only to a degree), the confrontation between the two seventeenth-century philosophers helps reveal why the rule of law is a problem, perhaps insoluble, for contractarian political theory.

Robert Burt defends a different democratic conception of the rule of law than either the neo-Hobbesian or the neo-Lockean one in chapter 4, and he explores its implications for the legitimacy of the death penalty. In Burt's view, as elaborated in *The Constitution in Conflict,* the democratic ideal confronts the perpetual possibility of internal contradiction deriving from its dual commitments to majority rule and to an antihierarchical principle of nondomination. Whenever a majority seeks to dominate a minority through the democratic process, democracy goes to war with itself. An institutional mechanism is needed to resolve the conflict; this is supplied, on Burt's account, by a conception of the rule of law that entitles a nonlegislative body such as a constitutional court continually to require legislatures to rethink and revamp policies that result in domination.[2]

In his chapter here Burt applies this jurisprudence to contemporary debates about the death penalty for murder. Arguing that a murderer clearly violates the democratic rights of his or her victims, Burt holds that they are entitled to defend themselves from the murderer via the sanction of the law. But in order to uphold democracy's commitment to the principle of nondomination, the dominant party—whether in legislative voting or in criminal law regulation—must not abandon the possibility of a future relationship based on mutuality with the dominated party. Inflicting death on the dominated party, no matter what past conduct might seem to warrant this infliction, constitutes a renunciation rather than a defense of the nondomination principle. Moreover, Burt contends that administration of the death penalty is inconsistent with democracy's commitment to nondomination in dealing with convicted murderers. Basing his argument on appeals to past social experience and psychoanalytic tenets in individual psychology, he contends that use of the death penalty is also likely to displace the nondomination principle in social relations generally between majorities and minorities.

Thus far we have been concerned with the tensions between the rule of law and other, democratic values. In part 2 the authors focus centrally on the centuries-old debate about the meaning of the rule of law itself. For the present generation many of the terms of this debate have been structured by Ronald Dworkin's seminal attack on the late H. L. A. Hart's legal positivism. Although Hart's argument was subtler and more complex than that of the classic nineteenth-century legal positivist John Austin, Hart had affirmed the basic positivist view that in every functioning legal order there will be an accepted test for determining which standards count as law and which do not. Dworkin challenged this, arguing that in complex legal systems such as Great Britain and the United States no such agreed-upon test exists and that as a result there is no sharp distinction between legal and moral standards, as the positivists had insisted there was.[3] Dworkin argued that the positivist thesis can seem plausible only if we focus on simple legal rules and statutes. In the real legal world, however, lawyers and judges argue and decide cases by appeal not only to such black letter rules but also to other sorts of standards that he described as legal principles. The scope for interpretation opened up by this reality was so extensive, Dworkin argued, that legal discretion could not be counted on to fill in the gaps where the law is silent or ambiguous; nor could it be reduced to some higher-order system of legal rules. Instead, he contended that any coherent jurisprudence must depend on a moral defense of the legal principles that infuse and shape the interpretation of statutes and legal arguments; hence his subsequent attempt to come up with a theory of interpretation to which the enduring integrity of the law is central.[4]

In chapter 5, Michael Walzer pursues the antipositivist case into the history of Jewish law; he demonstrates that a pluralistic written law can arise even in the absence of a pluralistic legal doctrine. The three separate legal codes contained in Exodus, Leviticus, and Deuteronomy differ in many significant respects, he notes, even though all three were understood to be the revealed commands of a single divine lawgiver. Walzer contends that the differences among the codes most likely reflect debates among the religious elites that compiled them. But the authors could not explicitly replace the codes or harmonize them with one another, he argues, because they could not acknowledge their own authorship of the divine law. "In principle they were articulating the content of the Sinai covenant; in practice they were deciding—more than once—what that should be." Such unacknowledged lawmaking continued throughout the medieval era, on Walzer's account. A pluralistic Jewish law evolved because of the conflicting ways in which rabbis understood and interpreted the authority of the divine lawgiver.

The room and need for judicial interpretation arises not only because of the indeterminacy of statutory and established law; in the West there is an equity tradition, traceable to Aristotle at least, which authorizes judges to depart from legal rules in order to do justice in particular cases.[5] Lawrence Solum takes up and defends a version of the Aristotelian view in chapter 6. He argues for a virtue-centered theory of judging on the grounds that only virtuous judges can be expected to exercise equitable powers well. They alone will have the necessary wisdom and judicial integrity to act with fidelity toward the purposes and principles immanent in the law.

Yet it was the claim that these immanent purposes and principles are indeterminate that the antipositivists had defended, a view that Stephen Macedo takes up and extends in his critique of Solum in chapter 7. Macedo agrees with Solum that legal rules do not always serve the ends of justice, since every case is

different whereas rules lump cases together. General rules of
law have advantages, in Macedo's view: they promote stability
and predictability, and they act as restraints on those with
power. But in extreme cases, at least, when following the rules
would result in a grave injustice, we want judges to have discretion. How can we manage, if not overcome, the resultant
tension?

Macedo is skeptical of Solum's answer for traditional liberal
reasons. He thinks that Solum both underdescribes the range of
virtues that would be necessary to accomplish the relevant task
and overestimates our capacity to secure judges who exhibit the
relevant virtues. Moreover, he argues that no amount of virtue
is likely to overcome our disagreements about how discretionary
power should be exercised. The practical wisdom Macedo advocates consists in accepting and managing, rather than seeking to
overcome, the tension between rules and discretion. This claim
leads Macedo to defend a moderate version of the conservative
critique of judicial activism. Resolving too many politically divi-
sive issues of legal interpretation on grounds of basic principle
could destabilize our politics, he argues in conclusion. We
should therefore understand and accept that the tension between law and discretion cannot be resolved, and draw the
appropriate moral that moderating judicial activism is desirable.

In chapter 8, Steven Burton also contests Solum's proposed
solution to the problem of judicial discretion. Arguing that par-
ticularist adjudication can never be reconciled with the rule of
law, he rejects the appeal to a virtue-centered theory as an
appropriate constraint on such particularism. However, he
makes the case that this need not commit us either to a legal
positivist or to a Dworkinian position. Rather, Burton defends
an open-ended, yet rule-bound, theory of adjudication. On this
view the law guides the process of adjudication by limiting the
kinds of reasons that may be taken into account by judges in
their exercise of judicial discretion. Specifically, it excludes ad
hominem reasons and "all moral and policy reasons not warranted by the conventional law as grounds for judicial decisions." In this way Burton acknowledges the decisive character
of Dworkin's critique of positivism, yet he comes up with a

response to it that is more strongly circumscribed by the letter of the law than is Dworkin's own solution.

Issues about the indeterminacy of laws and equitable discretion do not exhaust the circumstances in which the rule of law can be problematic. In part 3 the authors take up the constraints that rationality might reasonably be thought to require of the rule of law. If the rule of law is desirable partly because it is rational, then departures from that rule might also be desirable in the event that they can be shown to be rational. This is Russell Hardin's subject in chapter 9. "Does one who shares the morality behind the law have an obligation to obey the law from her own moral commitments?" he asks. His answer is a decisive no. The law may have the form or content it has, he argues, partly for epistemological reasons. Police, judges, and others in the justice system may have access to some kinds of knowledge that potential lawbreakers do not have, and they may be hampered by lack of other kinds of knowledge that these individuals have. For this reason, he contends, there may be circumstances in which it is right for a person to break a law, even when that person regards the law in question as morally justified. On the same account, Hardin concludes, we should not think it paradoxical to say that it can be right for the law to punish an individual who has acted rightly in breaking the law.

David Schmidtz contests this analysis in part in chapter 10. Distinguishing between morality as it applies to personal conduct and morality as it applies to institutional structure, he argues that morally justified institutional constraints are moral constraints of a particular sort. This is so notwithstanding the fact that they may conflict with obligations that derive from morality's personal strand. Schmidtz agrees with Hardin that differing information-gathering capacities can drive a wedge between what utilitarianism prescribes for institutions and what it prescribes for personal behavior, but, in contrast to Hardin, he argues that much of the divergence is accounted for by the fact that "utilitarian institutions are not formulated with utilitarian individuals in mind."

Jack Knight and Jim Johnson explore a different dimension of the relation between rationality and the rule of law in chapter

11, as they examine a number of recent efforts to employ rational choice models to support normative theories of statutory interpretation. These models assume that statutes are products of political competition, as a result of which individual preferences are aggregated into collective outcomes. The standard rational choice conclusion is that statutes generated by such processes are incoherent, if coherence is understood as reflecting a statement of the general will of the people in a democratic society. Knight and Johnson assess three attempts to salvage the legitimacy of statutes within the rational choice tradition: statutes conceived of as efficient contracts, statutes made coherent via appeals to conventional canons of interpretation, and statutes supplemented by appeal to public values at points where coherence is lacking. Knight and Johnson argue that each of the three proposals fails adequately to resolve the challenge presented by the public choice tradition, and they conclude with some suggestions concerning what such a resolution might involve.

William Eskridge and John Ferejohn defend a different model of rational statutory interpretation in chapter 12. They argue that a legal system satisfies the requirements of the rule of law if its commands are general, knowable, and performable. Like Knight and Johnson, they appeal to the rational choice tradition. Their contention is that democratic processes cannot be expected to produce statutes that are compatible with the rule of law as they have defined it. The task of courts, they argue, is to resolve the resulting tension. They examine various theories of how this might best be achieved, including the new textualist theories of Frank Easterbrook and Antonin Scalia, and Dworkin's strong normativism. Against these views they argue for the centrality of interpretive regimes to statutory interpretation. These are "collections of presumptions, canons, and methodologies that are held together by deeper conceptions of the nature of the political process." Whereas many recent students of interpretation contend that judges should take account of the structure and characteristic pathologies of legislatures in the course of interpreting the law, Eskridge and Ferejohn argue that legislators anticipate that courts will interpret statutes in certain characteristic and predictable ways, and that judges should take account of *that*. This leads Eskridge and Ferejohn to a defense of a version of the traditional legal process view against the new textualism, via novel discussions of the appropriate place of presumptions about legislative purposes and of the status of conventional canons of judicial interpretation.

Reasoned commitment to the rule of law is preeminently a liberal commitment, yet there are also tensions between liberalism and the rule of law, as the chapters in part 4, on the limits of the rule of law, remind us. In chapter 13, Richard Flathman explores this tension via an account of the ideology and practice of institutionalism, which, he says, "promotes order and regularity in human conduct and interactions." Thus characterized, he argues, institutionalism is both necessary to, and in conflict with, the liberal ideals of individuality, pluralism, and freedom. Flathman contends that the rule of law, which champions predictability through imperative command and mandatory obedience but is nevertheless widely valued by liberals, exemplifies this never fully resolvable tension within liberalism. By exploring ambiguities and dissonances within and surrounding the ideology of the rule of law, he urges liberals to adopt a cautious and distancing stance toward it, and toward institutionalism generally.

In contrast to Flathman, Gerald Gaus resolves the tension between liberalism and the rule of law in the latter's favor in our final chapter. He sketches a theory of the rule of law in which he shows how the disparate liberal commitments to formalism, substantive justice, the legal regulation of public authority, and the moral obligation to obey the law all fit together as justified aspects of a coherent account of the rule of law. The foundation of this theory is the fundamental liberal commitment to public justification of the principles of justice. Gaus contends that public reasoning is inconclusive, however, as to precisely which principles of justice are publicly justified and exactly how abstractly justified principles are to be applied to political practice. Because of this, he argues that liberal citizens committed publicly to justifying their demands on others are led to a certain sort of political authority—an umpire—to resolve their practical disputes about justice. This move inevitably

politicizes debates about the rule of law, bringing us full circle
to the arguments about democracy and the rule of law with
which we began.

## NOTES

1. 6 U.S. (1 Cranch) 137 (1803). The republican doctrine of separation of powers has distant historical roots, as has been demonstrated
brilliantly by J. G. A. Pocock in *The Machiavellian Moment: Florentine
Political Thought and the Atlantic Republican Tradition* (Princeton, N.J.:
Princeton University Press, 1975).

2. Robert A. Burt, *The Constitution in Conflict* (Cambridge, Mass:
Harvard University Press, 1992).

3. H. L. A. Hart, *The Concept of Law* (Oxford: Clarendon, 1961);
Ronald Dworkin, *Taking Rights Seriously* (Cambridge, Mass: Harvard
University Press, 1978).

4. Ronald Dworkin, *A Matter of Principle* (Cambridge, Mass: Harvard University Press, 1985), and *Law's Empire* (Cambridge, Mass: Harvard University Press, 1986).

5. Aristotle, *Nicomachean Ethics*, in *The Complete Works of Aristotle*,
Jonathan Barnes, ed. (Princeton, N.J.: Princeton University Press,
1984), 2:1795–97.

# PART I

# DEMOCRACY AND THE RULE OF LAW

# 1

# DEMOCRACY AND
# THE RULE OF LAW

## JEAN HAMPTON

Prominent Soviet supporters of Boris Yeltsin who defeated the coup of August 1991, when questioned by Western reporters, argued that its defeat vindicated the Soviet people's commitment to two important ideals: first, the ideal of democracy, and second, the ideal of the "rule of law." The thesis of this paper is that these two ideals are connected, and that we should understand contemporary democracy as a style of government quite unlike the ancient Greek democracies heavily criticized by early modern political theorists, insofar as it is based on the idea of the rule of law and not, as ancient Greek democracies were, on the rule of human will. Indeed, as I shall explain in what follows, it is because James Madison identified democracy as a species of will-directed human government that he was so concerned to deny that a United States under the Constitution would be an instance of it.

I shall explicate and defend my thesis in part by arguing against Thomas Hobbes's contention that all political societies must be founded on human will in order properly to be considered political societies. Hobbes maintained that it was logically impossible to have something called a government that was founded on a rule, or set of precepts, put forward in some kind of constitution or contract between the people and the ruler.

Ironically, I will argue that implicit in Hobbes's own contract method is the idea not only that law can be the ultimate governor in a political society but also that the ruling law can and should have what I will call a certain "democratic" content. In a strange way, one might even consider Hobbes the father of modern democracy, although he would have been horrified to have received such a title.

## I. THE TRADITIONAL DEFINITION OF DEMOCRACY

Consider Hobbes's definition of democracy, the main lines of which would be approved by political theorists of ancient Greece and Rome and the Middle Ages:

> The difference of Common-wealths, consisteth in the difference of the Soveraign or the Person representative of all and every one of the Multitude. And because the Soveraignty is either in one Man, or in an Assembly of more than one; and into that Assembly either every man hath right to enter, or not every one, but Certain men distinguished from the rest; it is manifest, there can be but Three kinds of Common-wealth. For the Representative must needs be One man, or More: and if more, then it is the Assembly of All, or but of a Part. When the Representative is One man, then is the Common-wealth a MONARCHY: when an Assembly of All that will come together, then it is a DEMOCRACY, or Popular Common-wealth: when an Assembly of a Part onely, then it is called an ARISTOCRACY. Other kind of Common-wealth there can be none: for either One, or More, or All must have the Soveraign Power (which I have shewn to be indivisible) entire.[1]

Note that Hobbes's categorization assumes that political authority is ultimately a human-directed phenomenon: the three kinds of political authority are merely three ways in which human beings can rule over others. Either all of them can rule, or only some of them, or only one of them. And when all of them rule, the resulting government is defined as a democracy. Thus for Hobbes, *democracy is a species of government based on human will— and in this case, the human will is constituted by all the people.*

Hobbes's definition of governments in terms of *how many humans are doing the ruling* is consciously based upon an argument to the effect that there cannot be a nonhuman, rule-based political authority. The best statement of this argument is to be found in *De Cive*, in the following passage:

> It is therefore manifest, that in every city there is some one man, or council, or court, who by right hath as great a power over each single citizen, as each man hath over himself considered out of that civil state; that is, supreme and absolute, to be limited only by the strength and forces of the city itself, and by nothing else in the world. For if his power were limited, that limitation must necessarily proceed from some greater power. For he that prescribes limits, must have a greater power than he who is confined by them. Now that confining power is either without limit, or is again restrained by some other greater than itself; and so we shall at length arrive to a power, which hath no other limit but that which is the *terminus ultimus* of the forces of all the citizens together. That same is called the supreme command; and if it be committed to a council, a supreme council, but if to one man, the supreme lord of the city.[2]

This "regress argument" is briefly summarized in a passage in *Leviathan:*

> [W]hosoever thinking Soveraign Power too great, will seek to make it lesse, must subject himselfe, to the Power, that can limit it; that is to say, to a greater.[3]

The conclusion of this argument is that in a political society there is a single source of power, beyond which no subject can appeal, and which is authorized to decide any question, resolve any dispute, no matter the content, the history, or the parties involved. This single source of power, called the "Sovereign," must be a kind of human will: either it is a single human will or a collective of human wills acting as one.

But hasn't Hobbes made an obvious mistake here? Even if we grant that a political society must be a "closed" system, with an ultimate authority, must that ultimate authority be human? Why can't it also be a constitution or set of laws, as Kelsen or H. L. A. Hart have argued, which acts as the "final decider" in the regime?[4]

In his expansion of the regress argument in *Leviathan*, Hobbes attempts to show that a final nonhuman decider is impossible. The problems of conflict and disorder that the political society is supposed to cure cannot be cured unless that political society rests on an ultimate and undivided *human* will. After all, argues Hobbes, in any controversy between human beings, only another human being is in a position to decide it, and to enforce that decision. A rule is inherently powerless; it only takes on life if it is interpreted, applied, and enforced by individuals. That set of human beings that has final say over what the rules are, how they should be applied, and how they should be enforced has ultimate control over what these rules actually *are*. *So human beings control the rules,* and not vice versa. Hence, if we agree with Hobbes that the central reason for having a political society is to resolve conflict, and if we agree with his observation that laws alone are unable to resolve anything because their meaning and their power over us are entirely a function of how they are defined, applied, and enforced, then we must accept the conclusion of the regress argument that only a regime with a final human decider who (either directly or through delegates) defines, applies, and enforces these laws is in a position to effect peace, and thus actually *be* a political society. And so, to those who propose that a constitution (limiting the power of a ruler) could be the final decider in a regime, Hobbes insists that this is not a viable form of polity because

> to be subject to Laws, is to be subject to the Common-wealth, that is to the Soveraign Representative, that is, to himselfe; which is not subjection, but freedom from the Lawes. Which errour, because it setteth the Lawes above the Soveraign, setteth also a *Judge* above him, and *a power to punish him;* which is to make a new Soveraign; and again for the same reason a third, to punish the second; and so continually without end, to the Confusion, and Dissolution of the Common-wealth.[5]

Note that Hobbes assumes that a political regime is only in place when one has an authority established that has the potential power to resolve all controversies that could potentially threaten the union. And he argues that laws cannot do this because their nature is such that they are just as able to generate conflict as to resolve it.

In part 2 of *Leviathan*, Hobbes elaborates on why he regards all laws, no matter their content, as worthless as an ultimate foundation of any political unit. Hobbes's position on the inefficacy of laws as governors is based on the following three beliefs:

1. Laws can never be rendered so completely clear that it is obvious to every human being what they mean. Hence they can themselves be the source of conflict unless there is a human being authorized to give the definitive interpretation of them. And if such a human being exists, then *he* is the ultimate authority, and not the laws he interprets, because he has control over them, rather than vice versa.

2. Laws can never be written so that their application to every situation is obvious to every human being. Thus, the question of how they are to be applied can generate controversy, which can only be resolved if a human being is authorized to decide their application in a definitive fashion.

3. Even if it were possible to define laws in a completely clear way, such that their application to any situation would be obvious, Hobbes would still maintain that human nature is such that those who stood to be disadvantaged by their application would be motivated by self-love to insist on defining them in some other, more advantageous way. So laws are often the source of conflict because of the way human nature responds to normative rules that get in the way of self-interest.

Relying on these three assumptions, Hobbes responds to opponents who argue, as Locke was to do later in the century, on behalf of rule-based (and sometimes morally motivated) limits on government power over the people it rules. First, to those who insist that there can and should be a contract between ruler and people, or else some sort of overarching constitution that defines and potentially limits the ruler's power, Hobbes replies in chapter 18 of *Leviathan* that this is merely an attempt to establish a set of rules as ultimate deciders in a regime, and is therefore doomed to fail because it does not incorporate into a political regime the kind of solution to the problem that such regimes are supposed to solve, namely, a final decider. Indeed, it not only neglects to incorporate that solution but also contributes to the social problem of disorder by interjecting into the social fabric yet another source of controversy.

Second, to those who want to divide sovereignty—for example, between a king and a parliament, or between a king, a parliament, and a court—Hobbes points out that sovereignty can only be divided via laws or rules setting out the division and the relative jurisdiction of each branch of government. So, argues Hobbes, if someone were to propose that, for example, sovereignty be divided into judicial, executive, and legislative units, he would be advocating, in effect,

> not government . . . not one independent Common-wealth, but three independent Factions; not one Representative Person, but three. In the Kingdome of God, there may be three Persons independent, without breach of unity in God that Reigneth; but where men Reigne, *that be subject to a diversity of opinion,* it cannot be so.[6]

So if the point of creating a political regime is to create an institution that will resolve all union-threatening controversy in a society, then one simply fails to create such an institution if one sets about to divide sovereignty, because such division must be accomplished by laws that are inevitably conflict generating.

Third and finally, if constitutional laws cannot be the final deciders of a political regime, this is even more true of moral laws. While Hobbes is willing to admit the existence of "laws of nature" that he regards as hypothetical imperatives dictating various forms of peaceful behavior that, when performed in concert with others, will promote peaceful and commodious living, once again he argues that, insofar as those laws are the subject of great controversy, they cannot be the final solution of conflict.

> All Laws, written, and unwritten, have need of Interpretation. The unwritten Law of Nature, though it be easy to such, as without partiality, and passion, make use of their naturall reason, and therefore leave the violators thereof without excuse; yet considering there be few, perhaps none, that in some cases are not blinded by self love, or some other passion, it is now become of all Laws the most obscure; and has consequently the greatest need of able Interpreters.[7]

So Hobbes would think it fruitless to try to amend or clarify moral rules intended as fundamental legal rules in a society so as to minimize conflict over how they are to be understood and applied because human nature makes the obvious response to them impossible when self-interest is at stake.

Let me restate Hobbes's regress argument so that we understand exactly what assumptions about laws and about human nature that argument rests upon:

1. A political institution exists if and only if it has the ability to resolve or forestall all conflict among human beings who interact in a certain territory.
2. An institution, purporting to be political, whose ultimate authority is some set of rules, whether moral rules, rules dividing power among branches of government, or rules limiting the power of political officials, cannot resolve conflict among human beings because these rules will themselves be the source of conflict, and this is because
   a) it is virtually impossible to define such rules clearly enough to eliminate all controversies about what they mean;
   b) it is virtually impossible to define rules clearly enough to eliminate all controversies about how and when they should be applied;
   c) human nature is such that, even if a rule is clear and easy to apply, if its application to one's own case is disadvantageous, one will strive to argue for a different application, thereby coming into conflict with those who are intent on understanding and applying it properly.
3. A political institution will be able to resolve all conflict only if total power (or sovereignty) is invested in a human will—the will of either one person or a group of persons or all the people.
4. Therefore, only those institutions in which total power is invested in a human will (in any of these three ways) can count as political institutions.

## II. WHO SHALL JUDGE?

Hobbes's argument is best understood as one salvo in a theoretical war waged in many sectors of European life during the seventeenth century concerning what kinds of government are possible. This was a frequent topic of discussion in the pamphlets written by politically interested people, from clergyman to lords, in seventeenth-century England. One pamphlet, written by Philip Hunton, which argued in favor of divided sovereignty, is particularly interesting because of the way it struggles with the issues raised by Hobbes's regress argument. Hunton maintained that England should divide powers between the king and the Parliament, with the king's power limited by the latter. However, he was aware that this position was attacked by royalists convinced that it was a recipe for anarchy. If the king is in effect a servant of the people insofar as he is subject to the power of Parliament, how can he hope to rule over them? Won't they ignore those of his rulings that they dislike, or remove him from power altogether if their self-interest so dictates? Hunton replies to this objection as follows:

> [I]f I convey an estate of Land to another, it doth not hold that after such conveyance I have a better estate remayning in me then that other, but rather the contrary; because what was in one is passed to the other: The servant who at the year of *Iubile* would . . . give his master a full Lordship over him: can we argue, that he had afterward more power over himselfe then his Master, because he gave his Master that power over him, by that act of Oeconomical Contract[?][8]

Hunton's idea seems to be that although the people are responsible for the king's power, nonetheless, when they create that power the people *give up* their right to govern themselves, and pass it entirely on to him. Nonetheless Hunton also wants to argue that the king's power is limited and subject, in part, to the control of Parliament. So what will happen if the king's behavior is perceived as extending beyond the legal prerogatives of his power? *Who decides* whether or not he has overstepped his bounds? Note that this last question asks for the person or persons entitled to apply what is in effect a rule defining the king's jurisdiction of power.

Hunton struggles mightily to answer the question. The decider, he notes, cannot be any foreign power, because if it were, the autonomy of the state would be destroyed. And one cannot grant the right to decide to the king himself, because that would, in effect, make the monarch absolute in power. Finally, he considers whether or not the people should judge the rule, *and he rejects this option also,* because this would turn the people into the ruler and make the king their servant, who could only govern them subject to their whims and pleasures (which are sufficiently dangerous to justify the creation of a ruling power over them in the first place). So in the end, Hunton says that in the kind of regime he would install in England, *no one* has the right to judge whether the monarch is abusing his powers! This is a remarkable example of intellectual honesty but seems so foolish as to indirectly make Hobbes's own case for him. The royalist Robert Filmer ridicules Hunton's position as follows: "Thus our Author hath caught himself in a plaine *dilemma:* if the King be judge, then he is no limited Monarch. If the people be judge, then he is no Monarch at all. So farewell *limited Monarchy,* nay farewell *all government* if there be no Judge."[9]

Hunton realized the unsatisfactory nature of this position, and thus tacked on the following codicil to it, maintaining that while the people cannot judge the ruler in any legal sense, they do have the *moral* right to judge him:

> And this power of judging argues not a superiority of those who Judge, over him who is Judged; for it is not Authoritative and Civill, but morall, residing in reasonable Creatures and lawfull for them to execute, because never devested and put off by any act in the constitution of a legall Government, but rather the reservation of it intended: For when they define the Superiour to a Law, and constitute no Power to Judge of his Excesses from that Law, it is evident they reserve to themselves, not a Formall Authoritative Power but a morall Power, such as they had originally before the Constitution of the Government; which must needs remaine, being not conveyed away in the Constitution.[10]

But the reader is puzzled: at first Hunton describes the king as the *master* of the people, who are his slaves, and now he is granting these slaves the moral right not only to judge the king's performance but also to depose him if they think it necessary!

Filmer attacks Hunton's position: "Thus at the last, every man is brought by this Doctrine of our Authors, to be his owne judge. And I also appeal to the consciences of mankinde, whether the end of this be not utter confusion, and Anarchy."[11]

Hobbes would argue that all of Hunton's problems stem from the fact that he would make government rest on a law defining and limiting a king's power. With any such government, one must ask the question, "Who shall judge the law?", and as the regress argument shows, either the answer to this question will establish who the *real* (human) authority in the regime is, insofar as it is the law's deciders who establish what will prevail in the regime, or it will show that there are no deciders of these laws, in which case the regime is doomed to collapse and thus cannot count as a genuine government. Note that if the decider is the king, then it is his will that is the foundation of the regime. But if the decider is the people, Hobbes would insist that the king can't be the ultimate ruler, since it is not he, but the people, who effectively constitute the human will calling the shots in the society. Hobbes has a dim view of the viability of democratic rule so understood, given that the people's tendency to misbehave or fail to coordinate effectively is the very reason for creating a political society in the first place. I suspect he would agree with James Madison, who maintained, in the context of explaining why the United States Constitution did not establish a democracy in the style of the Greeks, that "[d]emocracies have ever been spectacles of turbulence and contention: have ever been found incompatible with personal security or the rights of property; and have in general been as short in their lives, as they have been violent in their deaths."[12]

After the seventeenth century many theorists took Hobbes to be right. For example, it was commonplace in the nineteenth century to analyze modern regimes in the Hobbesian manner, by identifying the sovereign. Many believed this was easy to do in the case of Britain, insofar as Parliament by that time had become, to all intents and purposes, the sole legislative body in the country. But it was not easy to do for countries such as the United States, where the Supreme Court, the Congress, and the president are supposed to "share" power by performing separate (but equal) governmental functions. Indeed, the United States seems to be an example of a regime that Hobbes thought was impossible: namely, a regime in which sovereignty is divided according to an ultimate rule, which acts as a "final decider." If Hobbes is right that such a regime is impossible and that laws cannot rule, there must be an ultimate human decider somewhere in this country. Indeed, perhaps in this regime it would make sense to say that the decider is the will of the entire people. (And this may be the correct analysis of countries such as Britain, in which most of the members of Parliament are, after all, popularly elected.)

But if the people are continually called "sovereign" in these regimes, how does it make sense to consider the people "ruled"? Hunton's dilemma returns. If babysitters are hired to supervise a bunch of unruly children, and in reality the babysitters turn out to *be* the unruly children, the supervision is useless. And similarly, if the reason for creating a political institution is that people cannot govern themselves satisfactorily, and the political regime that is created is one in which the people rule, the exercise appears useless. James Buchanan, whose own contractarian analysis of the state gives the people the last word in government, calls this "the paradox of sovereignty":

> Men's universal thirst for freedom is a fact of history, and his ubiquitous reluctance to "be governed" insures that his putative masters, who are also men, face never-ending threats of rebellion against and disobedience to any rules that attempt to direct and order individual behavior.[13]

But the idea that each of us lives in a political regime under a master whom the people believe they are both able and right to master themselves when he gets out of line is not a benign paradox for theorists such as Hobbes; it is a straightforward inconsistency. We who live in regimes in which this seems to be true dismiss the charges of inconsistency without, however, understanding why we are justified in doing so, or indeed, why these regimes work, despite their paradoxical character. The fact that we have so little to say to defend our regimes against Hobbesian attack suggests that we don't yet understand how they work, why they cohere so well, and why they are capable of being highly stable, despite the force of Hobbes's attacks. In a curious way, we are in the same position as Philip Hunton: we know what polity we like, but we don't know how to defend it coherently against Hobbesian attacks.

### III. A HOBBESIAN RULE OF RECOGNITION

So we must understand the polity of the contemporary modern democracy better. To do so, let us begin with H. L. A. Hart's famous argument that a political society must have at least one rule, namely, the rule of recognition, which identifies what counts as law in that society. Hart's charge against Austin's positivist theory of law, namely, that it neglected to recognize the existence of the rule of recognition, is also an argument against Hobbes's entirely will-based analysis of government. Hobbes had hoped to avoid laws at the foundation of a regime, but in Hart's view, such an attempt is futile, because in each of the types of political regime Hobbes recognizes, there must be at least one law prevailing in order to identify who the sovereign is, and thus who has the power to decide all conflicts in a regime. That rule authorizes either one person or a group of persons or every person to make the law. Upon that rule rests the very fact that there is a political regime, and not simply a group of hoodlums with superior might ordering around a population.

To accommodate Hart's conclusion, therefore, we might amend the Hobbesian argument as follows:

> In order for a group of people to be considered to constitute a political society, there must be a rule of recognition identifying as law whatever arises from some kind of human will, whether that be a single person's will, or the will of some group less than the entire population, or the population. No other rule of recognition will result in the creation of a legal system, and therefore of genuinely effective law.

This revision attributes to Hobbes the position that the rule of recognition, in order to be understood to define a political regime, must have a certain content. His regress argument is therefore reinterpreted as a thesis about how the socially recognized and followed rule of recognition must identify law if government is to be created: namely, that it must specify the law as the product of some kind of human will.

But can we reconcile Hobbes's attack on governments founded in law with this revised position's reliance on the rule of recognition? Perhaps. Although Hobbes takes a dim view of the possibility of human beings cooperating in the interpretation of a rule, if the rule of recognition is as simple and straightforward as the revised position above would make it, then even Hobbes might think it possible for human beings to agree on what it means. This is particularly true in the case of monarchical government, where the rule might simply specify one individual as ruler.[14]

But must a rule of recognition have this form in order to define government effectively? And even if our post-Hartian Hobbes isn't right that a legal society *must* be so defined, is he right that it *ought* to be so defined if the ends of political society are to be effectively achieved?

## IV. The Stratification Solution

In order to begin the process of finding answers to these questions, I want to return to Buchanan's "paradox of being governed." I shall offer a solution to that paradox here,[15] and then go on to use it to evaluate the effectiveness of Hobbes's arguments against rules of recognition that rely either entirely or in part on something other than human will to define law. That evaluation will then allow us to analyze and defend an interpretation of the structure of modern democratic regimes.

This paradox should be solved in the same way that linguistic paradoxes are standardly solved: namely, by differentiating levels of inquiry and analysis. Consider the famous "liar's paradox," which one can illustrate with the sentence "This sentence is false." The sentence cannot be true when it tells us it is false; but if it is false, then given the assertion it is making, it would seem to be true. Tarski resolved this paradox by distinguishing two kinds of language, which he called the "object" language and the "meta" language. The meta language is used to talk about the object language but is not itself part of that language.

By understanding the predicates "is true" and "is false" to belong only to the meta language, one avoids the paradox. An assertion in the object language may not involve these words, which are properly employed only as part of evaluations at the meta level.

We can employ the same "stratification" solution to the paradox of being governed. Let us start by distinguishing two levels of government, the object level and the meta level. The object level is the level of laws made by those with legislative power in a regime: call this the level of the "legal system." That which defines this system is the rule of recognition—a rule that is part of the meta level, not the object level. Hart himself calls the rule of recognition a "secondary" rule, one that is about the "primary rules." So, as Hart noted, there are two kinds of laws in the legal system, the kind that defines what the system is, that is, the rule of recognition, and the kind that is created in the system, as specified by the system-defining rule. As I've discussed, if we revise Hobbes's regress argument along Hartian lines, that argument concludes that the system-defining rule must operate by identifying who the makers, interpreters, and enforcers of the primary (or "object") law are. Those who are not authorized by the rule of recognition to perform some aspect of governing would be appropriately considered "the ruled," pure and simple.

But how does such a rule of recognition, even if it has the kind of content Hobbes would recommend, get to be authoritative? And who is the person or group that shall judge whether those who are ruling have respected their role as defined by the rule of recognition? These are twentieth-century versions of the questions that troubled Hobbes and Hunton.

In a recent article, Jules Coleman argues that the rule of recognition is "authoritative only if there is a social practice in regard to it among relevant officials."[16] That is, it isn't authoritative insofar as it derives its validity from some higher law: "It is not valid or in some other sense correct; it just is."[17] Instead, to use Coleman's phrase, its authoritativeness is a "social fact," and he refers to the rule as a kind of social "convention."

Now surely Coleman is right that a rule of recognition is a social fact, one that sociologists or anthropologists or historians would be concerned to discover were they trying to understand the political society that it defined. But how is it that this social fact comes into existence, and how does that generation explain the authority of this social convention? Coleman's language above (which he takes to be suggested by Hart) seems to support the thesis that this fact is generated and maintained by the officials who are operating according to the rule of recognition. But surely this is to get the cart before the horse. The person who is identified as having a certain role in government by the rule of recognition doesn't make that law authoritative over her by obeying it; quite the contrary—it is *because* she understands it as authoritative over her that she obeys it as she performs that role. Of course, were she to fail to do so, she might be contributing to a weakening of that rule's authority. But whether or not this is true, if she does not obey it, she is flouting a law whose authority derives from something other than her prior obedience to it. This is only to say that, as Hart himself noted, the rule of recognition is a genuine *rule,* not a mere custom or social regularity but a normative requirement, and one that those who are empowered by it are obligated to respect.[18] So where does its normativity come from?

Hart himself suggests that its normativity comes from those who make up the regime when he discusses the source of the "acceptance" of the rule of recognition in a legal society: "Plainly, general acceptance [of the rule of recognition] is here a complex phenomenon, in a sense divided between official and ordinary citizens, who contribute to it in different ways."[19] Hart goes on to say that whereas the officials contribute by explicitly acknowledging what this law is, and what it means, as they play their roles in the system, in contrast, "The ordinary citizen manifests his acceptance largely by acquiescence in the results of these official operations."[20]

Now this last passage grants the people a role in maintaining the rule of recognition that appears to be quite passive—that is, acquiescence as opposed to active interpretation of its meaning. But elsewhere Hart suggests that "acquiescence" must be understood in a more active way, when he relates what is, in essence, a contractarian story to explain the origination and legitimacy of a legal system.[21] If a group of people were in a prelegal state, argues Hart, they would agree that, as a way of promoting order, instituting a government was desirable, and they would therefore create it by specifying a secondary rule—the rule of recognition—defining what would count as the primary rules in the legal society. This story essentially makes people the ultimate source of the legal system itself, and therefore the party that not only maintains it but also ultimately decides whether or not it will continue (and if so, under what form). The people's "acquiescence" is therefore analogous to the "acquiescence" of someone who has hired a lawyer to look after her affairs. The lawyer decides what to do, and acts under this person's authority, and as long as he does so satisfactorily, his client will be prepared to "acquiesce" in his decisions. But just as he holds his office only as long as she retains him in her service, so too does the ruler maintain his power only as long as the people retain him in their service (and indeed retain the very definition of the office he holds). So Hart's answer is that of a contractarian: the secondary rule has its source in and derives its authority from the people—including not only the officials who are rulers but also the people who are being ruled.

If the people are the source of the rules, mustn't they also be the ones who should judge it? Here we must beware: to say that "[t]he people who are ruled are also the ones who rule" is just as misleading as to say, "This sentence is false." To answer this question, we must specify *which* rules we're talking about. The people in most societies don't have the job of interpreting any of the primary or object rules. That job is performed by someone who occupies a certain legal office. But the people *do* decide the rule of recognition, and as they do so they are performing a meta-level action—that is, they are engaged in an action that is about the operation of the object level.

But have I solved the paradox of being governed by a mere verbal trick? I would insist that I have not, because the analysis I have just given doesn't merely generate labels, but does so in a way that allows us to *describe and understand the relationship between fundamentally different kinds of political activity*. Imagine a group of children who are playing a game of baseball in a vacant lot and who periodically stop the game to argue about the rules (they might want to make up new rules, argue about the interpretation of existing rules, or object to the application of the existing rules by the person they've appointed umpire). We know the difference between "playing baseball" and "arguing about the rules of baseball." And similarly, this analysis helps us to see the difference between "being subject to primary rules" and "participating in activities that seek to change how such rules are generated" in political societies. We are engaged in "being ruled" when we follow the law and experience sanctions set by legal authorities. And we are engaged in "interpreting the rule of recognition" either when we participate in activities that "create and maintain" our governments, or when we do what we can to overthrow them. I have discussed at length elsewhere the particular activities that constitute "creation and maintenance" of political structures: they can include everything from voting to doing jury duty to assisting in the punishment of those who have violated the primary laws to attempting to make constitutional changes (a process in which we behave most like the children arguing over the baseball rules in the vacant lot) to, perhaps most important, refraining from performing, advocating, or assisting in violent activities designed to overthrow the government.[22]

In a curious way, I think that this analysis might be what Philip Hunton was trying to get at in his remarks. He was right that no one in a political regime has the *legal* right to judge the fundamental rule of recognition defining the powers of government—that is, no one has that right in the "object legal system" itself, because at this level the rules are the foundation of government. But he was also right that the people have the "moral" right—or better, the "extralegal right"—to decide these rules in the sense that they have a right *outside* the legal system itself as they scrutinize the government at the meta level.

Why does the stratification analysis assume that the people are the ones who decide how well the object game is going at the meta level? Why doesn't it allow the possibility that it could be a right held only by a few individuals, or a small group? The answer to this question is, I would argue, implicit in the contractarian's methodology. One of the covert messages being sent by those, such as Hobbes, who justify the existence of the state on the basis of what we "could agree to," is that—in fact—

a state exists *only* because enough of the people who constitute it either have created it and/or continue to maintain it, which means they behave such that the rule of recognition does not change, or changes only minimally. Creating a political system is like creating a game: the creators set out the rules that provide for the roles each person will play in the game (and most of us play the role of "ruled" in the political system), and everyone plays his or her part for as long as a sufficient number are satisfied with how it's going. So, contractarians are saying that, in fact, a political system is the "people's game" because (whether or not rulers wish to acknowledge this fact) the people will decide how well the game is going, and in particular, how well any ruler is adhering to the rules defining the extent of his jurisdiction and power. And this is not a normative thesis, but *a descriptive thesis.* A political system isn't something built into nature, created by God, or designed and maintained by only a few individuals, who naturally rule other human beings in the way that a farmer rules over the animals in his herds. It is a thoroughly human institution, whose existence depends, in a variety of ways, on the behavior of those who constitute it.

This thesis was highly radical in the seventeenth century because it essentially insists that, as a matter of *fact,* the authority of the state is not something that can be derived from some sort of natural or innate authority possessed by some set of supposedly superior persons, nor is it something that is derived solely from the word of God. Instead, it maintains that the authority of the state is the creation of the people who constitute it (albeit perhaps also a creation that God endorses). The creation of the state is the creation of rules, or authoritative norms, that define the legal system and establish the obligations of those who would serve in it. Only officials who are empowered by this set of norms are correctly known as "legal authorities." Although no contractarian believes that *all* authorities are human creations (Locke maintained that parental authority was natural; and even Hobbes accepted that God's authority is natural and not a human creation), the thrust of their argument is that the authority of a *legal* system is a human invention—and yet one to which we nonetheless believe we owe great allegiance.

The issue of how far Hobbes should be understood to en-

dorse the conception of the state I have just described is complicated. I've been representing the contractarian methodology in
a very Lockean way—a way that Hobbes himself tried self-
consciously not to endorse. Hobbes wanted to say that when the
people create the government they *give up* their right to rule
themselves, so that they can never get it back, which means that
they can never be justified in staging a revolution to replace the
ruler. Or, in other words, he perceived the people as *alienating*
their right to govern themselves.[23] In contrast, Locke saw people not as giving up their right to rule to the persons they
named rulers, but rather as *entrusting* that right to the rulers,
fully prepared to take it back if they were not satisfied with their
rulers' use of it. On Locke's view, the people make the rulers
their *agents*.[24] Clearly Hart's contract argument is in the Lockean tradition. But remarkably, at a number of points in *Leviathan* Hobbes himself cannot resist an agency conception of political rule, at one point claiming,

> The obligation of Subjects to the Sovereign is understood to last
> as long, and no longer, [sic] than the power lasteth, by which he
> is able to protect them. For the right men have by Nature to
> protect themselves, when none else can protect them, can by no
> Covenant be relinquished.[25]

Such passages caused conservative royalists such as Bishop
Bramhall to label Hobbes's *Leviathan* a "rebel's catechism."[26]
But how can a philosopher who has maintained that the people
*give up* their right to govern themselves slip into language that
is supportive of rebellion? In my book I argue at length that an
alienation interpretation of the contract argument cannot be
consistently maintained by Hobbes, given his psychological assumptions—particularly the assumption that we will and ought
to do whatever we need to do to insure our preservation (which,
as Hobbes recognizes in the quotation above, might conceivably
require deposing the sovereign in certain circumstances).[27]

So both the premises of his argument and the contractarian
assumption that the state is the people's creation push Hobbes
in the direction of the main outlines of an agency approach.
The royalist Robert Filmer was surely right that if Hobbes
wanted to defend an absolutist government, his contractarian

method was exactly the wrong one to use to do it.[28] That method suggests not only a new descriptive account of the nature of a state but also a new understanding of the source of government's legitimacy. Indeed, it may even be the case, as I shall now explain, that these two implications of the contract method played a role in the development of the new concept of democratic polity in the eighteenth century.

## V. The Structure of a Modern Democracy

Let us now turn to the analysis of the structure of a modern democracy. What does the rule of recognition in a political society with this kind of polity look like? I will argue that it is substantially different from the kind of rule a post-Hartian Hobbes would endorse. In this section I will set out the central components of this rule, relying on the stratification analysis just developed. And in the next section, I will defend the analysis against Hobbesian attack.

In the old days, those theorists, such as Hobbes, Hunton, or John Locke, who maintained, contra the divine rights theorists, that it was the people, and not God, who established and legitimized political power, also assumed that, as a matter of fact (albeit perhaps not of right), what the people did when they didn't like a regime was to stage a revolution, preferably bloodless, in which rulers were overthrown and, if necessary (as in 1688), the political rules changed. But what if one could design a political system in which "revolution" was an organized and regular part of the political process? This is the idea that inspired the founders of modern democratic societies (and particularly the founders of the American polity); it is at the heart of the structure of contemporary democratic states.

Defenders of modern democracy self-consciously recognize that *political societies are created and maintained by the people who are ruled in them.* And as I've discussed, this creation-and-maintenance process involves the creation and maintenance of a set of authoritative norms that define the legal system and the obligations of the officials who work within it. However, *democracies operate so that the people have continual control over the process of creating and maintaining the regime.* In modern democracies, the people have created not only the "legal game" but also another game that defines how to play the "creation and maintenance" game. Let me explain.

Consider the standard coup: Ruler X has power because there is a rule, accepted by the people, that he is authorized to have it. But when some or all of the people no longer accept that rule, they engage in various power-retracting activities, and if enough people (or enough of the people who have most control over the present rulership convention) engage in these activities, Ruler X is gone. (So, for example, in the case of the Soviet coup, when too many people in powerful positions refused to obey orders—for example, Russian and Baltic soldiers in the army, political officers in various Soviet states, and various people involved in the economic life of the nation—the coup collapsed.) How such activities can come to be possible, and even coordinated despite the opposition of rulers, is a fascinating story; communication among opponents of a ruler is critical (and thus some pundits argued that one of the reasons the Soviet coup failed was the existence of the FAX machine). In another place I have described this kind of revolutionary activity at length and labeled it "convention-dissolving," in virtue of the fact that it unravels the convention defining who is to hold power—which is just to say that it destroys the society's rule of recognition.[29]

The experience of England in the seventeenth century was that political convention-dissolving could be difficult, lengthy, and even deadly dangerous for those involved in it. This lesson was not lost on the American revolutionaries. But what the framers essentially asked themselves was this: what if the people could get control of convention-dissolving activity—establishing rules that would actually allow it to occur on a periodic basis if the people so decided, and that would regulate it so that the dissolution would be as peaceful and orderly as possible? If there could be a "system of revolution" that was attached to the legal system, both rules and rulers could be changed quickly with minimal cost and disruption to the people. And the possibility of replacing them peacefully and painlessly would increase the people's control over the shape of their political game and thus allow them to better supervise their leaders (who would know that their being fired was not a particularly costly action for the people, and who would thus be under pressure, if they wanted to retain their jobs, to perform them as the people required). By and large, this "controlled convention-dissolving activity" involves what is commonly referred to as "voting," as I shall now explain.

Consider how the American Constitution works. This document not only sets up a certain kind of government, with offices that involve distinctive kinds of power and jurisdiction, but it also sets up rules for creating and dissolving conventions about *who* holds these offices. Through these rules our various government officials are empowered; but through these rules they can also be peacefully and effectively deprived of power. *Voting is therefore a form of controlled revolutionary activity.* Socialist radicals of the early twentieth century were right when they referred to votes as "paper stones."[30] Our elected "representatives" don't represent us in any literal sense—as if we were doing the ruling "through them." This is nonsense. They rule and we don't. But it is because we can easily deprive them of power—depose them, if you will—at certain regular intervals that they have (at least theoretically) the incentive to rule in a way responsive to our interests. Just like any other employee, if they want to keep their jobs they must work to the satisfaction of their employer. They therefore "represent" us in the way that any agent represents those who authorize her. In modern democratic regimes, representation is actually a form of agency.[31] Thus, those who would rule us are, in a democracy, in a continual competition with one another, attempting to gather votes that will, each hopes, be sufficient, according to the rules, to hire him or her as ruler. In democracies, more than in any other kind of regime, rulers don't have tenure.[32]

So our government is by the people, for the people, and of the people—except that this last preposition is misleading. Unlike in ancient Athens, most of us aren't actually in the government—only a few of us are. What makes this a government of the people is the fact that built into the rule of recognition are not only the rules that define the object political game but also rules that grant the people the power to create and dissolve portions of that object political game if they choose to do so with relatively little cost. Creating these rules is a novel way of extending the activity involved in creating and maintaining government. Such rules allow the people to play their "meta" role as definers of their political society in a more effective and controlled way. Those who fashioned modern democracies came to see that not only such activities as criminal punishment and tort litigation but also the very process of adding to or changing the political game itself could be made part of a larger conception of the "political game." Or, to put it another way, they discovered that revolutionary activity could be an everyday part of the operation of a political society. (Other democracies besides the United States might be better exemplars of this point; one thinks for example of Italy.)

To appreciate the precise structure of these regimes, we need to examine more closely the content of the rules of recognition that define them. As Hart appreciated, any rule of recognition is a *type* of rule—that is, it is a rule about rules, or what Hart calls a "secondary" rule. Now Hart notes that there are other secondary rules (about rules) that operate *within* a legal system, for example, contract rules (which are rules about how to create "private" transactional rules between two or more parties), or rules about how to make wills (which define rules about the distribution of property). The rule of recognition is not only a rule about rules, but more generally a rule about how to recognize and/or produce *any* rule in the legal system defined by it.

However, I will now argue that in a democracy, this rule is actually a *set* of rules that can be divided into types, as follows:

First, as Hart noted, this set of rules includes those rules that identify what is to count as the law in the object political regime. In democratic societies, these rules operate by defining offices that perform legislative, executive, and judicial functions, offices that, taken together, generate the primary laws in this society. Let me call such rules "structural" in virtue of the way they set out the institutions that perform these functions. They are, as Hart notes, a type of secondary (or meta) rule.

However, there is a second type of rule that Hart failed to explicitly recognize, and whose addition transforms any regime into a modern democracy. This type of rule defines how it is that the people control and/or change the operation of the

political regime as defined by the first type of rule, and it does
so in two ways. First, these rules dictate how the people install
or replace those who hold the offices defined by the structural
type of rule just discussed, through either direct or indirect
voting procedures. Second, these rules set out the procedures
for changing the rules that define these offices and the procedures for filling them. (For example, the U.S. Constitution sets
out an elaborate process for constitutional amendment.) By including these rules in the rule of recognition, the people not
only define the object political game but also determine the
system by which the people can revise that game, and under
what circumstances they will be warranted to do so. So with the
addition of these latter rules, the overall rule of recognition now
contains components that are *tertiary* as well as secondary: that
is, it contains rules about rules about rules (i.e., "meta meta
rules") insofar as it defines not merely the object political game
and the primary rules generated in that game, but also the
game of changing the object political game. Politics becomes a
three-tier, not merely a two-tier, activity.

Now all political societies have a three-tiered structure. What
makes democratic societies different is that *the way one engages in
third-tier activities is now governed by rules.* That is, in a nondemocratic regime, the citizen's role as a member of the population
that creates, maintains, or destroys the rule of recognition defining this object game is ill defined, often little understood,
often thwarted by the ruler to any extent possible, and something she and her fellow citizens "make up as they go along." In
a modern democracy, the citizen not only plays a role in the
object game and not only plays a role as a member of the
population that creates, maintains, and changes the rule of recognition defining the first game but also performs the latter role
according to well-defined procedures laid out in other parts of
the rule of recognition, procedures that can involve elections,
plebiscites, constitutional conventions, and so forth. And indeed, in some democracies, she plays the fourth-tier role of
creating, maintaining, or changing those rules that define these
election procedures, and that also define how to create, maintain, or destroy any other part of the rule of recognition. And
when she plays either of these last two roles, she is part of a

population that has taken it upon itself to structure and abide by rules that it uses to "revolutionize" the government.

Disgruntled members of a democratic regime are supposed to follow the procedures laid down by the rule of recognition for changing their rulers, or the offices they hold, or these procedures themselves. But they might not do so; and if they attempt to change the rule of recognition—including those rules that tell the population how to change rulers or offices in the regime—by taking certain actions (including violent actions) or by following procedures not laid down in that rule, they are engaging in what might be called "extralegal revolution." Such "old-fashioned" revolution is still possible in modern democratic states and occurs whenever the citizenry strives to revise or destroy the rule of recognition *without* respecting the rules it contains for carrying out a revision process. But insofar as the rule of recognition's procedures for revision are perceived as reasonable and are endorsed by most of the population, such revolutionaries will appear as opponents not only of the present rulers of the regime but also of the vast majority who support and maintain the way the rule of recognition defines the process of overseeing the regime's operation. Such a position makes their revolutionary activity unlikely to succeed, and contributes to what many see as the remarkable stability of modern democratic states.

There is one other type of rule that can be a constituent of a rule of recognition in modern democracies—but this type of rule need not be present in order for the regime to be appropriately called a democracy. It requires those who are to govern to do so in conformity to certain moral requirements. This type of rule is morally loaded to the extent that it partially articulates or partially points to a moral theory as the proper source of the content of object law created by the legislature. Coleman has rightly pointed out that there is no reason such rules cannot be part of (or even all of) the rule of recognition, and Randy Barnett argues that the presence of the Bill of Rights, and particularly the ninth amendment, indicates that the framers of the U.S. Constitution were convinced that moral reality was sufficiently clear to enable the American people to recognize and operate from that part of it circumscribed by these amendments.[33] Modern democracies do not have to incorporate such moral rules in order to be democracies, since their democratic structure is basically created by the tertiary rules discussed above. Nor do they need these rules to be explicitly written down in order for them to play an operational role in defining the nature of the object political society established by the rule of recognition. But they are a common part of many such societies, especially in written form, because they help to provide a moral yardstick that the people can use to judge the performance of those whom they are able to peacefully depose at the voting booth.

In my judgment the contribution of social contract arguments to the development of this modern conception of democracy is enormous. Historical documentation must await another paper, but consider that even though the image of an explicit social contract as the basis of government is make-believe, nonetheless that image must surely have generated in the minds of those who constructed modern democracies the idea that a well-run polity is one that recognizes and allows for the control of the people over that which is their creation—the political regime.

## VI. THE STABILITY OF MODERN DEMOCRACIES

Hobbes would certainly question how a rule of recognition with the democratic structure I have outlined could be either long lived or stable. After all, his regress argument establishes that the law alone, uninterpreted and unenforced, cannot rule. In a sense he would be right—the types of rules that together constitute the rule of recognition in modern democracies can govern only because the people of the political society understand them in more or less the same fashion and are prepared to do what is required to ensure that they are followed. So human will is behind the democractic rule of recognition, and the kinds of law making it up.

But one of the most important lessons we learn from the stratification analysis is that the particular kinds of behavior that human beings must perform to insure that a modern democractic political system survives are ones that all human beings—

even the "bad" ones—are capable of performing. As I've described, these behaviors all come under the rubric "maintaining the rule of recognition," and as people engage in these behaviors, they are engaged in a meta game of controlling the political game, which, in modern democracies, now includes procedures for revolution itself.[34] The people's control over this political game need not be tight; if the political system (and those who rule within it) is/are perceived as performing satisfactorily, public apathy is likely. This is Hart's "acquiescence." After all, why participate actively in meta activities if the political game is going well and the officials are performing (in the people's view) ably in interpreting the rule of recognition? However, such apathy can encourage power-hungry or incompetent government officials to make changes in the operation of that game and/or in the interpretation of that rule in ways that benefit them or the interest groups that they represent, and thus damage the people's ability to supervise them. (This can involve everything from trying to pack the Supreme Court to manipulating rules about campaign contributions in order to make incumbents' reelection highly likely.) As anyone who has been hurt by a bad lawyer will recognize, if the people fail to supervise their agents properly, they may wind up at their agents' mercy. Nonetheless, the object political game is the people's to lose.

But Hobbes would wonder why that loss wouldn't be inevitable, given that effective control of these agents is only possible when the population of the democratic regime by and large share a common understanding of what these normative conventions mean, so that they are able to reach a consensus on whether they are being followed and when they are being flouted. Despite the stratification analysis, this may seem problematic. Even assuming that the people are playing a meta role when they judge the officials of the regimes in which they live, nonetheless, as they play this role they will have to cooperate and agree with one another to a large degree about what components of the rule of recognition mean and how well the officials are playing the roles that this rule sets out. But this means the rule will have to be interpreted and enforced by the very people whose inability to cooperate and agree with one another is the fundamental reason for installing a government in the first place. So how can such a regime last for any length of time?

We can reply to these Hobbesian worries by pointing out that a modern democracy is explicitly designed to deal with and resolve the sort of disagreements about the performance of the rulers that Hobbes thought were inevitable. A democracy controls these disagreements, channels them into peaceful political paths, and makes the deposing of leaders rather easy if dissatisfaction is great. Rather than rely on a sovereign to banish such disagreement (a solution that post-Hobbesians thought unlikely to work, and in any case, unacceptable), the framers of modern democracies set up rules that would resolve disagreements about the performance of rulers through the use of various voting procedures. And although there is no voting procedure that can by itself persuade everyone that the outcome of the vote is the correct one, voting can provide a means of evaluating the operation of various parts of the object game that can strike people as "fair" in the sense that it grants everyone a say, and thus allows the opposition to state its case—even while leading in the end to a decision. And the opposition knows that this decision is reversible (in their favor) if they can garner enough votes for their side in the future, a fact that encourages them to remain supportive of the system that nonetheless produced, in their eyes, a bad outcome. Moreover, a society has a *democratic culture* when every citizen, including those with large differences in political outlook, can nonetheless follow and agree on the interpretation of those tertiary (or quaternary) constituents of the rule of recognition that set out procedures for resolving that controversy in favor of only one party.

Granted, in order for this style of government to work, the people must be in rough agreement about the correct interpretation of the meta rules defining these voting procedures. And even if the interpretation of these rules is, by and large, relegated to "expert" officials, the people must generally support their interpretive practices if the regime is to be stable and peaceful. Of course, one must remember that creating an object political game involves (as I've argued at length elsewhere[35]) the creation of a coercive policing power that, once installed, may be difficult to remove. (After all, those who govern are supposed to have more force than you, so that they will be able to prevail upon you were you to break the law. But such an advantage can also be used to undermine revolutionary activity against them.) So even considerable unhappiness in the population about how the tertiary rules are being interpreted may still be consistent with the stable and peaceful operation of the regime. Nonetheless, because even the policing power of a state relies on people either being actively involved in policing activities or else refraining from interfering with the operation of this policing power, the continued health of even this institution relies on the people's support of it and their ability to create and sustain at least some rough conventions about what rules mean and how rulers are doing. However, the success and stability of this style of government in the modern world is proof that at least this minimal cooperation is something human beings are quite capable of, contra Hobbes's cynical assertions to the contrary.

So, to summarize, modern democracies are highly successful in today's world because the remedy they propose for the disagreements that will inevitably accompany publicity about the private citizenry's evaluations of their government's performance is not the use of political coercion to try to banish all but one point of view, as Hobbes proposed, but the creation of (meta) rules that allow the people to reconcile their differing points of view, and to build those rules into the political process. And perhaps the increasing capacity of human beings to communicate and thus coordinate with one another has made this type of regime not only possible but also inevitable, given that governments based upon unconstrained human will cannot survive in a society where it is commonly known that dissatisfaction among the people is rampant. There is, of course, no guarantee that all such governments will remain stable and unified indefinitely, in part because there is no guarantee that the people will be able to maintain a commitment to following and commonly interpreting the meta rules defining how to reconcile their disagreements over its operation. But the fact that such highly stratified states are both possible and surprisingly robust permits us to be optimistic about both the future of fledgling democracies and the continued health of older ones, in the face of Hobbes's "proof" that such regimes fall quickly and inevitably into ruins.

## NOTES

1. *Leviathan*, chapter 19, paragraph 1, p. 94 of 1651 edition. (Henceforth, all page references in *Leviathan* will be to the 1651 edition, but I will also give the number of the paragraph of the chapter in which the passage occurs, to assist those whose editions do not preserve the pagination of the 1651 edition.)

2. See *The English Works of Thomas Hobbes*. Vol. 2, *De Cive*, ed. W. Molesworth (London: Bohn, 1840), chapter 6, para. 18, p. 88.

3. *Leviathan*, 20, 18, 107.

4. H. L. A. Hart, *The Concept of Law* (Oxford: Clarendon, 1961), 97–107; and Hans Kelsen, *The General Theory of Law and the State*, trans. Anders Wedberg (Cambridge, MA: Harvard University Press, 1945), 110–16.

5. *Leviathan*, 29, 9, 169.

6. *Leviathan*, 29, 16, 172.

7. *Leviathan*, 26, 21, 143.

8. Philip Hunton, *A Treatise of Monarchy* (London, 1643), 15–16.

9. Robert Filmer, *The Anarchy of a Limited or Mixed Monarchy* (London, 1648), 20; reprinted in *Patriarcha and Other Political Works by Robert Filmer*, ed. Peter Laslett (Oxford: Blackwell, 1949).

10. Hunton, *Treatise*, 18.

11. Filmer, *Anarchy*, 22.

12. From *The Federalist Papers*, Paper No. 10, written by Madison. (Quotation from Mentor edition [New York: New American Library, 1961], 81.)

13. James Buchanan, *The Limits of Liberty* (Chicago: University of Chicago Press, 1975), 92.

14. However, if this were all the rule did, then the political regime would last only as long as this ruler lived. There would be no rule requiring a certain procedure for transferring power. Moreover, if the rule established a democracy or aristocracy, the problem of succession would be removed, but we would now face the problem of defining how the aristocratic group or the entire population of citizenry must cooperate internally to create law. Rules would certainly be necessary

to clarify how this would be done; and such rules would be open to interpretive controversy. Hobbes fails to realize that democracies and aristocracies require rules of recognition with substantial content.

15. This solution is based on the one that I offered in chapter 9 of my *Hobbes and the Social Contract Tradition* (Cambridge: Cambridge University Press, 1986).

16. Jules Coleman, "Rules and Social Facts," *Harvard Journal of Law and Public Policy* 14, no. 3 (Summer 1991): 721.

17. Randy Barnett, "Unenumerated Constitutional Rights and the Rule of Law," *Harvard Journal of Law and Public Policy* 14, no. 3 (Summer 1991): 719.

18. Coleman himself sometimes characterizes the rule as a social "convention," but conventions are often normative in character (and indeed called "rules"), e.g., traffic conventions, conventions about constructing a legal document such as a will or a contract.

19. Hart, *Concept of Law*, 59.

20. Hart, *Concept of Law*, 60.

21. See Hart, *Concept of Law*, 89ff.

22. See my "The Contractarian Explanation of the State," in *Midwest Studies in Philosophy: The Philosophy of the Social Sciences*, ed. T. Ueling (Minneapolis: University of Minnesota Press, 1990).

23. I discuss the many passages in which Hobbes uses language suggesting alienation in chapter 5 of my *Hobbes and the Social Contract Tradition*.

24. Locke actually uses the metaphor of trust rather than of agency, but from the legal point of view, the latter relationship better captures Locke's own understanding of the ruler/subject relationship than the former. For more on this, see note 31 below.

25. *Leviathan*, 21, 21, 272.

26. Bishop John Bramhall, *The Catching of Leviathan . . . Appendix to Castigations of Mister Hobbes . . . Concerning Liberty and Universal Necessity* (London, 1658), 515.

27. See my *Hobbes and the Social Contract Tradition*, especially chapters 6–8.

28. As Filmer himself puts it, "I consent with him about the Rights of exercising government, but I cannot agree to his meanes of acquiring it. . . . [I] praise his building, and yet mislike his Foundation." From preface to *Observations concerning the Original of Government* (London, 1652); reprinted in Laslett, *Patriarcha* (see note 9 above).

29. See my "Contractarian Explanation of the State."

30. See the book *Paper Stones* by Adam Przeworski and John Sprague for a discussion of this term.

31. This is not unlike Hannah Pitkin's view of the nature of representation in modern democratic societies, as put forth in her book *The Concept of Representation* (Berkeley: University of California Press, 1967). However, Pitkin tends to use the metaphor of trust, and that metaphor is problematic. A trustor does not own that which is used on his behalf by the trustee. Moreover, unlike in an agent/client relationship, the trustee/trustor relationship is one in which the trustor does not have sufficient standing to fire the trustee, and is generally regarded as inferior to or less competent than the trustee, such that he must be subject to the trustee's care. (So children are assigned trustees; and in nineteenth-century England married women could only hold property in trust, in virtue of what was taken to be their inferior reasoning abilities.) The assumptions of the rights of citizens in modern democratic societies are at odds with the presumption of the trustor's incompetence.

32. I am grateful to Pasquale Pasquino for the tenure metaphor here.

33. See Coleman and R. Barnett, notes 16 and 17 above.

34. So members of Western democracies can never be considered subjects; the word is misused because at best one could say that they are subjects not to any political office holder but to rules that they have made, some of which give them control over the office holder.

35. See my "Contractarian Explanation of the State."

# 2

# CIVIL DISOBEDIENCE AND THE RULE OF LAW— A LOCKEAN INSIGHT

## CATHERINE VALCKE

### INTRODUCTION

Professor Hampton's response to the infinite regress objection voiced by Hobbes against the intelligibility of the rule of law is coherent and persuasive. Her argument is unlikely fully to satisfy participants in the social contract, however, for it fails to account for an important fact in the life of this contract, that is, civil disobedience.

Hampton does not address the issue of civil disobedience directly, but her remarks allow for some speculations. She explains that the terms of the social contract confine the citizens' control over the rulers to the *meta* level of political action (to borrow Tarski's typology, as she does), also referred to (in Hart's terms) as the level of design and application of *secondary* rules. She thus implies that they are without power with respect to the *object*-level, or *primary* rules. In other words, Hampton suggests that the citizens' only check is on the *process* of political decision making, that they must resign themselves to being entirely powerless as to the *product* of this process, namely, the substance of the law.

As civil disobedience emerges from the citizens' condemnation of the substance of legal rules, it is difficult to see how, if at all, this scheme could accommodate civil disobedience. One could try arguing in a formalistic fashion typical of private contract law reasoning that civil disobedience simply falls outside the scope of the social contract, so as to be neither condoned nor condemned by its terms. But this argument fails here because Hampton's model is not merely indifferent to the citizens' behavior toward legal rules; it requires that they conscientiously refrain from acting on their possible disapproval of these rules. In her model, therefore, any act of civil disobedience is a violation of the terms of the social contract.[1]

That is one possible contractarian interpretation of the relation between civil disobedience and the rule of law, and one that, moreover, will not be without appeal to a fair number of political actors. To those citizens who, like myself, are not content with granting such leeway to rulers in between elections, I want to offer another, one that builds civil disobedience into the social contract as a legitimate means for the citizens to exert some measure of control over the *output* of the political process.

In formulating this theory of civil disobedience, I will build heavily on the writings of John Locke, for two reasons. First, most of the ideas that form this theory can be found in Locke's *Two Treatises of Civil Government*[2] or in his *Letter concerning Toleration*,[3] albeit in no particular order or form of argument. As is the case with much of the secondary literature on Locke, therefore, this comment is intended as a reconstruction of what Locke might have written on the issue, rather than as an exercise in exegesis. Second, as Hampton states herself, the flavor of her own argument is distinctly Lockean,[4] and perhaps even more so than she suspects, for a close reading of the *Second Treatise* reveals that Locke clearly shares in Hampton's critique of Hobbes on this point, while he would, my argument will aim to show, in turn criticize Hampton's response as not quite daring enough. Indeed, Locke for one would want a system wherein the citizens' power over the rulers extends beyond the process of their empowerment to the means by which they exercise this power.

This comment is accordingly structured in two parts. Part 1 borrows from Locke to corroborate Hampton's critique of

Hobbes's infinite regress argument; part 2 draws on the same writings to carry her argument a little further, so as to reconcile civil disobedience with the rule of law.

## I. Locke's Critique of Hobbes on Political Participation

It is well known that Locke, like Hampton, disagreed with both Filmer and Hobbes on the question of the source of legitimate state authority. In fact, Locke's very purpose in writing the *Two Treatises of Government* was to counter the respective justifications the two royalists had formulated in support of unlimited state power.

In *Patriarcha*, Filmer had defended the omnipotence of the crown on deontological grounds, claiming that kings derive their title directly from God. Resolved to respond to Filmer on his own terms, Locke looked for an alternative to divine will as a source of moral legitimacy for state authority, and found it in Hobbes's idea of a social contract. But Hobbes's own motivation in introducing the social contract had been more pragmatic than deontological. He considered that any sovereign, even a tyrannical one, would in fact be better for everyone than none.[5] Leviathan's main claim to authority was thus merely that he appeared as the lesser of two evils.

Locke disagreed with Hobbes on this point. His own assessment of the costs and benefits of state authority differed from that of Hobbes largely because he chose a different baseline: Hobbes's state of nature was nothing short of a nightmare,[6] whereas that of Locke was relatively peaceful,[7] albeit not a state of pure bliss.[8] For Locke, therefore, whether or not civil society would be more desirable than the state of nature would depend on how well the officials would rule civil society. And surely, he warns repeatedly throughout the *Second Treatise*[9] that concentrating all powers in the hands of the sovereign is an ill-fated strategy. Hence, although Locke views the institution of civil society per se as a good idea, he insists that it is a risky operation whose success requires at a minimum that the institutors retain extensive and constant control over government.

Like Hobbes's defense of unlimited royal power, Locke's ar-

gument to the contrary is contractarian in that it too proceeds
from a particular interpretation of the social contract. As
Hampton explains,[10] Hobbes took the view that this contract
provided for nothing less than the abdication by all parties of
their right to rule themselves. Locke, in contrast, insists that we
should distinguish the right from the power to enforce, sanction, execute this right[11]—a distinction that Hobbes would
likely claim is unintelligible[12]—and then argues that only the
latter is transferrable, and thus transferred, from the individuals to the authority they nominate through the social contract.[13]
Only the power to sanction natural rights is transferrable in
Locke's view, for the rights themselves are fundamentally in-
alienable, as they are being held in trust for God.[14] Unlike
Hobbes's social contract, which provides a carte blanche to the
authority, that of Locke is no more than, in his own words, a
"trust," which, by definition, can be revoked by its creators upon
mismanagement by the trustees:

> [T]he Legislative being only a Fiduciary Power to act for certain
> ends, there remains still *in the People a Supream Power* to remove
> or *alter the Legislative,* when they find the *Legislative* act contrary
> to the trust reposed in them. For all *Power given with trust* for the
> attaining an *end,* being limited by that end, whenever that end
> is manifestly neglected, or opposed, the *trust* must necessarily
> be *forfeited.*[15]

In sum, Locke's simple response to Hobbes's objection to the
rule of law is that the search for ultimate authority does not
regress infinitely; it stops at the terms of the entrusting
agreement—or social contract, or rule of recognition—as interpreted and enforced by no other than the entrusting parties
themselves acting through their conscience on behalf of God:

> *Who shall be Judge* whether the Prince or Legislative act contrary
> to the Trust? . . . *The People shall be Judge;* for who shall be *Judge*
> whether his Trustee or Deputy acts well, and according to the
> Trust reposed in him, but he who deputes him, and must, by
> having deputed him have still a Power to discard him, when he
> fails in his Trust?[16]

The next question concerns *the way* the people must proceed
in revoking the sovereign's mandate, should they decide such

revocation is warranted. Locke argues that the use of force is then legitimate because, by the very fact of usurping the terms of its mandate, the sovereign has brought itself back into the state of nature toward the people, who, by the same token, have regained the power to punish those who transgress their rights.[17] Hence the right of revolution, bone of contention between Hobbes and Locke.[18]

But the significance of revolution proper, or forceful reversal of political power, in Locke's argument should not be overestimated. Admittedly, the revolutionary question is paramount in the *Two Treatises,* for they were written in reaction to the events of 1688. Yet, use of force is in no way essential to Locke's argument: although the dismantling of deficient political structures may legitimately be carried on through revolution proper, there are, Locke concedes, other ways of achieving the same result. One such way is that suggested by Hampton, namely, to build the right of revolution into the regime in the way of periodical elections. Not only do periodical elections minimize the cost and disruption for the people of dissolving the state, but they also present the other advantage, Locke believes (perhaps naively), of causing elected officials to be subjected to their own laws after their term in office expires, which further pressures them, while in office, "to take care, that they make them for the publick good." [19]

It is therefore with good reasons that Hampton characterizes her own answer to Hobbes's regress argument as "Lockean." [20] Yet, she may have underestimated the extent to which this is true, for Locke agreed not only that the rule of recognition contained in the social contract is the ultimate standard by which the rulers' performance is to be assessed but also that the institution of periodic elections is a judicious means for executing and enforcing this assessment. At this point, however, Locke and Hampton part company.

## II. A LOCKEAN THEORY OF POLITICAL PARTICIPATION

Several passages in the *Second Treatise* imply that Locke would want the citizens to retain more than just the means to control the *process* of creating and maintaining the regime—that he would want them to be in a position to control also the *product* of that process, that is, the object, the primary rules, the particular laws produced by the regime.[21] Those are the passages reminiscent of Aquinas, where Locke insists on the necessary correspondence of human legislation with the natural law. In section 136, for example, Locke quotes Hooker to suggest that "Laws Humane must be made according to the general Laws of Nature, and without contradiction to any positive Law of Scripture, otherwise they are ill made."[22] Those passages are important because, if Locke is serious about the correspondence of human legislation with the natural law—and there is no reason to believe he is not—it simply cannot be the case that he would be satisfied with a system that would have the citizens suffer immoral laws in between elections.

Fortunately, he does not have to be, for his concern can be accommodated through another slight modification of the terms of the social contract. This time, the modification consists of adding to the terms of the contract a requirement that the laws produced by the authority conform with certain guidelines, say, the rules of morality,[23] if they are to have binding force over the citizens. As a result, the citizens would be entitled, by the social contract, to resist laws that their conscience tells them are immoral. This meshes with Locke's own thoughts on the matter, as he clearly believed that the citizens are absolved from obeying immoral laws,[24] while he is otherwise largely silent on what happens in between election days.

Admittedly, Hampton does allow for the possibility of adding this morality clause to the social contract.[25] Indeed, as explained above,[26] the present discussion aims to build on, not contradict, hers. At this point, the only difference between our two models is that the morality clause is apparently merely optional in hers, whereas it is an integral part of the argument in mine. I write "apparently" because including the clause in the social contract in fact raises a serious problem, which both Hampton and I must resolve in order to retain the clause altogether, and which, moreover, will not be resolved merely by qualifying the clause as optional.

The problem is the following. Hobbes's objection to the intelligibility of the rule of law boils down to what Buchanan calls the "sovereignty paradox,"[27] that is, the paradox by which individuals in a polity want both to be governed and to govern the governors.[28] Professor Hampton suggested we solve the sovereignty paradox by maintaining a strict distinction between, on the one hand, the constitution of the regime and, on the other hand, the laws produced by that regime, and by confining popular check to the former. The morality clause does exactly the opposite: by allowing the citizens to disregard the laws they consider immoral, it extends their power beyond checking upon the constitution of the regime into assessing the product of this regime; it consolidates process and product, and thus eliminates the very distinction that supported the solution to the sovereignty paradox. In sum, when we try to enrich the social contract by adding the morality clause to its terms, we effectively revive the very problem that we wanted to solve in the first place.

Should we then conclude that Locke is fundamentally inconsistent when he insists on including this clause in the social contract? In the remainder of this comment, I will attempt to show that he is not. The solution I propose takes the form of a theory of civil disobedience, which I formulate in the following section, and defend as Lockean in the next one.

## A. The Theory

The theory proceeds from three assumptions. The first is that morality exists objectively as a law of nature. The second is that this law of nature, however real, is not in a form that is readily accessible to the human mind, so that the task of laying down its tenets in the form of positive legislation is not an easy one, particularly as we move down in levels of abstraction from broad principles to rules concrete enough to guide action in daily life. Rather, the moral, like the physical, laws of nature can only be properly decoded through a gradual process of trial and error, which entails that legal rules are always posited tentatively, subject to being subsequently discarded, corrected, and improved through some kind of feedback mechanism.[29]

Thirdly, I want to start out with the assumption that the

elected officials abide by the terms of the social contract in good faith, and hence truly endeavor to implement the law of nature in civil society. I will later relax this last assumption, as some may question its reality.

In light of these three assumptions, I propose to interpret the social contract as embodying a commitment on the part of all citizens to partake in the process of deciphering the law of nature, and on the part of the elected officials in turn to enforce the rules produced by this deciphering process. The salient point in this scenario is thus that, rather than granting to the officials the exclusivity in interpreting and enforcing the law of nature, it pictures the interpretive part of the process as a collective enterprise involving all citizens.

To be sure, the officials will be in charge of *initiating* the interpretive process, but the citizens will not be without a part to play. The officials will initiate the process by enacting laws of two kinds. One kind will be laws intended as prescriptions of the law of nature proper; the other will be laws that, although indifferent to the law of nature, are otherwise inherent to social organization. Rules of private law and criminal law are examples of the first kind. Crimes and torts may be condemned on moral grounds as violations of the principle of mutual respect. Similarly, the enforcement of contracts draws its moral justification from the principle that promises must be kept. In contrast, various rules designed to solve collective action problems are clearly indifferent to the law of nature.[30] For example, whether we drive on the right or left side of the road is a question of strict coordination devoid of moral significance, but is obviously in our interest to settle. Rules securing the production of certain public goods may similarly be argued to be morally neutral.[31]

What rules are mandated by the law of nature, what rules will serve efficient social organization, and how the two kinds interrelate (if at all) are questions for debate. For example, one might want to add to the first category laws mandating massive redistribution of resources on the argument that the principle of moral equality of all citizens dictates that we aim to even out physical inequalities. Likewise, one might want to question the reality of the individual preferences assumed to justify state production of a good presumed to be public.

All such questions will ultimately be left for the citizens to decide. Indeed, my scenario provides that, once the laws have been enacted by the officials, it falls to the citizens to assess the moral import and/or social efficiency of these laws. This the citizens will do by asking themselves whether the laws presented by the officials as moral conform to their idea of morality, and whether those presented as efficient are not in fact based on deficient information.

The citizens must then signal their approval or disapproval of the laws through obedience or disobedience. Their duty to manifest their disapproval stems from the commitment they made in the social contract to contribute to the lawmaking process. With respect to laws that are not indifferent to the law of nature, moreover, the citizens' duty to disobey those they believe are immoral is paramount, as this duty predates the social contract and cannot be renounced through it. In other words, because the very binding power of the social contract originates from the moral context in which it takes place (how could this contract be binding, but for a prior rule of morality that establishes the binding force of contracts?), this contract cannot conceivably provide its parties with a license to act immorally. That the officials enact a rule mandating immoral behavior is thus no excuse for the citizens to engage in that behavior.[32] Hence, whereas the citizens' duty to disobey laws they deem merely inefficient arises from the social contract itself, their duty to disobey laws they deem immoral emerges from the law of nature, and is thus prior to the social contract.

The citizens' disobedience to the laws will give incentives to the officials to modify these laws accordingly. These incentives will act in two ways. In an overt fashion, disobedience to the laws will provide the officials with advance warning of what might happen to them in the next elections, taking into account the extent of the disobedience and the importance of the laws under consideration. But disobedience will also have a more subtle and, at the same time, more immediate effect on lawmaking. By increasing the cost of enforcing the laws beyond officials' predictions, disobedience will force these officials to review their calculations and reconsider the opportunity of the laws in question. In this scenario, therefore, laws stand as tentative propositions of morality or efficiency, and civil disobedience acts as the feedback mechanism that allows for their gradual improvement or discard. Accordingly, lawmaking is a never-ending collective enterprise that progresses negatively, through the gradual elimination of mistakes.

Most importantly, however, this scenario rids us of Buchanan's sovereignty paradox, in that it does not entail that the citizens renege on the commitment they made in the social contract whenever they happen to dislike a law enacted by the officials they themselves put in power. Because civil disobedience is here performed—as the social contract provides—in all willingness to bear whatever legal sanction comes with the offense, it is no challenge to the officials' legislative authority. As such, it amounts to an application of the social contract, not to its breakdown.

The above discussion raises several questions, three of which I want to discuss in the remainder of this section. The first concerns the assumption of good faith on the part of the officials. If, as promised above, we relax this assumption and suppose now that the officials violate the terms of the social contract by declining to account for the citizens' disapproval of the laws, then the citizens should similarly be relieved from their contractual duties, that is, they should be relieved of any duties with respect to laws that are indifferent to the law of nature. Not so with respect to laws that are not indifferent to the law of nature, however, for, as explained above, the citizens' duties with regard to those stem from the law of nature itself, not from the social contract. In such cases, as in cases where official misconduct extends beyond certain laws to become systemic or even merely substantial, the only cure available to the citizens will be to remove the misbehaving officials from office, whether peacefully through the electoral process, or more forcefully through revolution.

The second question concerns the sanctions that the citizens are expected to undergo willingly when they engage in civil disobedience. It is unclear how much the citizens should be willing to give up for the sake of better laws. Should they, with Socrates, sacrifice their lives when such is the penalty mandated by the immoral law that they must disobey?

To their relief, this is unlikely, for, unlike Socrates' allegiance to the laws of Athens, the citizens' duty to obey the law here flows from the social contract; it is not inherent to membership in a polis. In the above scenario, indeed, the state is no more than the instrument chosen by the citizens to make their respective lives a little easier. As such, it is not intrinsically authoritative, but rather derives its authority from the social contract as act of will. Accordingly, it seems likely that the citizens would agree to put a limit on the sacrifices they are expected to make. It would indeed be peculiar to agree to give up one's life with the aim of making it better. Nonetheless, it may not be immoral to do so, for, as argued above,[33] the citizens' duty with respect to their lives and bodies is not absolute; God's mandate on this point is that they make the best out of them, as dictated by their conscience.

The last question I propose to discuss here is whether my model is applicable to political structures grounded in utility, rather than deontology, so as to resolve conflicts between individual- and institutional-level demands in contexts such as that described by Professor Hardin.[34] It is important to note that the reason the citizens in my model willingly undergo pain for the sake of the greater good of the community (here, morally better laws) is that they believe they are bound by extant rules of morality that transcend them. Would the model still work if sheer utility were therein substituted for this belief system?

Clearly, chances of success are extremely low if the citizens are *self-interested* utilitarians, for then a sweeping prisoner's dilemma will likely prevent civil disobedience from emerging. Indeed, because civil disobedience will only bring about legislative amendments if it is sufficiently widespread, it would be irrational for any one agent to incur costs unless she believes other agents will do the same, which is unlikely in a world of self-interested utilitarians.[35] In contrast, in a world of utilitarians who are not self-interested, the problem is no longer one of cooperation; it is merely one of coordination, which is aptly resolved through the social contract. Civil disobedience as collective information-gathering process is thus likely to break down only where the citizens perceive themselves as utilitarian and self-interested.[36]


## B. *The Theory as Lockean*

I now finally turn to the question of how much of the above discussion can properly be attributed to Locke. As explained in the introduction, Locke did not flesh out a whole theory of the relation of civil disobedience to the rule of law, although he did believe in both. He did nonetheless provide some of the elements included in my model, and it is those that I want to outline.

On the question of the accessibility of the law of nature to the human mind, Locke is somewhat inconsistent. Having written in section 12 of the *Second Treatise* that "it is certain there is [a law of nature], and that too, as intelligible and plain to a rational Creature, and a Studier of that Law, as the positive Laws of Common-wealths, nay possibly plainer," he then claims in section 136:

> [T]he Law of Nature being unwritten, and so no where to be found but in the minds of Men, they who through Passion or Interest shall mis-cite, or misapply it, cannot so easily be convinced of their mistake where there is no establish'd Judge. . . . To avoid these Inconveniencies which disorder Mens Properties in the state of Nature, Men unite into Societies, that they may have . . . *standing rules* to bound it, by which every one may know what is his.[37]

He may even have alluded to the evolutionary character of the interpretive process when he acknowledged, in section 156, that there are cases where the "variableness of humane affairs could not bear a steady fixed rule."

The confusion seems finally cleared by the following unequivocal statement taken from his *Letter concerning Toleration,* which statement reiterates the last point:

> But in this great variety of ways that men follow, it is still doubted which is this right one. Now neither the care of the Common-wealth, nor the right of enacting Laws, does discover this way

that leads to Heaven more certainly to the Magistrate, than every private mans Search and Study discovers it unto himself.[38]

With respect to the officials' legislative authority, Locke would probably insist that it is limited to the first kind of laws I list above, that is, laws that are dictated by the law of nature. For he describes the social contract as serving one, and only one, purpose, namely, the protection and enforcement of the citizens' natural rights of life, liberty, and property, and it is doubtful whether laws grounded in efficiency alone can be shoehorned into that denomination. But insofar as Locke's only disagreement with my model on this point concerns the content of the social contract, one would have to conclude, not that my model is inconsistent with Locke's theory of the state, but rather that it applies to other contractarian theories as well.

On the issue of civil disobedience, Locke is truly cryptic, perhaps because he was primarily concerned to defend another mode of control of the officials: forceful revolution. Nonetheless, he does suggest in the *Second Treatise* that revolution is appropriate where the officials act in bad faith,[39] which could be read as a roundabout way of allowing for other redress mechanisms when the problem is mistake rather than bad faith. This he in fact confirms in section 232, where Locke distinguishes *resistance* (of the positive laws) from *rebellion* (against the officials).

In contrast, he is quite explicit on the importance of bearing the sanctions of the offenses committed through civil disobedience, although not in the *Second Treatise,* where he insists that *"[n]o Man in Civil Society can be exempted from the Laws of it,"*[40] but then opposes Barclay's claim that resistance must be done "with Respect."[41] He later explains, "How to *resist Force without striking again,* or how to *strike with Reverence,* will need some Skill to make intelligible."[42] It is in the *Letter concerning Toleration* that Locke finally addresses the issue coherently. He there summarizes his views in the following, most revealing, fashion:

> *What if the Magistrate should enjoyn any thing by his Authority that appears unlawful to the Conscience of a private Person?* . . . I say, that such a private Person is to abstain from the Action that he judges

unlawful; and he is to undergo the Punishment, which it is not unlawful for him to bear. For the private judgment of any Person concerning a Law enacted in Political Matters, for the publick Good, does not take away the Obligation of the Law, nor deserve Dispensation. But if the Law indeed be concerning things that lie not within the Verge of the Magistrate's Authority . . . men are not in these cases obliged by the Law, against their Consciences.[43]

## CONCLUSION

I have tried to give an account of civil disobedience that reconciles one's duty to universal reason with one's duty to obey the law. This account rests on a view of morality as a transcendental law of nature that is accessible to the human mind, although not easily so. Civil disobedience, I argue, can be pictured as part of a collective lawmaking enterprise involving all citizens, an enterprise in which they bind themselves to take part through the social contract. In this scenario, laws are enacted by the officials as tentative statements of morality and/or efficiency, and then turned over to the citizens for their approval. Through civil disobedience, I suggest, the citizens manifest their disapproval, with the intent of pressuring the officials in turn to amend the statements accordingly. But civil disobedience does not here constitute a challenge to the officials' authority, and thus a violation of the rule of law, because, while disobeying, the citizens willingly undergo whatever penalty the officials have provided for the offense. By appealing to the social contract, therefore, it seems possible to combine the rule of law with individual autonomy within one and the same political system.

## NOTES

1. See Hampton's discussions of the role of moral theory in the citizens' assessment of "object law" (the substance of the legal rules) as indicative of the rulers' performance (Hampton, this volume, pp. 21–22). She is there careful to limit the citizens' power over the

rulers to, for example (p. 38), that of "peacefully depos[ing them] at the voting booth."

2. Peter Laslett, ed. (Cambridge: Cambridge University Press, 1988).

3. James H. Tully, ed. (Indianapolis: Hackett, 1983).

4. Hampton, this volume, p. 31.

5. *Leviathan,* at part II, chapter 18, para. 94, p. 238 (London: Penguin Books, 1985).

6. Id., part I, chapter 14, p. 189.

7. Secs. 4, 7, 19.

8. Secs. 21, 90.

9. "For he being suppos'd to have all . . . Power in himself alone, there is no Judge to be found, no Appeal lies open to any one, who may fairly, and indifferently, and with Authority decide, and from whose decision relief and redress may be expected of any Injury of Inconveniency, that may be suffered from the Prince or by his Order." Second Treatise, sec. 91. And to suggest that everyone would wish to be subjected to an all-powerful sovereign would, in Locke's view, be to suggest that, in certain cases, "[m]en are so foolish that they [would wish] to avoid what Mischiefs may be done them by *Pole-Cats,* or *Foxes,* but [would be] content, nay think it Safety, to be devoured by *Lions.*" Sec. 93. (Unless otherwise noted, all paragraph references hereinafter are to Locke's *Second Treatise.*) See also secs. 90, 131.

10. Hampton, this volume, p. 14.

11. "But though Men when they enter into Society, give up the Equality, Liberty, and Executive Power they had in the State of Nature . . . yet it being only with an intention in every one the better to preserve himself his Liberty and Property." Sec. 131.

12. *Leviathan,* at chapter 29, para. 9, p. 169.

13. "Man . . . hath by Nature a Power, not only to preserve his Property . . . against the Injuries and Attempts of other Men; but to judge of, and punish the breaches of that Law in others, as he is perswaded the Offence deserves, even with Death it self. . . . [T]here, and there only is *Political Society,* where every one of the Members hath quitted this natural Power, resign'd it up into the hands of the Community in all cases that exclude him not from appealing for Protection to the Law established by it. And thus all private judgement of every particular Member being excluded, the Community comes to be Umpire, by settled standing Rules, indifferent, and the same to all Parties; and by Men having Authority from the Community, for the execution of those Rules, decides all the differences that may happen

between any Members of that Society, concerning any matter of right; and punishes those Offences, which any Member hath committed against the Society, with such Penalties as the Law has established." Sec. 87. (Italics in original.)

14. "But though this be a *State of Liberty,* yet it is *not a State of Licence,* though Man in that State have an uncontroleable Liberty, to dispose of his Person or Possessions, yet he has not Liberty to destroy himself. . . . For Men being all the Workmanship of one Omnipotent, and infinitely wise Maker; All the Servants of one Sovereign Master, sent into the World by his order and about his business, they are his Property, whose Workmanship they are, made to last during his . . . Pleasure." Sec. 6. (Italics in original.) See also sec. 23.

Michael Zuckert rightly pointed out to me that Locke did not, however, view one's duty to preserve oneself as unconditional, as he writes of the slave, for example, that "whenever he finds the hardship of his Slavery out-weigh the value of his Life, 'tis in his Power, by resisting the Will of his Master, to draw on himself the Death he desires." Sec. 23. The duty of self-preservation should thus be interpreted as a duty to do the best possible with one's life and property in light of all circumstances, that is, to preserve one's life in all cases "but where some nobler use, than its bare Preservation calls for it." Sec. 6.

Concerning the social contract, however, since Locke believes that the very purpose of instituting civil society is to better protect individuals' natural rights to life, liberty, and property, it is unlikely this instiution could be deemed "noble" enough to warrant that individuals alienate these rights in favor of the authority through the social contract.

15. Sec. 149. See also sec. 132.

16. Sec. 240. (Italics in original.) To the same effect, see Locke's example of the soldier who could legitimately be required to "march up to the mouth of a Cannon, or stand in a Breach, where he is almost sure to perish" but could not similarly be required to give his superior "one penny of his Money" because "blind Obedience is necessary to that end for which the Commander has his Power, *viz.* the preservation of the rest; but the disposing of his Goods has nothing to do with it." Sec. 139. See also secs. 131, 168, 242–43.

17. "Whosoever uses *force without Right,* as every one does in Society, who does it without Law, puts himself into a *state of War* with those, against whom he so uses it, and in that state all former Ties are cancelled, all other Rights cease, and every one has a *Right* to defend

himself, and *to resist the Aggressor*." Sec. 232. (Italics in original.) See also sec. 202.

18. Sec. 155.

19. Sec. 143. See also sec. 138.

20. Hampton, this volume, p. 35.

21. For purposes of this comment, "primary rules," "legal rules," "laws," etc., refer to rules formulated by judges and legislators alike, as my arguments apply to both indiscriminately unless otherwise indicated.

22. Sec. 136, quoting Richard Hooker, *Of the Lawes of Ecclesiasticall Politie*, Book I, chapter I, sec. 10 (Keble ed. 1836). See also sec. 135: "The Obligations of the Law of Nature, cease not in Society but only in many Cases are drawn closer, and have by Humane Laws known Penalties annexed to them, to inforce their observation. Thus the *Legislators* as well as others. The *Rules* that they make for other Mens Actions, must, as well as their own and other Mens Actions, be conformable to the Law of Nature, *i.e.* to the Will of God, of which that is a Declaration, and the *fundamental Law of Nature* being *the preservation of Mankind,* no Humane Sanction can be good, or valid against it." (Italics in original.) To the same effect, see sec. 12.

23. "Rules and Social Facts," *Harvard Journal of Law & Public Policy* 14 (1991): 721.

24. At sec. 90, Locke quotes Hooker ("Eccl. Pol." 1. I. sec. 16) to suggest one is not obligated to obey the civil law when "there be reason shew'd which may necessarily inforce, that the Law of Reason, or of God, doth injoyn the contrary." See also secs. 208, 222. At sec. 21, he explains that whether or not obedience is required is for each individual to decide: "Where there is no Judge on Earth, the Appeal lies to God in Heaven. . . . Of that I my self can only be Judge in my own Conscience, as I will answer it at the great Day, to the Supream Judge of all Men."

25. Hampton, this volume, p. 37.

26. *Supra,* at 46.

27. *The Limits of Liberty* (1975), 92.

28. Russell Hardin discusses the same problem under a different label, namely, the "conflict between individual- and institutionnal-level demands." See Hardin, this volume, p. 223.

29. For more details on the applicability of the scientific method to lawmaking, see my "Hercules Revisited: An Evolutionary Model of Judicial Reasoning," *Mississippi Law Journal* 59 (1987): 1069.

30. To be sure, rules of private and criminal law can themselves be

interpreted as solutions to problems of collective action. Hobbes's own social contract has been interpreted as a means for individuals in the state of nature to solve their collective prisoner's dilemma. See J. Hampton, *Hobbes and the Social Contract Tradition* (Cambridge: Cambridge University Press, 1986). Similarly, detection and deterrence of crime can be seen as a public good, the production of which might be hampered by free riding. What sets these legal rules apart from those of the second kind is that they can be justified on moral grounds as well as on grounds of rational choice theory.

31. Rational choice theory and economics generally indeed proclaim themselves as morally neutral because they take individual preferences, moral or otherwise, as given. Whether they truly take individual preferences as given, and, even if they do, whether this starting point truly is morally neutral, are controversial questions which it will be for the citizens to debate, as I explain next in the text.

32. It is not here necessary that the citizens have a clear grasp of what is moral and immoral behavior in the circumstances; it is enough that one act to the best of one's conscience. Following Kant, I here take the view that an action can only be immoral if it can be perceived as such by the agent.

33. *Supra,* note 14 and accompanying text.

34. *Supra,* note 28. Hardin there describes the dilemmas faced by individuals when actions dictated by the maximization of their private utility clash with the demands of collective utility.

35. Note that it is here enough that the agent thinks that most *other* agents are self-interested utilitarians, even if *she* is committed to collective welfare.

36. Where citizens are self-interested but not utilitarians, the process is unlikely to break down either, for all that is here required is that the citizens have a reason for practicing disobedience that transcends the practice itself. Individuals concerned with, say, their own salvation will have reason to abide by God's law regardless of whether or not others share that concern and act accordingly.

37. (Italics in original.) To the same effect, see sec. 124.

38. At 36.

39. Sec. 20.

40. Sec. 94. (Italics in original.)

41. Sec. 233, quoting Barclay with disapproval, William Barclay *De Reguo et Regali Potestate* (Hanover, 1612).

42. Sec. 235. (Italics in original.)

43. At 48. (Italics in original.)

# 3

# HOBBES, LOCKE, AND
# THE PROBLEM OF
# THE RULE OF LAW

## MICHAEL P. ZUCKERT

A lasting legacy of the Warren and Burger eras of the U.S. Supreme Court has been renewed debate about the nature of rule of law. This debate has not merely claimed space in learned journals but has also contributed to the particularly acrimonious confirmation hearings on recent Supreme Court nominees like Robert Bork and Clarence Thomas. Although the debate is not without its complexities, two polar positions recur in one form or another within it, positions sometimes identified as Hobbesean and Lockean in character.

The so-called Hobbesean position, identified with the likes of Bork and Chief Justice Rehnquist, takes a positivist approach to law and an originalist approach to constitutional interpretation. The legitimate power of courts, including the Supreme Court, extends only to applying the law, with the law understood to be identifiable positive law of one sort or another. American positive law includes the Constitution, which the "Hobbeseans" concede to be supreme over other forms of law, but the Constitution must be used sparingly and with proper warrant when invoked to overturn the democratic will of the sovereign people as expressed in ordinary legislation. The "Hobbeseans" are partial, therefore, to Thayer's standard of judicial restraint, and to originalist interpretation.[1]

The sophisticated adherents of original intent jurisprudence do not "require that the judge know what the specific intention of the lawgiver was regarding the case at hand." Such a demand "would destroy all law." Rather, the originalist judge insists that in constitutional adjudication, "the text, structure and history of the Constitution provide him not with a conclusion but with a major premise. That major premise is a principle or stated value that the ratifiers wanted to protect against hostile legislation or executive action."[2] As Bork's subtitle ("The Political Seduction of the Law") indicates, the "Hobbeseans" define themselves as defenders of the rule of law and accuse devotees of more expansive approaches to law, constitution, and judicial role of being witting or unwitting enemies of the rule of law. To decide cases in a nonoriginalist manner, to find the "premises" or "values" for decisions elsewhere than in the text, structure, and history of the law itself is to substitute somebody's "value judgments"—normally those of the judges making the decision— for those "value judgments" that have attained the status of law and legitimacy. According to originalists, in other words, nonoriginalists commit the cardinal sin against the dominant constitutionalist tradition of Anglo-American law: they substitute the rule of men for the rule of law.

The "Lockeans," on the other hand, argue for a far more activist, nonoriginalist approach to the Constitution. "Lockeans" frequently appeal to some transcendent source of legal norms, such as nominee Clarence Thomas's invocation of natural law at his confirmation hearings. A good example of the "Lockean" alternative is a series of articles by Randy Barnett, who argues against Bork and his ilk that not only is judicial enforcement of unenumerated reserved rights compatible with the rule of law, but it is required by it.[3] Rule of law means exercise of publicly justifiable power. Public justifiability means or requires the application of moral standards, written or otherwise, to legislative output. Law is distinguished from acts of force precisely by its ability to withstand such scrutiny. It is not sufficient that law be authored by legitimate authority. The positivity of law, that is, its derivation from authorities designated by some "rule of recognition" (in H. L. A. Hart's term), is not sufficient to establish its lawfulness.

The "Lockeans" thus find the "Hobbeseans" to be, at best, mere formalists, affirming the external aspect of the rule of law but missing its inner core. At worst, the "Lockeans" suggest that the "Hobbesean" appeals to the positive law and original intent disguise a conservative political agenda. As Justice Brennan once urged, there are "political underpinnings," or at least political consequences, to the "Hobbesean" theory: "A position that upholds constitutional claims only if they were within the specific contemplation of the framers in effect establishes a presumption of resolving textual ambiguities against the claims of constitutional right."[4] Brennan and his "Lockean" allies thus turn the "Hobbeseans'" accusation back on itself: the originalists are themselves substituting the rule of men for the rule of law.

The "Lockeans," then, urge judges to test legislation against the moral standards that alone justify all acts of public authority. Open-ended constitutional provisions like the Ninth Amendment and the vaguer parts of the Fourteenth Amendment are seen as intimations within the positive law itself of the constitution drafters' acceptance of the "Lockean" conception of the rule of law. Thus these parts of the Constitution, rejected by Bork as mere "ink-blots," became for the "Lockeans" the very pillars of constitutional jurisprudence and the rule of law.

Most (although not all) partisans in our current legal wars accept the authority of the aspiration to the rule of law. Partisans on both sides express no less confidence that the rule of law is on their side and their side alone than warriors in hotter wars have claimed God as theirs and theirs alone. However, if we trace the issue back to the philosophic progenitors who stand to some extent as champions on each side of the controversy, we will not find, I think, that one or another of the combatants can rightly lay exclusive claim to forwarding the rule of law. Hobbes and Locke together point instead to the problematic character of the rule of law, a problematic embodied in the current conflict, but not resolved by either side.

## Hobbes and the Rule of Law

Although Jean Hampton's chapter, "Democracy and the Rule of Law," does not directly address the contemporary debate as sketched above, her argument has great relevance for it. Most significantly, perhaps, she challenges the very way in which the issue has been posed: her Hobbes is not the sponsor of a competitor to Locke's conception of rule of law, but a critic of the very idea thereof. The Hobbes who attempts to crush all soft-minded constitutionalists like Philip Hunton does not present a conception of the rule of law, but argues pointedly and forcefully against its logical and practical possibility. As she puts it on Hobbes's behalf, some will must always rule. Even when law seems to rule, there must be somebody to interpret and apply the law, and there must be somebody who has authority to resolve conflicts over the meaning or application of the law. It is the will of that somebody that rules, and not the law. This is the Hobbesean challenge to those like Hunton in his own time, Locke soon after, and Barnett and others today who seek a constitutionalist politics where the powers of the government are both limited and shared, as defined in a fundamental law of the Constitution.

She gives us here an authentic Hobbes; he does rail against the rule of law, just as she says. For this reason, I have used the term "Hobbesean" only with quotation marks to describe the provenance of the constitutional conservatism of Bork and the others. She reminds us, in other words, that it is not historically or philosophically accurate to describe contemporary originalists as Hobbeseans. The father would deny his alleged children, for they accept institutions and practices he either knew nothing of or cared nothing for. They, for example, view the Constitution as fundamental, ruling law when rightly used; they accept the complex American scheme of separation of powers that divides the legislative from the judicial power and arms the judiciary with the power to enforce the Constitution, including, among other things, the power to enforce enumerated, reserved rights. Hobbes more or less loudly sneers at all such things, or would do so if he could have imagined them.

For Hampton, then, the problem of the rule of law is the

problem posed by Hobbes in his "regress argument," but it is not the problem defined by the hand-to-hand contest of partisans of two quite different conceptions of the rule of law, one loosely associated with Hobbes and the other with Locke. There is only Lockean rule of law; Hampton implies that both parties to our current debates are Lockeans of one sort or another.

Plausible and persuasive as Hampton's interpretation is, there is, however, quite another way of reading Hobbes that brings him back within the orbit of rule-of-law thinking, and that gives point to identifying one position in our contemporary debates as loosely Hobbesean. Indeed, Michael Oakeshott, one of the most astute political philosophers of the twentieth century, goes so far as to identify Hobbes above all as the philosopher of rule of law.[5]

We can begin to resolve the paradox of Hobbes, the notorious philosopher of absolute sovereignty, as a philosopher of rule of law if we note the disparity between the way Hampton formulates the problematic of the rule of law and the way Hobbes himself does. For Hampton, the relevant contrast is between law and will—either rule of will, which her Hobbes endorses, or rule of law, which he rejects. Yet Hobbes himself does not formulate the issue in quite this way. According to Hobbes's formal definition, "Civill Law, is to every subject, those rules, which the commonwealth hath commanded him, by word, writing, or other sufficient sign of the will, to make use of, for the distinction of right, and wrong."[6] Law, in the more famous shorthand designation made famous within legal positivism, is the command or will of the sovereign.[7] At least within Hobbes's own conceptual frame, law and will stand not as opposites such that the rule of will automatically excludes the rule of law. The decisive distinction for Hobbes is, rather, that between public and private will. Law is public will, that is, the will of the public authorities, the sovereign, and rule of the public will is therefore identical with rule of law. Rule by public will promises to save human beings from the altogether unacceptable outcomes that rule by private wills typically produces. Hobbes's terrifying vision of the state of nature is an image of the unmitigated rule of private wills. The result is conflict, war, and the endangerment of all that human beings hold dear, that is, of all that they do will or might will.

The establishment of rule by public will, that is, rule of law, requires for Hobbes the rejection of everything we normally associate with the rule of law. When Hampton, for example, thinks of rule of law, she thinks of one or another form of constitutionalism—of a system in which some sort of fundamental law sets bounds to the powers of the ruling authorities, divides power among them, reserves rights to the people as such or to individuals, and establishes devices to enforce or implement these limits and reservations. Hobbes rejects divided authority and reserved rights.

Hampton rightly identifies the "regress argument" as an important part of his reasoning here, but there is a yet deeper level to his analysis.[8] The problem that requires political authority as its solution is precisely the problem of private wills—plural, partial, and conflicting private wills. The solution is to create an artificial public will, singular, comprehensive, and integral. Such a will is no doubt terrifying to contemplate; indeed, that is part of its point. The one dominating public will can possess not only the unity to establish a uniform rule "for the distinction of right, and wrong" in place of the multitudinous and conflicting private rules that would otherwise exist, but also the power to enforce that rule over the unruly private wills of the subjects.

Any efforts to limit that will, inspired by fear of it, must be resisted. To divide sovereign powers is to introduce into the ruling will a set of private interests—whatever partial concerns the various powers possess—that compromises the identity between the public will and the public as such. It also reintroduces into the heart of the public authority the conflicting private wills that led to the terrors of the state of nature in the first place. The result is civil war, even more devastating than the original state of nature. The sovereign powers are simply and essentially "inseparable."[9] No more may subjects reserve rights, that is, reserve a sphere of private will immune from the rule of public will. "Annexed to the Soveraigntie [is] the whole power of prescribing the rules, whereby every man may know, what goods he may enjoy, and what actions he may doe, without being molested by any of his fellow subjects."[10] There is, in other words, no private sphere of liberty or of property immune from legal control by the sovereign. For Hobbes, the rule of law means the *rule* of law as well as the rule of *law*.

Our contemporary "Hobbeseans," while not exactly agreeing with the master, do indeed incorporate Hobbeslike considerations into their approach to law. They insist on the authoritativeness of the sovereign authority—the people acting either through their normal democratic institutions, or in their higher constitutional capacity. Likewise, although they willingly accept a sphere of enumerated reserved rights that Hobbes would not, they nonetheless resist the introduction of private will into law interpreting, or, as it is redubbed in our post-Nietzschean age, they reject the importation of "values" not inserted into the law by the sovereign in one way or another.[11]

What is much clearer in Hobbes than in his semi-epigones, however, is the foundation that supports the whole. At this level, too, Hobbes's theory appears to be thoroughly paradoxical. The beginning and the end for Hobbes is the right of nature possessed by each equal human being. That right is "the liberty each man hath, to use his own power, as he will himselfe, for the preservation of his own nature."[12] For the sake of one's natural right one gives up, almost entirely, one's natural right. The exercise by each of his or her natural right (private will, private action) fails miserably at securing that to which each has a right, "the preservation of one's own nature": the state of nature is a state of war. To give up one's right so far as one is able is the means to secure that to which one has a right. Hobbes, in his own odd way, endorses the Christian maxim: one must lose oneself in order to find oneself. The purely formal or positivist notion of law at which Hobbes arrives is the result not of formal analysis of legal practice or legal concepts, but of a thinking through of the necessary means to the accomplishment of the substantive natural end of politics. In order to accomplish the substantive end, however, substance must give way entirely to form, or natural law and natural right must abdicate entirely to positive law and positive right.

## Locke and the Limits of the Rule of Law

Hobbes argues, in effect, that renunciation of all aspirations to constitutionalism as normally understood is a necessary condition for achievement of the rule of law. Hampton understands rule of law in the more standard sense of being close to or dependent on constitutionalism, and thus she fails to see Hobbes as a rule-of-law thinker at all. The brunt of her chapter shows how rule of law is possible on Lockean contractarian grounds despite the Hobbesean regress argument.

She argues that not only is the rule of law possible but also that modern democracies (as opposed to ancient ones) are based on this rule of law and not on the rule of will. Her response to Hobbes takes the following form: just as Tarski attempted to resolve logical paradoxes with the distinction between object and meta languages, so she proposes to refute Hobbes's regress argument via a distinction between object and meta levels of political authority. At the object level of the political system, the level of the operation of the ordinary institutions of government, a constitutionalist system of separated and divided authorities, with limited and defined powers, does indeed exist. At this level there is a governing rule, the rule of the Constitution and constitutional law.

The existence of the rule of law within the object-level political system does not deny the Hobbesean critique but departs from Hobbes in looking to a meta-level system for the resolution of conflicts that arise within the object level. At the meta level, the people, ultimately, have power to settle conflicts, authoritatively interpret, control (hire and fire) governors, and even change the entire structure of the object-level institutions. This is all done through a variety of practices, including elections, constitutional amendment powers, and even a right of revolution. Therefore, she replies to Hobbes, at the object level, at least, the rule of law prevails, and not as in previous systems (or, as Hobbes would have it, in all possible systems), the rule of some human will(s). So far as the system does ultimately depend on human will at the meta level, as she concedes it does, that human will operates quite differently than in earlier forms of democracy. It does not operate to govern on a regular basis, but only in a deferred way, to judge, correct, hire, and fire rulers.

As a response to Hobbes's regress argument, Hampton's argument must be judged only a partial success. On the decisive issue, she concedes Hobbes's point. She cannot replace rule of will by rule of law; perhaps her two-level system conceals to some degree the rule of will, but it is there, just where Hobbes said it must be. It remains a system of (democratic) sovereignty, a complicated form to be sure, but democratic sovereignty nonetheless. From Hobbes's perspective, it is not as important how things are labeled—meta or object—as it is to notice that human will stands as the necessary ultima ratio of the construct.

Her accomplishment might appear more impressive if one takes it out of the terms in which she has cast it—the conflict between rule of law and rule of will—and reformulates it instead in the terms suggested by Hobbes himself: she has attempted to show how constitutionalist rule of law is possible despite Hobbes's insistence that only government by an absolute sovereign can secure rule of law. In this she does, as she claims, proceed in a loosely Lockean manner.

I wonder, however, whether anything is gained by having recourse to the object/meta distinction in place of the conceptual solutions at which Locke himself and then his successors arrived. Locke saw his difference from Hobbes as lying precisely in his denial of the Hobbesean complete, or near-complete, cession of natural right by all the subjects in the covenant that produces the commonwealth. The cession of right in Locke is narrower, although how much so is difficult to establish without detailed textual analysis. However, the key conceptual breakthrough for Locke is relatively easily stated. In addition to their primary natural rights, human beings possess by nature another far-reaching right, the right to execute the law of nature. This executive power of the law of nature is given up entirely when a rational civil society is formed, but the primary natural rights are not.[13] Natural rights not surrendered form the foundation for limits on governmental power and ultimately for Locke's commitment to constitutionalist rule of law.

The Lockean solution received another formulation during

the course of the eighteenth century that is rather close to Hampton's Tarskian solution. Although the American founders were not the only ones to face the problem Hobbes posed, they were faced with it in especially severe ways, because they sought a system that divided authority in a particularly complex manner—federalism, separation of powers, reserved rights were all part of the constitutional scheme, and all fell afoul of the abstract logic of sovereignty and the practical "regress problem" Hobbes identified. Their solution was to distinguish between government and sovereignty. Sovereignty is to remain in the people, who, via the Constitution, empower different of their governments and parts of governments to different degrees. This corresponds, more or less, to Hampton's meta and object levels. The Americans differed from Hampton, to their advantage, I believe, in seeing that a conceptual solution was the mere beginning of what they needed. In addition, they developed a political science of the operation of institutions (at Hampton's object level) that would produce effective yet limited and safe government. *The Federalist* is an important text precisely because it develops such an institutional theory.

Locke surely is the patron of constitutionalist rule of law in Hampton's sense and even of rule of law as defended by "Lockeans" in our current legal debates. He relates to the latter group in his notion that government cannot reasonably be viewed as unlimited in its legitimate powers, but that all powers must, in principle, meet a justificatory test. In other words, Locke endorses the key elements of constitutionalist rule of law: separated and limited powers and reserved rights. Locke arrives at this position not merely by adumbrating a conceptual ground for resisting Hobbes's complete cession of natural right (e.g., Hampton's meta/object distinction, the distinction between ceding the executive power of the law of nature and the substantive rights, the distinction between sovereignty and government), but more importantly by presenting an analysis designed to show that the exercise of private will is not as such harmful.

According to Locke, Hobbes is most mistaken in believing that the good of each can be accomplished only through the in-principle complete substitution of public will for the private wills of the citizens. This is largely the accomplishment of his analysis of property, on the one hand, and religion, on the other. The reservation of property and liberty rights beyond anything Hobbes would admit derives from Locke's reanalysis of the role of material conditions in human existence and the insight that privately willed productive activity (labor, profit seeking) does not disrupt but rather knits together society by creating interdependence and wealth. Moreover, in his *Letter concerning Toleration* and other places, Locke shows that a privatizing solution to the religious problem, religious toleration, also better serves the cause of rights securing than does any kind of public solution. Religion is no longer to be the cement of society; the mutual interdependence of the division of labor and the joint subordination to secular but rational authority is, for the most part, to serve that function instead.[14]

Despite his sharp rejection of the Hobbesean means to their more or less common end, Locke's constitutionalist rule of law differs from Hobbes's in relatively subtle ways. Not only does Locke reject Hobbes's unliberal notion of the necessity of replacing private by public will, but he also refuses to grant the label "law" to any and all acts of the public will. "Tyranny is the exercise of power beyond right," and "when the governor . . . makes not the law, but his will the rule" at least one of the conditions in tyranny is satisfied.[15] Locke's doctrine of separation of powers is intimately connected to his revised doctrine of rule of law. He advocates a political structure quite different from Hobbes's: separated legislative and executive powers with strict legal subordination of the executive power. This arrangement is meant to establish rule of law in the full sense: unlike Hobbes's sovereign, who conjoins legislative and executive authority and whose every act of will is by definition law, Locke's arrangement means to require governance by standing law, that is, by general rules prescribed by the collective legislative body in advance. The legislature, barred from execution, is thus limited to general rule making. Hobbes's "absolute, arbitrary power, or governing without settled standing laws, can neither of them consist with the ends of society and government."[16] The executive, dealing with particulars, is limited to putting into effect the general rules, and remains subordinate to the legislature: "In all cases, whilst the government subsists, the legislature is the supreme power. For what can give laws to another, must needs be superior to him." [17]

Locke's doctrine of rule of law, although rightly seen as somehow standing in the background of the position taken by our contemporary "Lockeans," nonetheless differs from theirs in several decisive ways. Indeed, Locke ends up moving back toward Hobbes's nonconstitutionalist solution in many places, and thereby points toward the limits of any constitutionalist rule of law solution.

In the first place, Locke affirms an almost sovereign legislature. As Harvey Mansfield, Jr., has pointed out, "the rule of law for Locke clearly means the rule of the law-making power, not the ascendancy or inviolability of certain laws," and even less the legal ascendancy and inviolability of certain unwritten moral principles. [18] Locke has no law beyond the law to set limits to legislative power, and he has no body like the Supreme Court to enforce such a law or such limits. There are indeed certain principles governing the exercise of legislative power, for example, that it is to govern "by settled standing rules, indifferent, and the same to all parties," that it is not to delegate the legislative power, and that it is to respect the end (rights securing) for which it exists. [19] But Locke supplies no governmental body to impose such limits on the legislature, except perhaps the executive acting via its share in the legislative power, when it has such a share. In some respects, then, Locke is much less a "Lockean" than even committed "Hobbeseans" like Bork. The latter accept constitutional, enforceable limits on legislative power that Locke does not. Locke's supreme legislature is in many ways closer to Hobbes's sovereign than to current "Lockean" theory. [20]

Not only does Locke fail to secure rule of law in its modern version, "Hobbesean" or "Lockean," but he even retreats from rule of law in his own sense. Contrary to first impressions, the executive turns out not to be strictly subordinate to the legislative; the former possesses a prerogative power, which, remarkably, Locke describes as a "power to act according to discretion . . . without the prescription of the law, and sometimes even against it." [21] The standard of rightful action then is not law alone. Thus Locke does not simply endorse the old maxim, "Wherever law ends tyranny begins," but adds, "if the law be transgressed to another's harm."[22] Transgressions of law that help the community, despite being violations of the rule of law, are acceptable and, Locke suggests, even necessary. Locke rejects, in other words, a strictly constitutionalist approach to the fundamental powers of the commonwealth.

His liberation of the executive from strict subordination to the legislature of course reraises the difficult questions Hobbes had posed regarding all separation of powers schemes: who is to judge in case of conflict between the executive and the legislature? Locke's well-known answer is that "the people shall be judge." They shall judge in a variety of ways, including public opinion, general willingness to remain obedient to governmental actions, elections when those are relevant, and, finally, revolutions. The Constitution itself does not contain a means to resolve difficulties that arise within it.

Locke treats reserved rights in more or less the same way. Neither a Borkean nor a Brennanian Supreme Court second guesses the legislature's treatment of rights. Rights may be regulated for the sake of the public good, that is, for the sake of the general security of rights, but the judgments of the legislature are mostly taken to be determinative as to whether the public good is being served. Even with regard to the very central issue of taxation, the "legislative power" operates under the stricture that it may not tax a property owner "without his own consent." But this is achieved through the consent of the majority of representatives as apparently nonreviewable judgment that the public good warrants the imposition.[23] Reserved rights have a firmer presence for Locke than for Hobbes, but neither enumerated nor unenumerated reserved rights have the kind of presence they have, respectively, for our "Hobbeseans" and "Lockeans." Reserved rights for Locke lead to the demand that the legislature be a representative body. The rights make themselves felt as interests within institutions structured to give them presence. Not quite the same way as in Hobbes, but along similar lines, substance becomes process.

Yet substance never entirely becomes process for Locke, as it almost does for Hobbes. The executive through his prerogative power, as we have already seen, and the people through their right of revolution retain a residual empowerment through rights. If the process is oppressive, the people retain the right to throw it off in order to better protect their rights. Like the prerogative power, Locke's right of revolution escapes the bounds of rule of law, whether understood in Hobbes's, in his own, or in "Hobbesean" or "Lockean" terms. Locke's own solution to the problem of rights and the rule of law is certainly very far from that of contemporaries like Barnett. Locke's political philosophy thus culminates in a paradox as much as does Hobbes's: rule of law is necessary for the sake of securing rights, and yet securing rights requires (perhaps frequent) violation of rule of law. Locke does not appear to support those who believe that a rule-of-law system perfectly respectful of the underlying moral justification of law is possible.

## HOBBES, LOCKE, AND THE PROBLEM OF THE RULE OF LAW

Hobbes is not a "Hobbesean" and Locke is not a "Lockean" as these labels are being used here to describe polar positions taken in our current debates. If we turn the dialectical dial one twist further, however, we can restate these positions so that Hobbes and the "Hobbeseans," Locke and the "Lockeans" do align. The "Hobbeseans" are like Hobbes in maintaining that the ends of political power, whatever they may be, need to be buried in the means of politics. Justice is purely legal justice, and legal justice is achieved through honoring legitimate law, not just law as measured by any translegal standard. Our contemporary "Hobbeseans," like Bork, perhaps go even further in this direction than Hobbes, who, after all, affirmed a doctrine of natural right and natural law, that is, who had natural moral standards that provided the legitimating grounds for sovereign political authority. Bork and associates are more positivistic than Hobbes; beneath legal standards they discern nothing but arbitrary and variable "value judgments."

The "Lockeans" are like Locke in arguing the need for the end to have some abiding presence over and above all the positivities of law and process in which the ends are embedded. For Locke, this implies the extralegal prerogative power, on the one hand, and the extralegal right of resistance, on the other.

For the "Lockeans" this means the legitimacy or even necessity of direct judicial appeal to the morally justificatory principles that must be satisfied in order to legitimate all law. Hobbes and the "Hobbeseans" repose in a pure formalism. Locke and the "Lockeans" are dissatisfied with pure formalism.

Locke's own reason for rejecting Hobbes's formalism remains potent when translated into our current debate: a means cannot be cut free from its end. The moral rationale that justifies law remains always relevant to the actual law. It does not merely escort the lawmakers onto the dance floor and then retire to sit, all wallflowerlike, along the side while the authorities do what they will.

On the other hand, the rationale must retire for there to be genuine law. Moral argumentation tells us that we require law, and that law differs from moral aspiration precisely in having a definite human source in identifiable authorities and processes, and in having a specificity and concrete meaning beyond moral aspiration. Locke himself emphasized this. Even though he had no doubts about the natural moral standards that justify and constitute political power, he insists that the state of nature, the state without positive law, "wants an established, settled, known law, received and allowed by common consent to be the standard of right and wrong, and the common measure to decide all controversies between them."[24] The law of nature, or natural justice, does not provide a sufficient rule. That lack, according to Locke, makes the state of nature a very "inconvenient" state indeed.[25] Even Locke appreciates the force of Hobbes's argument regarding the need for "civill law." Locke here reminds us of the fundamental Hobbesean point too often forgotten by our contemporary "Lockeans." To reject the dogmatic positivism and relativism of Judge Bork does not automatically imply that judges have a claim to transcend law in the direction of their own best moral insights, as left-Lockeans like Michael Perry or right-Lockeans like Stephen Macedo believe.[26] So far as morality leads us to see the necessity for law, it must, as Hobbes insisted, retreat into the legal means and processes it established and justifies.

In a word, the debates between Hobbes and Locke and between "Hobbeseans" and "Lockeans" reveal the antinomy of the rule of law. We cannot proceed as the two parties to the current debates do, either as if there is no moral ground for law (or as if it does not matter at all), or as if there is an easy way to make the moral ground simply part of the legal order, simply embodied, that is, in a rule-of-law system. Perhaps the best solution possible is the one Abraham Lincoln articulated throughout his career: the moral end transcends and has higher dignity than the legal means, and yet the moral end never cancels the legal means. Law and morality coexist together, inseparably at one, inseparably at odds—dancers and wallflowers both.[27]

## NOTES

1. James Bradley Thayer, "The Origin and Scope of the American Doctrine of Constitutional Law," *Harvard Law Review* 7 (1893).

2. Robert Bork, *The Tempting of America: The Political Seduction of the Law* (New York: Simon and Schuster, Inc., 1990), 162–63.

3. E.g., Randy Barnett, "Foreword: The Ninth Amendment and Constitutional Legitimacy," *Chicago-Kent Law Review* 64 (1988): 37–65; Randy Barnett, "Foreword: Can Justice and the Rule of Law Be Reconciled?" *Harvard Journal of Law and Public Policy* 2 (1988): 597–624.

4. Speech by William J. Brennan, Jr., at Georgetown University, Oct. 12, 1985, reprinted in, *The Great Debate: Interpreting Our Written Constitution* (Washington, D.C.: The Federalist Society, 1987).

5. Michael Oakshott, "The Rule of Law," in Oakshott, *On History and Other Essays* (New York: Barnes and Noble, 1983), 157–64. Cf. also Harvey Mansfield, Jr., *Taming the Prince: The Ambivalence of Modern Executive Power* (New York: The Free Press, 1989), 177.

6. Thomas Hobbes, *Leviathan* (Cambridge: Cambridge University Press, 1991), ch. 26, p. 183.

7. Cf. Ibid., 197.

8. Hampton, "Democracy and the Rule of Law" this volume, p. 15.

9. Hobbes, *Leviathan*, ch. 18, p. 127.

10. Ibid., 125.

11. Cf. Friederich Nietzsche, *Twilight of the Idols*, ch. 5, "Morality as Anti-Nature"; cf. Bork, "Neutral Principles and Some First Amendment Problems," *Indiana Law Journal* 47 (1971): 10.

12. *Leviathan*, ch. 14, p. 91.

13. John Locke, *Two Treatises of Government* (Cambridge: Cambridge University Press, 1967), II, 127–31.

14. On the limits to Locke's secularism, see his *The Reasonableness of Christianity.* For a discussion thereof, see Michael P. Zuckert, "Locke and the Problem of Civil Religion," in Robert Horwitz, ed., *The Moral Foundations of the American Republic,* 3d ed. (Charlottesville, Va.: University Press of Virginia, 1986), 180–203.

15. Locke, *Two Treatises,* II, 199.

16. *Two Treatises,* II, 137; cf. 2:190.

17. *Two Treatises,* II, 150.

18. Mansfield, *Taming the Prince,* 200.

19. *Two Treatises,* II, 87, 135–42.

20. A good corrective to common views of Locke is Wilmoore Kendall, *John Locke and the Doctrine of Majority Rule* (Urbana, Ill.: University of Illinois Press, 1941).

21. *Two Treatises,* II, 160.

22. *Two Treatises,* II, 202.

23. *Two Treatises,* II, 138–40.

24. *Two Treatises,* II, 124.

25. Cf. Barnett, "Justice and the Rule of Law," 600–615.

26. Cf. Michael J. Perry, *Morality, Politics, and Law* (Oxford: Oxford University Press, 1988); Stephen Macedo, *The New Right versus the Constitution* (Washington, D.C.: Cato Institute, 1987); *Liberal Virtues* (Oxford: Oxford University Press, 1990). For a discussion of Perry's view of the relation between law and morality, see Michael P. Zuckert, "Review of Perry's *Morality, Politics, and Law*" in *Constitutional Commentary* 6 (1989): 446–59.

27. On Lincoln's "solution," see Harry V. Jaffa, *Crisis of the House Divided* (Garden City, N.Y.: Doubleday and Co., 1959); for one effort, but by no means the only possible one, to apply Lincoln's "solution" to American constitutionalism, see Alexander Bickel, *The Least Dangerous Branch* (New Haven, Conn.: Yale University Press, 1966).

# 4

# DEMOCRACY, EQUALITY, AND
# THE DEATH PENALTY

## ROBERT A. BURT

Imagine three of us in a common enterprise. You and I decide that he—let's call him Boy—should give his life in order to advance our goals. Boy objects. What can we say to justify this decision?

Democratic theory might suggest that we can invoke the principle of majority rule. Applying the standard of "one person, one vote," each of us three had an equal opportunity to cast the deciding vote. But it is not clear that this *ex ante* calculation is the only or the best criterion for vindicating the equality principle in democratic decision making. Boy can surely protest that, by imposing total deprivation on him, we have wrongfully denigrated his claim to equal status with us.

If we accept the proposition that democratic theory demands application of the equality principle throughout our relationship and not only at its formative moment (whether on entering some social contract or casting our first votes), then there is only one way that our communal decisions can be justified as truly democratic. That is if each of us agrees with all of the decisions that we reach.

The author is indebted to Bruce Ackerman, Jay Katz, Ted Marmor, and Eric Muller for their critical reading of this essay.

This unanimity imperative need not be embodied as a formal voting rule. Indeed, as a formal rule, unanimity would itself violate the equality principle by giving a veto to everyone and thereby permitting any one of us to impose his will on all the rest. This paradox does not, however, lead to the conclusion that majority rule is an adequate expression—or even the best practical approximation—of the equality principle. For many political disputes, majority rule suffices because the losers are in fact prepared to acquiesce in their loss, either because they are persuaded in open debate that they were wrong or because they see future electoral opportunities to recoup their loss by persuading others to join with them. For these disputes, majority rule is tolerable for the losers because they do not see themselves as permanently subjugated by the winners.

By this criterion, what can the two of us say to Boy to justify in democratic terms our decision to take his life? On its face, it might seem that nothing could justify this extreme deprivation. But imagine some additional facts: we are Boy's mother and father, he is our Boy, and we need his youthful strength to defend us against a foreign enemy intent on killing all of us; and so, in return for the nurturance we have given him, we ask him to risk, even to sacrifice, his life to save us. With these added facts, moreover, our majority decision to override his resistance no longer is an unfamiliar brutalization. It is a state-enacted military draft—a legislative enactment common in this country since the Civil War.

But do these added facts in themselves provide a basis in democratic theory for justifying the majority imposition on the dissenting minority? I would say not. These facts do offer a plausible set of arguments that the majority can advance with the hope of persuading the minority to acquiesce willingly; but without this concurrence, the demands of democratic theory are not met because the principle of equality at the core of this theory requires freely given consent as the basis of all political relations. Regarding the military draft, the minority might argue that its coerced loss of life ranks higher than the majority's wish to protect itself against a foreign enemy; but the majority could readily respond that its lives were equally at risk, that it could defend itself in no other way than to rely on the younger, stronger members of the group, and that these members owed this protection to their elders for past services rendered. In this specific context, the argument about applying the equality calculus is thus a standoff.

More fundamentally, any such clash of wills between a majority and minority creates this same conundrum within the terms of democratic theory. There is no way that the equality principle can be satisfied, that is, short of uncoerced consent on all sides. In response to stalemate, democratic theory does not require that one side bow to the demands of the other; equality demands that neither majority nor minority be forced to subjugate its will to that of the other. The theory does demand, however, that neither side regard the issue as closed until it is settled consensually and each of the disputants accordingly must accept the obligation of persistently trying to persuade rather than coerce one another.

This democratic obligation cannot be reduced to a clear-cut formula for practical application any more than unanimity can be adopted as a formal voting rule; the press of external events—the enemy at the gates of the city, for example—may create the dilemma that the equal status of some dissenters must inevitably be sacrificed to protect the status of others. But this necessary limit on the practical attainability of consensual dispute resolution does not mean that the equality principle must be revised to identify some circumstances where consent is no longer required. The equality principle cannot be thus amended without destroying its internal coherence.

## EQUALITY AND MUTUALITY

The practical problem points to a paradox within democratic theory. Though no formal resolution of the paradox is possible, democratic theory does identify obligatory ways of approaching it: all disputants are required to acknowledge that coerced resolutions are violations of the equality principle, to avoid any coercion when at all practicable, and to address one another always in a spirit of mutual persuasion and accommodation. This requirement cannot be adequately embodied in formal voting rules, whether such rules require majorities (supposedly adequate for "ordinary politics") or supermajorities (for "funda-mental matters" such as constitutional amendments). The dem-ocratic imperative can only be expressed as an ethos of mutual deference and accommodation that frames all social relations. Its observance by all disputants is the only way toward tolerable accommodation of the unresolvable paradox embedded in the equality principle.

American democracy has pretended, however, that this para-dox can be formally resolved. The pretension is embodied in the Supreme Court's role as the authoritative interpreter of the Constitution. In its adjudications, the Court regularly purports to identify precisely when a majority is or is not entitled to override minority opposition. Before the Civil War, the Court addressed this issue only in the context of relatively specific constitutional prohibitions against majority enactments, such as in the Bill of Rights; in the immediate wake of the war, the Fourteenth Amendment provided that "no state shall . . . deny to any person . . . the equal protection of the laws," thereby giving the Court apparent authority to adjudicate the applica-tion of the equality principle as such.[1] According to conven-tional constitutional doctrine, therefore, there is no paradox left hanging when the Court decides whether the majority is enti-tled to override the minority's dissent on any legislative matter; the Court purports to stand apart from the self-interested claims of the disputants and apply the constitutional calculus that measures the appropriate authority one side can have over the other, notwithstanding the absence of consent. There has been considerable dispute about the specific content of this judicial calculus—in contemporary terms, whether the judges are entitled to draw on their general conception of "fundamen-tal values" or must restrict their attention to some more nar-rowly specified "original intent" of the constitutional draftsmen. But the shared underlying premise of most participants in this jurisprudential debate is that, once the judges have applied the proper criteria, their calculation is authoritative and the losing litigants (whether the legislative majority or minority) have no legitimate complaint based simply on their refusal to consent to defeat.

There is, however, another and better way to view this judicial role. In its conventional robing, as the ultimate adjudicator of the Constitution, the Court serves functionally to disguise the paradox at the core of democratic principle and thereby (perhaps) to persuade the loser that he deserved to lose and should peaceably acquiesce. But this judicial role can be demystified and brought into harmony with the equality principle paradoxically, and thus properly, understood. Judges can see themselves not as the final adjudicators of the disputants' competing claims but rather as protectors of the equality principle whose goal is accomplished by promoting processes of mutual accommodation between the disputants—sometimes by reopening conflicts that had been conclusively resolved by majority rule, sometimes by refusing to overturn majority decisions precisely in order to direct the losing minority's attention to realistic prospects of redressing their losses elsewhere, sometimes by yet other means. There are myriad possibilities for this application of the judicial role; the important point lies not in the details but rather in the basic understanding that should lead judges to map their interventions with reference to this conception of democratic principle. If judges, that is, adequately understood that consent is the exclusive legitimizing touchstone in democratic theory, they would turn away from their own coercive impositions in the supposed service of democracy and look instead toward the many ways in which their adjudicative interventions can promote the ethos of mutuality among adversaries.

I have addressed all of this in my recent book, *The Constitution in Conflict*,[2] and will not rehearse the position. My concern here is not with the judicial role in constitutional adjudication but with the application of the paradoxical implications of the equality principle in another part of the legal system—the criminal law generally and the imposition of capital punishment specifically.

## MUTUALITY AND THE DEATH PENALTY

Return to our society of three: we two now claim Boy's life not to protect ourselves from an external enemy but as a response to Boy's own willful killing of his brother. Once again Boy objects. But this time the democratic equality principle appears to give us a direct justification for our disposition to override his dissent. Boy himself violated the principle by subjugating his victim and his wrongful action justifies our coercive rejoinder to reassert the integrity of equality as our organizing social norm. This justification is entirely persuasive for some coercive response to Boy's action, but it does not carry us the full way necessary to support our decision for capital punishment. The equality principle might seem adequate for this task as well, on the ground that Boy should simply get what he gave; but the calculus cannot be so simple.

The complexities were revealed in a recent dispute on the Supreme Court regarding the permissibility of providing so-called victim impact statements to juries deciding whether to impose capital punishment. During the past two decades, state legislatures have enacted many laws intended to enhance "victims' rights" by giving them greater protection in the workings of the criminal justice system.[3] For criminal sentencing proceedings, new laws were enacted providing that victims or their families were entitled to give formal presentations to the sentencing official, to speak on their own behalf about the magnitude of the injury inflicted on them by the convicted criminal. In 1987, by a five-to-four vote, the Supreme Court decided that victim impact statements could not be given to juries in death penalty cases; in 1991, with two new justices on the Court, this ruling was reversed by a six-to-three vote.[4] The core of the disagreement among the justices revolved around the calibration of equality between murderer and victim. The 1991 majority maintained that because the convicted murderer was entitled to provide evidence to the jury regarding all aspects of his life in order to inspire their sympathy, a full depiction of the victim's personal life should be given equal status in the sentencing jurors' minds (even if the murderer had known nothing of the victim's admirable traits or of the family and friends who depended on the victim). The 1987 majority was also concerned about equalizing the status of murderer and victim but relied on a different calculus; these justices maintained that the murderer was entitled to present his full life's story to the jury in order to obtain empathic identification from the jurors instead of revulsion and death at their hands, and that explicit portrayal of the victim's personal merits would overwhelm the jury's already strained capacity to see the murderer as a fellow human being rather than as a demon.

This disagreement between the 1987 and 1991 majorities mirrors the larger question about the existence of the death penalty itself: whether its talionic premise that one killing deserves another is an adequate justification, or whether this equalizing response is inconsistent with the democratic principle that insists on the equal worth of all human beings. In their internal debates since 1972, the Supreme Court justices have focused almost exclusively on whether the death penalty should be viewed as "cruel and unusual"; but this debate exemplifies the way in which obsessive attention to inscrutable constitutional language—in this case, the wording of the Eighth Amendment—diverts everyone's attention from the basic issues at stake. Arguments about whether capital punishment is more or less like some listing of "obviously cruel tortures" quickly descends to incommensurate gustatory claims. If some common vocabulary can be found for deliberating about the democratic justification for capital punishment, the equality principle has much greater promise (and, not incidentally, provides constitutional warrant for asking whether the Eighth Amendment's enigmatic stricture can be reexamined or given more precise content in light of the Fourteenth Amendment's equality guarantee).

Recasting the debate in equality terms does not, however, quickly or obviously resolve it. As in the smaller compass of the justices' disagreement about victim impact statements, different definitions of equality can be invoked on each side. Thus, even if we start with the premise that the fundamental democratic tenet is to assure equality for everyone, it is not obvious how a democratic regime should respond when one of its members grossly overrides another member's equal status. On behalf of capital punishment, the talionic imperative can be expressed quite plausibly: even if everyone has an a priori equal right to live, the murderer's wrongful taking of life has forfeited his claim to this equal status.[5] Evaluating this justification in equality terms leads to this further question: though it is axiomatic that a subjugated person is entitled by democratic theory to defend himself against this imposition, is he (or those acting on his behalf) entitled to impose an equivalent subjugation in return? Or is the victim obliged, in defending himself, to observe constraints based on the equality principle that his oppressor had disdained? Viewed in this perspective, the question of justifying capital punishment is no different in principle from evaluating any retaliation by any oppressed person in response to subjugative inequality imposed on him in any social relationship.

## EQUALITY, OPPRESSION, AND RETALIATION

Consider this example: for many years a legislative majority had overridden the wishes of a minority without even the pretense of attending to this minority's concerns; but after extensive changes in the voting population, the subjugated minority was able to form new electoral alliances that brought it into majority control. Is the newly dominant group entitled by democratic theory to impose equivalent degradations on its former oppressors now that it has repulsed their wrongful aggressions—to repay an "eye with an eye"? When the newly dominant group was a minority, it was clearly entitled to defend itself against majority depredations; democratic theory itself demanded that the then-majority was obliged to treat the minority respectfully by soliciting its consent rather than simply relying on coercion to accomplish its wishes. But now that the tables are turned, the new majority must see that if it disdains its past oppressors as it had been wrongfully treated, there would be nothing left between them remotely resembling democratic imperatives. The relationship on both sides would be avowedly based on coercion alone with no effort or even pro forma gesture from one side to the other appealing for common understanding and mutual respect. The hallmark of democracy, a consensual association among equals, would have no relevance to this social relationship, even as a guiding ideal.

This does not mean that the newly dominant majority is obliged to subordinate its interests to the old oppressors; they are as much entitled to vigorously defend themselves now as when they were an oppressed minority. But democratic theory does demand that everyone pursue self-interest in a way that achieves the greatest possible accommodation, in order to vindicate the basic premise of consensual equality; and this demand applies with special force against a legislative majority. Indeed, a minority is entitled by democratic theory to be more single minded in protecting itself than the majority, precisely because the minority's claims to equal status can so readily be overlooked by a self-absorbed majority. Conversely, a special obligation of self-restraint falls on the majority as such—even when (and perhaps especially when) the majority has just recently been transformed from, and still carries the wounds of, defensively embattled minority status.

## PUNISHMENT AND MAJORITY RULE

There is a direct analogy in this struggle between the new majority and its old oppressors and the conflict recurrently presented in the criminal law between a criminal and the once-helpless victim who now is able to invoke state police power to subdue his oppressor. The newly empowered victim is clearly authorized, by democratic theory, to apply coercion against the aggressor. But if we conclude that the crime victim is entitled to administer the identical measure of coercion that had been inflicted on him, we fall into the same fallacious conception of "tit-for-tat" equality invoked by a newly dominant electoral majority to justify retributive subjugation of its old antagonists.

The murderer acted immorally; but so did the once-dominant oppressive majority when it refused to extend any respect to the minority. Whatever distinctions might be drawn between the moral status of murder and political enslavement, in a democratic society the immorality of both actions are grounded in the same norm: that no one is entitled to subjugate another, that everyone is guaranteed equal respect. Moral outrage at the murderer or the enslaver might seem to justify an equivalent retaliation. But if democracy rests on the equality principle, democratic institutions must work to protect that principle—not to abandon it as a response to its transgression by one or another self-aggrandizing partisan.

The retaliatory force justified by the criminal law thus has the same place in democratic theory as majority rule. Each is a form of coercion and neither is legitimate as such. Criminal law penalties and majority rule are both rough expedients, tolerably consistent with the democratic equality principle only if all disputants (but most particularly, the dominant party) see their application of defensive coercion as a limited way station working ultimately toward the goal of a consensual relationship among acknowledged equals.

In the context of electoral politics, this means that the dominant majority should never abandon efforts to persuade the minority and should itself correspondingly remain open to persuasion from the minority—in a word, that everyone must see unanimity rather than majority rule in itself as the only democratically justified resolution for social conflict, no matter how practicably unattainable this goal might be. In the context of the criminal law, this same imperative means that the majority (that is, the victim allied with the state police power) must try not simply to constrain the aggressor against future depredations but to reform or rehabilitate him—that is, to persuade him to repudiate his wrongful subjugatory claims so that he might reenter a relationship of equal status with others.

In this rehabilitative effort, the dominant majority in the criminal justice system has an obligation to remain open to persuasion, which is equivalent to its obligation in electoral politics generally. In the criminal law as in electoral politics, no one is obliged to subordinate himself to another but only to seek concordance of interests; in the criminal law context specifically, murder must always involve the subjugation of one person by another and no one is obliged to acquiesce in this wrongdoing. But even here it is conceivable that a murderer could characterize his conduct or redefine the substance of the offense in exculpatory ways that, at the same time, more fully accommodate others' interests with his; and democratic theory requires that the dominant party remain visibly open to this possibility.

Unanimous resolution thus stands in criminal law as in electoral politics generally as the ultimate command of democratic theory—not that reconciliation and the restoration of a mutually respectful equal relationship between victim and criminal is practicably achievable in most cases but that the pursuit of this ideal must never be abandoned. This is the core reason why the death penalty violates democratic principle. Unlike even the harshest prison term, the death penalty is a flamboyantly visible proclamation that all social relations between victim and oppressor, between the dominant and subordinate parties, have been irreversibly severed. The murderer and his victim, of course, can never be restored to a mutually respectful equal relationship; the murderer has seen to that. But this regrettable reality is a practical constraint on the realization of the democratic ideal, not a rejection of the ideal itself on both sides of the relationship. When the victim—vicariously, through those acting on his behalf—rejects any possibility of reconciliation with his oppressor, then the practical constraint is elevated to a profession of principle: that is, a rejection of the democratic principle that reconciliation among adversaries is the ideal pursuit, no matter how impracticable that pursuit might appear.

This, then, is the deontological argument against capital punishment: that democratic principle, properly understood, is inherently inconsistent with the practice. There are also consequentialist concerns that follow from this argument—concerns that begin with the premise that the equality principle at the core of democratic theory should be the governing ethos of the American polity, and that lead to the conclusion that the legitimated existence of the death penalty in that polity is likely to undermine social commitment to the equality principle generally.

## THE WAGES OF DEATH

The central question in the consequentialist analysis is whether the death penalty's violence against democratic principle can be confined to social relations with murderers or, instead, whether this violence is likely to spread to other contexts. This question cannot be conclusively resolved but some suggestions seem more plausible than others. Abraham Lincoln's approach to this issue ranks high on this score, not only because of his iconic stature but also for more solid reasons.

Lincoln's warning was not addressed to capital punishment

but to the institution of slavery, which, as he saw, was also intrinsically opposed to democratic principle. Notwithstanding his principled concerns, however, Lincoln was not roused to action by the existence of slavery as such; his impetus came from congressional rejection in 1850 of the Missouri Compromise of 1820, which had restricted the spread of slavery into unsettled territories. Lincoln's view was that, although the Constitution accepted slavery, this was a political compromise understood as such in 1787, and that the founders implicitly acknowledged that slavery was inconsistent with democratic principle and should therefore ultimately be abolished. The Missouri Compromise, as Lincoln saw it, embodied this understanding whereas its subsequent repeal represented a direct axiomatic break with the equality principle that necessarily presented a pervasive threat to democracy.

This was the basis for Lincoln's famous prediction in his "House Divided" speech: "I believe this government cannot endure, permanently half slave and half free. . . . It will become all one thing or all the other. Either the opponents of slavery will arrest the further spread of it, and place it where the public mind shall rest in the belief that it is in the course of ultimate extinction; or its advocates will push it forward, till it shall become alike lawful in all the States, old as well as new, North as well as South."[6] Lincoln further believed that once the issue of principle had been framed as such, then the legitimation of slavery could not be confined to relations between blacks and whites but would spread throughout all social relations.[7]

Why should this occur? Why would there be an expansive dynamic that would inevitably go beyond the confines of black-white relations? Lincoln did not explain directly. But there are two explanatory facets of the slavery debate that lie behind Lincoln's reasoning (which are also directly analogous to the current status of capital punishment in American social practice). The first is the high visibility of axiomatic claims in Lincoln's day about whether slavery was justified in principle as compared to the prior regime of "tolerance" framed by uneasy ambivalence (even in the South itself).[8] This changed public status is also true of the contemporary American institution of capital punishment, which had been markedly declining in application and in public approbation for at least a century until the 1970s when, ironically, the Supreme Court's decision overturning all extant death penalty statutes led to an immediate resurgence in legislative action and public support.[9]

The second, related aspect is the aggressive implication of the proslavery (and pro–death penalty) position. Lincoln never enunciated the tenets of social psychology that led him to believe that the battle of principle regarding slavery, once joined as such, could not be stopped until one side or the other had entirely subjugated its adversary. But Lincoln and his generation illustrated these tenets by the example of their lives, by the way that increasingly unconstrained aggressions spread during the first half of the nineteenth century in relations between racial groups—both black/white and native American/white—to relations among whites, culminating in the extraordinary bloodletting of the Civil War.[10] This aggressive impetus, moreover, has not yet run its course in American social relations. Their experience of crushing defeat led white southerners to impose a retaliatory regime of humiliation and violence on blacks that was not simply reminiscent of but an intensified distillation of the most degrading aspects of enslavement. This regime was repudiated by white America only during this past generation. It is not yet clear, however, that this repudiation has come in time to arrest the strong impetus for a continued cycle of retaliatory aggressions from many black Americans still wounded by the living memories of their degradations. And fear among whites of this prospect—with an exaggerated force itself demarcating another gyre in the retaliatory cycle—appears to be an implicit aspect of the dramatic resurgence in public support for the death penalty following the precipitous decline between 1954 and 1970 when the prospects for racial reconciliation appeared salient.[11]

Our history thus illustrates an impetus for expansive subjugatory aggression that, if not ineluctable, is very difficult to keep within constraining boundaries. At this moment in American social relations, the death penalty—because of its visibility in our politics, the widely touted claims for its legitimacy, and its underlying inconsistency with the reconciliatory imperatives of democratic theory—appears to be a prominent instrument in the contemporary unfolding of a Gresham's law regarding coercion versus accommodation in social relations. Within the confines of the criminal justice system itself, this expansive dynamic has been visible during the past twenty years as the "rehabilitative ideal" has virtually vanished from the publicly offered justificatory rationales, to be replaced wholesale by an exclusively retributive conception of punishment. In concrete practical terms, this change in public vocabulary has been reflected by a dramatic increase in the numbers of prisoners—more than threefold multiplication since 1974—and the length of prison terms; the United States now has the highest rate of incarceration in the world, far surpassing South Africa in second place, and more than ten times the per capita rate of Japan or any Western European nation.[12] Throughout this same time, black men have constituted almost half of the prison population, both reflecting and reinforcing a "wide-spread perception of the American crime problem as one principally of race."[13] This perception in turn is a principal vehicle by which the increased embrace of subjugatory premises within the criminal justice system generally has been spreading to all social relations.

This account is suggestive, not conclusive, support for the proposition that the subjugatory impulses expressed in the death penalty cannot be confined to social relations with murderers. Added support for this proposition, also suggestive rather than conclusive, can be found in another source more directly pointed toward the psychological tenets that might explain the expansive character of subjugatory impulses generally, and might also specifically suggest why administration of the death penalty is more likely to reinforce rather than assuage the violence originally committed against the victim. This source lies in psychoanalytic precepts that guide the practice of psychotherapy for victims of past traumatic injuries.

These precepts direct our attention away from the social relations between victim and victimizer and focus instead on the internal representations of that relationship in the victim's mind. Psychoanalysis teaches that, especially when the trauma occurred during childhood, the victim's mental representations are not simply memories (or even suppressed memories) of the event but more fundamentally are incorporated into the victim's own sense of identity, through psychological mechanisms such as identification with the aggressor. Put in the vernacular, an abused child readily comes to believe not that "bad people did bad things to him," but that "he is bad because bad things happened." Unless this equation is altered, the child carries into adulthood not only a persistent sense of his victimization but also the more malignant conviction that he is somehow responsible for his abuse. The victim is thus locked in an endless struggle with himself (or with his own psychic structure)—a struggle that appears endless because the only route for escape from abuse seems somehow to require the destruction of his own psychic self-representation. Paradoxically, therefore, all efforts to assuage the pain of the remembered abuse are experienced by the victim as intensified violence against himself. For some victims, this psychological process induces self-lacerating paralysis. Others flee from acknowledging this heightened intrapsychic violence by the psychological defense mechanism of projecting inner feelings on external actors. In either event, whether this psychological struggle remains internalized and directed "against the self" or is projected outward onto external representations, the victim feels caught in an escalating cycle of violence that he is driven to act out against himself and/or others.

How can this cycle be interrupted, according to psychoanalytic precepts? A rationalist model would suggest that the victim be reeducated regarding the true source of his victimization, and this indeed has been a conventional understanding of psychotherapy: that the patient is encouraged, in the safe space of the therapist's consulting room, to reexperience his victimization and is brought to understand that he was not responsible but that it was a bad person who did bad things to him. In more general terms, this model portrays psychotherapy as a process by which the adult patient revisits his childhood and reevaluates through his mature rational capacities the events that he had previously misunderstood through his childish, irrational thinking. This, so the conventional understanding had it, was the meaning of Freud's famous dictum, "where id was, there ego shall come into being."

This conventional understanding does not, however, adequately convey the complexity or the true goal of the psychotherapeutic process. Cast in these rationalist terms, the therapeutic process itself becomes a repetition of rather than a release from the patient/victim's internalized struggle against himself—a war waged by the patient's "adult rational mind" against his "childish thinking." Freud's meaning has come to be understood much more in reconciliatory terms, that ego does not conquer id nor does id prevail over ego but that there should instead be an integration of, a mutuality between, these seemingly opposed elements (whether conceptualized as id/ego or as internalized representations of victim/victimizer, submission/domination, love/hate, etc.).[14]

This does not mean that the goal of psychotherapy is that the victim must forgive his oppressor; the goal is for the victim to relent in the struggle with his internal representations of his oppressor. Disentangling this internalization from the actual reality of the oppressor is, however, an exceedingly intricate process; and it may often be facilitated in practice if the victim can come to see his oppressor no longer as an all-powerful demon but as a human being comparable to himself. Reconciliation between victim and oppressor is not therefore a necessary therapeutic goal. But it is difficult for the victim to free himself from his own sense of grievance and his internally driven impetus for escalated violence against himself and others unless he is able to see his oppressor as no more (or less) powerful than himself.

One forceful representation of this wholesome comparability occurs when the victim can fully imagine himself able to forgive an oppressor who honestly acknowledges and repents his past wrongdoing. In actuality, of course, the oppressor may be so malicious or self-righteous in his subjugative posture that he never approaches the mutuality required for forgiveness. But for the victim's peace of mind, the oppressor's attitude is not the central concern. The key is the victim's own readiness, once safe in fact from repeated subjugation, to fully appreciate his safety by holding himself open to the possibility of reconciliation. Accordingly, the victim himself must not act in a way that excludes this possibility from actual realization.

There are obvious applications of these psychological tenets to the workings of the criminal law. In its ordinary structure, many aspects of the law comply with these tenets—most clearly in the dramatic setting of the criminal trial where the relative power of victim and criminal is not simply reversed from the original subjugatory acts but both instead are protected against one another. The precise scope of these mutual protections is, of course, subject to considerable controversy. But those who maintain that the victim's injury can be redressed by giving him (or the state acting on his behalf) the exact measure of the oppressor's coercive force—eye for eye, tooth for tooth—must do more than invoke equality as justification. This is not only a crude parody of equality in principle; it is a prescription in practice for unrelenting (and therefore escalating) warfare between victim and oppressor that does not free but more deeply ensnares the victim (and those acting on his behalf) in his subjugation. Of all such retaliatory subjugations that the criminal law might apply, the death penalty is the most vivid enactment of this mutually destructive social relationship. This is the core of the consequentialist argument against its application.

Another route—also not incontrovertible but strongly suggestive—leads to the same conclusion. The Book of Exodus records that as the Israelites crossed the Red Sea, they saw the water behind them close over the pursuing Egyptians and they "then sang [a] song unto the Lord" of celebration.[15] A midrash on this verse comments that angels in heaven heard the Israelites' song and they also began singing, but God said to them, "The Israelites sing because their lives have been saved. But you? My children are drowning. How can you sing?" And the Babylonian Talmud records that man is not alone in offering prayers but that God Himself prays, and His prayer is this: "May it be my will that my compassion conquers my anger, that my love overcomes my opposed disposition and that I will act toward my children mercifully and beyond the letter of the law."[16]

If this goal of forgiveness and reconciliation with wrongdoers is God's ambition not only for His angels but also for Himself, that surely is a recommendation for us. But if God Himself must pray for the will power to hold to this goal, that does suggest the difficulties involved for us who are only mortals.

## NOTES

1. This provision was extended to the national government by the Supreme Court in *Bolling v. Sharpe,* 347 U.S. 497 (1954), which overturned a congressionally enacted school segregation law for the District of Columbia at the same time that the Court invalidated similar state laws in *Brown v. Board of Education,* 347 U.S. 483 (1954).

2. Cambridge: Belknap Press of Harvard University Press, 1992.

3. Examples are new "rape shield" laws limiting defendants' ability to present evidence about the victims' past sexual experiences and laws requiring financial compensation to victims from public funds as well as from royalty payments to convicted criminals for movies or books about their crimes.

4. *Booth v. Maryland,* 482 U.S. 496 (1987); *Payne v. Tennessee,* 111 S.Ct. 2597 (1991). Between 1987 and 1991, Justices Powell and Brennan in the *Booth* majority were replaced by Justices Kennedy and Souter, who voted with the new majority in *Payne.*

5. On this score, it is notable that the Supreme Court has construed the Eighth Amendment to forbid the death penalty for any crime except murder. See *Coker v. Georgia,* 433 U.S. 585 (1977), *Enmund v. Florida,* 458 U.S. 782 (1982).

6. Abraham Lincoln, *Collected Works,* Roy Basler, ed. (New Brunswick, N.J.: Rutgers University Press, 1953), 2:461.

7. This was a recurrent argument Lincoln put forward in his 1858 debates with Stephen Douglas; see Harry Jaffa, *Crisis of the House Divided* (Garden City, N.J.: Doubleday, 1959), 336.

8. See William Freehling, *The Road to Disunion: Secessionists at Bay, 1776–1854* (New York: Oxford University Press, 1990).

9. *Furman v. Georgia,* 408 U.S. 238 (1972); see Franklin Zimring and Gordon Hawkins, *Capital Punishment and the American Agenda* (New York: Cambridge University Press, 1986), 26–49.

10. See my discussion of these trends and their interrelationships at op. cit. *supra* note 2, 155–99.

11. See Zimring and Hawkins, op. cit. *supra* note 9, 39. For powerful evidence of persistent racial bias in the administration of the death penalty, and equally powerful evidence of the Supreme Court's resis-

tance to acknowledging these facts, see *McCleskey v. Kemp*, 482 U.S. 920 (1987).

12. See *New York Times*, June 19, 1992, E4. See generally Robert Burt, "Cruelty, Hypocrisy, and the Rehabilitative Ideal in Corrections," in *International Journal of Law and Psychiatry* (1993, forthcoming).

13. Francis Allen, *The Decline of the Rehabilitative Ideal: Penal Policy and Social Purpose* (New Haven, Conn.: Yale University Press, 1981), 30. In 1974, of 215,661 prisoners in state and federal correctional institutions, approximately 98,200 were black (or 45.5%); in 1990, of 774,375 such prisoners, 367,122 (or 47.4%) were black. See U.S. Department of Justice, *Sourcebook of Criminal Justice Statistics, 1978* (1979), tables 6.27 and 6.59; and *Sourcebook, 1991* (1992), table 6.75.

14. See generally Hans Loewald, *Psychoanalysis and the History of the Individual* (New Haven, Conn.: Yale University Press, 1978); Jessica Benjamin, *The Bonds of Love: Psychoanalysis, Feminism, and the Problem of Domination* (New York: Pantheon, 1988); Jonathan Lear, *Love and Its Place in Nature: A Philosophical Interpretation of Freudian Psychoanalysis* (New York: Farrar, Straus, Giroux, 1990).

15. Exodus 15:1.

16. Tractate Berakhot 7a.

# PART II

# JUSTICE AND THE RULE OF LAW

# 5

# THE LEGAL CODES OF
# ANCIENT ISRAEL

## MICHAEL WALZER

## I

Notice the plural form: it is not only that the Bible contains
many laws but also, and more importantly, that it contains three
different legal codes. The many laws are easy to understand,
and it is equally easy to understand the popular wish that the
yoke of the covenant be less onerous. An old folktale claims that
on the day after the Sinai revelation, the Israelites rose early
and marched at double speed away from the mountain so that
they would not be given any more laws.[1] This did them no
good. Through history the laws kept piling up—not, however,
in the form of explicit additions and revisions to the covenant
code, Exodus 20–23, but in the form of two new codes: the
holiness code of Leviticus and the Deuteronomic code. Each of
these is described as if it too had been delivered at Sinai, and
yet no sustained or systematic effort is made, early or late, not
even at the time of canonization, to harmonize Leviticus and

An earlier version of this essay was presented as the Robert Cover Memorial
Lecture at Yale Law School in November 1991 and published in the *Yale Journal
of Law and the Humanities* in 1992. Biblical citations follow the form of *Tanakh: A
New Translation of the Holy Scriptures According to the Traditional Hebrew Text*
(Philadelphia: Jewish Publication Society, 1985) with some modifications.

Deuteronomy with Exodus. The three codes are significantly different in the range of social activities that they cover, the style in which they are written, and the substantive rules they establish. Yet all of them are divinely commanded by the same God. There has not been a succession of gods, each with his own law, as in other countries of the ancient Near East there was a succession of kings promulgating new and different legal codes, the most recent one replacing the one before. How can difference be explained when a single divine lawgiver rules eternally?

Trying to answer this question will lead me to ask a number of others, focused on the biblical writers' understanding of the law. I am less interested in the laws themselves with all their prescriptions and prohibitions than in the legal culture of ancient Israel, insofar as this can be read out of the biblical texts (we have no other sources, no court records, no independent accounts of procedures or cases). What emerges from the texts is a picture of a culture unusually pluralistic and a set of laws less subject to sovereign power and professional specialization than our own. The argumentative legalism of classical and medieval Jewry has its origins here—in the biblical codes and in the efforts of men and women, over many years, to live by them or to revise or escape them. But it is only the origins and not the later development that concerns me in this essay. For there is much to be learned from Israel's singular revelation, delivered by one divine lawgiver, recorded and preserved in three versions.

The documentary thesis provides an historical explanation of this "tripleness," which in its most general form I am inclined to accept: the three codes represent three different traditions, oral or written, dating from different periods, transmitted by different groups, brought together at some late date by unknown editors. I will draw upon this thesis in the course of my own argument, but it does not answer what is surely the hard and interesting question. Why were the different traditions *brought together,* set side by side, rather than serially replaced or rewritten and harmonized? How can we explain the survival of all three?

From a theological point of view, the three codes are literally inexplicable—and that is why the differences among them are never acknowledged in the text. No human lawmaking is recognized; hence there are no stipulated procedures for adding to the divinely revealed law or for revising it, let alone for replacing it. The rule of Deuteronomy 4:2, "You shall not add anything to what I command you or take anything away from it, but keep the commandments of the Lord," applies also, in principle, to the covenant code of Exodus and ought to have precluded the writing of Deuteronomy itself. And yet the writing went on and, as Michael Fishbane has demonstrated in an immensely learned study of "inner-biblical legal exegesis," argument, interpretation, and revision, in law courts and scribal schools, went along with it.[2] As soon as the first code was made known, a process began of adding and subtracting. In a sense, this is an entirely normal process of adaptation to social change. But since it is an unacknowledged process, it cannot have an acknowledged outcome. The adding and subtracting is surreptitious, and the result is a "divine word" inconsistent with itself.

It may well be, as some scholars think, that Deuteronomy was intended by its authors to replace earlier formulations of God's law—a self-conscious attempt to provide a new and alternative text.[3] In fact, the authors provided an additional text, which does not supplant but rather coexists with the earlier versions. The case is the same here as in the historical writings: the authors of Chronicles probably meant to replace the books of Samuel and Kings with their own expurgated history, heavily emphasizing the temple cult and the role of the priesthood. They must have hoped for readers who would find only their account available. But what they got from the beginning were readers like ourselves, for whom Chronicles is simply *another* account, oddly different from Samuel and Kings, but coexisting with it and laying claim to the same authority. The written history of God's people, like the codifications of God's law, cannot be supplanted. Each version pretends to be the only one, even though the quickest reading of the Bible as a whole exposes the pretense.

The failure of every attempt at replacement and the piling up of different versions of law and history give the Bible its special character. It is as if God presides over and therefore validates the different versions and also, necessarily, the disagreements they reflect. The disagreements cannot be openly recognized, but they also cannot be harmonized or written out of the text. They make further exegesis imperative since legal decisions and political and religious policies have to be justified in textual terms. New exegesis gives rise in turn to new disagreements. And again, because they cannot be acknowledged, the new disagreements also cannot be resolved.

The biblical text camouflages, as Fishbane writes, "the dependence of the divine word upon its human transmission and interpretation."[4] The camouflage conceals the divergence of interpretations and it also conceals the identities, the proper names and the social location, of the rival interpreters. Though we know the names of all the high priests and some of the royal scribes, the authors of the priestly code and of Deuteronomy are necessarily anonymous: officially, as it were, they do not exist. And because the interpreters cannot be identified, they cannot be ranked; it is not possible to establish the authority of some of them over others. So far as the text is concerned, the only author is God himself. But behind this God, covered by his authority and speaking in his name, stands a host of human authors who make the law by writing, reading, commenting on, and applying it. Priests, judges, scribes, and prophets: only the last of these tell us who they are and announce a new divine word; the others (the prophets, too, most of the time) read and revise the old words. No one has a monopoly on the production of new legal versions. Or, better, God's monopoly works against the consolidation of interpretive power in Israelite society and serves to legitimize the plurality of interpreters. These are the secret legislators of Israel. Had there been no doctrine of the divine word, their work would probably have been normalized, and some political or religious group would have seized control, establishing a monopoly on legal interpretation. But there could be no normalization so long as denial and, except for the prophets, anonymity were religiously required.

Eventually, centuries after the last of the biblical texts were written, the rabbis managed to establish an interpretive (and even, on some accounts, a legislative) monopoly—occasionally challenged, as by the medieval Karaites, but wonderfully effective over many years and across most of the diaspora. But this achievement depended on the claim that the law was now a human possession, no longer God's to give. Citing a line from Deuteronomy, the rabbis declared that "it is not in the heavens" (30:12), that is, its meaning had to be determined here on earth, by a majority of this or that rabbinic court.[5] What the Deuteronomic authors meant by this line, however, was something very different. They wanted to say that the law was easy to know, readily available not for interpretation but for obedience. One had only to study their text. They did not give the law an earthly location in order to justify their own legislative activity, for they did not, could not, acknowledge that activity. And therefore they could not prevent other people from doing—so long as the doing was denied—what they had done.

## II

Hence the three codes (and many scattered examples of independently announced law and legal exegesis)—all of them equally valid and simultaneously in force. The earliest is the covenant code of Exodus, which was probably, in one form or another, the law of the tribal confederation and the first kings.[6] Like the other codes, this one is nothing like a complete set of laws, and scholars have as yet found no principles of inclusion or arrangement. Leviticus is mostly new law, though its central section, the "holiness code" of chapters 19–25, goes over much of the ground covered in Exodus. The intense concern with sacrifice and purity suggests priestly authorship; the work was probably begun in the days of the first Temple but not finished, so most scholars claim, until the second Temple had been built and its cult established. It seems clear, though, that whoever wrote Deuteronomy knew many of the laws recorded in Leviticus, which must have existed in some earlier version by the seventh century. If Deuteronomy is, as Moshe Weinfeld has argued, the work of royal scribes (or of some group of scribes patronized by reformers in the court), then we have to imagine two contemporary but rival schools of secret legislators, writing new laws, revising old laws, and claiming that their work, too, had been delivered by God to Moses at Sinai.[7]

Deuteronomy is the crown of Israel's law: so, at least, academic commentators commonly conclude, sensing, perhaps, that the book is the work of writers rather like themselves. Principles of inclusion and arrangement are no more evident here than elsewhere,[8] but the book as a whole has the form of an intellectual composition, elaborately rhetorical, somewhat verbose, didactic, and—the anachronism is useful—ideological. Leviticus reads like a record of priestly practice, no doubt idealized. Deuteronomy is more programmatic, aiming self-consciously at religious and perhaps also at political reformation. Its laws have been called prophetic, humanitarian, secular, liberal, redistributive, and even feminist—though many of them seem remarkably unsuited to such adjectives. In any case, if Exodus is the law of the tribes, and Leviticus the law of the temple, Deuteronomy is the law of the nation or, more specifically perhaps, of the royal court and the capital city, which stand for the nation. We might think of it (anachronistically, again) as one of the earliest examples in Western history of the work of urban intellectuals.

It has often been said that Israelite law—the three codes taken together—is more "advanced," that is, more humanitarian, liberal, and so on, than that of other ancient peoples. Something like this is, indeed, the claim of the Deuteronomists themselves, who have Moses ask the assembled Israelites: "And what great nation has laws and rules as righteous as all this law that I set before you this day?" (Deut. 4:8).[9] Moses acknowledges here that other nations have legal codes, even if these are less righteous than Israel's; the others are not barbarians, like Kipling's "lesser breeds without the law." But they do not apparently receive their law directly from God. The seven Noachide laws are an invention of the rabbis. Except for the commandment of Genesis 9:6—"Whosoever sheds the blood of man, by man shall his blood be shed: for in His image did God make man"— there is no biblical account of a divine revelation to humankind generally or to the "nations," but only to Israel. Curiously, it is just this universal law against murder, as Moshe Greenberg has shown, that distinguishes Israel's criminal code from all the others that we know of in the ancient world. The other codes allow for monetary compensation in cases of murder, while the Bible insists on capital punishment.[10] Whether this is more righteous or more humanitarian is an open question, though the apparently related refusal of biblical legislators to punish crimes against property with death is certainly likely to appeal to modern readers.

In any case, the discovery and translation of more and more legal codes from both Mesopotamia and Asia Minor requires us to be skeptical of all apologetic and moralizing comparisons. It seems to be true that the rhetorical stress on social justice that marks the biblical codes has no precedent elsewhere—and the power of the prophetic writings, denouncing injustice, is also unequaled among Israel's neighbors: at least, nothing so strong has yet been found. Yet the substance of the biblical laws, especially the laws dealing with family and economy, is not in any sense singular or original; Israel's legislators were clearly working within a common Near Eastern legal tradition. The protection they provided for the weak—slaves, strangers, women—is sometimes greater than that provided in other ancient codes, sometimes not. The penalties they prescribed for violations of the laws are sometimes more lenient, sometimes more harsh. Social differentiation is considerably more rigid in the Babylonian laws than it is in Israel's, but national differences were more significant in Israel than in Babylonia.

### III

What is special about biblical law is not its substance but its sources and its presentation. I have already said something about divine provenance and the unexpectedly pluralizing effects of God's sole authorship. But there is also a more narrowly political point to be made about the doctrine of revelation—and then two points about the textual presentation of the law.

First, Israel's law is God's alone; it has no other possessive modifier. Above all, and in contrast to all the other Near Eastern codes, it is not the king's law. Despite the rich narrative accounts of Israel's monarchic period, writes Martin Noth, "we nowhere hear of the law-giving activity of the kings."[11] Nor is the law ever described as the work of an assembly of elders; nor, again, as a priestly codification, or a philosophical construction, or a judicial invention. Justice Holmes's maxim, that law is what the judges say it is, may in fact apply to ancient Israel as well as to modern America, but it would have been a literally inadmissible proposition among biblical writers. Politically, this means that everyone—kings, elders, priests, judges—is subject, indeed, equally subject, to the authority of the law. This is a matter of principle. The actual power relations prevailing in the community at any given time, of course, qualify or distort the expression of the principle. Nonetheless, principles are important, as we can see from the story of Ahab and Naboth in I Kings 21.

Ahab, who rules the northern kingdom of Israel, covets the vineyard of Naboth, which adjoins his palace grounds. He proposes to buy it, offering a "better vineyard" or a money payment. Naboth refuses, saying "The Lord forbid that I should give up to you the inheritance of my fathers." Indeed, the Lord does forbid it, according to laws delivered to Moses in the wilderness (Numbers 27 and 36). Ahab can do nothing: he goes home "dispirited and sullen," takes to his bed, turns his face to the wall. His wife, Jezebel, a Phoenician woman who worships Baal rather than Yahweh and does not know or respect Israel's law, contrives Naboth's murder. Ahab then seizes the vineyard and is confronted by the prophet Elijah, demanding, "Would you murder and take possession?" (I Kings 21:19). It is a wonderful scene, but I am more interested in Ahab's dispiritedness than in Elijah's righteous anger. The king implicitly acknowledges the laws of land tenure and thinks himself constrained by them. No way of changing the law is available to him.

The only people who might openly challenge and change the law are the prophets, who claim a direct relation to God. Moses, the first prophet, with the most direct relation, does add to the law he originally delivered—but only by bringing a case "before the Lord" (Numbers 27:5) and waiting until "the decision of the Lord should be declared" (Leviticus 24:12). The first of these passages is especially interesting because the case in question is initiated by the "daughters of Zelophehad," who speak before the congregation of Israel defending their right to inherit their father's land. God tells Moses that their plea is just and commands him to announce a new inheritance law.[12] The daughters seem more important here than the prophet, and the scene in which they appear suggests how the narrator views the accessibility of legal procedures and the popular character of legal argument. But the law is never again disputed so publicly. Nor did the later prophets have the authority to revise it in this open way.

Indeed, I know of only one passage in all the prophetic writings that seems to set the living word of the prophet against the written law. Here is Jeremiah speaking to the people of Jerusalem:

> How can you say, "We are wise,
> And we possess the law of the Lord"?
> Assuredly, for naught has the pen labored,
> For naught the scribes!
> The wise shall be put to shame,
> Shall be dismayed and caught;
> See, they reject the word of the Lord,
> So their wisdom amounts to nothing. (8:8–9)

These lines are both unusual and obscure: there is no specific "instruction" of the scribes that the prophet denies or cancels. He is probably more concerned with scribal wisdom than with the legal code. A better example of the prophet's relation to the law is provided by Jeremiah 17:21–22, where the laws of the Sabbath are amended or, as Jeremiah claims, elaborated: "Guard yourselves . . . against carrying burdens (or merchandise) on the Sabbath day, and bringing them through the gates of Jerusalem." No prohibition of "carrying" is recorded in the three codes.[13] But Jeremiah quickly adds: "Hallow the Sabbath, as I commanded your fathers," thus reading his amendment back into the original law. The prophet too is bound by the law; he cannot play the part of Max Weber's charismatic leader who proclaims: "The law is thus and so, but I say unto you . . ." Still, prophets do change the law without acknowledging what they are doing; and so do priests and scribes and judges. Kings cannot even do that; they can only break the law. They can put their hands on it, violently, but they cannot leave their intellectual or moral mark on it.[14]

## IV

The second distinctive feature of Israelite law is its radical embeddedness in a historical narrative. It is as if our own criminal and civil law were available to us only in repetitious but always slightly dissimilar passages interspersed throughout a history of the American Revolution. This historicism in part determines, in part qualifies, the law. Since the biblical narrative stretches only from the exodus to the conquest, Israelite kings play no part in it and, except for Deuteronomy 17, which anticipates and regulates kingly rule, they make no appearance in the legal texts. So it is not surprising that they are not among the acknowledged or even the unacknowledged interpreters of the law. Solomon is celebrated for wisdom, not legal knowledge. The account of deliverance from Egyptian slavery is the textual setting for an anti-authoritarian and a justice-oriented legalism. Future generations of Israelites are enjoined not only to study the law but also to retell the history. The legal texts refer regularly to the historical narrative and so invite interpretation in its terms. Hence the special force of the commandments about slaves, strangers, the poor and needy, widows and orphans. Babylonian and Assyrian kings, in the preambles to their own law codes, insist upon the protection they offer to these same groups, perhaps with reason. Yet this is *noblesse oblige*, the special task of the mighty. In Israel this task seems to be democratized; at least, it is rooted in a common experience of oppression and therefore available for democratization. When Amos, for example, denounces the practices he calls "grinding the face of the poor," he addresses himself to all Israel, not to the leaders of the community.

I hasten to add that the experience of Egyptian bondage did not lead Israelite legislators to abolish slavery. According to the covenantal and Deuteronomic codes, Hebrew slaves cannot be held longer than six years, a rule that effectively turns slavery into a form of limited indenture (Exodus 21:2–6; Deuteronomy 15:12–18—these two texts differ with regard to female slaves, a point I will come back to below). Nothing is said in either code about foreign slaves, however, for whom the seventh year presumably brings no release. Leviticus is explicit in permitting the permanent enslavement of foreigners: "they shall be your bondmen forever" (25:46), which must be the way Egypt's pharaoh thought about the children of Israel. Curiously, the Levitical standard for the treatment of the Israelite "bondman" is set by what appears to be an ethnically undifferentiated class: he is to be treated "as a hired servant and a sojourner." He must serve and sojourn, however, for forty-nine years, until the jubilee, rather than for only six years from the date of his purchase. He cannot be treated as harshly as a (foreign) slave since he belongs, along with all "free" Israelites, to God. Deuteronomy also recognizes the interethnic class of "hired servants" (wage workers) and explicitly demands equal treatment for all its members: "You shall not oppress a needy and destitute laborer whether a fellow countryman or a stranger" (24:14). Here the experience of Egyptian bondage is given a general application: "But you shall remember that you were a slave in Egypt." The Deuteronomic commandment not to return a fugitive slave ("He shall dwell with you in any place which he may choose" [23:16]) seems also to apply to foreigners, though scholars disagree about its exact meaning.[15]

V

The differences among the laws of slavery suggest an extended and serious argument—entirely appropriate in a community with a shared memory of bondage. The argument must have been as much about the experience as about the laws themselves: what moral and legal consequences followed from the remembrance of Egypt? What did it mean to be a vassal nation, a community of divine servants? To answer questions like these was to justify one or another understanding of the laws. And this brings me to the third distinctive feature of Israel's codes: many of the laws that they include are laws-with-reasons, justified laws. Nothing like this appears in any of the other Near Eastern legal codes. The great kings of Mesopotamia did not have to provide arguments for their laws. Nor, of course, does God. Many of God's laws, like theirs, are delivered without justification and seem—the laws of holiness and purity provide the clearest examples—entirely arbitrary. But the social and economic laws often come with reasons attached. Sometimes these refer directly to the historical narrative: "You shall not oppress a stranger: for you know the feelings of the stranger, having been strangers in the land of Egypt" (Exodus 23:9). Sometimes the justifications appeal to a more ordinary morality or, simply, to common sense:

> If you ... take your neighbor's garment to pledge [i.e., as a pawn], you must return it to him before the sun sets. It is his only clothing, the sole covering for his skin. In what else will he sleep? (Exodus 22:26–27)

> When you build a new house, then you shall make a parapet for your roof so that you do not bring bloodguilt on your house, if anyone should fall from there. (Deuteronomy 22:8)

The distinction between justified and unjustified law is, from a theoretical perspective, far more interesting than the more standard scholarly distinction between casuistic and apodictic law. Scholars have argued that the case law is common to the Bible and other ancient codes while the sharp imperatives of the apodictic form ("Thou shalt not. . . .") are more likely to be unique to Israel. But this is much disputed and of uncertain significance even if true. What David Weiss Halivni has called "the Jewish predilection for justified law," if it exists, is more important.[16] In the biblical texts, the predilection is only inter-mittently displayed. The reiterated phrase of Leviticus, "for I am the Lord your God," may provide a motive for obeying the laws, but it cannot be said to provide a substantive justification of their content. Laws-with-reasons appear often enough, how-ever, to call for an explanation: what is the reason for the reasons? One possible answer to this question is the strength of the covenantal idea. Because the covenant requires the people's consent, we might say, the laws must be justified. Even though the people have already given a "wholesale" consent—all that the Lord has spoken "we will obey" (Exodus 20:16)—Israel's legislators seem unwilling to rely entirely on that. They seek in addition something more specific and particularized, as if they have in mind a genuinely consensual community whose mem-bers know exactly what they are doing and why.

Yet perhaps the legislators are giving reasons first of all to one another and only incidentally to other members of the community. Another explanation of the justifying clauses in the biblical codes is that they reflect the actual discussions that went on within priestly or scribal or judicial circles. They are the textual residue of oral advocacy—of what was actually said in defense of legal reform and revision. The argumentative style of rabbinic law stands, I would suggest, at the end of a continuous development that has its beginnings here. But the beginning is very different from the end—and much harder for us to understand. How can we reconstruct the mindset that governed the earliest Israelite legal arguments? Whatever the sophistication and, as modern readers are likely to think, the humanism revealed in laws such as that of the pledge, biblical legislators were clearly open, as the rabbis generally were not, to the idea of direct divine intervention. When God intervened through the mysterious *urim* and *thummim*, for example, he did not give reasons. The word *torah*, which usually means instruction, testimony, law, or decision, also means oracle. Both priests and prophets delivered oracles, often unclear and always unargued. Like the answers to specific questions provided by the *urim* and *thummim*, these usually have to do with policy, not law. They are pronouncements about the future, warnings and foretellings, not legal rulings. Still, biblical law was worked out by people who believed in the warnings as well as the rulings, who had a sense of God's mysterious immediacy that was largely lost by the rabbinic age. The rabbis, some of them anyway, were openly skeptical about the possibility and even the desirability of divine intervention in their decision making.

Mindset aside, however, laws-with-reasons are not mysterious. Whether they are aimed at fellow or rival lawmakers or at ordinary citizens, they aim to persuade. From this aim, two things seem to follow about the biblical understanding of the law. First of all, this is not in any simple sense a legal positivist understanding. No doubt, God's law is authoritative because God is omnipotent, the sovereign of the universe. But no particular rendition or interpretation of the law is authoritative for this reason. Legal positivism "works" only when sovereign power is regularly and visibly deployed. But God's deployments, despite his omnipotence, are irregular and usually invisible. Hence his authority is effectively taken over by Israel's secret legislators. None of them (since the king is excluded) possesses anything like sovereign power, and so they are led to think about the law as something that requires argument.

And if there are arguments, there must also be standards to which the arguments appeal. Justified law implies the previous existence of ideas about justification—in the case of civil and criminal law, of ideas about justice. It appears that God himself is bound by these ideas, as Abraham tells him at Sodom: "Shall not the judge of all earth deal justly?" (Genesis 18:25). If God's power does not make law authoritative, neither does his righteousness make it just. The biblical writers were also not moral positivists. Moses' boast in Deuteronomy about the value of Israelite law carries the same implication as Abraham's rebuke: though the law is divinely delivered, divinely commanded, it does not determine but only realizes what is right. Or, alternatively, fails to realize what is right: for it is always possible that the reasons given for this or that law will be disputed—though never explicitly.

The effect of these disputes is, again, to pluralize the law. Old laws are not canceled, but rather new laws or revised versions of old ones are added. I have already suggested that the alternative process of replacement rather than addition characterizes other Near Eastern legal codes. Only among the Hittites, apparently, are the replacements made explicit (and only in a code without the usual royal preamble, perhaps designed for the use of jurists): "If someone blinds a free man or knocks out his teeth, formerly he would give one mina of silver, now he gives twenty shekels of silver and pledges his estate as security."[17] No reasons for the change are given, either because ordinary Hittites had no need to know or because the legislative authority of the king or his judges was never in question. A lone passage in the book of Ruth (4:7—"Now this was formerly done in Israel. . . .") reproduces the Hittite formula, though in the context of a case rather than a code. For the rest, additions and revisions are unacknowledged, and so, as with the Hittites, though perhaps for different reasons, mostly unjustified. We have to reconstruct the arguments that were probably made on the basis of justifi-cations offered in other cases. But there is one very nice exam-ple of an addition with reasons attached.

In Exodus 21:2–6, it is required that a Hebrew slave be set free in the seventh year of his servitude. He shall "go out free, without payment." The law is repeated in Deuteronomy with an important addition:

> When you send him free do not let him go away empty handed. Furnish him out of the flock and threshing floor, and out of your wine press which the Lord your God has blessed you, you shall give him. Remember that you were slaves in the land of Egypt.

The historical reference is especially appropriate here since the Israelites did not "go away empty handed" from Egypt (see Exodus 12:35–36). Surely they should behave toward their own kinfolk at least as well as the Egyptians behaved toward them. But this argument was apparently not entirely convincing, for the Deuteronomic authors add another: "It shall not seem hard for you when you set him free . . . for he has been worth a double hired servant to you" (15:18). Legal revisionism clearly involved economic as well as historical arguments.

Sometimes, it seems, these are also arguments of the sort that we would call ideological, arguments that reflect religious/political disagreements of a systematic kind. The slavery laws of Deuteronomy, for example, are clearly intended to improve the status of women, though the improvements are neither clearly marked out nor explicitly defended. The six-year limit, from which women were excepted in the Exodus code, now covers them in exactly the same way as men are covered. Male and female slaves are to be similarly treated, though nothing is said against their dissimilar treatment in times past. An even more intriguing example of what has been called Deuteronomy's "feminism" is the revision of the Tenth Commandment. This is the Exodus version:

> You shall not covet your neighbor's house, you shall not covet your neighbor's wife, nor his manservant nor his maidservant, nor his ox, nor his ass, nor anything that is your neighbor's. (20:14)

And this is the Deuteronomic version:

> Neither shall you desire your neighbor's wife. You shall not
> covet your neighbor's house, his field, or his manservant, or
> his maidservant, or his ox, or his ass, or anything that is your
> neighbor's. (5:21)

In the revised commandment, the wife is set apart, deliberately
taken out of the list of possessions, assigned, as it were, a verb of
her own. Again, no reason is given for the small but significant
change; if there was a protest, as by the daughters of Zelophehad, we are told nothing about it. This, the text insists, is what
God really commanded at Sinai. But it seems obvious that someone reading the earlier version of what God commanded did
not like it. We can only imagine what he, or she, said to his, or
her, fellow legislators.

<h1 style="text-align:center">VI</h1>

The existence of three codes means that Israel's legal tradition
was pluralist in character, encompassing (with what degree of
strain we do not know) argument and disagreement. The "predilection for justified law" enables us to see what the arguments
were probably like even if we cannot be sure of the settings in
which they were made or of the people involved. Ancient Israel
does not appear to have had any very developed conception of
citizenship. The biblical texts provide no doctrinal defense of—
they hardly seem to take an interest in—political participation.
But there clearly was a "participatory" legal culture. I do not
mean, necessarily, a culture of litigation, though access to the
courts appears to have been easy and the judges fairly busy if
not always fair in their business. The frequency with which they
are criticized by the prophets suggests the everyday importance
of their decisions. So does the commandment that comes at the
very beginning of Deuteronomy, set apart from all the others:
"You shall not be partial; but you will hear out high and low
alike" (1:17). Babylonian and Egyptian judges were probably
similarly enjoined; they do not seem, however, to have had to
listen to anything quite like a jeremiad when they failed to live
up to their responsibilities. But for our purposes here, litigation

and judicial integrity are less important than legislation and interpretive authority.

Here is what gives Israel's legal culture its distinctive—and, I might add, its enduring—character. From fairly early, a significant number of people, virtually the whole of the nation's intelligentsia, such as it was, and some subset of its ordinary members, were engaged in arguing about the law. The fact that they assigned their arguments to God we can take as piety or as presumption. Either way, the assignment legitimized their own activity. In principle they were articulating the content of the Sinai covenant; in practice they were deciding—more than once—what that content should be. Certainly, the decision-making process was political (and moral) as well as legal. But it was never understood or defended in political terms. Nor are procedures specified by which individuals were admitted to the process. Priests were born to their tasks, but there were many priests, and some of them obviously played a greater role than others. Judges were appointed by the king, but the texts also suggest that the elders of the people, chosen, perhaps, by the people, served at least in the local courts. Prophets were called by God, but we have only their own accounts of their calling. About the scribes, we know nothing at all. These are the people I have called the secret legislators of Israel—an elite, no doubt, but a very loosely structured elite, whose covenantal/legal consciousness was probably not entirely different from that of the nation at large.

The looseness of the structure had something to do with the tripleness of the codes—and both of these had something to do with a divine singularity that could not be imitated or even authoritatively represented anywhere in Israelite society. None of this, needless to say, gave rise to a pluralist *doctrine*. No biblical writer argued for the legitimacy of rival interpreters or of rival interpretations of the law. But as a group, the writers (authors, editors, scribes) left behind in the canonical texts a legacy of multiple and inconsistent codes and a record of unacknowledged interpretations and revisions. For reasons about which we can only speculate, they chose to live with this multiplicity, rejecting the two possible resolutions: serial replacement and editorial harmonization. The result of their choice was a written law that made possible those strange, open-ended legal conversations and arguments that constituted the oral law of later Judaism.

## NOTES

1. Louis Ginsberg, *The Legends of the Jews,* trans. Henrietta Szold (Philadelphia: Jewish Publication Society, 1910), 3:242.

2. Michael Fishbane, *Biblical Interpretation in Ancient Israel* (Oxford: Clarendon, 1985).

3. Joseph Blenkinsopp, in *Wisdom and Law in the Old Testament: The Ordering of Life in Israel and Early Judaism* (Oxford: Oxford University Press, 1983), 94, argues that Deuteronomy represents the first effort to create a "canonical" text—that is, a text that becomes the sole basis of continuing commentary and interpretation.

4. Fishbane, *Biblical Interpretation,* 272.

5. Baba Metzia 59b.

6. For an argument about the three codes and their probable historical settings, see Blenkinsopp, *Wisdom and Law,* chapters 4 and 5.

7. Moshe Weinfeld, *Deuteronomy and the Deuteronomic School* (Oxford: Clarendon, 1972), 179–89.

8. This has not deterred attempts to find or invent ordering principles that will account for the text as we have it. See, for example, Calum M. Carmichael, *The Laws of Deuteronomy* (Ithaca, N.Y.: Cornell University Press, 1974).

9. The text reads as if the author has a comparison or even a set of comparisons in mind, but it is impossible to say what other nations he is thinking of. For a modern comparison, arguing to a similar conclusion, see Leon Epsztein, *Social Justice in the Ancient Near East and the People of the Bible* (London: SCM Press, 1986).

10. I follow here the argument of Moshe Greenberg, "Some Postulates of Biblical Criminal Law," in Frederick Greenspahn, *Essential Papers on Israel and the Ancient Near East* (New York: New York University Press, 1991), 333–52.

11. Martin Noth, *The Laws in the Pentateuch* (London: SCM Press, 1984), 14.

12. But the daughters' victory is later compromised. See Numbers 36, and the discussion in Fishbane, *Biblical Interpretation,* 98–99, 104–5.

13. The case from Exodus 16:17–20 and Numbers 15:32–36 has to do with "gathering," not carrying.

14. One "statute" having to do with the equal division of booty is

attributed to David in I Samuel 30:25, but this was before David became king.

15. Jewish commentators commonly assume that the fugitive is a foreigner. See, for example, Ramban (Nachmanides), *Commentary on the Torah*, trans. C. B. Chavel (New York: Shilo, 1976), 5:287–88.

16. David Weiss Halivni, *Midrash, Mishnah, and Gemara: The Jewish Predilection for Justified Law* (Cambridge: Harvard University Press, 1986).

17. H. W. F. Saggs, *Civilization before Greece and Rome* (New Haven, Conn.: Yale University Press, 1989), 167.

# 6

# EQUITY AND
# THE RULE OF LAW

## LAWRENCE B. SOLUM

The rule of law, it is argued,
is preferable to that of any individual.
Aristotle, *Politics*

One important ideal of Western legal systems is captured by the phrase "the rule of law." A common interpretation of this ideal is expressed in the proposition that the rule of law requires a law of rules.[1] Another legal ideal is called "equity." This second ideal is frequently interpreted as the injunction that legal decision makers sometimes ought to depart from the rules in order to do justice in particular cases. If these interpretations are correct, the two ideals are in tension. The resolution of that tension at the level of theory is the project pursued in this essay. My claim is that properly understood, the practice of equity—of doing justice in particular cases under appropriate circumstances—is broadly consistent with the ideal of the rule of law.

My argument is Aristotelian and virtue centered. Departing from the rules in order to achieve particularized justice is consistent with the rule of law when legal decision makers possess certain judicial virtues—characteristics of mind and will that produce excellence in judging. One of the virtues of a good judge is judicial wisdom, the particularly adjudicatory form of the intellectual virtue of *phronēsis,* or practical wisdom. As a *phronimos,* or person of wisdom, an excellent judge can discern those situations in which a departure from the letter of the law is consistent with its spirit and hence with the rule of law. Although ambitious, my claim is not unqualified; even if guided by judicial wisdom, doing particularized justice will sometimes conflict with the values that underlie the rule of law.

## I. THE CONFLICT BETWEEN EQUITY AND
### THE RULE OF LAW

This section begins with an account of the rule of law that includes requirements of generality, publicity, and regularity. I then sketch a conception of equity as the practice of departing from the rules for particularized reasons. These conceptions of equity and the rule of law serve as the basis for an exploration of the tensions between the two ideals.

### A. *The Rule of Law*

The ideal of *the rule of law,* which can be traced back at least as far as Aristotle, is deeply embedded in the public political cultures of modern democratic societies. The importance of the ideal is reflected in its inclusion in the Universal Declaration of Human Rights of 1948: "it is essential if man is not to have recourse as a last resort, to rebellion against tyranny and oppression, that human rights should be protected by the Rule of Law." Although the ideal of the rule of law has been criticized on the ground that it is an ideological construct that masks power relationships, even Marxist critics may acknowledge that observance of the ideal can curb abuses by the ruling class.

An initial observation concerning the ideal of the rule of law is that there are several different conceptions of it. Indeed, the rule of law may not be a single concept at all; rather, it may be more accurate to understand the ideal of the rule of law as a set of ideals connected more by family resemblance than by a unifying conceptual structure. The purposes of this essay require neither a comprehensive survey of conceptions of the rule of law nor a resolution of debates about the contours of the ideal. A brief mapping of the territory will suffice.

Historically, the most influential account of the rule of law was offered by A. V. Dicey. His formulation incorporated three ideas: (1) the supremacy of regular law as opposed to arbitrary power, (2) equality before the law of all persons and classes, including government officials, and (3) the incorporation of constitutional law as a binding part of the ordinary law of the land.[2]

For the purposes of this essay, the rule of law can be conceived as the conjunction of seven requirements.[3] First, no extralegal commands are obligatory. The personal will or arbitrary decision of government officials should not serve as the basis for imposing legal detriments, including penal sanctions and civil judgments, on individuals. Second, actions by government and officials should be subject to regulation by general and public rules. Government officials should not be above the law, and the legality of government action should be subject to test by independent courts. The first two requirements specify the notion of "a rule of laws and not of men."

The remaining five requirements reflect a variety of concerns. Third, the legal system should meet the requirement of publicity. The laws should be known and expressly promulgated; no criminal penalties should be imposed for violation of rules that are not announced in advance. Fourth, the legal system should meet the requirement of generality: statutes and other legal rules should be general in statement and should not be aimed at particular individuals. Fifth, the legal system should meet the requirement of regularity: decisions should reflect the precept that similar cases should be treated similarly. Judges ought to justify the distinctions they make between persons by reference to the relevant legal rules and principles. Sixth, the legal system should provide fair and orderly procedures for the determination of cases. Seventh, the legal system should reflect the precept that ought implies can. The actions that the rules of law require and forbid should be of a kind that persons can reasonably be expected to do and to avoid. A legal system should recognize impossibility of performance as a defense, or at least a mitigating circumstance. Together, these seven requirements provide a conception that is representative of the variety of ideals that have been identified as part of the rule of law.

## B. Equity

*Equity* has acquired a number of meanings in contemporary legal discourse. Used by legal historians, "equity" refers to a distinct body of law that was once administered by the Court of Chancery in England and other common law countries. Used by some economists, the same term refers to considerations of distributive justice. I use the term "equity" to refer to the practice of doing particularized justice, when the just result is not required by, or is contrary to, the result required by the set of applicable legal rules.

Although much of what is called "equity" today is relatively rule bound, some modern American "equity" fits my definition. For example, Justice Douglas's opinion in *Hecht v. Bowles* stated, "The essence of equity jurisdiction has been the power of the Chancellor to do equity and to mold each decree to the necessities of the particular case."[4] In the view of conservative critics in the Reagan administration's Department of Justice, some federal judges have (mis)used their injunctive powers to depart from the rule of law and achieve particularized justice.[5]

The notion of equity as departure from the rules is rooted in Aristotle, and the best place to begin an exposition is with Aristotle's statement of the problem of equity and justice:

> What causes the difficulty is the fact that equity is just, but not what is legally just: it is a rectification of legal justice. The explanation of this is that all law is universal, and there are some things about which it is not possible to pronounce rightly in general terms; therefore in cases where it is necessary to make a general pronouncement, but impossible to do so rightly, the law takes account of the majority of cases, though not unaware that in this way errors are made. And the law is none the less right; because the error lies not in the law nor in the legislator but in the nature of the case; for the raw material of human behavior is essentially of this kind.[6]

This is the core of Aristotle's view of *epieikeia,* usually translated as "equity" or "fair-mindedness." As is frequently the case with Aristotle, the text is ambiguous. Aristotle and his contemporary expositors inform my account of equity, but I do not claim to have established a definitive interpretation of Aristotle's own view.

One characteristic of equity is that it involves a departure from the rules. Any general rule may be overinclusive or underinclusive with respect to the goal the rule is meant to achieve.[7] Equity corrects the law's generality by filling gaps in the law, by adjusting conflicts and tensions among legal provisions, and by making exceptions in cases in which the rule leads to unanticipated and unjust results. An equitable departure from the rules can relate to the intentions of legislators in two distinct ways. In some cases, doing equity requires the judge to realize the intention of the legislature. In other cases, it may require the judge to correct a defect in the law that the legislator did not or could not have anticipated—for example, in cases in which circumstances have changed or previously unknown facts have come to light.

A second characteristic of equity is its particularism.[8] Equity tailors the law to the requirements of the particular case. Understanding equity as a particularized practice allows us to distinguish it from other practices that involve a departure from legal rules. For example, equity is not identical to the resolution of conflicts between law and morality in favor of the latter. Judges might nullify a statute that legalized the practice of human slavery on the ground that slavery is always morally wrong. This is not an example of the practice of equity, because such a decision would not involve a departure from the rule on the basis of the facts of the *particular* case. Rather, the decision would be based on a general moral principle—for example, that wicked or immoral statutes should not be enforced.

## C. The Nature of the Conflict

An intuitive sense of the conflict between equity and the rule of law can be stated simply: the rule of law seems to require judges to follow the rules, whereas the practice of equity seems to permit departure from the rules. This intuition can be elaborated in three ways: first, through an analysis of the relevant concepts; second, at the level of moral argument; and third, by an examination of the relationship between rule and discretion in legal theory.

The first approach to the conflict between equity and rule of law is conceptual. The rule of law might be defined as a law of rules, but it usually is not. Rather, several features of the rule of law provide overlapping reasons for adjudicators to follow the rules when they decide cases. The first of these reasons is based on what I have called the requirement of *regularity*—the requirement that like cases be treated alike. This feature can cut both for and against the compatibility of the practice of equity with the rule of law. Since the practice of equity is predicated on unique features of the particular case, equity could be said to respect the requirement of legal regularity by treating different cases differently. The difficulty with this argument is that all cases differ in factual particulars. The key is to specify which similarities and differences should count. The requirement that like cases be treated alike requires judges to justify distinctions between persons in terms of the relevant legal rules and principles. To the extent that doing equity departs from the rules, it could be said to treat differently cases that are similar with respect to the features that should count. For this reason, the best view (at least provisionally) seems to be that equitable departure from legal rules violates the requirement of regularity.

The second reason for conflict is based on the requirement of *publicity*. The requirement that the laws be known and expressly promulgated would seem to direct judges to decide the cases that come before them according to rules that have been announced in advance. But the practice of equity is post hoc, done after the fact. The result required by equity may not be knowable until after all the parties have acted. This feature (seemingly) makes it impossible for persons subject to the law to guide their behavior by it.

The third reason for conflict is based on the requirement of *generality*. The rule of law requires the laws to be framed in general terms and forbids laws aimed at particular individuals. Equity does not involve the framing of legal rules aimed at

particular parties, but a judge doing equity will give reasons for
his decision that are based on the facts of the particular dispute
and not on rules framed in general terms. The practice of
equity is ad hoc, done on particular facts. The reasons given in
equity need not be particularized in the sense that they relate
only to named individuals. One can discuss the requirements of
justice in particular circumstances in impersonal terms. The
requirement of generality is more than a prohibition against the
decision of cases on the basis of reasons that are specific to
individual persons. Decision by general rules requires the judge
to fit the case within a category that encompasses a general
class of cases. Because equity requires judges to focus on the
uniqueness of particular fact patterns, there is tension between
the generality requirement and the practice of equity.

The second approach to the conflict between equity and the
rule of law is via the arguments of principle and policy that
support the rule of law. From a deontological perspective, the
practice of equity seems to violate a number of political or legal
rights of personhood and citizenship. Each requirement of the
rule of law can be restated as an individual political (and legal)
right that is potentially infringed when a judge departs from
public and general rules in order to do justice in a particular
case. For example, the requirements of publicity and generality
are reflected in the constitutional practice of the United States
by the right to due process of law and the constitutional prohibition of ex post facto laws and bills of attainder. Even though the
facts of a particular case may generate arguments for doing
equity in order to assure fairness to the winner, the loser in
such a case seems to have a legitimate complaint that her political rights have been infringed. Finally, the rule of law protects
the equality of citizens as lawmakers, by insuring that judges
do not substitute their own legislative preferences for those of
democratically elected officials in the guise of doing equity.

The case that the rule of law and equity are in conflict can
also be made from a consequentialist perspective. Initially, consequentialism may seem to support the practice of equity; doing
equity could be seen as departing from the rules in order to
produce good consequences in particular cases. There is, how-

ever, a consequentialist case to be made for the rule of law. The rule of law provides predictability, allowing individuals to plan their actions with knowledge of the legal consequences. The requirements of publicity and generality reduce the risk that adjudicators will use their discretion to obtain private gains at the expense of public goods. The practice of equity undermines the predictability and stability of the law and loosens the constraints against official abuse. From a consequentialist perspective the benefits of equity trade off against the benefits of the rule of law; the two are usually in tension. Consequentialism supports the practice of equity when the benefits produced by departure from the legal rule in the particular case outweigh the costs of instability, unpredictability, and risk of abuse.

The conflict between law and equity can be approached from a third direction, by considering the relation between rule and discretion in adjudication. The practice of equity can be conceived (at least as a working hypothesis) as an exercise of discretion by judges. H. L. A. Hart and Ronald Dworkin provide two "pictures" of the relationship between legal rules and discretion in adjudication, with two corresponding views of the nature of equity.

H. L. A. Hart's picture of the core and penumbra of legal rules mediates between two extreme positions. An extreme formalist might argue that all legal decisions are rule bound; an extreme realist could contend that all decisions are discretionary. On Hart's account, judges are constrained by the law in the decision of easy cases, within the core of a rule. In the penumbra, decisions are governed by the discretion of the judge.[9] The relationship of equity to Hart's picture differs in two classes of cases. In the first class, equity operates in the penumbra of a legal rule. Doing equity in the penumbra of the rules is simply the exercise of discretion—a normal event in Hart's picture. Equity is more problematic, however, in a second class of cases, when it operates to produce a result that is contrary to the rule's core meaning. For Hart, the rules have a core of determinate meaning because judicial practice in the core is consistent. Equity undermines the consistency of that practice and hence undermines the rule of law. Legal formalists could extend Hart's

point and argue that discretion and hence equity is never legitimate; at the other extreme, some legal realists might argue that
all decisions are discretionary and hence equitable in nature.

A second picture of the relationship between rule and discretion is contained in Ronald Dworkin's theory of law as integrity,
framed partly in response to Hart.[10] Dworkin rejects the notion
that judges have discretion, even in the penumbra of a legal
rule. Although particular legal rules may be ambiguous or contain gaps or conflict, the judge can still determine the right
answer in a particular case by appealing to the set of principles
that best fits and justifies the law as a whole. This procedure
provides the judge with a "metarule" that enables her to decide
each case in accordance with the law without directly resorting
to discretion or personal preference.

On one hand, one might say that Dworkin's picture reconciles equity with the rule of law. Doing equity is simply following
the metarule specified by law as integrity. The appearance that
equity is inconsistent with the rule of law is generated by a
misconception, that the law can be reduced to legal rules, when
in fact it includes principles as well. Thus, one could argue that
Dworkin explains equity as the application of legal principles
that modify the result that would obtain if the law consisted
only of rules.

On the other hand, one could say that Dworkin has simply
eliminated the idea of equity altogether, by arguing for an
expansive concept of the complete set of legal rules in which
every case should be decided according to general rules and
principles. Dworkinian "equity" is not focused on the unique
facts of the particular case. Rather, Dworkin's mythical judge,
Hercules, has the task of generating a set of "principles that fit,
not only the particular precedent to which some litigant directs
his attention, but all other judicial decisions within his general
jurisdiction and, indeed, statutes as well."[11] Hercules must be
very good at the construction of big theories, but nothing in
Dworkin's theory demands that he be sensitive to those facts of
particular cases that do not correspond to the requirements of
legal rules or principles. In a limited sense, Dworkin agrees with
the formalist that law is all a matter of rules (broadly under-

stood to include a coherence metarule) and that all discretionary attention to particulars (and hence equity) is illegitimate.

In sum, there are three ways to view the conflict between equity and the rule of law. First, the practice of equity violates the requirements of regularity, publicity, and generality, which are part of our concept of the rule of law. Second, at the level of political morality, the violation of these constraints can be seen as both unfair and harmful. Third, equity as a discretionary, fact-sensitive, and particularized practice is inconsistent with the role of general rules (and principles) in law as understood by Hart and Dworkin.

## II. A Virtue-Centered Theory of Judging

In the past three decades, there has been a revival of interest in Aristotelian moral theory, and especially in Aristotle's theory of the virtues.[12] To many modern ears, the term "virtue" *(aretē)* has lost its Aristotelian meaning. In Aristotle's sense, the virtues are human excellences. These dispositional qualities of character and intellect, such as courage and practical wisdom, produce human flourishing. In this section, I will sketch a virtue-centered theory of judging.[13]

### A. *The Structure of a Virtue-Centered Theory*

The essential point about a virtue-centered theory of judging is that it creates a conceptual link between the correctness of a legal decision and the decision that would be made by a virtuous judge. Three definitions specify the nature of the link. (1) *Virtuous Decision:* A legal decision is right if and only if a virtuous judge would make that decision under the circumstances. (2) *Virtuous Judge:* A virtuous judge is a person who occupies the legal role of adjudicator and possesses and acts in accord with the judicial virtues. (3) *Judicial Virtue:* A judicial virtue is a dispositional quality of mind or will that promotes excellence in judging. The judicial virtues include judicial intelligence, judicial wisdom, judicial integrity, judicial temperament, judicial impartiality, and justice.

Thus, on a virtue-centered theory of judging, good legal decisions are made in accord with the judicial virtues. But a virtue-centered theory of judging does not exclude a judge from considering legal rules or the consequences of particular decisions. Virtuous judges care about the rules. Fidelity to the law is an essential component of the virtue of judicial integrity. Moreover, virtuous judges care about the consequences that will flow from their decision in a particular case. The virtue of judicial wisdom includes the ability to assess the consequences of one's decisions and take them into proper account. A virtue-centered theory of judging permits a judge to attend to the considerations advanced by many rival theories. There remains an important difference, however. Legal formalism makes conformity with the legal rules criterial for a correct decision. Act-utilitarianism and its legal variants make the assessment of consequences criterial for the right legal result. A virtue-centered theory of judging allows and even insists that these activities are relevant but denies them criterial status.[14]

### B. The Judicial Virtues

The next step is an account of the judicial virtues. A good judge must possess six judicial virtues: (1) judicial intelligence, (2) judicial wisdom, (3) judicial integrity, (4) judicial temperament, (5) judicial impartiality, and (6) justice. The content of the judicial virtues can be specified by comparing and contrasting them with the general virtues—the qualities that anyone, including a judge, must possess in order to live a flourishing life. Some of the judicial virtues are simply the judicial possession of general virtues; judicial wisdom, for example, is simply a form of practical wisdom developed in and for the context of adjudication. Others are "differentiated virtues,"[15] character traits that are virtues only for persons who occupy the role of judge; judicial impartiality, for example, is not a virtue for someone who is not an adjudicator.

The first of the judicial virtues is a form of *sophia*, or theoretical wisdom. *Judicial intelligence* is excellence in understanding and theorizing about the law. A good judge must be learned in the law; she must have the ability to engage in sophisticated legal reasoning. Moreover, judges need the ability to grasp the facts of disputes that may involve other practical disciplines such as accounting or engineering. The talents conducive to theoretical wisdom in the law may be somewhat different from those that produce the analogous intellectual virtue in physics, philosophy, or microbiology.

The second virtue is *judicial wisdom,* a form of *phronēsis,* or practical wisdom. The good judge must possess practical wisdom in the choosing of legal ends and means. The person of practical wisdom knows which particular ends are worth pursuing and knows which means are best suited to achieve those ends. Judicial wisdom is simply the virtue of practical wisdom as applied to the choices that must be made by judges. The practically wise judge has developed excellence in discerning what goals to pursue in the particular case and excellence in choosing the means to accomplish those goals.

The third virtue is *judicial integrity.* The good judge must have a special concern for fidelity to law and for the coherence of law. Judicial integrity is what Aristotle would call a moral virtue, an aspect of character that creates a disposition to choose in a certain way. There is a close connection between the virtue of judicial integrity and the ideal of the rule of law. Without the virtue of judicial integrity, the values underlying the requirements of legal regularity, publicity, and generality would be threatened. The ability to set aside one's ambitions and one's political or moral preferences and decide on the basis of the law is a judicial virtue.

The fourth virtue is *judicial temperament.* The traditional concern in judicial selection with judicial temperament is illuminated by Aristotle's account of the virtue of good temper, or *prāotēs:* the disposition to anger that is proportionate to the provocation and the situation. The corresponding vices produce particularly bad results if possessed by a trial judge. Judge Hoffman's disproportionate rage in the Chicago Seven trial produced a spectacle that undermined public confidence in the orderly administration of justice. But being too slow to anger is also a judicial vice. A judge who fails to respond with appropriate outrage in the face of misconduct can have a similar, if less dramatic, effect. A courtroom that is out of control is almost as bad as one in which defendants are bound and gagged.

The fifth virtue is *judicial impartiality*. Judicial impartiality is the disposition to even-handed sympathy or empathy with the parties to a legal dispute: judges should not identify more strongly with the one side than with the other.[16] The degree of "partiality" or identification with the interests of the litigants that is appropriate to the role of judge is different from that which is appropriate to other situations. Parents should be partial to their children, and friends partial to one another. Judges should be partial to none but should possess an appropriate degree of sympathy and empathy with all who appear before them.

The sixth virtue is *justice*. A good judge must be disposed to give each party what she is due. In some cases, justice requires application of the legal rules, but in others, justice consists in departure from those rules. This relationship of the virtue of justice to legal rules will be developed in my discussion of the basis for reconciling equity with the ideal of the rule of law.

## C. The Moral Education of Judges

No formula that specifies the correct decision procedure for the resolution of cases will guarantee good judging unless the judge possesses the judicial virtues. But virtue, including judicial virtue, cannot be obtained quickly or through a sheer act of will. Aristotle believed that the intellectual virtues were inculcated through training and experience and that the moral virtues were developed by habit. His view provides insight into the acquisition of the judicial virtues as well.

An initial step in the moral education of a judge is simply a good upbringing and education, leading to acquisition of the general virtues. Further steps are legal training and practice. In common law systems, candidates for judicial office acquire the virtues of judicial intelligence, integrity, and wisdom by practicing law as an attorney or solicitor. (In other systems, judges may acquire their initial experience in a low-level judicial office.) The acquisition of the virtue of judicial impartiality, on the other hand, could take some time on the bench, away from the practice of law and partiality for one's clients. For these reasons, the best judges are likely to have practical experience, and the very best judges reach their full potential for judicial excellence only after they have spent some time on the bench.

The acquisition of judicial wisdom is particularly important for reconciling the practice of equity with the rule of law. Judicial wisdom is simply practical wisdom relevant to judging. It is most likely to be acquired through experience as a lawyer or judge, and in some cases through participation in politics. Legal practice allows the potential judge to develop a sense for what works as a practical matter and enables the potential judge to develop a sense of when the law is achieving something that is really worthwhile. Experience on the bench is likely to deepen this practical wisdom by exposing judges to a greater variety of experiences from a new perspective.

The sort of experience required for the development of judicial wisdom on the appellate bench may be different from that required for excellence in trial judges, especially in the case of the United States Supreme Court, which plays a special role in constitutional adjudication. The political role of Supreme Court Justices makes experience as a politician relevant to the development of judicial wisdom. Hugo Black and Earl Warren come to mind as justices known for their practical judgment, but the experience that shaped their wisdom was acquired in the sphere of politics as much as in the sphere of law.

## D. Some Considerations Favoring a Virtue-Centered Theory

So far, I have said little about the justifications for a virtue-centered theory of judging. There is a weak sense in which it is obvious that consideration of judicial virtue or character must be incorporated into a theory of judging. Almost no one thinks that character is completely irrelevant to being a good judge. Even if one believed that the correctness of legal decisions depends entirely on compliance with legal rules, one would want judges to possess the qualities of character necessary to follow the rules. A virtue-centered theory goes beyond this weak sense of the relevance of character to judging by making judicial virtue criterial for a correct decision. Folk wisdom and familiar examples lend plausibility to this strong view, although the support offered here falls short of a rigorous argument.

To begin, consider the paradigm of the good judge in Western culture. Solomon is not admired as a good judge because he followed the rules when he ordered the child cut in two. Quite the contrary. Nor is Solomon admired because he adhered to the correct decision procedure for deciding disputes; he is not the model for Dworkin's Hercules or for any other contemporary theory of judging. Solomon devised a solution to the case before him that responded to the particular dispute in a way that could never be duplicated. He is one of our paradigms of a *phronimos;* we say, "as wise as Solomon."

In addition, consider the qualities we admire in justices of the United States Supreme Court. Judgments about the members of the Court are politically contentious, but despite political disagreements, some justices are widely admired. John Marshall is not admired, I think, for adhering to an ideal decision procedure for the resolution of constitutional cases. The reasoning of *Marbury v. Madison* has been picked apart endlessly. One thing we do admire about Marshall's performance in *Marbury* is that he displayed practical wisdom by responding to the particular constellation of facts and political context in a way that fixed the practice of judicial review in the fabric of our political life. We admire him for his possession of judicial wisdom.

The case for a virtue-centered account of judging can also draw support from choice situations that are analogous to judging. Suppose that you have a serious illness and are confronted with two choices. You can choose to be treated by the book. Your physician will carefully follow the diagnosis and treatment prescribed by the most sophisticated and recent medical scholarship. Your second choice is for your physician to use her best practical judgment, deviating from the book on the basis of experience, intuitions, and hunches. Many of us would reasonably prefer that the physician not disengage her practical wisdom, despite our inability to offer a transparent account of its mechanism. (Assuming, of course, that we believe our physician possesses practical wisdom!) Admittedly, judging is unlike medical treatment in that the rule in the book will produce a winner and a loser. But law is not always a zero sum game. The community as a whole has a stake in assuring the best resolution of legal disputes.

These brief remarks about the plausibility of a virtue-centered theory of judging complete the exposition of the theory. I now turn to the central question: does a virtue-centered theory of judging allow us to reconcile the practice of equity with the ideal of the rule of law? If the answer is yes, we will have another, more programmatic reason to affirm a virtue-centered theory of judging.

### III. RECONCILING EQUITY AND THE RULE OF LAW

There is no mystical quality of virtuous decision that will dissolve the real tensions between some of the values that underlie the rule of law and some of the reasons that motivate the practice of equity. The fact that equity is done by a virtuous judge cannot change the fact that equity involves judges going beyond the letter of the law and will (sometimes) be less predictable than strict adherence to the letter of the rules might be. The practice of equity is consistent with the ideal of the rule of law at a fundamental level, but some tension remains.

As Aristotle understands the law, "the law *is* intelligence, it has its own rationality or *logos*."[17] But legal disputes cannot be resolved by the written laws themselves. To deal with a legal dispute, one must comprehend the case itself. It is only through an appreciation and understanding of the facts of a dispute that one can move to the question of what legal rules may apply. Legal perception, we might say, comes to the scene before legal judgment.[18]

For Aristotle, moral perception is informed by the virtues. Just as all moral actors differ in their ability to *see* the morally relevant dimensions of occasions for action, judges differ in their ability to *see* the salient features of a legal case. As Nancy Sherman puts it, "much of the work of virtue will rest in knowing how to construe the case, how to describe and classify what is before one."[19] The virtue most relevant to the possession of moral vision is *phronēsis,* or practical wisdom. *Phronēsis* is the intellectual component of the disposition to respond appropriately to particular situations; a *phronimos* is able to discern what is morally relevant about the situation.

Aristotle's view of moral perception is key to understanding his conception of equity.[20] Equity is the tailoring of the law to the demands of the particular situation. For this reason, equity can (or should) be done only by a *phronimos*, a judge with moral and legal vision. In my taxonomy, equity can (or should) only be done by an adjudicator who possesses the judicial virtues—most particularly, the virtues of judicial wisdom and judicial integrity.

Consider what happens when a judge who lacks these virtues attempts to do equity. Lacking judicial integrity, a judge who departs from the rules is likely to be imposing her own preferences and not the principles immanent in the law. Lacking judicial wisdom, a judge who attempts to do equity will not perceive the relevant features of the particular case and so in departing from the rule is more likely to do harm than good.

A virtue-centered account serves as the basis for three arguments that the practice of equity can be reconciled with the ideal of the rule of law: (1) done by a judge with judicial integrity, equity is not arbitrary departure from the rules; (2) an equitable decision can be more predictable and regular than strict adherence to the rules; (3) a limited practice of equity may actually increase adherence to the rules in the system as a whole. All three arguments may seem counterintuitive, and each requires further explanation.

First, when equity is done by a virtuous judge, departure from the rules is not the exercise of arbitrary discretion. An adjudicator with judicial integrity cares about the coherence of the law and is motivated to insure that her departure from the letter of the rules accords with their spirit. The purposes and values immanent in the law itself still hold sway, despite the departure from the letter of the law. As Judith Shklar summarized this point, "In Aristotle's account the single most important condition for the Rule of Law is the character one must impute to those who make lawful judgments. Justice is the constant disposition to act fairly and lawfully."[21]

The force of this first point may be obscured by the way

that many modern legal theorists divide adjudication between discretion and rule following. For example, Dworkin argues that even outside the core of a legal rule, decision always should be based on legal principles and should never be an exercise of discretion. Recall that Dworkin's mythical judge, Hercules, approaches a case by constructing the normative theory of law that best fits and justifies the political structure and legal doctrine of his community. From his normative theory of the law of his community, Hercules derives those rules and principles that apply to the particular case and then applies them.

There are two standpoints from which we can see the difference between Dworkin's views and a virtue-centered theory. First, from an external perspective, a virtue-centered view emphasizes the role of practical wisdom in organizing judicial perception. Dworkin's theory does not address the question of how judges find facts; he explicitly sets that issue aside.[22] But real judges, especially at the trial level, must be fact sensitive to make good decisions. A virtue-centered theory allows observers of the legal system to identify the capacities that a judge should possess in order to make good decisions.

Second, from an internal perspective, a virtue-centered theory gives guidance to judges who perceive that the application of the legal rules would result in injustice in particular cases. A judge who adopts a virtue-centered theory will pay heed to the particular constellation of facts that make up the case. A good judge will also possess the virtue of judicial integrity; she will carefully consider the values expressed in the ideal of the rule of law. If she comes to the conclusion that doing equity is appropriate under the circumstances, a virtue-centered theory tells her that she should exercise the virtue of practical wisdom and depart from the rules. By way of contrast, law as integrity forbids a departure from general rules and principles on the basis of a judge's perception that these universals fail to do justice in particular circumstances. From the perspective of a judge, a virtue-centered theory provides guidance where guidance is needed by indicating the circumstances in which the judge should engage in the practice of equity.

These differences between law as integrity and a virtue-centered theory can also be approached via a familiar criticism of law as integrity—that Hercules is a myth for two related reasons: (1) no real judge could construct the grand theory of the law that Hercules does, and (2) real judges decide cases instinctively without Hercules' theoretical deliberation. Dworkin acknowledges that these points are true of real judges, but denies that they have any force against his theory. Rather, "Hercules shows us the hidden structure of [real judges's] judgments and so lays these open to study and criticism."[23]

Dworkin's points can be expressed in Aristotelian terms. Legal decision making, at bottom, is the conjunction of theoretical wisdom and knowledge of the law. What judges really do ("the hidden structure") is to develop a theory of the law that fits and justifies existing legal practice. Dworkin saves the appearances—that judges frequently decide intuitively on the basis of "hunches" about correct outcomes rather than on the basis of elaborate theories—by two devices. First, judges develop working theories of the law as a whole over time. The working theories are unconsciously present and determine the content of their intuitive judgments or hunches. Second, because real judges are relatively slow when they engage in legal theory building, they develop "skills of craft husbandry and efficiency"[24] that enable them to reach conclusions without undertaking lines of theoretical reasoning that are unlikely to be fruitful. *Phronēsis*, or practical wisdom, is simply the name we give the unconscious exercise and efficient truncation of theoretical wisdom.

The virtue-centered account of the practice of equity denies that Dworkin's explanation is adequate to all the cases. *Phronēsis* is not simply unconscious or truncated theoretical wisdom. No matter how brilliant and learned in the law, Hercules would not be a very good judge if he lacked the experience of particulars that is required for practical wisdom.

This first argument for the compatibility of equity and the rule of law can be summarized as follows: a virtue-centered theory of judging incorporates Dworkin's insight that the law can guide decisions beyond the narrow confines of its letter, but it supplements Dworkin's explanation of the mechanism by which this process occurs. Virtue theory accepts that judges sometimes engage in Herculean theory building in order to construct legal principles but insists that judges with practical reason sometimes depart from the general rules and principles on the basis of their legal and moral perception of the facts of the particular case. This perception is guided by the judicial virtues, including, but not limited to, the virtue of judicial integrity. Concern for the coherence of the law as a whole constrains the way that a judge with practical wisdom will depart from the rules in order to do justice in a particular case.

The second argument for reconciliation of the rule of law with the practice of equity is that the notion of *moral and legal vision* that grounds the practice of equity is also necessary to understanding the application of legal rules.[25] Rule application can only take place after a judge comprehends the facts of the case. Moral and legal vision is required in order to reveal that a case is governed by a rule. For this reason, *both* the application of legal rules *and* the practice of equity require the virtue of judicial wisdom, or *phronēsis*.

This insight allows us to see how the practice of equity may actually reinforce, rather than undermine, the values of predictability and regularity that support the ideal of the rule of law. We all know that it is possible to produce arbitrary and unpredictable results by strictly adhering to the letter of the law. Perhaps the most familiar example of this phenomenon is the practice of labor unions disrupting a work environment by working to the book, adhering strictly to the letter but not the spirit of the rules. This takes us back to Aristotle's discussion of the basis for equity: no general rule can be framed with sufficient precision to yield the *expected* outcome in all particular cases. In some cases, the practice of equity will make outcomes conform to expectations and hence make the law more rather than less predictable.

The third argument for the reconciliation of law and equity is that the recognition of equity as a distinct practice may serve to increase the regularity and predictability of rule application in the legal system as a whole. Without a publicly acknowledged practice of equity, the pressure to do justice in particular cases may be relieved by loosening the constraints that legal rules place upon judicial decision in general. "Equity will out," we might say to summarize a point first made by Roscoe Pound.[26]

Undergirding this argument is the assumption that the degree to which a system of rules constrains the actual decisions made by adjudicators is a matter of social practice: a system can be tightly rule bound or loosely rule guided.[27] If equitable departure from legal rules is an accepted and acknowledged (but limited) exception within a general practice in which legal rules determine outcomes, then judges can tolerate the constraint of binding rules. Without this safety valve, judges will have good reason to engage in interpretive practices that give them considerable freedom of choice in every case and not just the exceptional one. Assuming that the pressure felt by judges to do justice in the cases that come before them is substantial (as I think it is), then the open practice of equity in a limited class of cases is likely to increase the adherence of the system as a whole to the requirements of the rule of law.

The three arguments that I have offered for the reconciliation of equity and the rule of law do not eliminate all of the tensions between them. There will be cases in which doing equity produces surprise or unfairness. Moreover, not all judges are virtuous. Allowing the practice of equity will permit some judges to act arbitrarily and unjustly. The decision whether to encourage the practice of equity should be made on the basis of prevailing social conditions and not solely on the general theoretical considerations explored in this essay. The fact that equity and the rule of law *can* be reconciled does not guarantee that they will be.

## IV. The Problem of Equity in a Pluralist Society

There are special difficulties with the practice of equity in a modern, pluralist society. In this section I address two objections to the legitimacy of a virtue-centered practice of equity in a modern, pluralist society: (1) that the justification of a virtue-centered theory of judging relies on premises derived from virtue-ethics that could not be accepted as reasonable by wide segments of the citizenry, and (2) that the virtue of judicial wisdom depends on elements of Aristotle's account of *phronēsis* that are embedded in deep and controversial views about moral psychology.

The first objection goes to the acceptability of a virtue-centered theory of judging for a pluralist society. At least since the Wars of Religion of the sixteenth century, Western societies have been characterized by strong and persistent disagreements about the nature of the good—a condition that John Rawls calls "the fact of pluralism."[28] Given this pluralism, respect for the freedom and equality of citizens requires that the basic institutions of society be justified by public reasons. The requirement of public reason rules out justifications that depend on the deep premises of particular moral or religious conceptions of the good. Public reasons include basic tools or reasoning such as logic and common sense, knowledge of facts that are not controversial and those established by science, and values that can be derived from the public political culture of our society.

Aristotle argued that the good is *eudaimonia,* or happiness. Some scholars contend that Aristotle's conception of a good life requires participation in philosophy or politics; others argue that Aristotle believed that happiness requires the pursuit of virtue for its own sake. However we interpret Aristotle, his views about the good life are controversial today; these views are not appropriate as the foundation of a theory of judging in a pluralist society.

Fortunately, a virtue-centered theory of judging need not rely on Aristotle's conception of the good. Although my exposition of a virtue-centered theory of judging has paralleled Aristotle's ethics, it is not the case that the former depends upon the latter. One way to see this is to recall a once-common reaction to Aristotle's ethics. It used to be said that Aristotle's theory was not a moral theory at all; rather, Aristotle had a theory of human flourishing or excellence that did not really answer the question of what is good or right. One could accept Aristotle's views as a conception of prudence, of how to live a successful life, without affirming prudence as a conception of the good. Likewise, one can accept a virtue-centered theory as an account of excellence in judging, without endorsing a virtue-centered theory of morality. Unless we affirm a strong version of natural law theory, our normative views about law are sufficiently distinct from our views about morality for us to accept legal theories that are not directly tied to our moral theories.

The second objection begins with the fact that a virtue-centered reconciliation of equity and the rule of law relies heavily on the concept of practical wisdom, or *phronēsis*. Wisdom is not a philosophical idea; it is a familiar part of folk psychology. The problem is that the common sense conception of practical wisdom seems somewhat obscure. One way of developing this objection is to pose a series of questions to the proponent of the proposition that judicial wisdom offers an explanation of equity that reconciles it with the rule of law. How does *phronēsis* work? What is the mechanism by which a virtuous judge is able to discern that the "spirit" of the law requires a deviation from its letter in a particular case? How can we tell the judges who do possess judicial wisdom from those who do not? The questions are pressing because without some account of *phronēsis*, a virtue-centered theory of judging is opened to the argument that it relies on the mystical vision or private intuitions of particular judges.

What is called for is an explanation of *phronēsis* in general and of judicial wisdom in particular. One route to an explanation would be to elaborate and defend the concept of practical wisdom from within Aristotle's moral psychology. This approach is problematic because reliance on deep premises in Aristotle's psychology is excluded by the requirement of public reason. Aristotle's theory relies on controversial premises about human nature and is embedded in his general views about biology and metaphysics.

Another strategy for explaining *phronēsis* is to rely on analogies to familiar experiences and on common sense. We can begin by exploring ordinary experiences that bear relevant similarities to practical wisdom. Take riding a bicycle. Very few of us could articulate a theory of the mechanism by which one is able to balance, pedal, and navigate—all at the same time. But somehow we do it. Moreover, no one seriously contends that we could do a better job of riding a bicycle by calculating expected utilities for each movement or following a set of rules or principles. These alternatives would likely result in a spill. In the case of bicycle riding, the appeal to intuitive knowledge that cannot be articulated is both persuasive and satisfying—as far as it goes. Recall that we have already examined a second analogy, the practice of medicine, in which practical wisdom does not reduce to a set of rules. The medical analogy suggests that we are comfortable with the idea of practical wisdom in choice situations that are relevantly similar to adjudication.

There are limits to the analogies to bicycle riding and medicine. After all, there are distinctions between judging and bicycle riding or treating a patient. Bicycle riding involves motor skills, muscle coordination, and a sense of balance; these processes might be thought to take place in the unconscious. Judicial decisions involve fact finding, legal reasoning, taking evidence, and other processes that seem to be conscious. Frequently these processes involve conscious deliberation: a mental activity that seems very far removed from balancing on a bike.

The validity of the analogy can be tested by considering the phenomenology of legal reasoning. When I think about a legal problem I do not find myself proceeding step by step through a deductive argument—at least not usually. Legal reasoning is much messier than that. In dealing with a difficult or complex problem, I get a flash of insight. Certain steps are so "obvious" that one does not see a need to articulate them, even when pressed for a step-by-step reconstruction of one's thought process. Perhaps legal reasoning is a lot more like riding a bicycle than it first seems. Physicians might say the same thing about diagnosis and treatment of illness. Medicine involves fact finding and reasoning, but it is not necessarily reducible to conscious deliberative processes.

The difficulty with this phenomenological argument is that it will not convince anyone who does not share my perception of what it is like to engage in legal reasoning. A judge might insist that she engages only in conscious activity when she does legal reasoning. "Every step is conscious," she reports. "None of that unconscious or intuitive stuff enters into *my* deliberations." Nonetheless, we can ask the question whether the mental processes that produce the experience of wholly conscious deliberation can really all be conscious. The answer must be negative. A truly complete deductive reconstruction of the legal reasoning required to think through any legal problem that is not trivial would be enormously lengthy; there is never time for conscious deliberation about all the definitions and stipulations, all the little, intuitively obvious steps, that we take for granted. One can see this quickly by trying to formalize completely the legal argument justifying the outcome in an appellate decision in a predicate logic, without leaving anything undefined and without fudging any of the steps.

No one can specify in any detail the mechanisms that underlie the intuitive, unconscious side of human reasoning. Consider the analogy to bicycle riding again. Here we also lack a full account of the mechanism, but the lack of such an account does not bother us as much as the lack of a mechanism for judicial wisdom does. Judicial decisions are politically contentious and are backed by the coercive power of the state. Requiring judges to decide on the basis of public reasons allows us to check their exercise of power. We have good reasons not to defer to a mystical vision possessed by wise judges. Our distrust is especially profound given that our views of politics and morality may be radically different from those of the supposedly virtuous adjudicator.

The lack of a precise account of the mechanism for practical wisdom does not entail that equitable decisions cannot be justified on the basis of public reason. There is a distinction between giving public justifications for judicial decisions and making such decisions exclusively on the basis of conscious deliberation from public reasons. A virtue-centered account of equity does not rule out offering public justifications for judicial decisions. Moreover, a virtue-centered account does not direct us to abstain from public evaluation of judges who render equitable decisions. Judges who cannot offer satisfactory explanations of their departures from the rules should be criticized and, if appropriate, subject to discipline or even removal from the bench. A virtue-centered account does suggest a certain division of critical labor. When the judge's explanation appeals to practicality and to her own experience, we ought to listen carefully to the criticisms and defenses offered by persons who also possess relevant experience. For this reason, appellate courts should include among their members significant numbers of experienced trial judges or lawyers. Equitable decisions should be reversed when they cannot be adequately justified.

## V. Conclusion

The rule of law is not a law of rules. The conception of law as a rule-bound practice is incomplete because it does not account for the role of judicial virtue in shaping legal perception. The practice of equity by a virtuous judge does not ignore the genuine importance of achieving regularity, publicity, and generality in the law. Fidelity to the letter of the law is part of the virtue of judicial integrity, but respect for legal rules is not the whole of judicial excellence. There are situations in which a judge with practical wisdom will perceive that adherence to the spirit of the law requires a departure from its letter. Sometimes justice and the rule of law require the practice of equity.[29]

## NOTES

1. The notion that the rule of law should be understood as a law of rules is expressed in a recent article by Justice Antonin Scalia. Antonin Scalia, "The Rule of Law as a Law of Rules," *University of Chicago Law Review* 56 (1989): 1175.

2. A. V. Dicey, *Introduction to the Study of the Law of the Constitution*, 10th ed. (London: Macmillan, 1960), 202–3.

3. My account of the rule of law draws on several sources. See John Rawls, *A Theory of Justice* (Cambridge, Mass.: Harvard University Press, 1971), 235–43; Lon Fuller, *The Morality of Law*, rev. ed. (New Haven, Conn.: Yale University Press, 1969), 33–94; Joseph Raz, "The Rule of Law and Its Virtue," *Law Quarterly Review* 93 (1977): 195; Geoffrey de Q. Walker, *The Rule of Law* (Melbourne: Melbourne University Press, 1988), 1–48.

4. *Hecht v. Bowles*, 321 U.S. 321, 329 (1944).

5. See United States Department of Justice, *Report to the Attorney General, Justice without Law: A Reconsideration of the "Broad Equitable Powers" of the Federal Courts* (Washington: Government Printing Office, 1988), 86–94, 161–66.

6. Aristotle, *The Ethics of Aristotle: The Nicomachean Ethics*, J. A. K. Thomson trans., rev. by Hugh Tredennick (Harmondsworth: Penguin, 1976), 1137$^b$9–37$^b$24. Page references to Aristotle's works are to Im-

manuel Bekker's 1831 edition of the Greek text. For a discussion of Aristotle's idea of equity, see Roger Shiner, "Aristotle's Theory of Equity," in *Justice, Law and Method in Plato and Aristotle*, (Edmonton, Alb.: Academic Printing and Publishing 1987): 173–191.

7. Frederick Schauer, *Playing by the Rules: A Philosophical Examination of Rule-Based Decision-Making in Law and Life* (Oxford: Clarendon, 1991), 31–34.

8. See id., 77–78.

9. H. L. A. Hart, *The Concept of Law* (Oxford: Oxford University Press, 1961), 121–50.

10. Ronald Dworkin, *Law's Empire* (Cambridge, Mass.: Harvard University Press, 1986).

11. Ronald Dworkin, "Hard Cases," in *Taking Rights Seriously* (Cambridge, Mass.: Harvard University Press, 1978), 116.

12. For an overview of virtue ethics, see Philippa Foot, *Virtues and Vices and Other Essays in Moral Philosophy* (Berkeley and California: University of California Press, 1978); Peter Geach, *The Virtues* (Cambridge: Cambridge University Press, 1977); James D. Wallace, *Virtues and Vices* (Ithaca, N.Y.: Cornell University Press, 1978); *Midwest Studies in Philosophy*. Vol. 13, *Ethical Theory: Character and Virtue*, Peter French, Theodore Uehling, Jr., and Howard Wettstein, eds. (Notre Dame, Ind.: University of Notre Dame Press, 1988); *Essays on Aristotle's Ethics*, A. Rorty, ed. (Berkeley and Los Angeles: University of California Press, 1980).

13. The approach suggested here is related to some other recent approaches to judging. See, e.g., Steven J. Burton, "Law as Practical Reason," *Southern California Law Review* 62 (1989): 747; Donald Brosnan, "Virtue Ethics in a Perfectionist Theory of Law and Justice," *Cardozo L. Rev.* 11 (1989): 335; Daniel A. Farber and Philip P. Frickey, "Practical Reason and the First Amendment," *UCLA L. Rev.* 34 (1987): 1615; Catharine Wells, "Tort Law as Corrective Justice," *Mich. L. Rev.* 88 (1990): 2348.

14. My account of a virtue-centered theory of judging borrows from Rosalind Hursthouse's exposition of virtue ethics. Rosalind Hursthouse, "Virtue Theory and Abortion," *Philosophy and Public Affairs* 20 (1991): 223–33.

15. Stephen Munzer, *A Theory of Property* (Cambridge: Cambridge University Press, 1990), 123.

16. See Stephen Macedo, *Liberal Virtues* (Oxford: Oxford University Press, 1990), 275.

17. Nancy Sherman, *The Fabric of Character* (Oxford: Oxford University Press, 1989), 15 (italicization added).

18. See Lawrence Blum, "Moral Perception and Particularity," *Ethics* 101 (1991): 702.

19. Nancy Sherman, *The Fabric of Character*, 29.

20. Shiner, "Aristotle's Theory of Equity," 184–87.

21. Judith Shklar, "Political Theory and the Rule of Law," in *The Rule of Law: Ideal or Ideology*, Allan Hutchinson and Patrick Monahan, eds. (Toronto: Carswell, 1987), 3.

22. See Ronald Dworkin, *Law's Empire*, 11–12.

23. Id., 265.

24. Id.

25. See Richard Posner, *The Problems of Jurisprudence* (Cambridge, Mass.: Harvard University Press, 1990), 142–43.

26. See Roscoe Pound, "The Decadence of Equity," *Colum. L. Rev.* 4 (1905): 23–24.

27. Frederick Schauer, "Rules and the Rule of Law," *Harvard Journal of Law and Public Policy* 14 (1991): 661–53.

28. John Rawls, *Political Liberalism* (New York, N.Y.: Columbia University Press, 1993): 212–54. John Rawls, "The Idea of an Overlapping Consensus," *Oxford Journal of Legal Studies* 7 (1987): 4; see also Lawrence Solum, "Pluralism and Modernity," *Chi.-Kent L. Rev.* 66 (1991): 93; Lawrence Solum, "Faith and Justice," *DePaul L. Rev.* 39 (1990): 1083.

29. I owe thanks to the editor of *Nomos* and the participants at the January 1992 meeting of the American Society for Political and Legal Philosophy for their comments and suggestions. I am also grateful to Scott Altman, Ken Anderson, Ronald Dworkin, Daniel Farber, Rosalind Hursthouse, Richard Kraut, Sharon Lloyd, Shelley Marks, Judge Richard Posner, and Frederick Schauer for reading and commenting on earlier drafts of this essay. My colleagues David Leonard, Gerry McLaughlin, John Nockleby, and Sam Pillsbury have been generous with helpful criticism.

# 7

# THE RULE OF LAW, JUSTICE, AND THE POLITICS OF MODERATION

## STEPHEN MACEDO

## I. INTRODUCTION: THE RULE OF LAW AND EQUITY

The rule of law is central to our notion of good government: it is one of our basic political commitments and ideals. Because it is so familiar, we are apt to forget that it is not simply an ideal: it is a practical ideal, a compromise between purer moral ideals such as justice and the practical limitations of human self-government. This is to say that the rule of law is neither a simple ideal nor simply an ideal. The tension between the rule of law and more exalted ideals like justice reminds us of the "in-betweenness" of our condition.[1] Good government means doing better than simply playing by the rules; it also means accepting that we should not try to do too much better.

More than anything else, the rule of law stands against arbi-

I am greatly indebted to Arthur Applebaum and Frederick Schauer for very useful comments and discussion, and to Frank Michelman for some basic challenges to which I've tried to respond. My thanks also to Peter Berkowitz, Walter F. Murphy, and Ian Shapiro for comments on an earlier draft. I would like to dedicate this paper to the memory of a colleague and mentor who did much to demystify and fortify the rule of law, along with many other liberal practices and institutions, Judith N. Shklar.

trariness and caprice: it regularizes political power and renders it impersonal, hence the phrase "the rule of law and not of men." It works by insisting that governments act through general, public rules made in advance of any prosecutions, rules that apply to public officials and citizens alike. The rule of law is often taken to require, or at least to gain strong support from, a higher or constitutional law that governs ordinary lawmaking, as well as politically independent courts of law to enforce this higher law against public officials.[2]

I will not follow those who would build into the rule of law not only the formal criteria and constitutional mechanisms referred to above, but also a commitment to the minimal state.[3] Although orderly freedom could not be achieved and preserved in a modern mass society without general, public rules to structure our interactions with others, the rule of law is also compatible with oppression: "no one may travel abroad" is a perfectly general rule.[4] One committed to the rule of law may also, moreover, embrace the welfare state, whose varied activities and enterprises may sometimes conflict with and compromise the rule of law, but certainly need not destroy it.

"Equity" has various meanings. The jurisdictional sense of equity refers to those bodies of law once handled by courts of equity or Chancery. My focus here is on two other closely related senses of equity, both of which introduce forms of discretion into the law (and I will tend to treat them together after introducing them separately).[5] Equity can refer to the practice of making *exceptions* to general rules, and so Solum says it "refers to the practice of doing particularized justice, when the just result is not required by, or is indeed contrary to, the results required by the set of applicable legal rules."[6] Whereas the rule of law checks arbitrariness with generality, equity notes that applying general rules rigidly causes injustice and hardship in particular cases. Equity mitigates the severity of general rules by relieving individuals of what turn out to be hard bargains, and otherwise fashioning remedies tailored to particular cases. As Aristotle put it:

> [T]he equitable is not just in the legal sense of "just" but as a corrective of what is legally just. The reason is that all law is universal, but there are some things about which it is not possible

> to speak in universal terms. Now, in situations where it is neces-
> sary to speak in universal terms but impossible to do so correctly,
> the law takes the majority of cases, fully realizing in what respect
> it misses the mark. . . . So in a situation in which the law speaks
> universally, but the case at issue happens to fall outside the
> universal formula, it is correct to rectify the shortcoming, in
> other words, the omission and mistake of the lawgiver due to the
> generality of his statement.[7]

Equity may, therefore, encourage us to make exceptions to
rules on the basis of background purposes, aims, and principles.

Equitable principles may come into play even when rules are
being followed, since background principles and purposes enter
into the interpretation of rules. Joseph Story described equity
as "the interpretation and limitation of the words of written law;
by construing them, not according to the letter, but according
to the reason and spirit of them."[8] Equity, as I will discuss it
here, stands for discretion: it helps temper both the rigid and
the mechanical application of rules. In the name of equity we
make exceptions to legal rules or interpret rules in light of
background principles and purposes.[9]

The proper grounds of equitable judgment are contested.
Some have held that equity stands for the invocation of reason
or natural right or some other source of higher law principles,
perhaps as in Justice Chase's famous insistence, in *Calder v. Bull*,
that laws must be interpreted in light of and limited by the "*vital
principles in our free Republican governments*" and "*the great first
principles of the social compact.*"[10] Others, like Story, emphasize
the extent to which legal equity should be tied to received precedents, principles, and rules, as well as the intentions of lawmakers. Story's motive is obvious enough: to restrain the discretion
of American judges, he sought to apply English legal usages
and constraints to American courts, a move that judicial conser-
vatives such as Gary L. McDowell heartily applaud. Properly
conceived, Story insists, equity conveys no great discretion to
judges, and has no room for considerations of conscience or
natural justice.[11]

McDowell, a New Right proponent of judicial restraint, argues that equitable principles should be, and for centuries were,
carefully defined and bound in Storyesque fashion in order to

control judicial discretion and arbitrariness. In the last half-century, and since *Brown v. Board of Education* (II) in particular, however, "social science speculation" has substituted for "precedent and principle," and equity has become an instrument by which the Supreme Court makes social policy—a task for which, according to McDowell, it is ill equipped. Judicial willfulness has supplanted the rule of law, flaunting the intentions of the framers and depriving the people's representatives of their rightful power to govern.[12]

McDowell hearkens back to Anti-Federalist warnings that the Constitution's broad moralistic language opened the way for judicial tyranny. The new federal courts, according to the Anti-Federalist "Brutus," were empowered to "explain the constitution according to the reasoning spirit of it, without being confined to the words or the letter." Brutus complained that the preamble's talk of "justice" and "the general welfare" would invite judges to interpret our fundamental law in light of the "reason and spirit of the constitution."[13]

The Federalists among the founding generation were not, of course, as fearful of judicial power as the Anti-Federalists and McDowell. Nor is it clear that British legal usages and norms are as relevant to us as McDowell suggests. British courts never, as Shannon Stimson argues, had the sort of political independence enjoyed by their American counterparts.[14] The American judiciary inherited not the limited political power of British courts, says Stimson, but the more politically expansive "judicial space" that had been carved out by colonial juries. Like colonial juries before them, American courts have long been independent sources of political judgment that help both check legislative tyranny and foster popular education and principled political dialogue.[15]

There is widespread agreement on the capital importance of rules to modern constitutional government. Rules need to be interpreted, however, and, as the foregoing discussion illustrates, there is ample conflict over the proper grounds and limits of discretion. How much discretion should decision makers have to shape or depart from rules in the name of principles, norms, and reasons that underlie and help justify those rules? How free should adjudicators be to interpret the letter in light of the spirit? And what are the legitimate grounds for construing the spirit of the law? Should judges be allowed to move beyond narrowly legal sources into the broader realm of morality and policy? Is it possible not to do so? What we need to ask is, how do we want power to be organized and to whom do we want to distribute it?[16] The tension between law and equity cannot, I will argue, be dispelled. Recognizing the need to accept and live with that tension furnishes an important lesson in political moderation.

## II. Rules and Purposes: The Essential Tension

Let us begin by considering an unsuccessful attempt to reconcile the rule of law and equity, an attempt handicapped by inattention to politics. Lawrence Solum, in his contribution to this volume, describes the tension between law and equity one-dimensionally, as a tension between generality and particularity. He seems transfixed by the fact that equity "requires judges to focus on the uniqueness of particular fact patterns."[17] But particularity is not the sole source of the tension between equity and rule following. After all, judges must always attend to particular fact patterns in order to decide which standing rules apply and how they apply. There is no option of leaving particular facts behind. Nor is it quite right to say that equitable departures from rules must be "based on the facts of the particular dispute" rather than on general moral principles.[18] The facts of a particular case, on their own, get us nowhere: general principles—of legality or morality or policy—must be brought to bear in order to justify any decision.

Solum sometimes talks as though the particularity of equity goes all the way down to the grounds for equitable exceptions: equity is inconsistent, he seems to say, not only with general rules but also with general principles.[19] But if the justifying grounds of an equitable judgment are as idiosyncratic as the facts of a particular case, it would be hard to see how equity could be anything but a prescription for arbitrariness. If equitable judgments were altogether particular they would not be publicly justified, since justification in a liberal democratic regime such as ours must involve the invocation of impersonal reasons and principles that we are prepared to extend to other similar cases (even if those cases are few and far between).[20] Equitable decisions depart from general rules, but they do not leave general principles behind.[21]

We should not make too much, therefore, of equity's characteristic particularity.[22] An equitable exception to a rule could be the basis for a new rule: future cases relevantly similar to today's exception will be treated in a like manner. Equity does not suspend the maxim "treat like cases alike." Every exception is a nascent rule.[23]

The conflict between generalized and particular considerations is not irrelevant to the tension between the rule of law and equity, of course, but we need to consider why it is that we often insist on the predominance of generality even when doing so leads to particular results that are less than optimal. The question is, why deploy rules that constrain the discretion of adjudicators or other decision makers? Why not deal with every case in its full particularity? Why not always apply rules flexibly? Why not always look through the rules at the underlying reasons and justifications and bring them to bear directly in each case, as would seem natural and just?

Let us remind ourselves of why rules are so important to the organization of social life. Rules do not serve the cause of fairness. No two cases are the same—though they may be similar—and yet rules lump cases together. General rules are necessarily both underinclusive and overinclusive. Indeed, as Frederick Schauer argues, we only take rules seriously insofar as they lead us to ignore relevant differences that matter. The price of rule-bound conduct is some measure of injustice in particular cases—not in some cases but in most cases.[24] The generality of rules never does full justice to the uniqueness of individual cases. Equity might temper the unfairness of a rule-bound system in extreme cases, but it cannot eliminate unfairness without eliminating rules altogether.

Suppose we wanted to make a simple "flat rate" income tax more equitable. Some measure of progressivity would help reflect people's ability to pay and what economists call the declining marginal utility of additional increments of income (an extra five thousand dollars per year matters a lot more to you if your annual income is ten thousand dollars than if it is fifty thousand dollars). Even so, income brackets still lump together house-holds whose ability to pay is really quite different. Additional complexity and greater equity can be achieved by providing exemptions for dependents, disabilities, and other factors. But perfect equity cannot be achieved unless each and every house-hold is assessed an amount determined by all of the relevant factors, which would be different in every case. A perfectly equitable system would require case by case assessments; the only rules applied would be perfectly flexible "rules of thumb."

Rules do not serve the cause of fairness: they entrench gener-alizations that are bound to distort individual cases. Rules are bound more or less to flaunt background principles and justifi-cations.[25] If rules are utterly transparent to their background justifications, and we may always invoke those background prin-ciples and bring them to bear in particular instances, then we have a regime of reasons and discretion rather than of rules. If we follow a rule only when it is the best thing to do, all things considered, then the rule is a mere "rule of thumb" and what we have is decision-making discretion rather than rule-bound conduct.[26]

Rules do not, therefore, serve the cause of fairness and they do not lead to the best results in particular cases, but they serve a number of other values.[27] General rules foster the virtues of reliance, predictability, and stability: by reducing variance in individual cases, they allow individuals and associations to plan their lives and avoid running afoul of the law. Rules allow us to economize on time and so promote efficiency by relieving us of the need to deliberate on every occasion on the full range of relevant considerations. Rules allow communities to allocate power, to coordinate individual actions, and to direct individu-als toward common ends. The power of rules to coordinate might even increase the power of communities to achieve their purposes (rules can be "enabling constraints," as Bernie Yack puts it[28]). General rules might even promote community by emphasizing commonalities and downplaying differences.[29]

Perhaps most importantly, rules help us avoid errors arising from the prejudice, ignorance, and incompetence of decision makers. When we curtail discretion by insisting on rule-bound

behavior, we sacrifice opportunities for truly virtuoso performances and fine-tuned treatment (indeed, the more rule-bound
an office or role, the less likely it is to attract truly outstanding
individuals), but we also avoid suffering the idiocies, corruption,
and abuse that will occur when knaves and fools have leeway.

Adam Smith made so much of humankind's tendency toward
"partiality" and "the delusions of self-love" that he virtually
equated ethical conduct with a strict adherence to general rules
of conduct, especially in our dealings with others: "The rules of
justice are accurate in the highest degree, and admit of no
exceptions or modifications." While some flexibility might be
allowed with regard to virtues such as etiquette, "it is otherwise
with regard to justice: the man who in that refines the least, and
adheres with the most obstinate stedfastness to the general rules
themselves, is the most commendable, and the most to be depended upon." To begin making exceptions for oneself is to
court ruin: "When once we begin to give way to such refine-
ments, there is no enormity so gross of which we may not be
capable."[30] And the reason is simply that

> [n]one but those of the happiest mould are capable of suiting,
> with exact justness, their sentiments and behaviour to the small-
> est differences of situation, and of acting upon all occasions with
> the most delicate and accurate proprietly. The coarse clay of
> which the bulk of mankind are formed, cannot be wrought up
> to such perfection. There is scarce any man, however, who by
> discipline, education, and example, may not be so impressed with
> a regard to general rules, as to act upon almost every occasion
> with tolerable decency, and through the whole of his life to avoid
> any considerable degree of blame.[31]

It is not coincidental that so intense a reverence for rule following is exhibited by the great theorist of the modern mass, commercial society: a society, inevitably, of strangers.

So powerful in everyday thinking is the rule-bound notion of
uprightness that it often seems to overwhelm more particularized conceptions of fair or just treatment. The reason for this is
probably precisely that which Smith supplies: our suspicion of
"situational ethics" and of judgments tailored to particular facts
stems from our awareness of the difficulty of attaining an impartial point of view. Knowing how hard it is to attain impartial-

ity in one's own judgments, we also know that it is costly to
monitor in the judgments of others. We distrust ourselves and
others and so regard rule following as the key to moral conduct
in normal circumstances. While rule following may be the best
we can do, it is a practical long-term strategy that builds on an
account of the infirmities of practical reasonableness and self-
control. It trades off suboptimal performances in particular cases for the sake of rule-promoted virtues like stability,
predictability, and a rough long-term approximation to good
conduct.

Rule-bound conduct gains psychological support from the
comfort we experience in being treated the same way as others
with whom we identify (our cohort). Equal treatment within
groups or classes certainly reduces negotiation and information
costs, and it cuts down on opportunities for misrepresentation
and manipulation. Rules help keep authority impersonal and
reduce opportunities for favoritism. Adherence to known rules
helps reduce suspicion and the need for surveillance to which
suspicion gives rise. For all these reasons rules allow for the
kinds of gross interpersonal comparisons in which we can take
comfort: I may not be getting as much money as I would like
and think I deserve, but at least I make the same as everyone
else with my level of seniority in my department. Rules do not
promote real justice or fairness, but rules promote feelings of
fairness based on the kind of simple, visible, rough and ready
comparisons that people commonly rely upon because they are
easy to make. General rules allow us to see rather easily that a
kind of rough and ready justice is being done.

If all this is right, then governance by general rules will, in
many instances, reduce the amount of dissensus and conflict.
General rules treat people equally on the basis of a narrow
range of considerations. By excluding many factors from a
given decision or allocational scheme, general rules help eliminate many potential grounds for interpersonal comparison and
the perceptions of unfairness that are bound to follow. All-
things-considered judgments, on the other hand, open a
Pandora's box of possible grounds for self-preference and suspicion. As Harvey C. Mansfield, Jr., observes: "When law en-

counters human stubbornness, it resorts to universality and asserts: you are no different from anyone else."[32] Conflict can be curbed, therefore, if we all agree to accept general rules.[33]

Just how strong is the trade-off between justice and the rule of law? It might be argued, contrary to what has been implied here, that the trade-off is a weak one: general rules do not do justice in particular cases, but they are the best way to insure that justice is maximized across many cases and over time.[34] And yet, we do not govern via general rules merely for the sake of maximizing justice overall; we deploy generality in order to pursue aims that compete with justice. Generality gains support from our desire to economize on the time it would take to look into every case: we sometimes consider it simply not worth our while to learn as much as we would need to know in order to do justice in every case.[35] General rules promote values such as stability and community coordination, as we saw above, and these values have nothing to do with justice. The tradeoff between justice and general rules is often, therefore, a strong one.

Our willingness to compromise justice will vary from one set of decisions to another. It is one thing to set faculty salary levels entirely on the basis of seniority, quite another to give tenure to everyone who makes it through seven years on the job. It is one thing to lump different people together in the tax code only on the basis of income levels and a few other rough-and-ready criteria, quite another to inflict the death penalty without an extensive and painstaking inquiry into particular circumstances. Our willingness to accept even the weak version of the trade-off between rules and justice depends on the seriousness of the decisions at hand.

The values promoted by rule following are not absolute. Within some limits and on at least some grounds we want most rule followers to have discretion in particular instances. The crucial trade-off is between rigid rule-bound behavior and a more flexible regard for rules that is sensitive not only to the particularities of the case but also to the broader values and aims underlying the system of rules as a whole. That trade-off will be reflected in the weight of the presumption that attaches to a rule in the face of arguments, from equity or justice or other background aims, pointing to a contrary decision.[36]

Many debates over the proper nature of constitutional interpretation owe something to the tensions, canvassed above, between the rule of law and equity: questions about the legitimate grounds and norms of interpretation, questions of constraint and discretion, and questions about the distribution of authority among institutions (founders, legislatures, executives, judges, etc.) and across time. Advocates of judicial restraint, like McDowell, want to keep the grounds of interpretation narrow: bounded and defined by precedent, tradition, professional practice, and, perhaps most importantly, the intentions of lawmakers. Advocates of restraint hope to exclude broad considerations of political morality and policy, which are seen as subjective and "political." Defining the interpretive grounds narrowly is meant to confine judicial discretion, though it is far from obvious that the historical sources favored by the New Right yield clear answers.[37] Nor are those narrow sources the only obvious or natural grounds for interpreting rules. When we argue over the rules of baseball, as Schauer points out, no one insists that we ask what Abner Doubleday intended. It might be far better for judges to interpret rules and make exceptions on the basis of their best judgments about reasonable purposes and good justifications.

Proponents of a relatively robust judicial role often argue that moral principles are among the legitimate interpretive grounds. It is significant for Ronald Dworkin, for example, that the framers wrote into the Constitution, not particular conceptions of equality, liberty, and due process, but general abstract concepts of those ideas, leaving it to later interpreters to think about the meaning of these concepts for themselves.[38] The framers could, after all, be specific when they wanted to be (they said the president must be thirty-five years old, not "mature"). Where broad language was chosen we can take that as a deliberate delegation to the future to interpret in light not only of constitutional text, structure, and precedent, but also of our own best thinking about equality, due process, and other broad constitutional principles. Sotirios A. Barber seconds this thought, adding that the best way to vindicate the Constitution's claim to supremacy is to read it as the preamble suggests, as an attempt to approximate justice, liberty, and the general welfare—not historical notions of these concepts but our best understanding of the real things.[39]

At base, of course, everyone who weighs in on these interpretive controversies is advancing a practical judgment about how our constitutional government will go best. In the end, even a die-hard defender of the authority of history like Robert H. Bork seems to regard political science as the ultimate court of appeal.[40] For Bork, courts must be constrained not because of what the framers said but because courts are subject to political pathologies: they are all too apt to fall under the sway of intellectual elites who will use them to win political battles without going to the trouble of persuading the people and winning elections.

There is no abstract or contextless answer to the question of how best to balance the competing demands of rules and discretion, or law and equity. Political morality is important, but that source must be consulted along with, and in the context of, an historically informed account of our confidence in different institutions. While "mechanical" rule following in any complex endeavor is impossible, we can foster more or less discretion, discretion of different kinds, and various patterns of deference and self-assertion. That said, it seems hard to imagine that the tension between law and equity will be anything other than basic and ineliminable. Not all would agree, however, and it will be instructive to consider why.

### III. Public Virtue: Solution or Problem?

In his essay in this volume, Lawrence Solum suggests that the rule of law and equity can be reconciled if we select judges virtuous enough to recognize when exceptions to the rules are justified: wise, prudent judges can be trusted to depart from the letter of the law when circumstances justify. The virtuous judge (one with theoretical wisdom, judicial integrity, practical wisdom, and a sense of justice) seeks to respect received rules, but is not blind to the need to look past the letter to the spirit or purpose of law.[41] But Solum's theoretical reconciliation of the tension between the rule of law and equity is merely that: theoretical.

The proper working of the rule of law does indeed depend upon a certain measure of virtue in judges, as Solum says, but it also depends on a broader range of virtues as well. Like many other law professors, Solum writes as though the legal system is the creature of judges. Judges and courts do not, however, operate in a political vacuum. Law is the creature of judges, legislators, executives, and citizens (among others). We must account for the whole range of virtues required to sustain the rule of law. Once we have done that, it should be apparent that in politics, virtue is not merely part of the solution, it is also a problem: it is, in many ways, precisely the problem to which the rule of law is a response. As we shall see, even virtue in abundance remains a political problem.

Rule following requires uprightness and impartiality, and these surely are among the judicial virtues. And since mechanical and rigid rule following is unlikely to be acceptable, adjudicators should also be capable of interpreting rules in light of evident purposes, at least to discern the circumstances to which they apply and to make exceptions in extreme instances. Even Story, McDowell, and Bork will not deny that we need virtuous judges.

Much of what we have said about rules and discretion applies to executives as well as judges. Executives must also interpret laws—constitutional and statutory—to discern their duty. And executives, like judges, should be able sometimes to act without a rule or even against the rules, as John Locke famously described in his discussion of prerogative (which is "nothing but the power of doing publick good without a Rule"[42]). Emergencies arise, after all, and it is the executive (a single will, always on duty, and capable of speedy and energetic action) who meets them most directly: "many accidents may happen, wherein a strict and rigid observance of the Laws may do harm."[43]

The executive—with speed, vigor, and the armed might of the polity—is a far more dangerous branch than the judiciary. We must hope that executives use their discretion to "preserve, protect, and defend" the going order, and not to supplant or subvert it. The office is designed to attract spirited individuals prepared to do quite nasty things on our behalf and, we hope, only on our behalf. The executive office must be capacious enough to attract persons of great ambition but not, we hope, so capacious, unstructured, and exhilarating as to provoke subversion.[44] That's the rub, of course: taming the prince, but not too much.[45]

As rule makers, legislators might seem exempt from the tension we have described, but legislation is no exercise in pure discretion. Rules define the proper mode of lawmaking, and there are aims and purposes of legitimate lawmaking (though these, like Article 1 of the Constitution, are often underenforced). The idea of the rule of law itself imposes important constraints on lawmakers: to govern in tolerably general, prospective terms.[46]

The rule of law also depends upon citizen virtue. All three branches, and the rule of law itself, stand, in Alexander Bickel's phrase, at "the bar of politics."[47] The ultimate conformity of our institutions with the norms of legality and the limits of permissible discretion depends on a populace capable of supporting a tolerable balance of rules and discretion, and of making judgments in particular cases (distinguishing a Lincoln from a Nixon, for example). As Publius tells us, constitutional constraints mean little without the support of popular opinion.[48] Liberal constitutionalism has an irreducible republican element.

The rule of law, then, does not dispense with the need for virtue in judges, executives, legislators, and citizens. It would be a mistake, however, to think that this observation provides a way of reconciling the rule of law and equity, as Solum seems to suggest. Political virtue is not an easy thing to come by, and our liberal, commercial republic does not make its promotion a high priority. Nor is democracy a very good way of insuring that the virtuous are chosen for office. Even judges, though among our most respected public officials, do not enjoy universal confidence: "a judge is just a lawyer who is friends with a governor," is how one of my colleagues once put it.[49] Such a quip may go too far, but it is no better to regard virtue as a political panacea.

Virtue is not wholly neglected in or unavailable to liberal, democratic, commercial republics, but its supply will be inadequate to reconcile the tension between discretion and rule-bound constraint. This problem is not peculiar to modern republics; after all, even Aristotle was not prepared to invoke virtue (alone) as a solution to the problem of political rule. Aristotle did not think (as Solum seems to) that Aristotelian virtue allows us to reconcile the rule of law and equity. Only in the realm of the ideal does virtue rule for Aristotle: only there are the good citizen and the good man the same. In practice he advises even kingships (rule by the one best person) to govern according to law.[50]

Aristotle's practically best regime is mixed: a compromise between virtue, wealth, and equal freedom that places a high value on stability and moderation. In the mixed regime, Aristotle emphasizes the importance of law, not because it is the way of allowing virtue to rule, but because of the practical difficulties of rule by the virtuous. "One who asks law to rule . . . is held to be asking god and intellect alone to rule, while one who asks man adds the beast. Desire . . . and spiritedness pervert the best men. Law is intellect without appetite."[51] Which is not to say that in practice law can be intellect without appetite: law must be made and administered by people, after all.[52] Partiality and self-preference are pervasive political problems for Aristotle: these may be constrained and moderated by laws and other institutions, but they must also be accommodated to some degree. Virtue is not unimportant in Aristotle's politics, but it is not a solution to all political conflicts. If virtue is a problem for the mixed constitution Aristotle envisaged, it is certainly going to be a problem for a democratic, permissive, mass, commercial society like our own.

Even if we were to find highly virtuous executives or judges at one point in time—individuals worthy of wide interpretive latitude—that would not necessarily make us better off in the long run. Locke noted that the reign of good princes is most dangerous to the liberty of their subjects.[53] We trust good leaders with a great deal of discretion, but doing so enhances the powers of their office and so of their successors in office, who might be bums or worse, and it helps undermine norms of rule following with long-term value. By bending the normal rules,

Lincoln and Franklin Roosevelt helped prepare the way for figures such as Richard Nixon and Oliver North—as Nixon himself has suggested:

> Lincoln pointed out, when he was under criticism for denying habeas corpus and taking very strong actions during the Civil War—he said there are some actions which, under normal circumstances would be illegal, become legal if the president orders them because of the security of the country. And, for example, that would cover the wire-tapping to stop the leaks, which we did engage in.[54]

Great executives like Lincoln and FDR create precedents that lie about like loaded guns, there to be picked up by those who would sink below rather than rise above the normal rules.[55] These long-term costs need to be taken account of before we applaud exercises of discretion that seem well justified in particular circumstances.

The same is true for judges. Robert Bork lauds the statesmanship of John Marshall, accepting that Marshall was an activist judge who used his office politically to help consolidate Hamilton's vision of the founding. Marshall's creativity was necessary and justifiable, according to Bork, because the founding was not yet complete. But later justices must not aspire to Marshallian creativity. Bork's originalism is, indeed, designed to prevent judges from aspiring to a Marshallian stature: "it would be a mistake for us to take Marshall's performance, in all its aspects, as a model for judges now that the basic structure and unity of our nation have been accepted."[56] Our times do not call for judicial statesmanship; according to Bork, we face no moral and political imperatives equivalent to those of consolidating the nation's founding. And yet, there is Marshall: his words enshrined in every casebook, inspiring his most ambitious successors to strive toward or even surpass his statesmanship and renown. Frank Michelman concludes a spirited encomium to retired Supreme Court Justice William Brennan with the line: "He is a framer."[57]

Now that's unsettling. Brennan's critics might say that Michelman captures all too accurately Brennan's mission, and his lack of fidelity to law. It is just such a suspicion—that judicial activism leaves law behind—that leads Bork to regard appeals to an activist Court as no more legitimate than appeals to the joint chiefs of staff. Lucky for us, Bork would probably say, that the Warren Court had no armies at its disposal.

We are far better off, on the conservative view, if our mediocre leaders stick to the normal rules. Crises may arise, of course, when extraordinary virtues are needed—the kinds of virtues that chafe at mere rule following. Such virtues will, however, be appropriate for executives rather than judges: executives properly enjoy forms and levels of discretion (especially in national security affairs) not extended to the other branches. One prince, a Borkian conservative would argue, is enough. The Court is in no position to save the nation from political crises, as it has demonstrated when it has tried (as in *Dred Scott*).[58]

The question of whether we are better off with mediocre, plodding judges enforcing settled rules and exercising modest, gap-filling forms of discretion, or with brilliant judges, slicing through the rule-governed thicket to advance underlying principles and ideals, is palpably partisan. The conservative plea for judicial restraint rests on a complacent assessment of our current condition, and is eminently questionable. One might argue that the promises of the founding and the Civil War have not been realized for blacks, women, gays, and other oppressed groups in our society. One might argue that the moral and constitutional imperatives of the 1960s *were* powerful enough to warrant the activist invocation of purposes and principles that the Warren Court engaged in. The preservation of basic constitutional principles, especially as they concern the basic interests of minority groups, cannot be left entirely to the elected branches of government. By invoking background principles and ideals, interpreters such as Justice Brennan help us progressively realize the aspirations of the founding, as Michelman implies.

Whatever one thinks of Justice Brennan or Robert Bork, it must be admitted that virtue does not eliminate the tension between rule following and discretion. There is an irreducibly partisan dimension to the problem of whether to support stability or change. One person's virtuoso public servant—cutting through the legalistic thicket to advance the causes of justice and equality—is another's subverter of law in the cause of a partisan political agenda.

All ought to admit, however, that given deep political disagreement on underlying moral aspirations and aims, some degree of stability and moderation ought to be built into the system, especially with regard to the interpretation of our basic law. All should concede that if every judge aspired to be a "framer," the law would lose all semblance of nonpartisanship and neutrality: it would become one more partisan, political battleground and its ordering function would be destroyed. At some point, the equitable engagement in flexible and morally based constitutional interpretation could breed erratic and eccentric constitutional norms, and political chaos.

We may, after all, agree upon a particular rule without agreeing at all on background principles and underlying moral aspirations (consider the alliance of feminists and "family-values" advocates supporting antipornography statutes). Coalitions develop in favor of particular rules for reasons that may be very different and even radically opposed. Different judges (and other public officials) are liable, therefore, to have very different conceptions of how to interpret and advance underlying aims and purposes. The issue of constraint and discretion is not simply partisan, therefore, at least among those prepared to concede that we must live with our disagreements and govern via institutions that promote some measure of stability and moderation. Up to a point, even liberal activists are generally prepared to concede something to conservatism.

Virtue turns out—even when we can secure it—to be not simply a solution but also a problem. It is a problem because departures from the normal rules can help breed more such departures, and today's virtuoso president or judge may help loosen the constraints that protect us from tomorrow's crook or tyrant. It is a problem, as well, because the very description of what the virtue of a judge or executive consists in will depend in part upon partisan judgments about what good government consists in.

These problems go to the heart of the tension between the rule of law and equity: the aspiration to advance the ends and reasons that underlie and justify the law might become destructive of law itself. The desire to do justice today in particular cases should be restrained in the name of the many practical reasons supporting a rule-bound system of mutual restraint and settled expectations.[59] These include our desire to restrain even great leaders on the grounds that their successors may be quite otherwise, and the recognition that background principles of justice are matters about which we are liable to disagree. This suggests that there are forms of moral virtue that are misplaced in politics, or that in politics, virtue needs to be kept in its place.

Let us consider this problem from the point of view of citizens. Could an excess of citizen virtue ever be a problem? When we think about citizen virtue in our regime, we are liable to think of preferring the good of the whole over personal and partisan interests, or we might identify virtuous citizens with the pursuit of liberal justice. Virtuous citizens make sacrifices in a war effort, march for civil rights, or do other things in the name of generalized moral concerns rather than mere self-interest. And yet, it might be that a love of justice can pervert citizen virtue.

Consider Lawrence Friedman's depiction of our changing understanding of the aims of law. What has occurred, Friedman argues, is not a litigation explosion so much as a qualitative change in our expectations about what law should achieve for us. In the nineteenth century, legal liability, due process, and other protective practices were not extended very widely. People accepted the routineness of uncompensated losses: there simply was no general expectation that third parties were to be held responsible when losses occurred.[60] Likewise, the exercise of authority in a host of institutions (schools, prisons, families) was not subjected to rigorous public scrutiny or oversight. Sanctions meted out by authorities within various institutions were not expected to comply with anything like our understanding of due process.[61]

During the twentieth century we have witnessed, Friedman contends, the rise of a "security state" supported by a growing popular belief in "total justice." Someone or some institution must be held responsible for every accident or loss, and all losses should be fully compensated. And those subject to authority should have elaborate opportunities for due process in order to assert their rights. Friedman does not decry the rise of the security state: it might foster certain forms of inefficiency but it supports, he astutely observes, a new ideal of expressive individualism. More secure expectations allow us to develop and express our individuality without having to worry about many of the ever-present vulnerabilities that were accepted in the nineteenth century.

The demand for "total justice" goes too far. The expectation that no loss should go uncompensated, that someone or some institution should be held responsible for every accident, that elaborate due process should be available whenever authority is exercised, could represent (or become) a kind of immoderate longing for perfect justice in every case. As Friedman suggests, "Modern rights . . . are pushy, expansive and bold," and a wide variety of political claims are advanced in terms of rights, which are, by their nature, not easily subject to compromise.[62] And Mary Ann Glendon argues that American "rights talk" has indeed become pathological:

> It is set apart from rights discourse in other liberal democracies by its starkness and simplicity, its prodigality in bestowing the rights label, its legalistic character, its exaggerated absoluteness, its hyperindividualism, its insularity, and its silence with respect to personal, civic, and collective responsibilities.[63]

On Glendon's account, compromise, moderation, a sense of responsibility to others, and obligation to the community are all swept aside by rights-driven demands. Such demands may well be at odds with the rule of law, which, as we have seen, accepts unfairness in individual cases in the name of predictability, efficiency, stability, and other values promoted by a regime of general rules.

A possible response to the argument developed thus far would be that the political problem is not with virtue, but with a simplistically moralistic or rights-centered conception of virtue. Citizen virtue is not moral virtue but political virtue: it is, as Aristotle would say, relative to the regime.[64] And in a regime of laws, one important citizen virtue is a willingness to support the laws even though they do not measure up to one's ideal of justice pure and simple. It is a kind of practical wisdom to know that justice should not always be preferred to the laws, and to know that total justice is unattainable. The most reasonable thing is to acknowledge the need to constrain the exercise of reason in particular cases.[65]

There may indeed be a kind of practical wisdom, a supreme political virtue, that stands over and above both rule-bound conduct and moral virtue. The possession of political virtue so understood would not, however, reconcile the rule of law and equity. Political virtue as practical wisdom would consist, indeed, in knowing how to manage the tension between law and equity, or rules and discretion, giving due weight to each. The practically wise person would fairly weigh the demands of justice and the other moral ideals that underlie our Constitution, while recognizing that we should not strive too hard to do justice in individual cases because at some point that striving disrupts the system of general rules, settled expectations, and reasonable consensus.[66] Practical wisdom would consist, therefore, in preserving rather than dispelling the tensions we have described, and in recognizing these as permanent features of our politics.

## IV. CONCLUSION: CONSERVATIVE CRITICS REVISITED

The tension between the rule of law and equity is powerful, basic, and essential to self-government. That tension is practical and political: it may be possible to imagine formalistic, theoretical ways of reconciling these notions, but in anything short of utopian circumstances, it will remain. Its existence reminds us of the "in-betweenness" of our politics: that we should strive for justice, but not too much; that we should play by the rules, but keep one eye on the reasons and aspirations that justify those rules.

If we want to know how *we* should think about managing the tension between law and equity or rules and discretion, then we need to consider the particular characteristics of our politics, and the aptitudes and disabilities of our institutions. In the spirit of that political moderation that, I have argued, is a political virtue, I conclude by returning to those conservative concerns about judicial activism (roundly criticized by the present author among others) and suggest that these concerns—at least in a moderate form—are not wholly groundless. Let us sketch two versions of the conservative complaint: one radical but implausible, another more moderate and worthy of consideration.

Proponents of the radical version argue for restraint based on a decidedly Hobbesian rendering of our democracy, in which the people are sovereign. On this model, democracy is founded on the notion that we are all equal in virtue (or that we must regard ourselves as such for the sake of peace), and political legitimacy is founded wholly on consent. None can justify putting his or her partisan political opinions above those of others; all must submit to democratic procedures that require that we persuade one another and thus treat one another as equally reasonable. The judiciary is fundamentally anomalous in this skeptical democracy.

Judicial activism—especially when it is based on a straightforward resort to moral principles—treats some people as more than equally reasonable: it treats some people's moral views as more worthy than others'. It is, as such, an affront to democratic equality, and one that the people are bound to resent. Our liberal "cultural elite" is all too tempted to resort to claims of moral superiority and to the courts, to flaunt democratic procedures and the hard road of popular persuasion.[67] And the courts are all too apt to accept the flattering invitation and to place themselves above democratic choice. The courts will, in this way, fan popular resentments and undermine a sovereign people's self-restrained commitment to constitutional forms and individual rights.

This radical critique combines a too-Hobbesian view of the moral foundations of our politics with a suspiciously classical view of class conflict (it all comes down, a little too easily, to the few and the many). The result is a good story, but not one that fits our polity very well. Where is the great upsurge of popular resentment against the Court? And where is the popular jealousy on behalf of the power of elected officials? Given that there are much higher levels of popular confidence in the Supreme Court than in Congress, the frequent tendency to de-

scribe the Court as an "anomalous" undemocratic institution—
an institution whose legitimacy is compromised and uncertain—
appears to be peculiarly academic, and groundless.

A second, more moderate and plausible story better supports
worries about judicial power. The political resort to courts and
to individual rights-claims is not a fundamental assault on our
moral equality or government by consent: we share common
commitments not just to popular rule but to a liberal public
morality and constitutional limits. The political independence
and institutional structure of the courts make them a vital part
of our political order, better able than the political branches to
weigh and protect rights-claims. To be effective, moreover,
courts must secure the cooperation of other political actors and
citizens. Even so, judicial review can help sharpen and concen-
trate morally principled conflicts that much of the rest of our
political system works to fragment and moderate. Power is frag-
mented and checked through bicameralism, federalism, and the
separation of powers. A commercial republic helps encourage
relatively temperate, compromisable material interests, and an
extended republic helps fragment and moderate those interests
still further. Fairly large single-member congressional districts
require compromise and coalition building. The two-party system overrepresents middle-of-the-road views. In all these ways
and others our institutions press toward stability, moderation,
incremental change, and a fair degree of consensus.

In courts, however, principled considerations can be expressed much more cleanly, and there too one side can achieve
something closer to total victory. Victories won in court, moreover, may bypass the arduous process of democratic deliberation and persuasion, thereby provoking resistance, resentment,
and instability.[68] Armed with the power of injunction, moreover, courts have increasingly acted not simply to strike down
constitutionally offensive laws, but peremptorily to devise far-
reaching settlements and to impose them on the polity.[69] Adding insult to injury, the courts have often justified themselves in
the language of "high-minded moral certainty, . . . inflamed
rhetoric and self-proclaimed moral rectitude."[70] The relative
permanence of court decisions may also fan frustration. The
problem is not, on this moderate critique, that the Court is in

some fundamental sense illegitimate, but rather that transferring too many political issues to the courts may force relatively undigested changes on the polity. The process could feed on itself: settling political issues through the courts today may invite others to do the same tomorrow. If the courts and the Constitution become, moreover, mere partisan arenas—vehicles for advancing one's partisan agenda—then these vital guardians of constitutional limits may be undermined.[71]

This moderate story is plausible: the balance of principle and prudence could be wrecked by overzealous judicial moralists. Resorting to the courts too readily and frequently could destroy the kind of long-term political capital that we associate with the rule of law: stability, mutual self-restraint, and political moderation. It may be right to worry, with Mary Ann Glendon, about the extreme rhetoric often employed by opposing sides on morally charged issues before the courts, rhetoric that implies that "the losers, their points of view, and their way of life are being read right out of society."[72] With Robert A. Burt, it might be well to recall that dialogue, accommodation, mutual respect, and reasonable consensus need to be cultivated, even with southern segregationists, for a democracy ultimately depends upon widespread consent.[73]

The moderate right critique of judicial power is not radically misguided, but it does seem overstated. The Supreme Court and the Constitution appear to enjoy high degrees of legitimacy and respect, and even the highly controversial decision in *Roe v. Wade* has not provoked anything approaching a real political crisis. There is a danger, too, in placing too much emphasis on the need for accommodation and compromise: these provide incentives for foot dragging and threats of social conflict in the face of urgent moral demands, such as that of desegregation. While we must search for good reasons and a reasonable consensus, we should rarely wait for anything like unanimous agreement before insisting on respect for basic rights.

The concerns that lie behind the moderate call for judicial restraint are not groundless, however, and need to be met on their own terms. Proponents of activism ought to acknowledge that the Court should not act simply and whenever constitutional principle suggests that it should: though hardly a novel observation, it is worth remembering that the courts must also marshall their political capital, secure a reasonable consensus for their decisions, and consider the political stresses and strains their decisions may cause.

In politics—which is where courts are—both principle and prudence must have their say. The tension between law and equity, between rules and discretion, helps remind us that constitutional principle and particularized justice must be weighed against our long-term interests in rules, reasonable consensus, and moderation. It is worth remembering—if not always heeding—the moderate proponents of restraint.

## NOTES

1. Harvey C. Mansfield, Jr., "Constitutionalism and the Rule of Law," *Harvard Journal of Law and Public Policy* 8 (1985): 323–26, 324.

2. See the helpful accounts in Lawrence B. Solum, "Equity and the Rule of Law," 120; and Gerald Gaus, "Public Reason and the Rule of Law," 328.

3. See Friederich Hayek, *Law, Legislation, and Liberty.* Vol. 2, *The Mirage of Social Justice* (Chicago: University of Chicago Press, 1978); Michael Oakeshott, "The Rule of Law," in *On History and Other Essays* (Oxford: Blackwell, 1983), and *On Human Conduct* (Oxford: Clarendon, 1985), essay 3.

4. As Judith N. Shklar points out in criticizing Hayek, *Legalism: Law, Morals, and Political Trials* (Cambridge, Mass.: Harvard University Press, 1986), 24.

5. I am indebted to Frank Michelman for urging upon me the importance of distinguishing these senses of equity, though he may not agree with my subsequent treatment of them.

6. Solum, "Equity and the Rule of Law," 123.

7. *Nichomachean Ethics,* 1137b 10–30, trans. Martin Ostwald (Indianapolis: Bobbs-Merrill, 1978), 141–42. Gary L. McDowell has an instructive account of equity, *Equity and the Constitution* (Chicago: University of Chicago Press, 1982), 18.

8. Joseph Story, *Commentaries on Equity Jurisprudence as Administered in England and America,* vol. 1 (Littleton, Colo.: Rothman, 1988), 6.

9. I agree with Frederick Schauer that there is no difference between making an exception to a rule and changing that rule. "Exceptions," *University of Chicago Law Review* 58 (1991): 871–99, esp. 893–99.

One could argue that in the reason sense of equity the very meaning of a rule is at stake, whereas in the exception sense the rule's meaning is clear but there is a question about whether the rule should be applied. This seems to me contrived: surely, part of a rule's meaning is an account of when it should not be applied. If there is a question as to whether an exception should be made, then a rule's meaning is not clear. When an exception is drawn on the basis of background principles and reasons, then the rule's meaning has changed. I am indebted to Frank Michelman here, who I believe would dissent from this account.

10. 3 Dall. 386 (1798).

11. Story, *Commentaries on Equity,* 17.

12. *Brown v. Board of Education of Topeka,* 349 U.S. 294 (1955); McDowell, *Equity,* 8–9, 97–110.

13. Brutus, Letter XI of January 31, 1788, in Herbert J. Storing, ed., *The Anti-Federalist* (Chicago: University of Chicago Press, 1985), 164–66; and see McDowell, *Equity,* 43.

14. Shannon C. Stimson, *The American Revolution in the Law: Anglo-American Jurisprudence before John Marshall* (New York: Macmillan, 1990), 10–14 and *passim.*

15. Ibid., 133–48.

16. To confer power on judges is not necessarily to take it away from legislators. As Frank Michelman suggested to me, lawmakers could be frustrated and immobilized if they had to mark out the precise contours of a rule in advance, or to revisit each rule every time it became apparent that reasonable exceptions needed to be made, or the scope of a rule needed to be clarified. Judicial discretion can increase legislative power. As I have heard Jeffrey Tulis argue, we should not think of political power as a fixed pie to be divided up. Lawmakers may be all too eager to fob controversial issues off on the courts, as Theodore J. Lowi points out in *The End of Liberalism: The Second Republic of the United States,* 2d ed. (New York: Norton, 1979); and see the instructive discussion in Mark A. Graber, "The Non-Majoritarian Difficulty: Legislative Deference to the Judiciary" (unpublished paper, presented at the 1992 Annual Meeting of the American Political Science Association).

17. Solum, "Equity and the Rule of Law," 126.

18. Ibid., 125.

19. Solum says that equity is at work when rules are nullified "on the basis of the facts of the *particular* case," but not when a decision is "based on a general moral principle." See his remarks on slavery, "Equity and the Rule of Law," 124.

20. On public justification see my "The Politics of Justification," *Political Theory* 18 (May 1990): 280–304.

21. As Frederick Schauer puts it, "even a particularistic decision-making procedure employs prescriptive generalizations. . . . [B]oth species of decision-making, the particularistic and the rule-based, project the generalizations of the past onto the realities of that past's future." *Playing by the Rules: A Philosophical Examination of Rule-Based Decision-Making in Law and in Life* (Oxford: Clarendon, 1991), 78.

22. As I believe Solum does. This overemphasis on particularism leads Solum to advance some strange criticisms of Dworkin. Solum suggests that legal principles, in Dworkin's scheme, are general, even universal principles, so when Dworkin corrects rules on the basis of legal principles, this does not count as an exercise of equity. See Solum, "Equity and the Rule of Law," 128–29, 138. This is a bit contrived. On any account of discretion there will be principles that allow us to pick out those particular cases in which rules should not apply. Those principles will often be relatively abstract and they will, as in Dworkin's scheme, apply to more than this particular case. Admittedly, Solum sometimes suggests that equitable principles need not be particular-ized, at least "in the sense that they relate only to named individuals" (125–26).

23. Schauer supports this claim; see "Exceptions."

24. Schauer, *Playing,* 136–37. Equity and the rule of law are funda-mentally consistent, Solum says, "but some tension remains" (135). The tension seems quite fundamental to me.

25. On rules as entrenched generalizations, see Schauer, *Playing,* ch. 3.

26. Ibid., 177–78.

27. This paragraph draws on Schauer's excellent account, ibid., ch. 7.

28. Bernard Yack, "Toward a Free Marketplace of Social Institu-tions: Roberto Unger's 'Super-Liberal' Theory of Emancipation," *Har-vard Law Review* 101 (1988): 1961–77, 1967–68.

29. A point made to me by Fred Schauer.

30. Adam Smith, *Theory of Moral Sentiments,* ed. D. D. Raphael and A. L. Macfie (Oxford: Clarendon, 1979), 159, 175.

31. Ibid., 162–63.

32. Harvey C. Mansfield, Jr., *Taming the Prince: The Ambivalence of Modern Executive Power* (New York: Free Press, 1989), 127.

33. Stephen Holmes argues that by narrowing the agenda in the face of intractable disagreement we can improve our ability to govern

across other areas of life. See Stephen Holmes, "Gag Rules or the Politics of Omission," in *Constitutionalism and Democracy*, ed. J. Elster and R. Slagstad (Cambridge University Press, 1988), 19–58.

34. A point made to me by Gerald Dworkin.

35. See the instructive discussion in Russell Hardin, "My University's Yacht: Morality and the Rule of Law."

36. A point made to me by Fred Schauer.

37. For a critique of the jurisprudence of original intent, see my *The New Right v. the Constitution,* 2d ed. (Washington, D.C.: Cato Institute, 1987). It should be acknowledged, of course, that many of the constraints on judges and other decision makers are not the product of the materials with which they deal, but of the institutions and structures of interaction within which they are socialized and within which they operate; see the important remarks in Martha S. Feldman, "Social Limits to Discretion: An Organizational Perspective," in *The Uses of Discretion,* ed. Keith Hawkins (New York: Oxford, 1992).

38. Ronald Dworkin, *Taking Rights Seriously* (Cambridge, Mass.: Harvard University Press, 1977), 134–36.

39. Sotirios A. Barber, *On What the Constitution Means* (Baltimore, Md.: Johns Hopkins University Press, 1984), ch. 1.

40. Robert H. Bork, *The Tempting of America* (New York: Free Press, 1990), 1–11 and *passim.*

41. Solum, "Equity and the Rule of Law," section II.b.

42. John Locke, *Two Treatises of Government,* ed. P. Laslett (New York: Mentor, 1965), 425 (*Second Treatise,* par. 166).

43. Ibid., 421; and see the excellent discussions contained in Joseph M. Bessette and Jeffrey K. Tulis, *The Presidency in the Constitutional Order* (Baton Rouge: Louisiana State University Press, 1981).

44. On all this see the young Lincoln's warning: beware persons of great ambition, those who aspire to the greatness of political founders. Such ambition is dangerous in a settled constitutional order, for once the founding is complete such ambitions can only be realized through the destruction of what others have created. The respectable middle classes, Lincoln warned, need to guard against persons of great ambition ("the tribe of the eagle and the lion") and revere the law; in "The Perpetuation of Our Political Institutions: Address before the Young Men's Lyceum of Springfield, Illinois," January 27, 1838 (in *Abraham Lincoln: His Speeches and Writings,* ed. Roy P. Basler (New York: Da Capo, 1990). That, of course, cannot be the whole of Lincoln's teaching, for he scorned peace-preserving compromises (such as that of Stephen Douglas) at odds with the commitment progressively to realize

human equality; see *The Lincoln-Douglas Debates of 1858*, ed. Robert W. Johannsen (New York: Oxford University Press, 1978).

45. See Mansfield's important account, *Taming the Prince.*

46. For an important account, see Kenneth Winston, "Toward a Liberal Conception of Legislation," in NOMOS XXV: *Liberal Democracy*, R. Pennock and J. Chapman, eds. (Albany: New York University Press, 1983).

47. Alexander Bickel, *The Least Dangerous Branch: The Supreme Court at the Bar of Politics*, 2d ed. (New Haven, Conn.: Yale University Press, 1986). I have not, of course, exhausted the forms of virtue needed in a liberal regime: bureaucrats, for example, also face problems of constraint and discretion similar to those discussed here; see Feldman, "Social Limits to Discretion."

48. See *The Federalist* #84, and *passim.*

49. As Judith Shklar once said to me.

50. Aristotle, *Politics*, book 3.

51. Ibid., bk. 3, ch. 16.

52. As Bernard Yack points out, the preceding quotation comes at the end of Aristotle's summary of the arguments made by the proponents of rule by law. In practice, as Yack rightly emphasizes, Aristotle is aware that law constrains the exercise of practical reason; see Yack, *The Problems of a Political Animal: A Reinterpretation of Aristotelian Political Philosophy* (forthcoming), ch. 6.

53. Locke, *Second Treatise*, 424–25, paragraph 166.

54. Transcript from the television program "Richard Nixon Reflects: An American Interests Special," hosted by Morton Kondracke, air date May 4, 1990, distributed by News Transcripts, Inc., Washington, D.C., p. 24.

55. This was one of Justice Robert Jackson's worries about providing a judicial imprimatur for the forced internment of Japanese-Americans during World War II; see *Korematsu v. United States*, 323 U.S. 214 (1944).

56. Bork, *Tempting*, 28; and see 21–28.

57. Frank I. Michelman, "Super Liberal: Romance, Community, and Tradition in William J. Brennan, Jr.'s Constitutional Thought," *Virginia Law Review* 77 (1991): 1261–1332.

58. *Dred Scott v. Sandford*, 60 U.S. 393 (1856).

59. Economists call this a problem of "time inconsistency"; see Herb Taylor, "Time Inconsistency: A Potential Problem for Policymakers," *Business Review* (Federal Reserve Bank of Philadelphia), March/April 1985, 3–12. I am indebted to Randy Krozsner for discussions of these matters.

60. Lawrence Friedman, *Total Justice* (New York: Sage, 1985), ch. 4.

61. Ibid., ch. 5.

62. Ibid., 120.

63. Mary Ann Glendon, *Rights Talk: The Impoverishment of Our Political Discourse* (New York: Free Press, 1991), x. Glendon's worries gain support from Neal Devins, "Fundamentalist Christian Educators v. State: An Inevitable Compromise," *George Washington University Law Review* 60 (1992): 818–40, esp. 824.

64. *Politics*, book 3, ch. 4: only in the ideally best regime are the good citizen and the good person the same.

65. Solum talks about *phronesis* but, again, particularity is at center stage and politics is missing; "Equity and the Rule of Law," 135.

66. As Bernard Yack puts it, "Law then is, for Aristotle, a limit on the exercise of practical reason that is derived from reason itself." *Political Animal*, ch. 6.

67. Bork, *Tempting*, 112 and *passim*.

68. As Harvey C. Mansfield, Jr., charges was the case with regard to affirmative action; "The Underhandedness of Affirmative Action," in Russell Nieli, ed., *Racial Preference and Racial Justice* (Washington, D.C.: Ethics and Public Policy Center, 1991).

69. Having enjoined enforcement of discriminatory state laws, McDowell argues that further enforcement should be left to legislatures; *Equity*, 109–10. Robert A. Burt also worries about authoritarian and peremptory judicial injunctions that bypass deliberation and consensus building; see *The Constitution in Conflict* (Cambridge, Mass.: Harvard University Press, 1992), ch. 1.

70. Burt, *Constitution in Conflict*, 25.

71. Assuming that courts are "vital guardians," which has been disputed, see Gerald Rosenberg, *The Hollow Hope* (Chicago: University of Chicago Press, 1991).

72. Glendon, *Rights Talk*, 156. See also the important questions about the adequacy of rights discourse to the issue of abortion in particular, in Kim Lane Scheppele, "Constitutionalizing Abortion," unpublished paper presented at the American Political Science Association, Chicago, 1992.

73. Burt, *Constitution in Conflict*, 2–6, 18–33, 348–52 and *passim*.

# 8

# PARTICULARISM, DISCRETION, AND THE RULE OF LAW

## STEVEN J. BURTON

In "Equity and the Rule of Law,"[1] Professor Solum begins to develop an Aristotelian, "virtue-centered" theory of adjudication that responds to modern and liberal concerns about constraining judges from abuses of power while allowing them to do justice under the law. The addition to the literature of an Aristotelian theory of adjudication is a valuable contribution. I find myself in agreement with the direction of his effort in two general ways. First, the project is one within law as practical reason.[2] Too much American legal theory is confined to the theoretical questions introduced by Oliver Wendell Holmes, Jr., and continued by the legal realists and their heirs in law and economics and critical legal studies. Important as descriptive and explanatory theory often is, one should not forget that judges are actors within a legal system and that the law is supposed to guide their conduct. Second, Solum endorses a balancing approach to adjudication, allowing judges to take into account and weigh a variety of competing considerations in a case. The main alternative is to insist on a hierarchy of legal and other authorities or sources to ensure that the law will determine a correct result in a lawsuit whenever it governs at all. I

I thank Ken Kress and Serena Stier for their comments on the manuscript.

fully agree with Solum's insistence that the law does not consist only of result-determining rules, but may legitimately require judges to exercise discretion in cases.[3] In the extended family of theories of adjudication, our general approaches are siblings.

I am not persuaded, however, that Solum has reached his most important goal: "to reconcile the practice of equity with the rule of law."[4] I think this goal is crucial. I will not discuss Solum's interpretation of Aristotle or the general arguments against Aristotelian ethics. What matters is whether Solum advances a sound theory of adjudication, or part of one. Nor will I discuss at length whether deriving a theory of judging from a classical theory of general ethics will tell us anything distinctive about the ethics of judging in courts of law or will respond adequately to modern political concerns. I will focus specifically on "equity" in adjudication and its relationship to the rule of law. This topic is of wide contemporary interest. What Solum calls "equity" bears resemblances both to judicial discretion generally and to particularistic modes of judging advocated recently by some feminist legal theorists. The problem posed by the rule of law is important whether, with Ronald Dworkin, one comes to bury judicial discretion[5] or, with the feminists, one comes to enlarge and praise it.[6]

I will discuss three questions in this essay: (1) What is the challenge posed to the practice of equity by the rule of law? (2) Does Solum's virtue-centered theory of judging respond adequately to the challenge? (3) Is there a better way to understand and respond to this kind of challenge? In the third part, I will offer an alternative understanding of the problem and suggest how, without falling into particularism, judicial discretion can be brought within the rule of law.

## I. The Challenge

The rule of law is a political ideal. As I understand it, the ideal is the part of a modern political theory that sets forth certain conditions for legitimate action by government officials.[7] Our present interest concerns the conditions under which judicial action is justified and deserves respect. The rule of law implies that such action is justified only when it is in accordance with the law (while allowing for additional conditions). It is the basis in political theory for specific demands that the law constrain judges and other officials. The rule of law supposes that legal constraints on official action are necessary to support a government of limited power, a separation of powers among its parts, and a citizenry that realizes a high degree of liberty.

The rule of law is a controversial political ideal. Some versions are more expansive than others. Dworkin has written that the rule of law requires nothing less than that a community is ruled by an accurate public conception of individual rights.[8] Michael Moore has given a more complex substantive account emphasizing six "rule of law values"—separation of powers, equality and formal justice, liberty and notice, substantive fairness, procedural fairness, and efficient administration.[9] To these thinkers, the emphasis is on the "law" in the rule of law, and "law" is given a nonpositivist interpretation that makes conformity to the rule of law perhaps sufficient for a just legal system. Lon Fuller's classic account is less substantive. His rule of law requires the norms of a legal system to be general in scope, public, announced in advance, clear in meaning, enacted in conformity with existing laws, possible to obey, stable, and enforced in accordance with their meaning.[10] Similarly, John Rawls elaborates the rule of law based in a conception of formal justice requiring "the regular and impartial administration of public rules."[11] A narrower and more formal view was advanced by Friedrich von Hayek, who claimed that the rule of law "means that government in all its actions is bound by rules fixed and announced beforehand—rules which make it possible to foresee with fair certainty how the authority will use its coercive powers in given circumstances."[12] To von Hayek, the power of the state should never be used except as required by predictable rules announced in advance. It does not matter to the rule of law, on his view, what the content of the rules may be. The emphasis is on the "rule" in the rule of law, leading Justice Antonin Scalia to announce that the rule of law generally requires a law of rules.[13]

Equity, on the other hand, is a less frequently analyzed idea. In ordinary usage, "equity" is often a virtual synonym for simple fairness or reasonableness in one's conduct toward others, as when one refrains ex gratia from insisting on his or her rights. This conception has little relevance in adjudication because a judge adjudicates the rights of others. Jurisprudentially speaking, equity has a more specialized meaning. The idea is generally traced to Aristotle, who offered it as a corrective to a well-known vice of stated legal rules. In his terms, "about some things it is not possible to make a universal statement which will be correct."[14] In contemporary terms, we would say that rules as stated tend to be over and underinclusive with respect to the just result and with respect to their own background justifications.[15] When a case arises "which is not covered by the universal statement," Aristotle wrote, "then it is right . . . to say what the legislator himself would have said had he been present, and would have put into his law if he had known."[16] Equity secured a major place in Anglo-American legal history when the courts of law were supplemented with courts of equity in response to the rigidities of the old English writ system. Here, the courts of equity were to do justice in cases where the law failed of its purpose. Solum defines "equity" as "the practice of doing particularized justice, when the just result is not required by, or is contrary to, the set of applicable legal rules."[17]

What is the challenge posed to equity by the rule of law? The answer depends on which conceptions of the rule of law and of equity one employs. Let us keep things simple but adequate for evaluating Solum's arguments. The rule of law, understood in its formal aspect, might require (1) a law of rules only, where rules are understood to require results in cases. Or the rule of law might require (2) a law of rules and principles only, with "principles" here referring to the familiar Dworkinian idea of attractive moral principles implicit in the legal practice, which principles provide reasons for judicial decisions. Equity might involve (A) decision as a matter of principle, roughly in the Dworkinian fashion, or (B) decision as a matter of particulars, eschewing abstract standards in favor of an "immersion in particulars."[18] On this simplified analysis, there are four possible relationships between equity and the rule of law, as indicated at Table 8.1.

Solum's paper seems ambivalent about which of these possible conflicts he seeks to reconcile. Law sometimes is treated as a

*Table 8.1*

Equity

|  | (A) Principled | (B) Particularist |
|---|---|---|
| (1) Rules Only | NO | NO |
| (2) Rules/Principles | YES<br>(Dworkin) | NO<br>(Solum) |

matter of rules that determine the legal results in cases (1), as when he speaks of equity departing from the "letter of the law."[19] The conclusion, and much of the energy of the piece, is aimed at formalistic conceptions of the rule of law as a law of result-determining rules. At other times law is treated as a matter of rules and principles (2), as when he states that the rule of law requires judges to "justify the distinctions they make between persons by reference to the relevant legal rules and principles."[20] Equity sometimes is treated as a matter of principles implicit in the law (A), as when Solum defends equity because it is consistent with the "spirit" of the laws by contrast with their "letter."[21] At other times, and most often, equity is treated as a matter of particulars (B), as when he distinguishes his views from Dworkin's by contrasting equity as particularized justice with both rules and principles of law.[22]

We can understand the challenge posed to equity by the rule of law within this simple framework. There is an obvious problem in two cases—when the rule of law requires a law of result-determining rules and equity involves decision as a matter of principles (1A) or particulars (1B). Neither principles nor particulars are rules in this sense. It follows from this conception of the rule of law that equity is out of bounds. Moreover, there is an analogous problem if the rule of law requires a law of rules and principles while equity is a matter of particulars (2B). Particulars are neither rules nor principles. Under this conception of the rule of law, then, judges may not decide cases as a matter of particulars. Again, there is no logical room for reconciling equity with the rule of law. Reconciliation of one possible conflict can be accomplished easily: if the rule of law allows decision according to rules and principles and equity is confined to decision according to principles (2A), then a practice of equity is allowed by the rule of law. Any conflict between rules and principles would be a problem within the rule of law, not between the rule of law and something else. This is a more or less Dworkinian solution.

The challenge posed to equity by the rule of law is sharp when the rule of law includes rules and principles while equity is a matter of particulars (2B). The same problem for particularism is implicated in other cases, but clarity of presentation is served by setting these cases aside. They go the way of the primary case anyway. On this interpretation, we can proceed to question whether Solum's virtue-centered theory of judging meets the most interesting challenge—bringing particularism within the rule of law.

## II. Particularism and the Rule of Law

The chief feature of a virtue-centered theory of judging lies in its definition of a correct legal decision: "A legal decision is right if and only if a virtuous judge would make that decision under the circumstances."[23] A virtuous judge is "a person who occupies the legal role of adjudicator and possesses and acts in accord with the judicial virtues"—intelligence, wisdom, integrity, temperament, impartiality, and justice.[24] The virtues are understood as dispositional qualities of mind and character or goodwill. Character is the more important for present purposes. Character may be understood simply as a person's distinctive ensemble of dispositions to choose or act in habitual ways in various circumstances that may arise. A virtue-centered theory of judging relies on the judicial character—not general rules, principles, or policies of the law—to produce responsible judgments. Hence, any virtue-centered theory inclines toward the kind of particularism that Solum embraces.

Dispositions of character are conditioned and cultivated over a lifetime. As Solum suggests, some dispositions are cultivated in one's professional activities.[25] Which dispositions are developed, however, may depend on the legal culture, which may or may not provide a suitable environment for growing good judges. For lawyers in some legal cultures, emphasis may be placed on the virtues of good judgment, attention to detail, patience, independence, honesty, initiative, open-mindedness, and persistence.[26] These traits would seem to be helpful in growing good judges. In parts of the current practice in the United States, however, it seems that the professional "virtues" involve a contrasting list: aggressiveness, competitiveness, opportunism, few scruples, ambition, greed, strategic savvy, and the like. We should remember that the judicial virtues may or may not be developed through participation in the practice of law. One may learn, rather, to locate the loopholes and exploit them to the advantage of the client, self, firm, or political groups with which one identifies.[27] To be sure, in judicial selection, we should prize those candidates who have cultivated lawyerly virtues that are akin to the judicial virtues.[28] The question here, however, is not about judicial selection.

## Solum's Arguments

Solum makes three arguments to reconcile equity with the rule of law. First, he claims, "when equity is done by a virtuous judge, departure from the rules is not the exercise of arbitrary discretion."[29] The argument is that a judge with judicial integrity "cares" about the coherence of the law and is "motivated" to insure that his departure from the letter accords with the spirit of the laws. Thus, "the purposes and values immanent in the law itself still hold sway, despite the departure from the letter of the law."[30]

There are three problems with this argument for the nonarbitrariness of equity. First, accordance with the spirit of the laws when departing from their letter shows nonarbitrariness in a Dworkinian way. This argument is apt when the rule of law is understood as a law of result-determining rules and equity is a matter of principles (2A). But Solum's goal is to reconcile a practice of equity qua particularism with the rule of law. There is no argument here for the nonarbitrariness of that kind of equity, though Solum's particularism is his basis for distinguishing his theory from Dworkin's. A second problem is that Solum needs a stronger claim than one about judicial caring and motivation. The rule of law requires that judges *act* nonarbitrarily, in accordance with the law; it does not raise questions only about their sincerity and goodwill, which do not suffice to justify the official use of coercion.[31] The third problem is that the claim is limited to equity *when done by a virtuous judge*. But the rule of law is important precisely because we cannot count on our judges to be virtuous. Solum here concedes that the practice of equity will be arbitrary when the rule of law is most needed. Perhaps he is less interested in reconciling equity with the rule of law than in showing that, when our judges are virtuous, we do not need the rule of law.

Solum's second argument for the consistency of equity and the rule of law is that "the notion of moral and legal vision that grounds the practice of equity is also necessary to understanding the application of legal rules. . . . [B]oth the application of legal rules *and* the practice of equity require the virtue of judicial wisdom."[32] No doubt Aristotelian insights figure in a sound theory of judging under law. For example, thinking about moral perception might be helpful in understanding what it is to spot a legal issue. Moreover, any theory of judging that analyzes the law as rules, or rules and principles, or policies, should confront Aristotle's question of what "moves" the actor to act in accordance with those abstract standards.[33] However, it is doubtful that only a *phronimos* can apply legal rules correctly. Even if this were true, the second argument is fallacious. A may be necessary to x and necessary to y. This does not establish that x is consistent with y. B may also be necessary to x at the same time that not-B is necessary to y. If this is so, x and y are inconsistent. Thus, moral vision may be necessary for doing equity and also for applying legal rules. The rule of law nonetheless may be satisfied only if a judge follows the rules while equity is done only if the judge departs from the rules. I happen to think that something like this is the case. The rule of law is not just a cluster of political values. These values support a norm that requires judges at the least to justify their decisions in the rules, principles, and policies of the law.

Solum's third argument fares a little better. It is that "the recognition of equity as a distinct practice may serve to increase the regularity and predictability of rule application in the legal system as a whole."[34] This consequentialist argument supposes that there is substantial pressure on judges to do justice in particular cases. Unless relieved by allowing a practice of equity, this pressure would lead to interpretative practices undermining the integrity of the rules generally. My experience suggests that there is something to this empirical claim. Like Solum's first argument, however, it is better directed at the challenge posed when law is conceived as result-determining rules while equity is a matter of principles or particulars. The pressure is probably less when laws are interpreted intelligently in accordance with their background justifications, not blindly in accordance with their literal meanings. In any event, it remains unclear to me how particularism increases the integrity of rule application. Solum's equity licenses a departure from the rules whenever a judge thinks they lead to unjust results. Does this not turn governing rules into mere suggestions or rules of thumb?

### Two Hurdles

If Solum's three arguments do not do the job, could better virtue-centered arguments be developed to reconcile equity qua particularism with the rule of law? I am skeptical. At least two major hurdles must be overcome.

The first hurdle is understanding how a decision "on the particular facts" can be justified and nonarbitrary at all. Solum speaks of "particularized reasons."[35] He suggests that "equitable decisions should be reversed when they cannot be adequately justified."[36] Solum's main view of equity, however, is highly particularistic. He is not advocating the substitution of moral standards for legal standards when the law leads to unjust results, nor is he advocating a purposive and context-sensitive application of legal rules and principles.[37] His equity is "ad hoc, done on particular facts,"[38] "predicated on unique features of the particular case."[39] So, it should be asked, how is it possible for the particulars of cases to be justifying reasons for action at all?

The particulars of a case are plain facts. They are inert in that, as such, they carry no normative force. They constitute the circumstances for judicial action but are not themselves reasons for action or, more to the point, legal reasons. A fact in a case can become a reason for action when combined with a general standard of conduct. To give a mundane example, when Michael Motorist encounters a red traffic light, he encounters a fact in the circumstances of his action. The colored light carries no implication for what he should do until it is combined with a general standard. Thus, if all motorists should stop on encountering a red traffic light, Michael should stop. Until some such standard is introduced into the picture, it would be silly for Michael to change his conduct because he sees a colored light. The general standard makes the colored light also a legally *relevant* fact in the circumstances because it is a *reason* to stop—a signal. Michael's action then might be reasoned and his action nonarbitrary with respect to that standard. Only then might Michael's action be *justified*.

If the rule of law requires, as I think it does, that official decisions be justified in law, and therefore be reasoned and nonarbitrary with respect to general legal standards, then the rule of law excludes decision as a matter of particulars. I do not know how otherwise to think about treating like cases alike or applying a rule consistently (though it is not always necessary for a judge to make the general standard explicit).[40] There may be some people who directly intuit justice in particular cases; I am too often puzzled to be one of them. Even for them, however, justification would require more than a report of the intuition. It would require an argument from an appropriate general standard of conduct.

The second hurdle for a virtue-centered theory of judging involves two ways in which the challenge posed to equity by the rule of law reappears in virtue talk. I assume that Solum is correct that a virtue-centered theory would hold at base that a "legal decision is right if and only if a virtuous judge would make that decision under the circumstances."[41] One problem is that this is a counterfactual proposition offered as a definition of the right-making characteristics of a judicial decision. But it doesn't do any work. Arguments about what a virtuous judge would decide will replay all of the arguments about what a right legal decision is. So we may as well focus directly on the decision and its proper grounds, not on a hypothetical person making it. Another problem arises once a plausible list of judicial virtues is given. Even apart from the tendency for competing lists to proliferate, the virtues on any list are likely to involve conflicting dispositions in important cases. In Solum's scheme, for example, judicial integrity requires fidelity to the law, including the "ability to set aside one's ambitions and one's political or moral preferences and decide on the basis of the law."[42] A judge with judicial wisdom "has developed excellence in discerning what goals to pursue in the particular case and excellence in choosing the means to accomplish those goals."[43] A virtue-centered theory of judging seems merely to reframe the challenge posed to equity by the rule of law as a challenge posed to judicial wisdom by judicial integrity. To reconcile the latter challenge again involves us in all of the arguments we would make about equity and the rule of law directly.

Within law as practical reason, the basic fact is that persons act in circumstances for reasons. The law guides conduct by providing persons with reasons for action.[44] By focusing on a judge's character, a virtue-centered theory of judging moves the focus from reasons for action to persons and their dispositional properties. I see no advantage in that. Focusing exclusively on the character (and intelligence) of the person does not clarify the relationship between the law and judicial conduct. It takes *the law* out of the rule of law.

## III. Discretion and the Rule of Law

Is there a better way to understand and respond to the challenge posed to equity by the rule of law? What has been said thus far requires a reformulation of the question. "Equity" should not be understood as particularism. No plausible theory of law treats law as a matter of particulars. Therefore, the rule of law rules out decision as a matter of particulars. Yet a problem remains. Equity is in any event discretionary; as Solum uses it, it amounts to a broad judicial discretion. The interesting problem, I suggest, continues to be the one raised most powerfully by Dworkin—reconciling judicial discretion with the rule of law. I will suggest here that there is a way to do this without supplanting judicial discretion with a right answer thesis like Dworkin's.

## The Force of Law

Discretion is the power to choose between two or more courses of action each of which is thought of as lawful.[45] The law may confer a discretionary power on a decision maker, as when the law of appeals commits a question to the trial court's discretion. Judges also have discretion when the law is indeterminate with respect to results. The indeterminacy debate stimulated by the critical legal studies movement is helpful to understanding discretion. The arguments of Kress, Solum, and others suffice in my view to justify rejecting the radical indeterminacy thesis, which claims that the law is pervasively indeterminate.[46] At the other extreme, few hold a complete determinacy thesis, which would claim that the law determines a single right result in all possible cases. Most of us are somewhere in between these extremes. Descriptively, we think that judges sometimes have discretion, not that they always do or never do. Normatively, we think that some mix of rule and discretion is optimal: it is hard to defend a legal system that would squeeze all discretion out of judicial decision making, as by having a closure rule requiring judgment for the defendant whenever the law is indeterminate. This centrist position is noticeably undertheorized in contemporary jurisprudence.

The most popular conceptions of law allow no room for judicial discretion within the rule of law. These conceptions insist that the law count for nought unless it determines the result in a case.[47] Strong legal formalism thus continues to dominate the discussion despite the ridicule heaped upon it for decades. For H.L.A. Hart, the law consists of result-determining rules; other cases are left ungoverned by the law. For many legal realists, decisions are dependent on personal or policy preferences because outcomes are not determined by the legal rules. The critical legal studies movement's indeterminacy thesis is thought to be an embarrassment to "liberal legalism" only on the assumption that the law must dictate results. Dworkin's right answer thesis is a way of claiming that the law succeeds in principle in determining results. To be sure, there are differences here concerning the means by which and the extent to which the law determines results, if it does. There is, however, implicit agreement that judges can fulfill their duty to uphold the law only if the law determines the outcome in cases.

If the law must dictate the result in a case or count for nought, and discretion exists when two or more results are permitted by the law, then the exercise of discretion must not be governed by the law. And if it is not governed by the law, there can be no way to bring judicial discretion within the rule of law. Discretion must be lawless.

I want to contest the idea that the law must dictate a result and, consequently, that judicial discretion cannot be brought within the rule of law. To say that the law must dictate results is to take a position on the question of the *force* of law, by contrast with its form, grounds, content, and function. We are speaking here of a normative force, not a causal force that produces effects without intervening rational deliberation. Significantly, there are different kinds of normative force. A legal standard can (claim to) have absolute or conclusive force because it requires a particular action regardless of other considerations. This is the idea of the law dictating a result. As Dworkin taught us,[48] a legal standard also can provide a reason to be taken into account and weighed along with other relevant reasons. And, as Joseph Raz taught us,[49] a legal standard can exclude some kinds of reasons from those upon which a person ought to act. Rules, principles, and policies can guide conduct by changing the relevant reasons for action without determining a particular result: they can add or remove a reason that tips the balance of reasons in legal deliberations. The law can be most powerful if it both provides a legal reason for an action and excludes most or all other kinds of reasons, as when a traffic law makes a red light a reason for a motorist to stop and excludes from consideration any desire to get somewhere quickly and the driver's independent sense of safety.[50] However, it is not necessary for a law to dictate results for it to guide conduct.

A crucial distinction in thinking about the law and discretion, then, is between conceptions that make it necessary for law that it generate determinate results and those that make it necessary only that the law provide reasons to be weighed. Another crucial distinction is between included and excluded reasons for judicial action. Now reconsider judicial discretion on the assumption that the law provides reasons to be weighed and excludes from judicial purview all but legal reasons.

## Lawful Discretion

To begin, we should ask a neglected question: what do judges have when they have discretion? We can distinguish three alternative conceptions of discretion—the "anything goes," "extralegal standards," and "legal reasons" alternatives. We should consider whether discretion can be reconciled with the rule of law in relation to each of these three alternatives.

The first alternative supposes that, when a judge has discretion, anything goes. This seems to be the assumption when it is claimed, in skeptical legal realist fashion, that judges decide whatever they want to decide when the law is unclear (and it is often or always unclear). A number of similar claims are currently popular. It may be claimed in neopragmatist fashion that judges should decide cases as best they can, taking into account any consideration they think relevant.[51] Or it may be urged that legal indeterminacies be exploited to further the judge's prior political commitments.[52] Judicial discretion consequently may be thought to signify that a judge may decide on the basis of personal or political preferences or interests, or felt identification with the parties in particular situations—on ad hominem reasons. Strong legal formalism might be attractive if this were the only alternative to result-determining rules. But two others are available.

The second possible standard governing judicial discretion is the extralegal standards alternative. It supposes that a judge with discretion should reach the best decision on the basis of relevant nonlegal standards, such as those of sound political morality or social policy. By contrast with an "anything goes" alternative, this one restricts the reasons available in judging to those that could justify a decision. It excludes ad hominem considerations, preserving impartiality even when the law is indeterminate. This alternative captures the moderate legal realist claim that judges decide and should decide on the basis of implicit legal policies whenever the rules are indeterminate. It expresses the views of Hart and Raz that a judge with discretion has no legal duties, but should reach the best decision.[53] It is Dworkin's main foil.[54]

The third possible standard governing judicial discretion is the legal reasons alternative, which is developed in my recent book, *Judging in Good Faith*. On this view, the law guides judicial deliberations by constraining the reasons that properly enter. The law is understood as a guide to conduct that admits and excludes reasons for judicial action. As the extralegal standards alternative excludes ad hominem reasons, this alternative excludes both ad hominem reasons and all moral and policy reasons not warranted by the conventional law as grounds for judicial decisions. Legal reasons for judicial action may include both reasons created by the law and independent reasons the law authorizes judges to act on. The possibility thus arises that the judicial duty to uphold the law requires a judge to act on reasons provided by the law, and not on other reasons, even when exercising discretion. Judges would be under a duty to weigh competing legal reasons without recourse to other kinds of reasons.

Neither the anything goes nor extralegal standards alternatives can be brought within the rule of law, even when the law is regarded as a provider of legal reasons, not necessarily results. Both involve reasons outside the law, which reasons are not warranted by the law as grounds for judicial decisions. Ad hominem reasons are excluded from judicial purview by requirements of impartiality in judging. Ad hominem and (unwarranted) extralegal moral or policy reasons are excluded by the judicial duty to uphold the law. Judges do not act under a default rule that leaves them free to do whatever they want to do in the absence of a determinate legal directive to act otherwise. The default rule for them is a duty to uphold the law in all cases; demands for lawful conduct do not evaporate when a judge has discretion.

The legal reasons alternative is a different story. It understands the judicial duty to uphold the law to require judges to act on reasons provided by the law, and not on other reasons, even when exercising discretion. The legal reasons alternative fits easily within a conception of the law as a provider of legal reasons. It consequently fits easily within a conception of the rule of law that understands the law in this way. In principle, judicial discretion can be reconciled with the rule of law when the law constrains the set of reasons upon which judges act lawfully. This insight generates the good faith thesis: "the judicial duty to uphold the law requires judges to act on the reasons provided by the law and not on reasons excluded by judicial duty or the law's standards."[55]

It may be questioned whether judges can weigh conflicting legal reasons in a case without recourse to other kinds of reasons for the grounds of weight. To begin a reply, turn the question around: how can judges weigh conflicting legal reasons with recourse to other kinds of reasons? Consider a case in which the legal reasons have conflicting implications for judicial action. The legal realist will seek the grounds of weight first in extralegal reasons of morality or policy. The problem of weight may recur, however, because moral and policy considerations may also generate incompatible implications for action with no privileged tie breaker. The legal realist then may turn to ad hominem reasons for the grounds of weight. These kinds of reasons are excluded from judicial deliberations by all accounts, even when a judge has discretion. Were ad hominem reasons to be included, however, they also would conflict with each other. Presumably one should act on the better ones. What then would be the grounds for favoring some over others? Demanding fresh grounds for the weight of a reason at each appearance of conflict leads into a regress or vicious circle. It is not a way to render the grounds of weight intelligible.

We can avoid the regress by distinguishing analytically the identification of relevant reasons from the consideration of their weight in judicial deliberations. When we do this, it should become apparent that *all* of the relevant reasons enter a deliberation at the identification stage. It makes no sense to suppose that only some relevant reasons enter, with others held back to enter only as the grounds of weight. If this is right, the grounds of weight must be internal to the congeries of reasons thus identified.

This internality of the grounds of weight makes sense because, as any lawyer knows, the importance of a legal reason ebbs and flows depending on the congeries of reasons in which it is embedded, even while the law remains unchanged. To illustrate, assume that a motor vehicle left the road and damaged a storefront.[56] In a tort action, the fact that the operator had an epileptic seizure at that moment looms large, all else being equal, as a reason to find that the motorist was not negligent. The fact of the seizure seems less weighty, as an exculpatory reason, when it turns out that the motorist did not take antiseizure medication that day. Not having taken antiseizure medication, in turn, is crucial if the motorist had a history of epilepsy and was under a prescription to take the medication regularly. But it shrinks in significance if the motorist had not had a bout with epilepsy for many years. In the same context, the mere fact that an epileptic was operating a motor vehicle probably is insignificant, but gains salience if the motorist's medical history includes many epileptic seizures even while properly medicated.

Consequently, no reason can be weighed until all relevant reasons have been identified. Once all relevant reasons have been identified, no fresh reasons can enter to serve as the grounds of weight. Irrelevant reasons are irrelevant. The lawful weight of each legal reason must be a function of the other legal reasons. So we should conceive of the grounds for weight as a ring of relevant reasons impinging on a decision, not a linear regress in search of a result-determining foundation. There is a dash of pragmatism here, allowing a purposive responsiveness to the congeries of facts in cases, within a guiding framework of law. But it is not particularism because it insists that facts are relevant—are legal reasons—due to general standards of conduct warranted by the law as grounds for judicial decisions.

*Rule of Law Values*

An objection to my approach might rest on the values supporting the rule of law, questioning whether the kind of discretion I
would permit leaves these values inadequately realized. It might
focus on three clusters of values justifying the rule of law—
public accountability, liberty, and regularity.

Public accountability is a key aspect of the rule of law. Virtue-
centered and particularistic theories of judging, which require
only the sincerity of well-qualified judges, do not afford an
object for public evaluation of judicial performance. A similar
argument might be aimed at the good faith thesis. On this
approach, judges are permitted to reach different conclusions
due solely to differences in their judgments of weight. It might
be argued that discretion can be used as a cover. A judge with
guile might counterfeit the weights to reach a decision desired
on improper grounds.

A judge conceivably might approach the law as a bull-headed
lawyer would approach a contract he wants to break. Such a
judge might be dissuaded from advancing his own agenda only
by the kind of determinacy of results required by strong legal
formalism, if then. But even a modicum of sensitivity to the
diversity of ways in which facts can combine themselves counsels
a rejection of such formalism, especially as a definition of what
it means for the law to constrain judges. Nor should it serve as
a criterion for public accountability. The laws in any system can
be result determining and nondiscretionary or reason providing, leaving discretion to judges. Public accountability can be
understood in two ways parallel to these two ways of understanding the force of the law. Public accountability might require a judge to show that he or she reached the single right
result determined by the law or only to show that discretion
was exercised for the right kinds of reasons. If I am right that
the law yields reasons, not necessarily results, it should follow
that public accountability requires a judge to show only that
discretion was exercised properly. Our theory of public accountability for judges should conform to our theory of adjudication in this respect.

The relation between liberty and determinate law is often

thought to anchor the rule of law. Rawls, among others, highlights this aspect:

> A legal system is a coercive order of public rules addressed to rational persons for the purpose of regulating their conduct and providing the framework for social cooperation. When these rules are just they establish a basis for legitimate expectations. They constitute the grounds upon which persons can rely on one another and rightly object when their expectations are not fulfilled. If the bases of these claims are unsure, so are the boundaries of men's liberties.[57]

Von Hayek and others make similar points. A rule of determinate law is attractive in theory because it is thought to enhance (negative) liberty by letting everyone know when the public force may fall on them. Individuals can adjust their conduct accordingly, relying on the state to leave them unencumbered in all other respects.

This virtue of determinate law, however, is not a constant property of all laws. It may be most important when transactions are planned and people both know the law and rely on it, as in many real property transactions. It may be unimportant when advance planning is not a realistic part of the picture, as in many tort or discrimination contexts. My claims about judicial discretion are conceptual and intended to show that discretion is compatible with the rule of law. They do not uphold discretion as an ideal for all kinds of cases. We can have determinate laws when determinacy is possible and is more important than the countervailing considerations. Liberty surely should count in the balance when designing laws. But liberty is not a political value that dominates all others in all circumstances.[58] Hence it is not a sufficient ground for insisting that judicial discretion is always unacceptable.

Albert Venn Dicey made nonarbitrariness central to the idea of a rule of law:

> [T]he Rule of Law means "the absolute supremacy or predominance of regular law as opposed to the influence of arbitrary power, and excludes the existence of arbitrariness, or prerogative, or even of wide discretionary authority on the part of the government."[59]

A separation of powers clearly requires that the law constrain each official to a regular domain of action. Those who take the rule of law to require that the law dictate results tend to understand the required regularity on one of two metaphors involving a chain, neither of which permits discretion. First, those who follow the Holmesian theoretical approach to jurisprudence see the relationship of a legal standard to the result in a case as a causal chain.[60] Hart's lessons about the internal point of view suffice to justify rejecting a causal understanding of the rule of law. From the judicial standpoint, the law guides the conduct of agents who are free of inevitable causal chains and responsible for their actions. Second, those obsessed with legal formalism and its negation tend to see the connection as a deductive chain. Von Hayek, for example, claims that judicial decisions "must be deducible from the rules of law and from those circumstances to which the law refers and which can be known to the parties concerned."[61] But enough has been said against the possibility of such legal formalism that no rehearsal of the arguments is required here.

The rule of law should be understood, rather, on the metaphor of an authorization chain, which is more like a chain of command than the chains that control a wild beast.[62] This kind of chain begins with the broad set of all possible reasons for action, divided into all kinds—good reasons and bad ones, selfish reasons and generous ones, deontological reasons and consequentialist ones, and so on. It narrows at the first legal stage, where the lawmaker is authorized to act only on a subset of all possible reasons, as provided by a theory of legislation. Legitimate reasons for legislative action are limited by excluding, for example, all reasons of financial gain to the legislator. At the next stage, the lawmaking can be understood as a further exclusion of reasons, leaving a subset of reasons upon which a law-interpreting and law-applying official is authorized to act. Accordingly, looking at each step down an authorization chain, we see the set of all possible reasons progressively restricted as the law demarcates the next official's legal reasons for action and excludes other reasons. Looking up the authorization chain, we see the set of legitimate reasons for action progressively expand for each official.

The rule of law should be understood to require official action in accordance with the law, understood as a provider of legal reasons for action within a complex authorization chain.[63] When the rule of law is so understood, there is no requirement of either causal or deductive determinacy. At the same time, there is no tolerance for judicial arbitrariness or abuse of power. At the judge's end of the chain, there well may be reasons supporting two incompatible actions. Either action, however, is in an important sense nonarbitrary just because it is supported by legal reasons. Indeed, the difficulty of judicial decision in hard cases arises precisely because each action is amply supported by legal reasons. Judicial discretion is cabined within deliberations structured and guided by the law, which admits and excludes the reasons for a judicial decision and requires those reasons to be weighed in good faith. The primary concern of the rule of law is that the reasons for judicial action all be warranted by the law as grounds for judicial decisions.

## CONCLUSION

Professor Solum has, I think, raised a difficult and important question. Equity, understood as a kind of judicial discretion, is widely practiced within our tradition. At the same time, judicial discretion is not obviously compatible with the rule of law. I do not think that a particularistic, virtue-centered theory of adjudication solves the problem. I do think that the problem can be solved by analyzing the rule of law, the law, and the judicial duty to uphold the law in terms of reasons for action. I am only too aware that my brief remarks here do not suffice to give a complete argument for my position. I can only refer the reader to the more extensive argument available in *Judging in Good Faith.*

## NOTES

1. Solum, "Equity and the Rule of Law," this volume.
2. Steven J. Burton, "Law as Practical Reason," *Southern California Law Review* 62 (1989): 747–93.

3. See generally Steven J. Burton, *Judging in Good Faith* (Cambridge: Cambridge University Press, 1992).

4. Solum, "Equity and the Rule of Law," at 135.

5. Ronald Dworkin, *Taking Rights Seriously* (Cambridge, Mass.: Harvard University Press, 1977), 31–38, 81–130.

6. See generally Martha Minow, "Foreword: Justice Engendered," *Harvard Law Review* 101 (1987): 10–95; Judith Resnik, "On the Bias: Feminist Reconsiderations of the Aspirations for Our Judges," *Southern California Law Review* 61 (1988): 1877–1944; Suzanna Sherry, "The Gender of Judges," *Law and Inequality* 4 (1986): 159–69. For a contrasting approach, see Martha Minow and Elizabeth V. Spelman, "In Context," *Southern California Law Review* 63 (1990): 1597–1652 (admitting the need for abstract aspects of reasoning).

7. Legitimate action here is a normative concept, signaling that action is justified and deserves respect. Legitimacy should be distinguished from legitimation, which signals that people *believe* that government action is justified whether or not it is justified. Legitimation is an explanatory, predictive, or descriptive concept appropriate to a sociological theory of government. See Alan Hyde, "The Concept of Legitimation in the Sociology of Law," *Wisconsin Law Review* (1983): 379–426.

8. Ronald Dworkin, *A Matter of Principle* (Cambridge, Mass.: Harvard University Press, 1985), 11–12.

9. Michael S. Moore, "A Natural Law Theory of Interpretation," *Southern California Law Review* 58 (1985): 277–398, at 313–18.

10. Lon L. Fuller, *The Morality of Law,* rev. ed. (New Haven, Conn.: Yale University Press, 1969), 33–94.

11. J. Rawls, *A Theory of Justice* (Cambridge, Mass.: Harvard University Press, 1972), 235.

12. Friedrich A. Hayek, *The Road to Serfdom* (Chicago: University of Chicago Press, 1944), 54.

13. Antonin Scalia, "The Rule of Law as a Law of Rules," *University of Chicago Law Review* 56 (1989): 1175–88.

14. Aristotle, *Nicomachean Ethics,* in *The Basic Works of Aristotle,* ed. Richard McKeon (New York: Random House, 1941), 1019–20 (1137[b]).

15. For example, Duncan Kennedy, "Form and Substance in Private Law Adjudication," *Harvard Law Review* 89 (1976): 1685–1778, at 1687–1701; Schauer, "Formalism," *Yale Law Journal* 97 (1988): 509–48.

16. Aristotle, *Nicomachean Ethics,* 1019–20 (1137[b]).

17. Solum, "Equity and the Rule of Law," at 123.

18. E.g., Minow, "Foreword: Justice Engendered," at 92.

19. Solum, "Equity and the Rule of Law," at 120, 127, 136, 145.

20. Id., at 122.

21. Id., at 120, 127, 136, 145.

22. Id., at 137–38.

23. Id., at 129.

24. Id.

25. Id., at 132–33.

26. See, for example, Anthony T. Kronman, "Living in the Law," *University of Chicago Law Review* 54 (1987): 835–76.

27. See Duncan Kennedy, "Freedom and Constraint in Adjudication: A Critical Phenomenology," *Journal of Legal Education* 36 (1987): 518–62.

28. See Lawrence Solum, "Comment: The Virtues and Vices of a Judge: An Aristotelian Guide to Judicial Selection," *Southern California Law Review* 61 (1988): 1735–56.

29. Solum, "Equity and the Rule of Law," at 136.

30. Id.

31. Steven J. Burton, "Law, Obligation, and a Good Faith Claim of Justice," *California Law Review* 73 (1985): 1956–83 (review essay of Philip Soper, *A Theory of Law* [Cambridge, Mass.: Harvard University Press, 1984]). ?

32. Solum, "Equity and the Rule of Law," at 139.

33. See Burton, *Judging in Good Faith*, 157–66.

34. Solum, "Equity and the Rule of Law," at 139.

35. Id., at 121.

36. Id., at 145.

37. Id., at 124–26.

38. Id., at 126.

39. Id.

40. See Melvin A. Eisenberg, *The Nature of the Common Law* (Cambridge, Mass.: Harvard University Press, 1988), 83–96.

41. Solum, "Equity and the Rule of Law," at 129, 133.

42. Id., at 131.

43. Id.

44. Burton, *Judging in Good Faith*, 37–50.

45. Henry M. Hart, Jr., and Albert M. Sacks, *The Legal Process: Basic Problems in the Making and Application of Law,* tent. ed. (Cambridge, Mass.: Harvard Law School, 1958), 162.

46. Ken Kress, "Legal Indeterminacy," *California Law Review* 77 (1989): 283–337; Lawrence Solum, "On the Indeterminacy Critique: Critiquing Critical Dogma," *University of Chicago Law Review* 54 (1987): 462–503.

47. E.g., Dworkin, *Taking Rights Seriously*, 24, 36; Duncan Kennedy, "Legal Formality," *Journal of Legal Studies* 2 (1973): 351–98, at 355.

48. Dworkin, *Taking Rights Seriously*.

49. See Joseph Raz, *Practical Reason and Norms* (London: Hutchinson, 1975), 25–28, 35–45.

50. See Joseph Raz, *The Authority of Law* (Oxford: Clarendon, 1979), 18, 21–23; Joseph Raz, *The Morality of Freedom* (Oxford: Clarendon, 1986), 38–69. See also H. L. A. Hart, *Essays on Bentham* (Oxford: Clarendon, 1982), 243–68.

51. Richard A. Posner, *The Problems of Jurisprudence* (Cambridge, Mass.: Harvard University Press, 1990), 232.

52. Kennedy, "Freedom and Constraint."

53. H. L. A. Hart, "Introduction," in *Essays in Jurisprudence and Philosophy*, ed. H. L. A. Hart (Oxford: Clarendon, 1983), 1–18, at 6; H. L. A. Hart, *The Concept of Law* (Oxford: Clarendon, 1961), 120–32; H. L. A. Hart, *Essays on Bentham* (Oxford: Clarendon, 1982), 161; Joseph Raz, *The Authority of Law* (Oxford: Clarendon, 1979), 67–68, 70–77, 90–97, 180–209.

54. Ronald Dworkin, *Law's Empire* (Cambridge, Mass.: Belknap Press of Harvard University Press, 1985), 108–14.

55. Burton, *Judging in Good Faith*, 36–37.

56. See *Hammontree v. Jenner*, 20 Cal. App. 3d 528 (1971).

57. Rawls, *A Theory of Justice*, 235.

58. See Isaiah Berlin, *Four Essays on Liberty* (Oxford: Oxford University Press, 1968).

59. Albert Venn Dicey, *Introduction to the Study of the Law of the Constitution*, 8th ed. (London: Macmillan, 1915), 198.

60. See Oliver Wendell Holmes, Jr., *The Common Law*, ed. Mark D. Howe (Boston: Little, Brown, 1963), 5.

61. Friedrich A. Hayek, *The Constitution of Liberty* (Chicago: University of Chicago Press, 1960), 213–14. See also Posner, *The Problems of Jurisprudence*, 43.

62. Burton, *Judging in Good Faith*, 152–57.

63. I do not wish to imply that the chain flows from some "basic norm" along one dimension from the citizenry to the judge. More likely, the chain would form a complex web of authorizations along the lines suggested in Joseph Raz, *The Concept of a Legal System*, 2d ed. (Oxford: Clarendon, 1980), 93–167.

# PART III

# RATIONALITY AND THE RULE OF LAW

# 9

# MY UNIVERSITY'S YACHT: MORALITY AND THE RULE OF LAW

## RUSSELL HARDIN

### THE MORALITY OF LAW

The long-running debate over the putative moral obligation to obey the law seems, in recent decades, to be sparked by the generally accepted fact that much of the content of actual law is conventional and is not deducible from moral first principles. Yet, this conventional content seemingly becomes right, so that one should abide by the *rule* of law. Varied arguments have been proposed to back this claim. In recent decades it is commonly supposed that no argument will do the trick.[1]

The question whether there is a moral obligation to obey the law is typically posed as though one may have a particular morality that the law may violate. For example, a utilitarian or a Kantian cannot be obligated or have a duty to obey a Nazi government's laws where these are utterly immoral by utilitar-

For comments on earlier drafts, I wish to thank Paul Bullen, Wendy Gordon, Hanna Gray, John Ferejohn, David Schmidtz, and participants in the informal Wednesday evening moral and political theory seminar at the University of Chicago, the Legal Theory workshop of the Law Faculty at the University of Toronto, and the January 1992 meeting of the American Society for Political and Legal Philosophy.

ian or Kantian principles. Despite its virtually total neglect, however, a more difficult issue is whether one has *eo ipso* a moral obligation to obey a law that is derived *from one's own moral principles*.[2] The vast standard literature on whether one has an obligation to obey the law asks and answers that question almost entirely in the abstract, as though the issue were whether anyone and everyone can have the same obligation. To put the issue in this abstract form one must assume a unique answer to the question of what is moral, as though the issues between utilitarians, Kantians, Aristotelians, and others are settled, or one must assume there is a metatheoretic reason for thinking the law is separate from moral theory.

Instead of posing the question of legal obligation at the most general, abstract level, I wish to ask whether one who shares the apparent morality of a given law or legal system is therefore morally bound to obey the law. *Even in this most congenial case for a moral obligation to obey the law, the answer is often no.*

In the justification of law there are two compelling classes of normative claims we can make. First, we may be able to say directly that something is wrong, as many would want to say killing under certain circumstances is wrong. Such claims may be grounded in any standard moral theory, including utilitarianism, various rationalist deontologies, contractarianism, virtue theory, the ethics of caring, and, of course, atheoretical intuitionism for those who just happen to know right from wrong or good from bad. And second, we may be able to say that a particular institutional arrangement for handling social interactions is right. We may then say that particular actions are wrong by arguing indirectly through the institutional arrangement. Consequentialist moral and political theories such as utilitarianism and John Rawls's theory of justice, in its concern with distribution, generally give such overarching normative defenses of institutions.

We might associate the first class of direct claims with Hume's category of natural duties that we can more or less see on their face in relevant situations, and associate the second class of indirect institutional claims with Hume's artificial duties.[3] Artificial duties are duties that could be otherwise if we had other particular institutional arrangements, which might work just as well as the arrangements we do have. For example, the traffic laws of England and the United States differ in many ways, but drivers in either country may reasonably be thought bound to that nation's laws.

The striking fact is that these two classes of justifications can yield conflicting conclusions even when they both derive from the same basic moral principle or theory. We generally must have institutions to regulate various interactions. They are often useful for handling motivational problems, as legal institutions do. And they are generally necessary for determining relevant facts, as police investigation and trials do. The second, epistemological, consideration is of greater interest here. The legal system may have capacities for discovering facts that individuals cannot match. But it may also face constraints on gathering and using information that individuals, including individuals in the legal system, need not face in a particular case. Legislative enactments may address certain kinds of fact, such as average tendencies of the population, while ignoring other kinds, such as idiosyncratic personal preferences. Not only the legislature but also implementing agencies may have much better access to the former kinds of fact than to the latter. Conflicts between direct and institutional claims of rightness may arise when an individual has better specific knowledge than relevant institutions can have or can generally be expected to have. There may even be conflicts when the individual has poorer knowledge.

Although I will generally address arguments to utilitarian justifications, justifications from other moral principles may be supposed to have similar structures. This is not an issue that has been of great concern to exponents of certain theories, and one cannot be sure of the structures of some theories. Utilitarianism is grounded in some notion of welfare, which applies as well at institutional and individual levels. Even at the individual level, a utilitarian must take account of the welfare of others in justifying her actions. Contractarian consent, in the rationalist variant of most contemporary contractarianism, is inherently about institutional-level choices. It would be preposterous in general to apply rationalist consent theory to ordinary dyadic exchanges and then to enforce the "agreement" (although parents may often do this for—or to?—their children when they impose resolutions on their children that they think the children would accept if only they knew enough to understand the issue). Therefore, unless a rationalist contractarian theory is coupled with something beyond a principle of agreement,[4] say, with fairness, or it justifies some consequentialist general principle, it may not be subject to the conflict I address here. But if it escapes this conflict, its advocates should avoid falling into con- tractarian discussions of morality at the individual level. Liber- tarian consent, because it must always be actual, applies identi- cally at both levels, although it may be incapacitated at the institutional level by the near-impossibility of universal agreement. Fairness may have very different content at the two levels, although I will assume it is not a bifurcated notion. If it is bifurcated, fairness theorists face a difficult task in elucidating the notion.

Finally, although I do not focus on it here, the problem of conflict of motivations is central to institutionalist moves. One can consistently say that, for one's own interests, the best ar- rangement for handling some problem would be a law that would be enforced, even against oneself, and yet also say that it would be in one's own interest to try to dodge that law when happenstance allows. The success of a legal order may turn on getting individuals to act for their more general collective inter- est and to overcome their momentary particular interests, typi- cally by establishing incentives to change the latter.[5] Indeed, that is the central purpose of the legal order in Hobbes's theory of sovereignty, which gives a clear introduction to the institu- tionalist structure of a combined moral and legal theory. If self- interest is taken as a general moral principle,[6] its main problem in bridging from institutions to individuals would presumably not be epistemological but motivational. *The issue I address here, however, is the problem that arises when the motivational problem is absent because we are focusing on individuals who share the moral vision of the law.*

## HOBBESIAN LEGAL ORDER

I have discussed the strategic structure of Hobbes's theory of sovereignty elsewhere and will not spell it out fully here.[7] In brief, Hobbes supposes that life without government would be so bad that all would happily accept any government in preference to continued anarchy. This is sometimes seen as a resolution of a prisoner's dilemma. In fact, Hobbes's portrayal of life without order imposed by government is the constant failure of exchange in various dyadic prisoner's dilemmas. Lack of political order is not simply a superversion of failed exchange. It is a matter of coordinating on some form of government to bring order to us. Included in the order that we get is, of course, the power of sanctions to coerce peaceful behavior as the government thinks necessary. Yet, each of us would have assented to government with such sanctioning power as better for each of us than disorder. It is to our mutual advantage to have coercive government. Hence, the strategic problem we face when we choose government over disorder is merely a coordination of all of us on an outcome we all prefer to disorder.

The Hobbesian choice is not a pure coordination, because, although we may all prefer any of several possible governments to no government, you may prefer democracy while I prefer aristocracy. But the choice is not impure merely in the sense that, whatever regime we choose, some will freeride by violating the law while others abide by it. What no one of us can do is face a different system of law with different expected probabilities of punishment for violations than others face. That is what we coordinate on: a system for and a level of effectiveness of law enforcement. (The level we choose or get may seem far more draconian for the risk averse than for daredevils.) I cannot meaningfully freeride on our creation or maintenance of government by, say, secretly crossing my fingers while voting the government in. Once it is in, that is the end of it. The Hobbesian choice of a system of government and law is relatively complete: we coordinate on a whole system, including its organization of sanctions for illegal actions. No one can freeride on the general choice, although one might freeride on others within the system, if one can successfully avoid sanction. Hence, Hobbes's general problem is simply one of coordination on a system, not of collective action with all its enticement to freeriding.

If Hobbes's vision of anarchy, including the anarchy of revolutionary times when government fails, is compelling, then his account fits the problem of maintenance of an extant government against revolutionary threats better than it fits the problem of choosing an initial government. We can all more readily coordinate on the unique extant government than on any of the many possible forms of government we might create out of our anarchy. Mutual advantage is essentially the central moral claim for Hobbesian order. We obey a particular government because failure of the government through revolution will be worse for virtually all of us, at least for all of us in the present generation.

We may go further with the Hobbesian argument to apply it even to a particular legal rule when considered *ex ante*. We can justify many rules as an expected improvement for everyone. Hence, *ex ante* the adoption of a rule may be a matter of simple coordination. However, when the rule is applied in a particular case, the interaction it governs may be partly or entirely conflictual. But in general the Hobbesian argument applies to the overall choice of government, not to particular laws.

The central strategic problem at the core of law is well implicated in Hobbes's partly positive, partly normative theory of sovereignty and law. Here my purpose is not to argue further for this Hobbesian vision of the law [8] but merely to accept it in broad outline and then investigate what it means for life on the ground under law. The genius of Hobbes's solution is to recognize that we might find order to be an intermediate good on which virtually all could coordinate *ex ante* to justify government. When we face a particular legal rule, however, the interaction it governs may be partly or entirely conflictual. It is only in the vastly larger context of the need for capacity to resolve such interactions that we can speak of the shared interest in coordination. *Law in its applications is almost entirely marginal, while in its Hobbesian justification it is inherently holistic.*

In this respect, Hobbes is not alone. Many of the contemporary justifications of law are really justifications of a legal system, not of particular applications of laws. Indeed, I think we must generally want justification to be at the systemic and institutional levels, not at the individual level. That is true despite my view that all that matters is individuals and their welfare. There is no intrinsic value in the law or in any particular law, and there is no intrinsic value in a given state or legal order. There is only the value that comes to individuals.

The strategic problem in Hobbes's theory infects many other theories as well. But it may not affect all. For example, one of the leading candidate theories of law and government in our time is some variant of contractarianism. In its most common contemporary variant, contractarianism is Kantian and rationalist; it is grounded in what one ought to consent to, not in what anyone either actually or tacitly has consented to.[9] The object of rationalist contractarian thought is the form of government. Once that form is put in place, it should run on its own without constant recourse to direct contractarian devices. Indeed, the choice of form should be influenced by understandings of what could be made to work, which, in societies with which we are familiar, is unlikely to include ongoing contractarian commitments. If an individual should do a personal assessment of what it would ideally be contractarian to do, that assessment could be contrary to what the constitutional arrangements stipulate in many contexts. But a theory that allows such individual revision might be rejected by most rationalist contractarians.[10]

In an institutionalist account, there is no conceptual connection between what system would be good and what I ought to do, but only a contingent, causal connection. Hence, contingently it can happen that what the system requires of me is not what I ought to do. It may have been a recognition that there is no conceptual connection that led Hobbes to make a connection merely through the threat of sanction.[11] In any case, Hobbes's and John Austin's view of the definitive role of sanctions in law is not merely a psychological claim about human nature or moral incapacity. Rather, they claim that sanction is conceptually implied by their justification for law. Law is justified more or less holistically, not piecemeal. To connect the holistic system to piecemeal contexts in which individuals act, Hobbes and Austin think sanctions are necessary. This is a conceptual, not a moral, move.

To show that Hobbes and Austin are wrong, one who shares their institutionalist perspective must show that something other than sanction could make the holistic and piecemeal justifications match. The successful creation of Socialist man or the widespread belief in the divine inspiration of the law and the intention of the deity to punish in the afterlife for legal infractions in this life would be adequate if they could generally be made to work. In smaller communities, the pressure of social rebuke might work well enough to take the place of legal sanctions. But this is a device that, for the sanctioned individual, is closely related to legal sanctions. Hobbes, who inadequately understood social norms in ongoing small-scale interactions, would rule this device out as ineffective, whereas Austin, with a richer understanding of informal possibilities, would count this device as part of a broader range of devices for maintaining social order.

All of these alternatives to legal sanction seem to fail for positive reasons, at least in large-scale modern societies. Yet it is a commonplace claim that the law or, more broadly, social order stands on the moral commitments of the populace. Indeed, this claim is at the core of the Parsonian sociological vision. It is at the core because it is a dogma, an assumption from which much of the Parsonian world follows. It is not something demonstrated in its own right or shown to follow from anything else. Daniel Bell says, "The ultimate support for any social system is the acceptance by the population of a moral justification."[12] If this is meant in any strong sense, it is an astonishing claim. Perhaps Bell means very little. The "a" in "a moral justification" might be a different moral justification for each of many groups of citizens. Or perhaps the "a" is meant more strongly as "a single." Then there must at least be a core of consensus. For the United States, to which one might suppose Bell meant to apply the claim, one may reasonably doubt even that much. The core of moral and political consensus may be an empty domain. Various fundamentalist religious groups and various racial superiority groups seem to agree with some of us about nothing, not even procedurally. They may use and insist on using civil libertarian procedures to protect their own interests, but they would immediately abrogate them in dealing with others.

It is plausible that the only consensus we have, and we do not always have even it, is that which Hobbes claims. We almost all prefer order to anarchy. But, as already noted, that is no very specific point of agreement; it does not uniquely select out a form of government for us. And there are times when even this much is not in agreement—or, rather, when some think the risk of tumbling into anarchy, as the result of challenging the political order, is outweighed by the potential gains. Something like this must have been the view of many in the times of the American Revolution and the Civil War. It may also have been the view of some in the time of the black power and anti–Vietnam War movements and of many in (now formerly) Communist nations in recent years.

Is the Hobbesian minimalist's consensus adequate for Bell's thesis? Surely not. That thesis is reduced to the empirical assertion that order serves our individual interest better than the alternative. Moreover, such a consensus still fails to motivate individuals in the face of actual laws, even individuals who go further and agree with the laws in principle. For this purpose, there is no serious candidate to replace sanction at the conceptual core of the law.

## No Parking

The most straightforward objection to the obligation to obey the law is to claim that it would be moral in some context to violate the clear law. It is an easy claim to make. Perhaps it is best to make it with a real-world example, preferably a trivial example that will not provoke disagreement about its actual structure. Suppose we have no-parking areas so that, for quick errands or emergencies, people may stand briefly while doing their business. Unless there is someone in a waiting car who will move it when directed to by a police officer, the car gets a ticket. Obviously, this is inefficient for those who do not otherwise need or want to have a second person along for the errand. Moreover, if it were possible for me to know no one else would need a particular space for a brief stay, it would be efficient in a narrow sense for me to park there without fear of causing disruption and without need of an extra person. It is only at the global level of determining what information system we will use for allocating no-parking spaces to brief parkers that it would be inefficient for me to park there.

Suppose I know that today the police are pulled off their

usual duties of ticketing minor traffic offenses to provide crowd control and protection for visiting dignitaries during a major political march and demonstration. I am confident there is negligible chance of a ticket for my illegally parking while I do an errand. Moreover, suppose that the considerations that bring me to need to do the errand are exceptional and that I would want the system to be able to exempt people in such dire straits from having to obey the parking laws—if the institutional burden of handling such exemptions were not egregious. My moral theory might be based on consent, fairness, or utility. And the law could be built on my background moral theory, which, contrary to the law, tells me to park. Indeed, it might even tell me to park on occasions when I could expect a ticket but when I would think the benefits of parking outweighed not only the likely benefits of keeping the space free for others but also the cost of my fine.

The claim that I might morally violate the law may seem devastating to the thesis that there is an obligation to obey the law. But in the parking case and in many others, all that is at stake is roughly the ancient concern with equity. The law cannot be sufficiently detailed to get everything right. Hence, ideally there should be the possibility of overriding the letter of the law to adjust for hardship or perverse implications. I can morally violate the parking law precisely because I can credibly think legal authorities would agree with my formally illegal choice. There may be practical obstacles to invoking equity and it may nevertheless be right for the individual to violate the law when the individual acts from the same moral principles as those that lie behind the law.

Equity depends on the possibility of bringing relevant officials and lawbreakers to common knowledge and understanding of the formally illegal action. Once the case is clearly understood, sanctions may be waived, perhaps already by the apprehending police officer, perhaps only by the court. For many reasons, however, it might be impossible to make the issues clear. What should happen then? Let us turn to cases in which it is generally implausible, even incoherent, to say that equity should govern violations of the law that are apparently moral.

## MY UNIVERSITY'S YACHT

Under recently changed laws in the United States, the expenses of using a yacht cannot be charged to federal government grants for research. A few years ago, using a yacht was permitted, just as using a resort hotel for an intensive meeting is permitted, and one might imagine there were cases in which using yachts for research conferences was less expensive than using hotels or conference centers. The reason a university should now not charge federal research grants with expenses for the use of a yacht is not that such economic considerations have changed. The reason is that it is now illegal to charge federal expenses to a yacht and the university will be subject to sanction if it does.

Here there may be no person who is forbidden from the action; there may be only the institution. I, as a federal research grant holder, should not let expenses for use of a yacht be charged to my grant.[13] Various officials in the comptroller's office should also not allow such charges to go through.

Has any of us been immoral if we let such expenses be charged to the federal account? Suppose we are all utilitarian and we all want the results of our actions to be utilitarian.[14] Moreover, if we have looked at the evidence, we might all agree that, while our particular use of a yacht would be fully utilitarian (it would be cheaper and more effective than using a hotel in Oakland), the availability of federal funds to cover for yachts invites abuse that can best be blocked by simply outlawing any yacht charges to a federal account. There is therefore no disagreement on moral principles or on what the law ought to be.

Perhaps such expenses do go through nevertheless because, say, of flaws in the revision of auditing procedures after the change in the law that newly prohibits yacht expenses. And perhaps I as a professor cannot seriously be thought competent to know the federal rules—I do not even know the rules for obtaining a degree in my department. After all, my whole understanding of the world is that division of labor is welfare enhancing, and I entrust university financial matters to my grants office and to the comptroller, whose specialty is to keep up with relevant rules. I cannot keep up with all the federal rules that apply to me (who can?), and the rule on yachts may have been changed since my last grant. If grant holders could handle all these matters well enough on their own, there would be no need for the massive bureaucracy of auditors and so forth. Although I have to grit my teeth to write it, it may be utilitarian to have such a bureaucracy. And it may be utilitarian for most grant holders to be relatively ignorant of the finer rules of what can and cannot be charged to direct and indirect costs.

Our action in charging yacht expenses might therefore be entirely a matter of incompetence, not of venality. We did nothing morally wrong, only legally wrong. Moreover, we might stand back to look over what we did, including the changes in auditing practices in response to changes in the law, and conclude that reasonable, moral people would have done what we did. Against the possibility of future failings, we might be able to say nothing more than that certain people should be even more assiduous in their jobs than they evidently were this time. Perhaps even Congressman John Dingell would have to agree in a private moment that our actions overall were morally right, although illegal.[15]

In this case, as in many others, a moral theory such as utilitarianism may direct our construction of the law even while it also directs our individual violation of the law. The morality at the foundations of the law may be identical in principle to my personal morality but strategic and informational considerations lead to conflict between the two in practice. In the case of the yacht expenses, both applications of moral reasoning face constraints on information that are peculiar to the relevant agency. Congress imposes a prohibition because its members suppose the Internal Revenue Service and federal granting agencies cannot adequately discriminate between reasonable and unreasonable uses of yachts.[16] And my university and I face ordinary problems of institutional knowledge and monitoring. Gathering information and monitoring actions, of course, do not come free and must therefore be done at a reasonable level that will not be perfect in some ideal sense.[17]

The conflict between the moral reasons for the law and those for my actions can be merely empirical and not at all moral theoretic. The derivation of what behavior is required differs for the two cases (legal mandate versus individual choice) principally because of differences in the epistemological capacities of institutions and individuals. In that sense, the difference is merely empirical. The same moral principle gives the police, judges, jurors, and free agents the same advice on how to deal with available knowledge. Conflict occurs when these different parties to the judgment of the same individual action have conflicting factual assessments of causal relations. That conflict finally undercuts any claim that my actions under the law are bound by moral obligation. In some contexts, they are bound only by whatever sanction is in the law. In those contexts, to say that my actions are bound by moral obligation to the law under my moral theory is effectively to say that my theory must have an exception clause that turns moral judgment over to institutions in relevant circumstances.

In the cases of my university's yacht expenses and of my parking in a no-parking zone, there are two different problems of knowledge. In the yacht case, the problem at the time of the infraction is with my (or the university comptroller's) passive knowledge, knowledge that was already gained at an earlier time but that may be wrong. This problem may have effect only because of the common organizational problem of less-than-perfect auditing and control, a similarly passive problem. In the no-parking case, I actively know what the law says I should do and yet I violate it. Yet in both cases, my actions could flow from moral considerations. In the yacht case those considerations are *ex ante* because, before I ever charged the yacht expenses, I chose to invest time in other activities that I might have put into learning the government's grant rules. In the no-parking case, those considerations may be in direct assessment of the relative merits of following and violating the law.

In the yacht case, I fail to abide by the law when I would follow it if only I knew better. The problem is that I have traded off the limited moral value of knowing better for the supposedly greater moral value of doing other things, such as teaching, when time and intellect do not permit perfection in everything at once. In the no-parking case, even in the face of adequate knowledge of the law, I should actively act against the law if I directly follow the moral injunction that grounds the law. In such cases, the threat of sanction may be applied independently of whether there is good reason to do what brings down the sanction. For example, one might see that potentially sanctioned action would be best for the institution and the society in this instance. Hence, the connection via sanction may actually violate positive causal connections.

Finally, suppose—what has not been a charge against Stanford—that relevant officials at Stanford were fully aware of the change in law that made it no longer legal to charge their yacht expenses to federal grants, but that they did so anyway. Perhaps they reasoned that the change in the law was not really intended for them, but was intended to stop abuses by business executives who were suspected of charging yachts to tax deductible business expenses partly in order to increase their personal rewards tax free. As a tax-exempt corporation, Stanford could not abuse the tax laws to offset some of the costs of owning a yacht for occasional personal pleasures. And perhaps it was genuinely putting the yacht to good use for research and conference purposes by providing cheaper and better conferences for their federal grants.

The Stanford officials' act of charging yacht expenses was then illegal. But was it immoral? When the charges were supposed to be from error of a kind one can expect in large bureaucratic organizations—error due to reasonable choices about how careful to be with audits and so forth—they were not necessarily immoral. M. B. E. Smith seems to hold with "most people" that an illegal action is a matter for moral concern only if it is wrong on grounds other than its illegality.[18] It may be extremely difficult to make a case against Stanford's charging its yacht to federal indirect cost accounts on the grounds of general welfare, fairness, or other standard moral principles. On Smith's dictum, then, Stanford's officials were not morally wrong even if they deliberately flouted the new law. Against Smith's view, we might deem Stanford's actions immoral for the reason that the judgment involved a conflict between Stanford's interests and its commitment to moral resolution. For psychological reasons, we might think people should defer such judgments to other parties or, as in this case, to the law written by relatively neutral parties. This is still partially an empirical and not merely a moral claim.

Nevertheless, one might think it possible that, despite the conflict of motivations, one can sometimes rightly say the weight of evidence in favor of the morality of violating the law is overwhelming. For example, if in Stanford's case the deliberate flouting of the law on yachts led Congress to rewrite the laws to make such action legal, we might suppose Stanford officials were right to violate the law. Those who think such action by Congress implausible may conclude that Stanford wrongly violated the law and should be properly punished.

## Fairness

A standard criticism of utilitarianism is that it leads to self-contradictory implications—that the utilitarian thing to do is sometimes not utilitarian.[19] The conflicts in the accounts of yacht expenses and no-parking violations might therefore be supposed peculiar to utilitarianism. They are not. They are a function of the institutionalism of the law in a utilitarian theory of law, not of the theory's utilitarianism per se. Other moral theories of the law are similarly institutionalist. Indeed, virtually every standard theory of law, except perhaps intuitionist variants of natural law, is inherently institutionalist. These theories also generate conflicts between what is morally justified in the law and what an individual might be morally justified to do. The chief reason for the conflict, as in the cases above, is the differences in the epistemological capacities of institutions and individuals.

Briefly consider other theories. A moral theory based in autonomy, such as many recent authors propose, may yield similar conflicts between individual and institutional requirements. Joseph Raz, who is strongly committed to autonomy, evidently holds that, if autonomy is to underlie the law, the concern with autonomy must be consequentialist.[20] We need institutions to enhance autonomy, but those institutions will, as in the argument above, have different epistemological capacities than individuals have. They may therefore be expected sometimes to reach different conclusions about what ought to be done than an individual committed to autonomy might reach.[21]

Suppose we have a system of legal entitlements based on principles of fairness. And suppose those entitlements affect income and wealth, largely in an egalitarian direction. I may fully share the moral commitment to fairness that underlies our law. But I may also have a child, a relation, or merely an acquaintance who, on evidence I think compelling, has been slighted by our entitlements program. Although the evidence is compelling to me, it may be that, for reasons of, say, procedural fairness, it cannot be used by the institution or that the institution would be incapable of gathering such information without gross distortion. I therefore may act from considerations of fairness to violate the law to correct for the miscarriage of fairness by the law.

Charles Beitz recognizes the possibility of conflicts of fairness in democratic voting procedures even when these are grounded in fairness. He concludes that, if we have properly designed our voting institutions from the relevant principle of fairness, then I do not have grounds for complaint if my lot is unfair from some abstract perspective.[22] That is to say, the empirical constraints on what institutions can be designed and how well they can work partially determine what it is right for me to get from the institutions. Similarly, if we choose a distribution of wealth and other basic goods on the basis of Rawlsian principles, then I have no ground for complaint if my share is relatively paltry. It is the system of distribution that must be fair, not the instances.

Despite the apparent problem that fairness may have with conflict between institutional- and individual-level assessments of its duties, fairness has been proposed as the overarching ground for obedience to many—but not all—laws. Suppose the utilitarian as such is not bound to many particular laws, such as parking laws. One might argue from fairness that all are bound to what any are bound to. H. L. A. Hart makes such an argument for cases of mutual advantage, and one can plausibly argue that parking restrictions are for mutual advantage.[23] But then we must wonder whether the fairness criterion, which applies to the whole system of law, can meaningfully apply to a particular application of it.[24]

Theorists other than those committed to fairness can reject Hart's argument from mutual advantage as simply not consistent with their moral principles. For example, the law of restitution in the United States seems to reject Hart's argument from mutual advantage. According to the *Restatement of the Law of Restitution,* "A person who, incidentally to the performance of his own duty or to the protection or the improvement of his own things, has conferred a benefit upon another, is not thereby entitled to a contribution."[25] The *Restatement* is virtually libertarian or actual-consent-contractarian on this matter. It requires prior consent from me for me to owe you any contribution toward the costs of the order you provide to our mutual benefit.

Those committed to fairness might, if the move works, actually escape the conflict between institutional- and individual-level moral conflict. To achieve fairness overall, we create institutions. Once these are in place, they contingently affect what it is fair for individuals to do. The existence of utilitarian institutions also affects what it is utilitarian for an individual to do, but this is merely a causal relation that adds institutional effects to the range of impacts one must assess to justify one's actions. For the fairness theorist, the creation of fair institutions partly constitutes what it is fair to do.

Again, Hart argues that, if our law serves the mutual advantage of all of us and some obey it, then it is only fair for the rest of us to obey it. Does Hart's move work? Rawls seems to think it does. But Hart may since have rejected it.[26] Robert Nozick rejects it for the libertarian reason that it could be thought to apply to someone who shared in the mutual advantage of some institutional arrangement but who did not actively consent to the burdens of that arrangement.[27] This objection might be compelling if we were striving to find an overarching principle to apply to all moral and legal theories. But if our principle of an obligation from fairness is only to apply to those committed to fairness, something like Hart's move may work, at least prima facie. It may work not because institutions trump individual considerations, but because they help to constitute some of these.

Although the logical structure of the argument from fairness for an obligation to abide by legal institutions grounded in fairness is consistent with that principle, the argument still does not carry the day. All it does is add extra weight to the claim that abiding by law is fair. That still leaves open the possibility that the totality of fairness considerations available to an individual trumps the fairness of following the law. Hence, the fairness theorist cannot escape the problem of the utilitarian or other moral theorist. Institutions are required in order to achieve greater fairness or greater welfare because institutions have capacities for making things happen that individuals, acting spontaneously, do not have. But their capacities come at the cost of partially offsetting incapacities that individuals may not have. We cannot trick our way out of this empirical conflict with a conceptual move.

The discussion here of moral theories of law other than a utilitarian theory is admittedly sketchy. Unfortunately, that is largely because these theories are so far very sketchy. Few of them have been brought down to ground and applied systematically to real institutional problems. Beitz's treatment of political equality in a fairness theory is nearly unique in its focus on institutional possibilities. In contrast, there are extensive utilitarian accounts of such grounded problems. Not surprisingly, therefore, there are also remarkably many criticisms of utilitarianism that are far less sketchy than the slight account I have given here of other theories. It is much easier to do more than sketch a criticism when the theory under review is highly articulated and occasionally even fairly precise.[28]

## Irresolvable Conflict

Apparently we cannot salvage a general claim to obey the law even for those who share the morality that might underlie the law. We may move these people closer to obedience by imposing sanctions for disobedience, just as we may affect the behavior of those who reject the morality of the law, even if this is little more than *ex ante* mutual advantage as it is in Hobbes's theory.

But sanctions are likely only to raise the level of obedience, not to make it perfect. And, for any standard moral theory, at some point we must think greater severity of sanctions would be worse—no longer utilitarian, no longer fair, or no longer rationally consensual.

The conflict between individual- and institutional-level moral demands is a strategic conflict. Because "ought" implies "can," what either an individual or an institution ought to do depends on what it can do. For empirical epistemological reasons they can often do quite different things and they cannot match each other. Hence, what each ought to do need not be what both ought to do. But the differences in moral requirements are not moral theoretic—the same general moral principles can apply to both individuals and institutions.

Can we bridge the conflict? No. Or at least we cannot do so in principle, although we might be able to in some particular cases. We cannot do so in principle because we get into the conflict by applying to its fullest the moral principle we have. Once at impasse, we have no further resources for addressing our problem. All we can do is attempt to bridge the gap between the epistemological capacities of our institutions and relevant individuals. Whether we can succeed in that move is not a subject for conceptual or logical analysis within our moral theory. It is out in the empirical world, where the need for institutions arises.

It is plausible that some institutions should be designed to include devices to block action from contrary individual motivations, including moral motivations, by its own office holders. For example, there may be good strategic reasons for blocking officials from being able to hear claims for moral justifications for violations of laws or agency rules. If they cannot hear such claims, they will be less likely to bend before false claims. Or perhaps officials can reasonably be expected to master the rules they enforce but not to master all the evidential tasks necessary for justifying violations of those rules. In either case, we might expect better results on our moral theory from strong constraints on official actions to conform to the law. This is particularly true if individuals have incentive to seek special treatment and to rationalize their illegal actions, even though they need not actively think they rationalize but may think they are fully committed to relevant moral principles. But, again, such claims are about empirical matters and are not part of moral theory beyond the constraint they may impose on what is possible.

We might nevertheless suppose legal institutions could, under perhaps exceptional circumstances, correct for their own incapacities. Suppose I have acted from utilitarian motives in breaking the law. If arrested and brought to trial, I might put my own utilitarian assessments up as a defense. The court could then hear my evidence and act on it to do what the institution might have wanted to do if not for its epistemological incapacities. But the court might still finally face incapacities that I do not, and it might reject the claimed utilitarianism of my move. Its sanction might then apply to one who acted rightly. We face a pragmatic contradiction. The contradiction does not turn on internal conceptual problems, but only on contingent facts. At bottom, it can be moral to break even a moral law. And, on the same principle of right, it can be right for the law to punish an individual who has acted rightly.

## NOTES

1. For example, see M. B. E. Smith, "Is There a Prima Facie Obligation to Obey the Law?" *Yale Law Journal* 82 (1973): 950–76; and A. John Simmons, *Political Obligation* (Princeton, N.J.: Princeton University Press, 1979). Tony Honoré argues against Smith and Simmons for an obligation to obey the law in *"Nécessité Oblige,"* in Honoré, *Making Law Bind* (Oxford: Oxford University Press, 1987), 115–38. His chief argument is that of H. L. A. Hart, cited below.

2. An alternative view is that there is something about law that gives us an obligation to obey it independently of our own personal moral principles. This view is implausible if law is a means—for example, a means of achieving or maintaining order. H. L. A. Hart raises such a view in "Are There Any Natural Rights?" *Philosophical Review* 64 (1955): 175–91, at 185.

3. David Hume, *A Treatise of Human Nature* (first published London: Noon and Longman, 1739–40), bk. 3, esp. pts. 1 and 2.

4. Thomas Scanlon characterizes his contractarian vision as moti-

vated strictly by commitment to reasonable agreement. Scanlon, "Contractualism and Utilitarianism," in Amartya Sen and Bernard Williams, eds., *Utilitarianism and Beyond* (Cambridge: Cambridge University Press, 1982), 103–28, at 115n. Although Scanlon evidently thinks contractualist arguments are counter to utilitarianism, one plausible ground of reasonable agreement is the overall welfare effects of the choices before us.

5. Viktor Vanberg and James M. Buchanan, "Rational Choice and Moral Order," *Analyse und Kritik* 10 (1988): 138–60, distinguish between a person's constitutional and action interests.

6. As David Gauthier wishes to do in *Morals by Agreement* (Oxford: Oxford University Press, 1986).

7. Russell Hardin, "Hobbesian Political Order," *Political Theory* 19 (May 1991): 156–80, and "The Morality of Law and Economics," *Law and Philosophy* 11 (November 1992): 331–384.

8. I do argue for it in Hardin, "Hobbesian Political Order" and "The Morality of Law and Economics."

9. See further, Russell Hardin, "To Rule in No Matters, To Obey in All: Democracy and Autonomy," *Contemporary Philosophy* 13, no. 12 (November–December 1991): 1–7.

10. Consider one particular problem with such revision. We might agree, either in the rationalist sense of many contemporary contractarians or actually and *ex ante,* to contractarian restrictions on possible exchanges. For example, we might suppose that certain classes of exchanges lead to exploitation that blocks more productive or beneficial exchanges. We could not then resolve a particular potential, restricted exchange by dyadic appeal to the contractarian principle, because the restriction is grounded in a whole-society contractarian principle and is specifically desirable *only because the dyadic appeal produces contrary results.* A contractarian argument in defense of the original restriction on these exchanges just is a denial of the permissibility of subsequently making such exchanges. For fuller discussion, see Russell Hardin, *Morality within the Limits of Reason* (Chicago: University of Chicago Press, 1988), 108–13.

11. This move may, however, simply reflect a supposition that there are no moral constraints at work at all. Against this supposition, however, is Hobbes's concern with mutual advantage.

12. Daniel Bell, *The Cultural Contradictions of Capitalism* (London: Heinemann, 1976), 77.

13. In fact, my university has no yacht. My university's president at the time of this writing, Hanna Gray, said that to her knowledge we did not even have a rowboat.

14. One can construct similar arguments for other institutionalist moral theories.

15. In return, we should agree, even in a public hearing, that our actions in violating the grant rules were legally wrong and should be corrected.

16. They may also rightly worry that the public cannot discriminate enough even to recognize a category of reasonable uses of yachts at public expense.

17. Even the National Science Foundation in its auditing practices recognizes the trade-off between costs and effectiveness of auditing (*Science* 254 [4 October 1991]: 24).

18. Smith, "Is There a Prima Facie Obligation to Obey the Law?" 975.

19. These claims are generally silly (Hardin, *Morality within the Limits of Reason,* 22–29). Many of these claims come from the Monty Python school of moral philosophy, but they may get much of their impetus from vague recognition of the conflict between institutional and individual choices.

20. Joseph Raz, *The Morality of Freedom* (Oxford: Oxford University Press, 1986), 408.

21. Unfortunately, autonomy theory is not yet well developed beyond assertions that autonomy is superior to, say, welfare as a moral principle. One cannot say very much about how autonomy works through legal institutions until autonomy theorists deepen the theory. There are beginnings, often little more than hints, in some of the contributions to John Christman, ed., *The Inner Citadel: Essays on Individual Autonomy* (New York: Oxford University Press, 1989), and in Gerald Dworkin, *The Theory and Practice of Autonomy* (Cambridge: Cambridge University Press, 1988), Lawrence Haworth, *Autonomy: An Essay in Philosophical Psychology and Ethics* (New Haven, Conn.: Yale University Press, 1986), Raz, *The Morality of Freedom,* 367–429, and elsewhere.

22. Charles Beitz, *Political Equality* (Princeton, N.J.: Princeton University Press, 1989), 191.

23. Hart, "Are There Any Natural Rights?" 185.

24. Russell Hardin, "Sanction and Obligation," *Monist* 68 (July 1985): 403–18, esp. 415–16. In addition, of course, there may be issues of equity, because the particular laws may be insufficiently nuanced to capture all the interests at stake or to represent these fairly.

25. The *Restatement of the Law of Restitution* (St. Paul, Minn.: American Law Institute, 1983/1937), chap. 3, §106, p. 445.

26. Conversation (June 1982) about why he did not include "Are There Any Natural Rights?" in his essay collection, H. L. A. Hart,

*Essays in Jurisprudence and Philosophy* (Oxford: Oxford University Press, 1983). Hart generally dismisses the earlier (1955) essay (ibid., 16–17), but he also restates the argument from *fairness to those who follow the law* in "Problems of the Philosophy of Law," in Paul Edwards, ed., *The Encyclopedia of Philosophy* (New York: Macmillan, 1967), 6: 264–76, at 275.

27. Robert Nozick, *Anarchy, State, and Utopia* (New York: Basic, 1974), 90–95. For further discussion, see Hardin, "Sanction and Obligation," esp. 413–16, and Russell Hardin, "Rationally Justifying Political Coercion," *Journal of Philosophical Research* 15 (May 1990): 79–91.

28. See further, Hardin, "The Morality of Law and Economics," esp. 112–16.

# 10

# THE INSTITUTION
# OF MORALITY

## DAVID SCHMIDTZ

### I. Constructing a Moral Theory

Most of my own research lately has been on what philosophers sometimes call the "why be moral" question. What, if anything, gives people reason to be moral? This chapter considers how institutions might play a role in answering the question, and whether there is a sense in which institutions, like persons, can be moral or immoral. What would make an institution moral? Maybe this: an institution could be moral by virtue of giving *people* a reason to be moral. That line of thought led me to conclusions that in many respects are like Russell Hardin's. This chapter outlines the broader theory that pulls me in that direction. It is about how moral constraints work when they work through institutions.

Modern ethical theories are supposed to help guide individ-

This chapter applies a general theory developed in my book, *Rational Choice and Moral Agency*. I thank Princeton University Press for permission to use that material here. I am also grateful to the Institute for Humane Studies at George Mason University for financial support in the form of an F. Leroy Hill Summer Research Fellowship. For helpful comments, I thank Elizabeth Willott and participants at the 1992 American Society for Political and Legal Philosophy conference in San Antonio, especially Jules Coleman, Amy Gutmann, and Russell Hardin.

ual action. Unfortunately, the most familiar utilitarian and deontological theories tend to address us as if we lived in a cultural, economic, and political vacuum. When such theories are
abstracted from the institutional context in which real-world
individuals operate, they are not as helpful as they could be
even when it comes to guiding individual action, let alone when
it comes to assessing the morality of institutions. I want a theory
that directly concerns itself with the morality of institutions, and
yet is recognizable as a moral theory in the sense of taking a
position on how individuals ought to act in an institutional
context.

My approach to constructing a moral theory begins by bor-
rowing from H. L. A. Hart.[1] Hart's legal theory distinguishes
between primary and secondary legal rules. Primary rules comprise what we normally think of as the law. Secondary rules,
especially *rules of recognition,* are rules we use to determine what
the law is. I believe a fully worked-out moral theory also operates on two levels. Morality consists largely of rules of conduct,
primary rules, that are moral analogs of law. Moral theorists,
though, generally do not take it upon themselves to propose
rules of conduct. More typically, what they are looking to find in
the course of their theorizing is a rule of recognition for morals.

What would a rule of recognition for morals be like? Modern
ethical theory begins with a *fundamental explanatory principle,* a
principle that explains what makes a thing moral. A fundamental explanatory principle becomes a rule of recognition when
applied to a particular subject matter, such as acts, rules, conventions, laws, institutions, character traits, and so on.

For example, utilitarianism's fundamental explanatory principle is the principle of utility: X is moral if and only if X
maximizes utility. We produce the different flavors of utilitarianism by replacing X with a specific subject matter. Thus, *act*
utilitarianism lets the utilitarian explanatory principle range
over actions themselves. Act utilitarianism's *recognition rule* (i.e.,
an act is right if and only if it maximizes utility) then translates
directly into act utilitarianism's single *rule of conduct:* maximize
utility. *Rule* utilitarianism applies the utilitarian explanatory
principle to sets of rules of conduct, or action guides for short.
The resulting recognition rule states that following a particular

action guide is right if and only if following that action guide has more utility than would following any alternative action guide. Of course, the utility-maximizing action guide might boil down to a single rule of conduct that says "maximize utility." Then again, it might not.

So, that is how I view the structure of moral theory. Before we proceed, let me note that there must, of course, be a crucial disanalogy between rules of recognition for morals and for laws. Legal positivism is the thesis that a rule of recognition could correctly pick out a rule of conduct as legal even though that rule is immoral. There can be no such thing as moral positivism, though, because it is not possible for a rule of recognition to correctly pick out a rule of conduct as moral when that rule is not moral. It may not be essential to laws that they have an inner morality, but we cannot entertain any similar agnosticism about morality itself.

## II. Moral Dualism

One of Professor Hardin's main insights is that we can sometimes be morally justified in breaking a morally justified law. I think that is right, but what sort of theory best accommodates this insight? I think the way to go is to acknowledge that morality ranges over more than one subject matter. One strand of morality ranges over the assessment of *personal conduct*. A second strand ranges over the assessment of *institutional structures* that regulate personal conduct in a social setting. What makes the two strands essentially distinct is not that their fundamental explanatory principles are different. They might not be. The essential and uncontroversial distinction is made in terms of the *subject* of normative assessment. One strand concerns personal conduct; the other concerns social structure.

So, how does this dualistic framework help us to explain and generalize Professor Hardin's idea that individuals can have a utilitarian justification for breaking the law even if the law is justified on utilitarian grounds? For one thing, the framework reveals that even if the two strands begin with identical explanatory principles, the two strands cannot possibly produce identical recognition rules. The two recognition rules are formed by applying fundamental explanatory principles to two essentially distinct subject matters. Therefore, even if the explanatory principles are identical, you still get different recognition rules. And so you still can get conflict. The dualistic framework shows that this potential for conflict is independent of the nature of morality's fundamental explanatory principles. The potential is inherent in the structure of morality—in the fact that the elements of morality's action guide come from more than one source.

Professor Hardin goes on to say, "the conflict between the moral reasons for the law and those for my actions can be merely empirical and not at all moral theoretic" (216). Professor Hardin's point, as I understand it, is that even if the same fundamental explanatory principle applies to both personal conduct and institutional structure, the conclusions it yields may conflict, primarily because institutions are constituted under epistemological conditions that are radically different from those that face individual decision makers. I do not deny that epistemological considerations create a potential for conflict independently of the character of morality's fundamental explanatory principles. Nor do I deny that, as soon as we identify morality's explanatory principles, the extent and nature of the actual conflict will be an empirical issue. Nevertheless, the question of which explanatory principles we are given in the first place is a question of moral theory. And the nature and extent of the conflict between morality's two strands depends on which explanatory principles we are given. The *potential* for conflict is independent of morality's explanatory principles, but whether there is *actual* conflict in a given case is very much dependent on morality's explanatory principles.

Further, although the potential for conflict is independent of morality's explanatory principles, it does not follow from this that the potential for conflict is independent of moral theory per se. On the contrary, moral theories have structure as well as content, and the structure of moral theory can and does have a bearing on the potential for conflict. For example, there is a potential for conflict implied by the supposition that both laws and personal conduct are subject to moral evaluation. I realize that this supposition pertains only to the structure of morality and not to the content of its explanatory principles, but I would still call it a matter of moral theory. At any rate, it does not look like a merely empirical issue to me.

Let me add that if both explanatory principles were utilitarian, that would be a particularly explosive combination. The principle of utility as applied to *personal conduct* notoriously leaves room for nothing else. No supererogatory acts, no deontic obligations, nothing. When it comes to meshing with the principle underlying the institutional strand, a utilitarian explanatory principle will conflict with anything, even itself.

I do not make these points as an adversary of utilitarianism. Although I doubt that either strand's fundamental explanatory principle is precisely utilitarian; and although I doubt that the two principles are identical, I do think both principles are *teleological*. Many people (philosophers, anyway) assume that teleological explanatory principles could produce only instrumental rules of conduct. This is a mistake, because there could easily be, and in fact are, teleological reasons for adopting rules of conduct some of which have the status of categorical constraints. This point is more obvious when applied to morality's institutional strand. For example, there are perfectly good teleological reasons why no legal system has ever rejected a prohibition of murder in favor of requiring murder minimization. Legislators who want to minimize murders are well advised to simply prohibit it. Teleological explanatory principles can and often do yield categorical rules of conduct, and this fact becomes all the more obvious when we realize that morality has multiple strands, and that one of them pertains to the subject of institutional structure.

In any event, I think human institutions have normative stature only insofar as they serve the ends of human agents, and only in proportion to how generally they serve the ends of human agents. Institutions are not persons. They are not ends in themselves. Their normative status is a matter of degree, and is contingent on how they function.[2]

To give an example, municipal parking regulations might have normative force by virtue of comprising an institution that generally serves the ends of human agents. Parking regulations can have this normative force, however, without entailing that individual agents have a decisive reason to conform to such regulations in a given case. The degree of normative force of real-world regulations is such as to leave open the possibility of cases where people have decisive reasons to disregard pertinent regulations. Regulations have their normative force in virtue of giving reasons for action in a broad range of cases. The reasons for action that they provide will not always be decisive.

But can regulations have any normative force at all? On this question, I worry that Professor Hardin and I might be passing like ships in the night. He seems to think that institutions as such are normatively inert. They can affect calculations about what an individual utilitarian should do, but that is it. In contrast, I think that a morally justified institutional constraint is a moral constraint. We impose various constraints on our behavior from the inside out, so to speak, and some of those constraints are moral constraints. In addition, we are subject to constraints imposed on us from the outside in, and some of those are moral constraints too. They comprise a separate strand of morality, but they are nonetheless part of morality. There seems to be a basic difference here between Professor Hardin's view and mine. I do not know which of us has the burden of proof. In any event, I will not try to carry that burden here. Either way, I think much of Professor Hardin's argument goes through, but agreeing that the argument is sound does not preclude having different ways of interpreting the conclusion.

At any rate, as I see it, moral constraints working through social structure often rule out particular actions regardless of whether they would otherwise be called for by morality's personal strand. There are constraints against murder, for example. Such constraints serve the common good as they work through social structure. In my view, this is one way of explaining why such constraints are moral constraints.[3] When an explanatory principle applying to personal conduct yields a different conclusion about murder in a given case, we have a conflict between morality's two strands. Does the institutional strand give way to the personal strand in such a case? Sometimes it might, but I see no reason to think it would do so in a systematic way. I agree that we can sometimes be morally justified in breaking a morally justified law, but we do not provide a justification for breaking a morally justified law merely by point-ing out that personal and institutional morality have come into conflict. The personal strand does not trump the institutional strand. I do not think either strand is more fundamental or more weighty than the other.

Professor Hardin might object to the view that the personal strand is merely one strand among others on the grounds that "to say that my actions are bound by moral obligation to the law under my moral theory is effectively to say that my theory must have an exception clause that turns moral judgment over to institutions in relevant circumstances" (217). But how bad would it be for a moral theory to have such an exception clause? After all, as Professor Hardin says, epistemological circum-stances vary. The individual's are not always ideal. Further, there is an alternative reading of what it means to say that a law is morally binding. Deferring to institutions need not involve turning moral judgment over to institutions, for it may be that some aspects of moral judgment are not the province of the personal strand in the first place. Rather, some aspects of moral judgment may involve trying to discern whether a constraint embedded in an institutional structure is a genuine moral con-straint. And if a person judges that a structurally embedded constraint is a genuine moral constraint (perhaps because the individual judges that the constraint works through the institu-tion in a way that serves the common good), then the person concludes that he or she is under a moral constraint. No abdica-tion of responsibility for moral judgment is implied.

### III. How Institutions Serve the Common Good

One source of the conflict between utilitarian institutions and a utilitarian personal morality (supposing for argument's sake that personal morality could be utilitarian) lies in the fact that the rules of utilitarian institutions are formulated to handle normal cases. They are not formulated in anticipation of all the peculiar contingencies a utilitarian agent might face in a particular case. They cannot be. According to Professor Hardin, "the chief reason for the conflict is the differences in the episte-mological capacities of institutions and individuals" (219).

Differing epistemological circumstances are indeed crucial, and I like (and will not try to improve upon) the way in which Professor Hardin explains how they work. What I question is the idea that epistemological circumstance is the *chief* source of conflict. Earlier, Professor Hardin had said that "if self-interest is taken as a moral principle, [the law's] main problem in bridging from institutions to individuals would presumably not be epistemological but motivational. The issue I address here, however, is the problem that arises when the motivational problem is absent because we are focusing on individuals who share the moral vision of the law" (208; emphasis omitted).

I have mixed feelings about this way of framing the issue, for I think that at the institutional level there is no such thing as motivational problems being absent. Professor Hardin says a motivational problem arises if we take self-interest as a moral principle, but motivational problems are not conditional on what we take to be a moral principle. Motivational problems arise no matter what we take to be a moral principle. Nor can we say, even in a hypothetical setting, that the motivational problem is absent *because* we focus on people who share the moral vision of the law. Even if there are utilitarians who share a utilitarian vision of the law, we cannot infer that a motivational problem does not arise. It does arise, for the utilitarians in question speak for themselves, not for their neighbors. And because not all neighbors are utilitarians, that changes what can count as a utilitarian vision of the law. When utilitarians create laws, it is not their intention to be talking merely to themselves. They are creating laws to govern their present and future neighbors as well as themselves, which means they have to address actual and potential motivational problems.

Therefore, another broad source of moral conflict—and this is the point I really want to stress—lies in the fact that utilitarian institutions are not formulated with *utilitarian agents* in mind. Institutions impose certain constraints on us, constraints on what we can do to others. Many utilitarians consider it a mystery why morality would incorporate any constraints beyond a requirement to do all and only that which maximizes the good.[4] But really, there is no mystery at all as to why morality's *institutional strand* incorporates constraints. Morality (as it works through institutions) constrains the good's pursuit because the good is pursued by individuals, and individuals do not pursue the good in an impartial manner. If the good is to be realized, then institutions—legal, political, economic, and cultural institutions—must put individuals in such a position that their pursuit of the good in a partial manner is conducive to the good's production in general.

There are reasons why utilitarian law does not consist of a simple injunction to maximize utility.[5] Institutionalizing an injunction to maximize utility would not maximize utility. It would not come remotely close to maximizing utility. The reason for this goes beyond epistemological considerations to the fact that individuals are not utilitarian in the first place.

Maybe morality's personal strand *is* utilitarian, but that does not change the fact that most persons are not utilitarians. You cannot assume people will serve the common good just because you have some theory that says they *should*. Unfortunately, it is not unusual for theorists to draw conclusions about which institutions would work well on the basis of suppositions about which institutions would work well if people acted as the theory says they should. (Professor Hardin's books are a welcome exception to the rule.) Then, when such institutions turn out to be catastrophes, the blame is pinned on flaws in human nature. This is a mistake. Morality's institutional strand responds to people as they are, not to people as the personal strand says they should be.[6]

If I could push a button that would make all people dedicate themselves to maximizing aggregate utility, I might do it. It is hard to say because such a thought experiment is beyond my imagination. I suppose I would push a button to make people more reluctant to impose negative externalities on each other, for I have a more concrete idea about what that would be like. In any event, the important point is that there is no button to push, and people are not dedicated to maximizing utility. Whatever an institution's purpose is, it cannot serve its purpose merely by giving human agents commands or helpful hints about how to serve its purpose. People have purposes of their own. They will not serve the institution's purpose unless doing so serves their purposes too. Whatever we think of deontology as a moral theory, the descriptive fact remains that people are ends in themselves. People formulate and execute their own plans. Institutions that ignore this descriptive fact function badly.

And that tells us a lot about which institutional constraints serve the common good. Since institutions are not agents themselves, they cannot be said to act in the way human agents act. Some people would say that institutions are or can be agents in a sense. I have no great quarrel with this idea. I insist only that institutions and human agents cannot be said to act in the same way. Institutions act, if they act, by moving people, whereas people act by moving themselves. If institutions serve the common good at all, they do it not by acting but rather by influencing the behavior of human agents. Therefore, if morality serves a purpose, and especially if it serves a purpose as it works through interpersonal constraints embedded in social structure, it must serve its purpose through the effect it has on the opportunities, incentives, and expectations of individual agents.

Professor Hardin describes the Hobbesian justification of law as holistic, whereas a moral obligation to obey the law emerges only within "the piecemeal contexts in which individuals act." He says that "[i]n an institutionalist account, there is no conceptual connection between what system would be good and what I ought to do, but only a contingent, causal connection. Hence, contingently it can happen that what the system requires of me is not what I ought to do. . . . To show that Hobbes and Austin are wrong, one who shares their institutionalist perspective must show that something other than sanction could make the holistic and piecemeal justifications match" (211). I agree with Hardin's conclusion that what the system requires of me need not be what I ought to do. I am less sure about his premise. Is there no more than a circumstantial connection between what system would be good and what I ought to do?

Consider what it would take for a system to serve the common good. On my view, since a system has effects only through the effect it has on individual opportunities, expectations, and incentives, a system cannot serve the common good unless it gives individuals reasons to act in ways that serve the common good. Thus, the connection between holistic and piecemeal utilitarian justifications is more than a matter of empirical circumstance. There is a conceptual connection as well. A system serves the common good in a holistic way precisely by systematically giving individuals reasons to serve the common good in a piecemeal way.

But consider how this sort of connection might frustrate a committed utilitarian. The system's holistic justification lies in how it closes the gap between self-interest and the common good in piecemeal contexts, but for an agent who starts out more than willing to serve the common good, the ways in which the system acts to close the gap can be an obstruction. For example, a restriction against using federal funds to buy yachts is holistically justified by virtue of reducing opportunities for people to act against the common good. But in reducing opportunities to act against the common good, it also reduces opportunities to act for the common good.

Given that morality has to work through human agents to serve its purpose, it follows that moral social structures do not make the kind of demands of human agents that would serve the common good only if compliance could be taken for granted. Morality as it works through institutions does not merely *ask* people to serve the common good; a moral institution gives them *reasons*. Morality plays strategically. What it actually asks, when it asks us through social structures, is something calculated to produce the attainable pattern of compliance that best serves its purpose.

Lest this point seem excessively obvious, let me draw attention to how it distinguishes my theory from a couple of popular alternatives. Rule utilitarianism asks what set of rules would have the most utility *if embraced by a moral agent.* In the version defended by John Harsanyi,[7] the principle of utility is used to identify the moral code that would have more expected utility than any other logically possible moral code if it was followed by all rational and morally motivated people. In contrast, I am asking what set of institutions has the most utility given that average citizens are not going to embrace utilitarian rules of conduct any time soon. Rule utilitarianism is a theory about how individuals should act, whereas my theory is a theory about morality's institutional strand. The institutional strand of my theory steps back to ask how agents will actually react to the social structures in which those interpersonal constraints are embedded. We need constraints because people pursue their own projects, and not always with an eye to how those projects affect others. Constraints are not just for agents who want to be moral, but for all of us. A moral social structure will be formulated so as to channel as effectively as possible the activities of moral, amoral, and immoral people alike. So, my theory is not utilitarian in any familiar sense, despite incorporating an institutional strand that begins with the principle of utility.

My theory is perhaps closer to Thomas Nagel's, insofar as Nagel also sees a need for a theory about the morality of institutions, one that moderates the demands of the impersonal point of view. Moderation is called for, Nagel seems to say, because the impersonal point of view owes it to the personal point of view to give the latter some room. It would be extremely difficult to follow up this suggestion with anything specific, though, and Nagel, by his own admission, has yet to do so.[8] In contrast, I am saying the impersonal point of view owes it to *itself* to give the personal point of view some room. I do not agree that "any system must be justified twice, . . . both from the point of view of what would be impersonally desirable and from the point of view of what can be reasonably demanded of individuals."[9] Expressing my disagreement with Nagel in Nagelian terms, I think a system need only be impersonally justified, and that the personal perspective is important when it comes to justifying systems only because it has practical implications that bear on what system can be impersonally justified.

Nor is my theory contractarian, although I can see how it might seem contractarian to readers who share my view that contractarian grounds for moral endorsement are fundamentally teleological.[10] Contemporary contractarians derive conclusions about the legitimacy of interpersonal constraints by asking whether rational bargainers in a state of nature would agree to accept those constraints. But as David Gauthier rightly remarks, "the genuinely problematic element in a contractarian theory is not the introduction of morality, but the step from hypothetical agreement to actual moral constraint."[11] Contractarians generally seem to think ethics ought to work like this. First, we figure out what people would agree to, which tells us what morality's rules of conduct are. Second, we figure out how to get people to comply with the terms of the agreement. Edward McClennen says, "I share Gauthier's commitment to a contractarian approach to morality, and I think it is possible to interpret moral principles as principles upon which rational self-interested persons can agree. I also share his view that it is crucial to such a project to show that rational persons will dispose themselves to choose in a cooperative manner." [12] As John Rawls put it, "persons in the original position assume that the principles they acknowledge, whatever they are, will be strictly complied with and followed by everyone. Thus, the principles of justice that result are those defining a perfectly just society, given favorable conditions. With the presumption of strict compliance, we arrive at a certain ideal conception." [13] Compliance problems are something we take up when we do "nonideal" theory.

That has to be wrong. The compliance problem is not the second step. It is not something that can be set aside as a task for so-called nonideal theory. The compliance problem is an integral part of the first step. [14] When one chooses a set of rules, one chooses a particular compliance problem along with it. Therefore, we cannot begin to know whether instituting a given set of rules will be mutually advantageous unless we know how bad its associated compliance problem will be. We cannot say whether an agreement is mutually advantageous, and we certainly cannot say that what emerges from it will be *just,* until we know what will emerge from it. And knowing what will emerge from it is a matter of knowing what pattern of compliance will emerge from it.

A given system may look like it would be advantageous for Kantian noumenal selves (as Rawls [15] envisions them). This does not, however, imply that the same system would be mutually advantageous for flesh and blood people. If a system must be genuinely advantageous as a condition of being just, then showing that it would be advantageous for noumenal selves hardly begins to show that it is just. Instead, we should ask whether a system would induce flesh and blood agents to act in mutually advantageous ways.

There will of course be some system the worst off members

of which are in fact better off than the worst off members would be in any alternative system,[16] and I do not deny that having such a property would be of great moral significance. My point is only that the system having this property will be one that faces its compliance problems squarely. The system that actually makes the worst off as well off as possible will not be even remotely like a regime that tries to enforce a formal principle of distribution like "Distribute so as to make the worst off as well off as possible." The compliance problems created by trying to enforce such a principle would be a nightmare for everyone but those in charge.

Theorizing that abstracts from compliance problems gives us a fantasy, perhaps, something pleasing to imagine. But it does not give us an ideal; it will not give us something to aim at. It will not be something to which anyone faced with real-world compliance problems should aspire. (An ideal need not be attainable, but it must be something to which we should aspire.) We choose a set of institutions together with its own particular expected pattern of compliance. To abstract from compliance problems is to abstract from the fact that the agents for whom we devise institutions are human.

Utilitarian institutions do not try to ensure that each person is maximizing utility. Rather, they try to produce a pattern of behavior, a pattern that serves the common good even though it consists largely of suboptimal actions. There is a sense in which human agents can often act on the understanding that their chosen course of action is their best available alternative. Institutions cannot optimize in any similarly straightforward way. Institutions can only induce patterns. Moral institutions do not depend on people acting against their interests. Moral institutions serve the common good by treating moral motivation as the scarce resource that it is, as something that cannot be taken for granted. Therefore, if the constraints that utilitarian institutions impose on a genuinely utilitarian agent seem like a hindrance,[17] we should not be at all surprised, for the rules of utilitarian institutions are formulated not so much to facilitate the projects of utilitarians but rather to channel the projects of quasi-egoists in such a way that even the projects of quasi-egoists end up serving the common good.

## NOTES

1. H. L. A. Hart, *The Concept of Law* (Oxford: Clarendon, 1961), 89–93.

2. Indeed, as Professor Hardin notes, Joseph Raz goes so far as to say that an institution's concern with autonomy *must* be consequentialist. See *The Morality of Freedom* (Oxford: Oxford University Press, 1986), 408; emphasis added. Raz is right, for institutions are not ends in themselves. They command respect only in virtue of what they do.

3. I also believe this account can explain why there would be prohibitions against murder even in the state of nature. Even in the state of nature, there can be rudimentary social structures that serve the common good, such as the de facto peace that consists of no one having yet fired the first shot. Thus, I believe that there are morally justified constraints embedded in social structure even in the state of nature. And as I say in the text, I believe morally justified constraints are moral constraints. But that is a story for another time.

4. For example, see Shelly Kagan, *The Limits of Morality* (New York: Oxford University Press, 1989), 121–27. Samuel Scheffler has also expressed this view, despite having a theory that departs from utilitarianism in other respects. See *The Rejection of Consequentialism* (New York: Oxford University Press, 1982), 129.

5. Perhaps such an injunction could not be simple. Would some official have a mandate to enforce an injunction to maximize utility? But wouldn't that mandate be inconsistent with the official being bound by the injunction? Suffice it to say that not all of a system's wheels can be turned by the principle of utility. If the system is to have any utility, then someone somewhere has to be bound by an action guide consisting of something other than the principle of utility. (That action guide could be grounded in the principle of utility as an explanatory principle, but that is not the same thing.)

6. The institutional strand does, however, respond to people as they are *on behalf of what they could be,* and thus it can respond to people on behalf of what the personal strand says they should aim to become. So, the nature of the personal strand can help shape the institutional strand's rules of conduct because insofar as the personal strand enjoins people to pursue a certain reflective conception of their own interests, this will help to flesh out an interpretation of 'common good' as it enters into the formulation of the institutional strand's explanatory principle. See chapter 8 of my *Rational Choice and Moral Agency.*

7. "Does Reason Tell Us What Moral Code to Follow and, Indeed, to Follow Any Moral Code at All?" *Ethics* (1985): 44.

8. *Equality and Partiality* (New York: Oxford University Press, 1991), 3.

9. Ibid, 31.

10. See my "Justifying the State," *Ethics* 101 (1990): 89–102.

11. *Morals by Agreement* (Oxford: Oxford University Press, 1986), 9.

12. "Constrained Maximization and Resolute Choice," *Social Philosophy and Policy* 5 (1988): 96

13. *A Theory of Justice* (Cambridge, Mass.: Belknap, 1971), 351.

14. In passing, note that hypothetical agreement is *not* an essential part of the first step. If we can correctly predict that people will react to an emerging social structure in a mutually advantageous way, then that settles the question of whether the emerging social structure will be mutually advantageous. Alternatively, if we are talking about circumstances where consent per se is morally important, hypothetical consent will be no substitute for the real thing. See Schmidtz, "Justifying the State."

15. "Kantian Constructivism in Moral Theory," *Journal of Philosophy* 77 (1980): 515–72.

16. Rawls, *Theory of Justice* (at 302) offers this as a principle of justice for institutions.

17. The hindrance might be ameliorated to the extent that utilitarian judges have and use a certain latitude for judicial discretion to let genuinely utilitarian lawbreakers off the hook. See Larry Solum's essay in this volume. But this can only be of minor consequence, because most action, utilitarian or otherwise, does not lead to court cases. It is merely constrained by pertinent institutions, and sometimes those constraints will be a hindrance.

# 11

# PUBLIC CHOICE AND THE RULE OF LAW: RATIONAL CHOICE THEORIES OF STATUTORY INTERPRETATION

## JACK KNIGHT AND JAMES JOHNSON

### I. INTRODUCTION

In this chapter we consider a number of recent efforts to employ rational choice models to support normative theories of statutory interpretation.[1] These efforts are grounded in the public choice tradition, which has developed a conception of politics in a democratic society that calls into question many of the bases of the legitimacy of the rule of law. This tradition has been interpreted to argue that statutes, as the product of political competition that aggregates individual preferences into collective outcomes, are incoherent as a statement of the general will of the people in a democratic society.[2] What makes these new efforts especially important is that they attempt to incorporate the conclusions of the public choice tradition in theories of how courts should interpret statutes. In doing so, they seek to salvage the normative legitimacy of the rule of law in a demo-

We share equal responsibility for any errors and equal credit for any insights in this chapter.

244

cratic society in the face of the public choice challenge to that legitimacy.

Several approaches have been proposed to resolve the incoherence problem and to sustain the legitimacy of statutory interpretation. Two types of arguments are offered in support of the different approaches: (1) that the proposed approaches are best able to aid the courts in furthering the underlying purposes of democratically elected officials; and (2) that the approaches will produce better and more coherent legislation because of the interactive effects of the courts on the actions of legislatures. What we consider here is whether these public choice-based theories of statutory interpretation sustain a claim that the judicial interpretations are entitled to normative legitimacy.

In the next section we briefly sketch the nature of the problem as formulated by the public choice literature. In sections 3 and 4 we consider three proposals for how courts can develop a coherent vision of statutory enactments of the legislature. In the third section we assess to what extent these proposals are successful in meeting the challenge to democratic legitimacy. In the fourth section we consider the extent to which courts that adopt one of these approaches can have a salutary effect on the nature of the legislative process and, thus, enhance legitimacy.

## II. THE ROLE OF COURTS IN A DEMOCRACY

"What is the best way for a court to act in a democracy?"[3] This is the question that motivates much of the recent rational choice work on judicial interpretation. In matters of a constitutional nature, the question can imply a tension between democracy and the rule of law: when constitutional review of statutes leads to a court overturning the enactments of democratically elected officials. In matters of statutory interpretation, the question can be interpreted to imply a tension, but it can also be seen to envision a close relationship between democracy and the rule of law: when courts are asked to discern the meaning of a statute enacted by elected legislators. In the constitutional case, the legitimacy of judicial decision making rests on the connection between the court's decision and the Constitution; in statutory cases, the legitimacy rests on the connection between the court's interpretation and the actions of the elected representatives of the people.

Note here that, in the case of statutory law, the underlying legitimacy of the court's decision rests on the democratic process itself. This introduces two distinct questions. First, how, and under what conditions, do democratic procedures bestow legitimacy on law? Second, if democracy is the source of legitimacy, from whence do the interpretations and pronouncements of nondemocratic bodies derive their legitimacy? While the questions are distinct, the answer to the second is dependent on the answer to the first. If the conditions have been satisfied for democratic procedures to produce normatively legitimate statutes, then the court's interpretations of those statutes will also be legitimate as long as they relate in the proper way to the actions of elected officials. If the conditions have not been satisfied, then the question becomes one of whether there is something the court can do to enhance the legitimacy of statutes by relating its decision to those actions of legislators most likely to bestow legitimacy.

The key phrase here is "relate in the proper way." In their chapter in this volume, Eskridge and Ferejohn divide contemporary jurisprudential theories of statutory interpretation into three basic categories: original intent (interpretation should be consistent with the original intent of the enacting legislature), new textualism (interpretation should be consistent with the language of the text), and dynamic (interpretation should reflect the fact that statutes change over time to accommodate changes in society's norms and values.)[4] Each of these approaches establishes a different way for the court's decision to relate to the actions of elected officials. But, for our purposes here, it is sufficient to note that all of the approaches rest on some fundamental notion that courts will derive their legitimacy in statutory interpretation by trying to relate their decisions to the underlying purposes of democratically elected officials.

Conceptualizing the problem of legitimacy in this way allows us to see the argumentative strategy of rational choice theories of statutory interpretation. These accounts establish with considerable clarity the complicated relationship between these two questions of legitimacy. Since the first question focuses on the democratic process itself, some account of how democratic procedures produce legitimacy must be offered. Each of the rational choice accounts is stymied in this effort by the challenges of the public choice literature. Thus, the key to their attempts to offer a normative theory of statutory interpretation rests on their ability to recommend a method of judicial decision making that will connect a court's decisions to those actions of legislators that will overcome the problems raised by the public choice critique of democracy.

Most rational choice accounts make an argument for the legitimacy of law that is based on the production of law through proper institutional procedures: if the law is the product of fair, public procedures, then it is entitled to some form of special consideration. This resolution is theoretically grounded in these accounts' notion of democracy and is aligned with the legal process school of jurisprudence.[5] Ferejohn and Weingast present the most fully developed formulation of this argument. Consider the following passage, in which they set out the problem of the legitimacy of the rule of law:

> The rule of law ... requires that conduct be regulated by a system of impartial public rules whose consequences can be foreseen and anticipated. Such a system must be coherent if it is to have predictable consequences for individuals. The design of an optimal "coherence" test remains a central question in jurisprudence, but most versions require at least some degree of rationality: that legal commands be understood as rational requirements imposed by the state for some comprehensible purpose, a purpose of a sort that could actually be held by a single individual. Classical collective choice theory suggests that this coherence is, in principle, unobtainable in a democratic state.[6]

The main thrust of the passage is that law produced by a democratic body lacks the coherence necessary for it to have normative force.

The major results of the public choice literature are well known.[7] Democracy is treated as a process by which individual preferences are aggregated into a collective decision, either a specific outcome or an ordering of the preferences of the group. Many early theorems, the most seminal of which is Arrow's Impossibility Theorem, demonstrate that any aggregation mechanism that satisfies some standard conditions of fairness will fail at times to produce a coherent collective ordering. In the case of majority rule procedures, additional studies show that the conditions for the existence of a majority rule equilibrium, defined by Riker and Weingast as "a social choice such that individuals in the group, each acting to achieve the highest obtainable outcomes in his or her preference order, will arrive at a given social choice and, once arrived, will have no incentive to look for something better,"[8] are very restrictive. These results imply that democratic procedures will produce cycling at the level of group preferences and, therefore, that the outcomes of such a process will be highly contingent on the particular institutional procedures (e.g., who sets the agenda) under which the decision is made. This contingency leads to the conclusion that political outcomes are the product of strategic manipulation and that democracy is merely a process of political competition. Such a conclusion undermines the claim that the products of the democratic process represent the collective interest and are therefore infused with normative legitimacy.

Thus, theories of statutory interpretation that rest their views of the legislative process on the lessons of public choice theory face considerable obstacles in establishing conditions under which democratic procedures can bestow normative legitimacy on statutes. Nonetheless, these various accounts seek to maintain a relationship between democracy and the legitimacy of statutory law. For example, Ferejohn and Weingast opt for what they say is a "practical" solution based on what democracy requires of the rule of law: "the commands issued by a sovereign and fairly chosen legislature have some claim to be obeyed by a democratic people. And this is true even of a legislature long since deceased."[9] Thus, the product of a democratic legislature is entitled to some special deference from the people and, therefore, from the courts. In an important way this shifts the burden of establishing legitimacy onto the courts: the task for the courts here is to find an interpretive strategy that will (1) enhance the coherence of legislative pronouncements by discerning the underlying purpose of the legislators and (2) justify the claims of legitimacy.

To see how this shifting of the burden works, we can briefly consider Judge Frank Easterbrook's recommendation that judges act as "honest agents" of the legislature.[10] On this account, insofar as courts advance the intent of the enacting legislature, judicial pronouncements can claim legitimacy. Furthermore, it locates the judiciary within the lawmaking process in such a way that by adopting particular interpretive stances it can be seen as enhancing or hindering deliberative activity within legislative bodies.

An initial problem with this recommendation seems related to the challenge of public choice theory. An agent, after all, presupposes a principal.[11] The public choice results on incoherence and instability appear to rule out treating legislatures in such an "anthropomorphic fashion."[12] There thus is a tension here as well as in the other accounts between the view of the court as an agent of the legislature and skepticism about whether the legislature possesses the requisite coherence to be a principal.

But Judge Easterbrook dispels much of this tension by reformulating the way courts conceive of the legislative process. He recommends that

> [j]udges must be honest agents of the political branches. They carry out decisions they do not make. Judges who appreciate the economics of legislation and the markets will be good agents as well as honest ones. Good agents reduce the costs of implementing laws. Reduce the cost of anything and you get more. So good judges make it easier for the political branches to strike compromises, to enact new laws.[13]

By recommending that, in addition to being "honest" agents, courts be "good" ones as well, he suggests how, by shifting metaphors, public choice-based theories of statutory interpretation might mitigate the tension mentioned above. A good agent facilitates *contracting* by legislative *bargainers*. With this change of metaphor—from aggregation to contracting and bargaining—the supposed incoherence of the legislative process becomes tractable.

### III. Potential Solutions to the Coherence Problem

The Easterbrook example represents merely one of a number of ways that recent rational choice accounts have proposed to enhance the coherence of statutes. In the next two sections we consider three such alternatives: (1) statutes as contracts, (2) statutes as bargains that are enhanced by conventions, and (3) statutes as pronouncements that are supplemented by public values. In this section we assess the alternatives in terms of their ability to highlight and emphasize aspects of the legislative process that enhance the coherence and legitimacy of statutes. In the next section we briefly consider the extent to which they enhance the legitimacy of the democratic process through their effects on legislative deliberation.

### *Contracts*

Many rational choice accounts treat statutes as contracts that codify agreements generated by bargaining processes within a legislature.[14] On this view the task of statutory interpretation is consistently to identify and support the intent of the particular coalition comprised of legislators who are parties to the original statutory bargain.[15] This, of course, raises an obvious difficulty in that a coalition can no more have a unified purpose or expectation than can a larger legislative body. One strength of this approach is that it squarely faces this difficulty and generates a rather interesting set of interpretive canons intended to identify those members of the enacting coalition whose preferences were especially important in shaping particular statutory bargains. The expressed preferences and expectations of these "pivotal" actors become the key to reconstructing legislative intent.[16]

McNollgast justifies the focus on "pivotal" legislative actors through an analysis of how different interpretive stances adopted by the courts can effect legislative decision making. They use a consequentialist normative criterion to discriminate among the various possible interpretive stances. Here the analogy between producing statutes on the one hand and contracting on the other exerts considerable force. That interpretive stance that best works to "facilitate legislative agreements and insure the efficiency of the legislative process" by enforcing original expectations and constraining strategic communication is deemed superior.[17] A view of courts as agents, both honest and good, of the legislature obviously fits comfortably here.

An honest agent is concerned with the expectations and preferences of the original parties. In statutory interpretation this means that courts should, within constraints imposed by the strategic setting in which they find themselves, rule on behalf of the *enacting* rather than the current or *sitting* legislature. This distinction allows us to see that while the court may in fact act contrary to the "majoritarian whims" of the current legislature, it does so in the name of an earlier majority. It is by establishing this connection to the intent of the enacting legislative coalition that Ferejohn and Weingast hope to establish the legitimacy of judicial pronouncements and, thereby, "provide a practical response to the theoretical tension between law and democracy."[18]

Unfortunately, the laws-as-contracts approach fails adequately to resolve the coherence problem. This becomes apparent if we look more closely at the interpretive canons that McNollgast suggests will enable the court to determine the intent of the enacting legislature. Recall that these canons focus less on the goals and expectations articulated by "ardent supporters" of legislation than on the role of "pivotal" legislators. Specifically, these canons focus attention on the compromises and accommodations that ardent legislators are forced to make in order to garner the support of pivotal members.[19] This is where the difficulty arises. In theory, pivotal legislators are those who hold veto power over bills by virtue of the key decision-making positions that they occupy. In practice this more often than not means that pivotal legislators are members of "non-representative committees with gate-keeping authority."[20] What makes the authority of such committees legitimate? Absent a persuasive answer to this question, the law-as-contracts effort to establish the legitimacy of judicial pronouncements founders.

On this account, the courts, insofar as they act as honest and

good agents, are viewed as strengthening rather than obstruct-
ing democratic processes. This is because

> enhancing the efficacy of statutes is a fundamental value in a
> democracy because formally enacted statutes, *produced according
> to public and fair procedures,* are the best expressions of public
> judgements.[21]

Thus, the legitimacy of democratic outcomes presupposes that
they can be understood as produced by normatively justifiable
procedures. Efforts to treat laws as contracts face a particularly
discomfiting quandary here. On the one hand they need to
establish the fairness of legislative structures and processes. And
on the other, their own account of these structures and processes raises serious doubts about whether they can plausibly be
characterized as fair. For in the first place the occupants of key
committee assignments, upon whom the interpretive canons
proposed by this approach center, emerge as "pivotal" members
via strategic political competition that is arbitrary from a normative perspective.

More importantly, if the legitimacy of the law is contingent
on the institutional procedures that produce it, then the analysis
shifts to the character of the institutional procedures. The key
to the question of legitimacy focuses on an explanation of how
the procedures, such as congressional committees and norms,
were established. The legislative procedures upon which this
claim rests are the product of bargaining by legislators with
varying degrees of influence on the process. Thus they are the
product of the same political process that produces other laws.
If the procedures are the product of a political process that is
dominated by the various asymmetries of power that characterize a society, why should those institutions be entitled to any
special normative deference? And why should such a set of
procedures bestow legitimacy on the fruits of that process?[22]
The statutes-as-contracts approach must justify the claim that
these legislative contracts are more than the mere product of
strategic politics. Resting the claim on a set of institutional procedures that is itself a political phenomenon will not satisfy
this requirement.

## Bargains and Conventions

Eskridge and Ferejohn understand that there are weaknesses in the statutes-as-contracts approach to statutory interpretation. They reject the contract metaphor on the grounds that, unlike bilateral contracts, statutes have "third-party effects."[23] By this they mean to emphasize the content of legislation and the fact that statutes can produce harms for some actors. In doing so, they place greater emphasis on the bargaining aspect of the legislative process and highlight the thoroughly political nature of these statutes. Given the distributional effects of these statutes, they reject a reliance on efficiency as the criterion by which courts can enhance the coherence of legislation. At this level their understanding is clearly an advance over the statutes-as-contracts approach.

To address the incoherence and legitimacy problems, they recommend that courts should adopt interpretive conventions that are welfare enhancing and that will encourage the nonstrategic aspects of legislative behavior. Here their justification for this recommendation is somewhat unclear. On the one hand, they also introduce the efficiency like benefits of conventions:

> the canons are conventions ... and ... the practice of using them can allow agents, in this case legislators, to coordinate their behavior in ways that would not be possible, or as easy, without them. A canon is *efficient* if its use permits the drafting and enacting of legislation that improves everyone's well-being relative to not using a canon. Two canons are *equivalent* if they permit the actors to attain identical levels of utility or well-being. Thus, we can now set forth our central idea about the canons: where each set of canons is efficient and all are equivalent, legislative agents should be indifferent as to which set of canons is employed in the courts as long as one of them is.[24]

And they emphasize these effects in their claim that such conventions will produce a legislative environment (in which legislators can make clear and credible *ex ante* commitments as to their interpretations of the meaning of the statutes they propose) that creates greater incentives for nonstrategic and more deliberative behavior.[25]

On the other hand, they acknowledge that these conventions themselves can have distributive effects and that, therefore, they must be justified on independent normative grounds:

> we view the choice of interpretive methods and specifically the choice of canons as a choice among alternative conventions, and recognize that alternative sets of canons may lead to distributions of welfare that cannot be compared according to an efficiency criterion. The choice and defense of interpretive conventions requires normative grounding and, as efficiency notions are evidently too weak to do the job, such grounding must be sought elsewhere in political theory.[26]

Thus, the general welfare-enhancing effects of interpretive conventions will be insufficient for a justification of these conventions as a resolution of the problems of legitimacy.

This leads us to the question, what would be a sufficient justification for a court to employ a particular interpretive convention? For a specific convention to enhance the legitimacy of statutes, it must be justified on some grounds independent of its political nature. Eskridge and Ferejohn do not take up this question, but it is, as they readily acknowledge, essential to their more general enterprise. They hint at an answer when they suggest that their proposal for interpretive conventions is in the spirit of recent proposals that interpretive canons should incorporate "public values" in statutory interpretation.[27] By turning to an assessment of these proposals, we can see how difficult a task it is to justify distribution-effecting conventions on nonpolitical grounds.

### Public Values

This third approach to the question of how courts might enhance the coherence and legitimacy of statutes recommends that courts interpret such statutes in the context of the dominant public values that are relevant to the purpose of the statute. Whether formulated in terms of republican values[28] or prevailing social norms,[29] the various approaches that can be categorized under this heading share a belief that courts should interpret statutes as consistent with the prevailing ethical principles and values in a community. This assumption that legislators seek to instantiate statutes with these prevailing values allows courts to discern the underlying purpose and to enhance the coherence of those statutes.

The important question to ask here is, what justifies the use of these principles by a nondemocratic body to impose meaning on a statute? That is, what is it about such principles that would lend legitimacy to statutes that were interpreted as instantiating such principles? Most accounts that advocate the use of such public values fail to answer these questions. One exception, however, is Posner's justification of this approach to judicial decision making in his more general argument in support of a pragmatic jurisprudence. While he differs from some of the other proponents in the exact principles he would employ, his account serves as the most complete existing attempt to justify the public values approach.[30] Posner bases his justification on the existence of a "social consensus" around these principles.[31] Thus, on his pragmatic account, the legitimacy of judicial decision making is a function of the extent to which there is a social consensus on the purposes and goals upon which the law is based.

Given the increasingly heterogenous nature of modern society, it is highly unlikely that a social consensus will exist regarding ethical principles that might ground the interpretation of statutes. Judges who invoke consensus to justify their interpretations thus have a difficult case to make against charges that their actions are merely political and thus lacking in legitimacy. In any event, the more fundamental question of why a social consensus should make ethical principles a source of legitimacy in statutory interpretation cases remains to be answered.

In what sense can consensus provide justification? Consider two alternatives. First, a social consensus might be the basis of some agreement-based account: the ethical principle is legitimate *because* there is a social consensus on it. Posner himself acknowledges the weaknesses of this line of argument.[32] The clear objection is that consensus can be produced by power asymmetries and not through free and uncoerced choice. The power relations can work at the level of maintenance (where the

dominant groups in society maintain an apparent consensus
through the threat of retaliation, or the expectation of a possible retaliation, against deviations from that consensus) or at the
level of the original development of the consensus (where the
convergence on a particular ethical convention was the product
of the asymmetries of power in a society). On either account,
the objection undercuts a consent-based justification of ethical
principles. If the "social consensus" is a function of force and
not free commitment, we cannot draw normative inferences
from the existence of a mere convergence on a particular ethical position.

While Posner would seem to accept such a objection, he
nevertheless maintains that social consensus is a source of legitimacy. In several places in his analysis he emphasizes the idea
that "causes and justifications need not coincide."[33] Thus, if the
social consensus can be a source of a justification different from
that of the agreement-based variety, the fact that the consensus
was originally the product of power asymmetries need not defeat the other justifications.

From this perspective, we should consider an alternative answer to the question of what consensus tells us about justification—it may be evidence of the value of an ethical principle,
value that courts may invoke as a way of producing support for
their decisions. Here the justification is a practical one. Regardless of the origin of the convergence of society on a particular
ethical principle, we may come to learn that the principle has
socially desirable properties. These properties may serve as part
of a pragmatist justification of judicial decisions.

Posner offers such an argument in support of "wealth-maximization" as an ethical principle that *should* form the basis of
common law decision making. As evidence in support of the
argument that wealth-maximization is a principle upon which
there is wide consensus in everyday practice, he offers the precedents of the existing common law:

> [Judges] fashion the common law out of customary practices, out
> of ideas borrowed from statutes and from other legal systems
> (for example, Roman law), and out of their own conceptions of
> public policy. The law they created exhibits, according to the
> economic theory that I am expounding, a remarkable (although

not total . . .) substantive consistency. It is as if the judges *wanted* to adopt the rules, procedures, and case outcomes that would maximize society's wealth.[34]

We want to set aside the question of whether Posner's claim that the common law instantiates the wealth-maximization principle is an accurate one. This has been the subject of exhaustive debate. For our purposes the important feature of this argument is the role that the evidence of convergence in the evolution of the common law might play in a justification of the ethical principle. The key to this kind of justification rests not so much on the fact that judges decided previous cases in a particular way, but rather on the fact that the consequences of those decisions were deemed sufficiently desirable that they were replicated and expanded over time. For Posner, the evidence of a consensus, or convergence, on a particular principle is evidence that such a principle has shown its instrumental value by the fact that it has withstood the "test of time."[35] On this account, principles that have demonstrated over time their utility in the face of competing principles are entitled to some presumption as to their socially desirable character.

Here consensus lends support to a judge's justification of her reading of the underlying purposes and goals in a practical way: the goals must be socially valuable or they would not have persisted over time in the face of conflicting principles. This notion, central to the pragmatic program, is an example of the common intuition that a phenomenon that survives an evolutionary process demonstrates in doing so its functional value. Yet this common intuition is open to challenge; its plausibility depends on the specific conditions under which the historical process takes place. For this to be a good justification of the judge's choice of principles, the conditions that make the test of time a meaningful criterion must be satisfied.

We can see more clearly exactly what these conditions are by briefly considering Posner's argument that a pragmatic judge should make an open inquiry into the consequences of her actions in the course of making a decision. The emphasis on open inquiry raises questions about the level of discretion available to judges. In response to these questions, Posner must defend this recommendation of a wide-ranging inquiry against the claim that such discretion increases the political dimension and threatens the legitimacy of the law. In fact, he argues just the opposite: "the tools of practical reason can resolve many common law issues with tolerable definiteness, so that the judge does not have to fall back on personal values or raw politics."[36] This argument rests implicitly on the following claim: the resources that a judge would invoke in the process of reasoning practically about a difficult legal question are sufficiently definite and clear that two judges from different political positions would converge on the same answer to that question. Thus, the plausibility of this argument hinges on the nature of the resources that a judge invokes in the process of practical reasoning.

What distinguishes resources that are legally sound from those that are merely political? Here again we see the importance of the "test of time" criterion for the pragmatic program. Posner offers an answer to this question in terms of legal precedent. He acknowledges at first that a precedent is merely an earlier judicial decision. Taken in isolation the decision in difficult cases is a political act. Thus, for judicial precedents to be more than mere politics, they have to meet some nonpolitical standard. Posner argues that some precedents meet this standard and acquire a more authoritative status over time:

> One thing that can solidify a precedent—that can make it authoritative (or more authoritative) rather than just a source of information—is its endorsement by many judges over a substantial period of time. Other things being equal, a conclusion to which a number of different individuals have come—a conclusion (better, a hypothesis) that has survived continual retesting—is entitled to more deference than the conclusion of a single individual. So time can help stabilize legal doctrine. Notice that, from this perspective, the more diverse the judiciary, the more its rulings invite unforced agreement, ungrudging deference.[37]

Thus, the key to legal soundness in this case rests on the survival of certain precedents in the competition of judicial decisions. The fact that a judicial decision has been tested and subsequently embraced by other judges somehow transforms the initial political act and provides it with some more authoritative status.

Questions of the use of such publicly shared principles are answered with reference to those principles that have survived in an open and unforced competition of ideas. In Posner's example, the legitimacy of pragmatic judicial decisions depends on the case one can make about the nature of that competition, about the conditions under which certain ideas come to achieve a consensus. If they are not satisfied (and we have suggested a major reason why they would not be in a modern heterogeneous society), we see no reason to distinguish a pragmatist decision from any other political act.

Our analysis of Posner's argument shows that the more general claim that courts can enhance the legitimacy of statutes through the use of public values rests on a claim about the underlying nature of the principles that these courts employ. On Posner's account, judges should be constrained by (or, at the very least, should show special deference to) those principles that satisfy certain criteria. The main criteria are social consensus and survivability in the test of time. Both rest on the existence of free and open inquiry that produces rules and knowledge that people accept and continue to reaffirm in uncoerced ways. If the rules and principles invoked by pragmatic judges are, in fact, the product of such free inquiry and uncoerced choice, then pragmatic decisions are distinguishable from mere politics.

But we must always remember that social *convergence* on principles and rules does not imply social *consensus*. The problem for this argument lies in the extreme difficulty in establishing and maintaining the conditions necessary for the kind of free and open inquiry that would give political decisions some nonpolitical justification. When these conditions are not established, we see nothing that gives the products of time and convergence any normative significance other than its political one. Thus, unless such conditions are met, neither the use of interpretive conventions nor the invocation of "public" values will adequately resolve the legitimacy problems raised by a reliance on a public choice theory of legislative politics.

## IV. The Effects of Interpretive Approaches on the Quality of Legislation

Each of these three approaches sees itself as contributing to a basically Madisonian version of democratic deliberation. The court, on this view, can, by adopting one rather than another interpretive posture, enhance or diminish the deliberative processes within the legislative branch.[38] Along these lines, these approaches see courts, insofar as judges interpret statutes in a way that creates incentives for behavior that is not narrowly political, as enhancing legislative deliberation and, thus, increasing the legitimacy of statutes. So these rational choice accounts might turn to the incipient theory of democratic deliberation as a way out of the quandary imposed by public choice theory.

But we are doubtful that such a move would be successful. The Madisonian perspective defended by some rational choice accounts takes a mechanical view of democratic deliberation. It sees courts as providing incentives that might ameliorate the propensity of legislators to act strategically.[39] This comports with the checks and balances notion of interbranch relations defended by Madison.[40] But it is not obviously sufficient to establish that legislative processes generate "legal commands understood as *rational requirements* imposed by the state for some comprehensible purpose."[41]

We think that it may be possible to elaborate a notion of democratic deliberation that could meet this last requirement. Such a notion would focus less on the impact of judicial strategies on deliberative processes within the legislature than on an interbranch process of persuasion and debate. In this sense it is consistent with views of deliberation sketched by advocates of the Constitution in which the courts serve as "an intermediate body between the people and the legislature."[42] And it extends notions of deliberation implicit in the writings of some contributors to these rational choice accounts.[43] Perhaps most importantly, such a view would evade the apprehensions of rational choice theorists who presume that deliberation derives legitimacy from some relation, however attenuated, to a preexisting popular will.[44] Although we cannot elaborate this view here, we would defend a vision of democratic deliberation that derives legitimacy instead from processes of free and reasoned de-bate.[45] In our view deliberation aims not to induce consensus over values or preferences but, more modestly, to establish agreement over the dimensions of the debate.[46]

This idealized view of deliberation is consistent with a con-ception of how the law actually works in a democratic society. Such a conception must take account of the challenge that both public choice theory and the realities of strategic political behav-ior raise for the legitimacy of statutory law. While it resembles views that see the court as engaged in "a continuing colloquy with the political institutions and with society at large," we do not contend that the court "in fact" fulfills this deliberative role.[47] Rather, our view is that such an idealized process of reasoned argument both identifies the source from which legal rules derive whatever normative force they may have and pro-vides a view of what "democracy requires of courts" that can serve as a critical vantage point from which to assess the short-comings of extant legal practices.

## NOTES

1. See Daniel Farber and Philip Frickey, *Law and Public Choice* (Chicago: University of Chicago Press, 1991), as well as symposia in the *Virginia Law Review* 74 (1988), *Georgetown Law Journal* 80 (1992), *The Journal of Law, Economics, and Organization* 6 (1990) and 8 (1992), and *The International Review of Law and Economics* 12 (1992).

2. William Riker, *Liberalism against Populism* (Prospect Heights, Ill.: Waveland, 1982).

3. John Ferejohn and Barry Weingast, "Limitation of Statutes: Strategic Statutory Interpretation," *Georgetown Law Journal* 80 (1992): 565–82, at 573.

4. William Eskridge and John Ferejohn, "Politics, Interpretation, and the Rule of Law," this volume.

5. Henry Hart and Albert Sacks, *The Legal Process* (Cambridge, Mass.: Harvard University Press, 1958).

6. John Ferejohn and Barry Weingast, "Limitation of Statutes," 568; see also Ferejohn and Weingast, "A Positive Theory of Statutory Interpretation," *International Review of Law and Economics* 12 (1992): 263–79.

7. For those who are unfamiliar with the logic of public choice,

Farber and Frickey offer a concise account of the standard results with special emphasis on the implications for questions of legal interpretation.

8. William Riker and Barry Weingast, "Constitutional Regulation of Legislative Choice," *Virginia Law Review* 74 (1988): 373–402, at 373–74.

9. Ferejohn and Weingast, "A Positive Theory of Statutory Interpretation," 4.

10. This is explicit in Ferejohn and Weingast, "A Positive Theory of Statutory Interpretation," and it is implicit, in ways that we note below, in McNollgast, "Positive Canons: The Role of Legislative Bargains in Statutory Interpretation," *Georgetown Law Journal* 80 (1992): 705–42.

11. The principal-agent literature does not necessarily present an obstacle to viewing courts as agents. Arrow, for example, acknowledges the possibility that an agent might represent multiple principals. See Kenneth Arrow, "The Economics of Agency," in *Principals and Agents,* ed. J. Pratt and R. Zeckhauser (Cambridge, Mass.: Harvard Business School Press, 1985).

12. Ferejohn and Weingast, "Limitation of Statutes," 571, 567–68.

13. Frank Easterbrook, "The Supreme Court, 1983 Term—Foreword: The Court and the Economic System," *Harvard Law Review* 98 (1984): 4–60, at 60.

14. McNollgast, 706; Easterbrook, "Foreword: The Court and the Economic System," 15; Daniel Farber, "Legislative Deals and Statutory Bequests," *Minnesota Law Review* 75 (1991): 667–89.

15. McNollgast, 705, 725; Ferejohn and Weingast, "Limitation of Statutes." The purpose of interpretation on this view is not activist in the sense of courts assembling policy preferences. Rather, it springs from the recognition that any contract will have ambiguities that require resolution. See McNollgast, 709, n. 11.

16. McNollgast, 707–8, 718–27.

17. McNollgast, 710.

18. Ferejohn and Weingast, "Limitation of Statutes," 580.

19. McNollgast, 707, 711–12, 728.

20. Ferejohn and Weingast, "A Positive Theory of Statutory Interpretation," 22; "Limitation of Statutes," 580.

21. Ferejohn and Weingast, "Limitation of Statutes," 567; emphasis added.

22. For an account of institutional emergence and change that makes this point more generally, see Jack Knight, *Institutions and Social Conflict* (Cambridge: Cambridge University Press, 1992).

23. Eskridge and Ferejohn, 281.

24. Eskridge and Ferejohn, 283.

25. Eskridge and Ferejohn, 283.

26. Eskridge and Ferejohn, 282.

27. Eskridge and Ferejohn, 282.

28. Cass Sunstein, *After the Rights Revolution* (Cambridge, Mass.: Harvard University Press, 1990); Farber and Frickey, *Law and Public Choice.*

29. William Eskridge, "Public Values in Statutory Interpretation," *University of Pennsylvania Law Review* 137 (1989): 1007–1103; Richard Posner, *The Problems of Jurisprudence* (Cambridge, Mass.: Harvard University Press, 1990).

30. Although Posner casts most of the argument we consider here explicitly in terms of common law cases, the justification of the use of public values in statutory cases follows the same basic logic. In "Pragmatism, Realism, and the Politics of Legal Theory" (unpublished manuscript), we argue that Posner's pragmatic program for statutory interpretation reduces, in the face of his acceptance of the public choice conception of legislative politics, to his program for common law decision making.

31. Posner, 243.

32. Posner, 126.

33. Posner, 126, 194, 240.

34. Posner, 355–56; author's emphasis.

35. Posner, 112–22.

36. Posner, 255.

37. Posner, 117–18.

38. Eskridge and Ferejohn characterize this as aspects of a process of selecting equilibrium strategies in a game between the courts and the legislature. They argue that "any satisfactory theory of legislatures must contain a specification of the interpretive regime. Otherwise, legislators wouldn't be able to know what they were voting on, or to form coherent strategies for casting their votes" (268). Thus, they conclude that "interpretive regimes can be seen as 'causing' or 'inducing' legislative behavior" (273).

39. Ferejohn and Weingast ("Limitation of Statutes" 565, 566, 581) are concerned with the propensity of legislators to pursue reelection at the expense of lawmaking. McNollgast (713, 717, 741) is concerned with the propensity of legislators to introduce language in order to influence subsequent interpretations of legislation.

40. See *Federalist* 51, in Jacob Cooke, ed., *The Federalist* (Middletown, Conn.: Wesleyan University Press, 1961).

41. Ferejohn and Weingast, "Limitation of Statutes," 568; emphasis added.

42. In this mediating role, of course, the courts exercise "neither Force nor Will, but merely judgement" (Hamilton, *Federalist* 78).

43. Eskridge, "Reneging on History?" *California Law Review* 79 (1991): 613–84, at 666. In particular it would allow us to take seriously the claim made by these theorists that "the composition and preferences of these various agents cannot be taken as fixed and immutable" (Ferejohn and Weingast, "Limitation of Statutes," 566). See also Eskridge, "Reneging on History?" 656.

44. See Riker; also Jules Coleman and John Ferejohn, "Democracy and Social Choice," *Ethics* 97 (1986): 6–25; also Ferejohn and Weingast, "Limitation of Statutes," 569–70.

45. Bernard Manin, "On Legitimacy and Political Deliberation," *Political Theory* 15 (1987): 338–68; Joshua Cohen, "Deliberation and Democratic Legitimacy," in A. Hamlin and P. Pettit, eds., *The Good Polity* (New York: Blackwell, 1989). For a more complete development of this discussion of the possibilities of democratic deliberation, see Jack Knight and James Johnson, "Aggregation and Deliberation: On the Possibility of Democratic Legitimacy," *Political Theory*, forthcoming.

46. Our position here seems to converge with that sketched by Farber and Frickey, 55–56.

47. Alexander Bickel, *The Least Dangerous Branch* (New Haven, Conn.: Yale University Press, 1962), 240.

# 12

# POLITICS, INTERPRETATION, AND THE RULE OF LAW

## WILLIAM N. ESKRIDGE, JR. AND JOHN FEREJOHN

### I. INTRODUCTION

We may say that a legal system satisfies the requirements of the rule of law if its commands are general, knowable, and performable.[1] Generality is the requirement that the content of law not depend on particulars such as the identities of the subjects; it is sometimes said to require that that law be rulelike (even if it is not explicitly expressed as a system of rules).[2] Knowability requires that law be publicly promulgated and that changes in it be prospective in their effect.[3] Performability is the requirement that individuals could act in ways that satisfy its commands—particularly, that it not be contradictory or violate physical or other constraints on action. While no actual legal system could fully satisfy all these demands—indeed, generality seems transparently to conflict with knowability—we hold the rule of law as a normative standard with which to evaluate the regulation of our public life. Its virtues are rooted in elemental requirements of justice (a source of all three requirements) and efficiency (by allowing individuals and public bodies to rely on the anticipated operation of the legal system when making allocative choices among alternative courses of action).

At the same time, we value democratic institutions that can freely make or change laws as we or our legitimately elected representatives decide. But what assurance is there that such free and unfettered institutions will produce general, knowable, coherent, and complete systems of law? What assurance is there that a democratic government will exhibit rule of law features? There are several theoretical reasons for doubting the possibility of a reconciliation. Most elementally, there is no a priori reason to believe that an individual acting over time will make stable or coherent choices. The problems of dynamic consistency and commitment are ubiquitous and unavoidable even for single individuals. Secondly, the identity of the sovereign— democratic or otherwise—changes over time, and there is no reason to believe that sovereign desires, as opposed to actions, will be stable. Finally, the results of social choice theory and positive political theory suggest that, except under very unusual circumstances, even minimally democratic institutions will produce incoherent, unstable, and morally arbitrary sets of commands even within a static context.[4]

We can see therefore that there is a deep tension between sovereignty and lawlikeness. Moreover, the tension between democracy and law is especially profound in the sense that it puts our strongly held normative beliefs in popular sovereignty directly into conflict with our equally strong attraction to justice. While this tension is theoretically unresolvable, practically it can be ameliorated in several ways. On one reading of our constitutional traditions, we have tried historically to structure our institutions in such a way that they preserve some responsiveness to public desires while still remaining responsive to the requirements of justice. In effect, this has led the founders and their heirs to try to check majoritarian impulses by imposing institutional requirements such as bicamerality, executive veto, and special majority requirements, each of which has the effect of limiting somewhat the incoherence of the system of majority commands. At the same time, we have tried to remedy the ill effects of democratic impulses by allowing the judiciary some authority to make the system of (incoherent) commands more lawlike through interpretation and construction. Indeed, the justice-based requirement of generality is a virtual guarantee of judicial discretion.

While these two constitutional methods might seem distinct, they are both attempts explicitly or implicity to arrange institutions and therefore institutional incentives in such a way as to ameliorate the tension between democratic rule and law by reducing the incoherence of legislated outcomes.[5] Unfortunately, there is no reason to believe that limitations on majorities of the sort found in modern constitutions could be sufficient to eliminate statutory incoherence.[6] Moreover, the courts themselves remain chronically vulnerable to political forces within the constitutional structure, and judicial rulings, insofar as they are aimed to increase lawlikeness, must often be countermajoritian and therefore politically unpopular.[7] Is there any reason to think that courts so embedded in a political structure will work to bring coherence and justice to law?[8]

There seems to be no purely institutional justification for such faith. It is hard to see how either the conditions of their employment and tenure, or institutional protections for their decisions, would automatically produce judges oriented to lawlikeness. An assurance, if one is to be forthcoming, must come from some other source, and we suggest that this source may be found in what we shall call *interpretive regimes*, which are systems of norms or conventions that regulate the interpretation of legal materials, including statutes. The norms in an interpretive regime tell courts and citizens how strings of words in statutory commands will be interpreted and applied to cases, what presumptions will be entertained as to the scope and effect of legal commands, and what auxiliary materials will be employed to resolve ambiguities. Interpretive regimes are not arbitrary collections of norms but typically rest on conceptions of public life and the political process—that is, on political theories—and they inherit some of their persuasive powers from being so grounded. The hypothesis we explore is that the integrity of an interpretive regime provides some degree of insulation against political forces surrounding courts, and can work to increase lawlikeness. Having said that, we believe that regimes can be critically evaluated with respect to their capacities simultaneously to enhance the democratic and lawlike properties of our public life.

In this chapter we develop the idea of an interpretive regime as a set of conventions that restrain and regulate judicial action. Regimes are conventional in that they are partially arbitrary rules for interpreting legislation. Viable conventions must permit law to be general, knowable, and performable, while at the same time respectful of legislative acts. They should also be politically robust and self-enforcing so that legislators, executives, and judges can believe they will be employed. And they should be democracy enhancing in the sense of encouraging legislative deliberation. Nevertheless, interpretive regimes will have distributional consequences as well, so that the grounds for choosing among them, therefore, must in the end remain political.

We argue that the effects of interpretive regimes are profound and ubiquitous. For example, any satisfactory theory of legislatures must contain a specification of the interpretive regime. Otherwise, legislators wouldn't be able to know what they were voting on, or to form coherent strategies for casting their votes. Shifts in regimes, if they can be identified, ought therefore to have profound effects on both the quality of legislation and legislative deliberation. In turn, interpretive regimes should affect the sorts of tasks the government can undertake.

We also ask whether (and how) a well-specified theory of interpretation requires or rests on a theory of the legislative process. We could, to be sure, propose the same kind of answer that we gave to the first question: insofar as court interpretations can (and sometimes do) provoke congressional reactions, judicial interpretation must rest on anticipations of congressional responses.[9] A main goal of this chapter is to explore answers to this second question more deeply in order to get a clearer idea of how we might explain the evolution of interpretive systems.

## II. Political Theory and Interpretive Regimes

Interpretive regimes are made up of norms and conventions governing the interpretation of legal materials. These elements are generally unified according to shared conceptions of public life and politics. For example, one conception of politics holds that there is a (possibly unique) set of "just" laws—laws that would optimally regulate social behavior in ways that permit the living of good lives by citizens—appropriate to the body politic. Democratically elected legislators are well motivated to identify these rules and embody them in statutes (insofar as they are able to overcome their own frailties), and democratic executives and judges seek willingly to read and implement these statutes in light of the underlying conception of justice. Because of the coherence of natural law, statutory law will tend to be coherent as well, with inconsistencies traceable to judicially correctable cognitive "errors." This idea of "natural law" as regulative of actual law rests on two assumptions: first, that a coherent shared conception of justice exists and is sufficiently complete to guide the formation of law; second, that democratic institutions—legislatures, agencies, and courts—are both competent and well motivated to identify and implement it.

A second, more institutional, approach is perhaps more common—one that recognizes that very different normative expectations surround legislatures and courts. While legislatures are designed to give statutory expression to public opinion in an open and responsive fashion, courts have a special responsibility and competence to find generality (rules), coherence, and lawlikeness in statutes, even when (especially when) statutes themselves fail to possess these properties. The legal process view requires that courts find ways to interpret legislative statutes, which permits them to be lawlike while respecting the authority of their provenance.[10] The authority of law, on this view, rests both on its lawlikeness and on its institutional pedigree.[11] Inevitably, the expectation that courts treat law as general, stable, and coherent sometimes conflicts with the requirement that they respect the commands of the other branches. The special duty of courts to resolve these conflicting claims, so it is said, requires that they be insulated from other institutions and social forces in order that their members be provided with protections from democratic and other temptations.

Central to both these approaches is the idea that what the legislature does is systematically related to what the law is, but the nature of the connection is profoundly different. On the natural law account, courts and legislatures are both engaged in a cognitive or epistemic enterprise. The legislature seeks to identify and enact a system of laws that is already coherent; courts are engaged in applying received legislative statutes to factual situations, and employ statutes as one window, among others available to them, on the natural law. Judicial deference to legislatures would be based only on the relative cognitive competence of legislatures to discover what law requires.

On the legal process view, legislative action contains volitional as well as cognitive aspects. Courts are to exhibit deference to legislative actions because representatives are institutionally competent and motivated to express public sentiment. Unless there is evidence of constitutional distortions in the expression of public sentiment, courts should not try to look behind legislative actions. If the resulting legislative commands are incoherent, courts must find ways maximally to give them force, subject to the constraints of lawlikeness. One way to do this is to interpret statutes as having purposes, not on the ground that they "really" do, but because such an interpretive principle best supports a rule of law within a democratic society.

These two conceptions of politics differ fundamentally in the matter of how courts are to regard legislative action. On the first conception, the legislature is engaged in cognition; in the nature of such activity, its perceptions can be wrong and justifiably may be corrected. Insofar as the information base for the correction is made known to legislatures, they can be expected to concur in the judicial decision. On the second view, however, the legislature is signaling the courts as to the desires and wishes of its members or their constituents and must, on ordinary grounds of institutional competence, be presumed to be correct in its assessments.[12] The grounds for judicial correction rest not on a theory of legislative "error" but on an appeal either to what the Constitution or formal justice requires, or to the requirement that the law be presumed to be coherent.

### III. Legislation and Interpretation

The past quarter-century has brought a great increase in interest among political scientists in the way that legislatures work. Beginning in the late 1950s, the number of empirical investigations of legislative behavior began to multiply. Early studies often focused on how individual members of legislatures decided how to vote in formal roll calls. Over the next few decades, increased attention was paid to the internal structures of legislatures—committees, party leadership institutions, and caucuses of various sorts—and to an effort to understand how legislators behaved in these venues as well. Many of these early investigations tried to understand congressional practices as sociological/organizational phenomena: complex sets of norms, beliefs, and roles that supported and sustained both the institutions and acceptable standards of behavior. These studies often saw the production of legislation as more or less instrumental to maintaining integrated institutional structures.

These early empirical and theoretical investigations have been followed, more recently, by efforts to understand how legislative institutions coordinate the activities of ambitious politicians anxious to pursue their own separate goals. This work, rooted to some extent in social choice theory as well as in game theory, has sought to understand the ways in which the production of legislative products—including statutes—can be understood as the product of the interaction of economic agents. Like the empirical work that preceded and informed it, much of the modern theory of legislatures pays attention to their complex internal structures and attempts to see how it is that such institutions affect legislative behavior and the production of legislation. And, as in the earlier theories, legislation is only one of the products of a legislature, and not necessarily the most important one from the members' points of view.

Within the legal profession, there has been increasing interest in theories of statutory interpretation—what we have called interpretive regimes—over the past half-century. To a certain extent, this interest is fueled by practical concerns—most of what lawyers do in the modern regulatory state rests intimately upon the interpretation of ambiguous, contradictory, or incomplete statutes. But the interest is broadly abstract as well — traceable both to changing understandings of language and linguistic convention and to an appreciation of the stakes involved — and during the 1980s theories of statutory interpretation blossomed like dandelions in springtime.[13]

Before the 1980s, most theories of statutory interpretation emphasized the original intent or purpose of the legislators enacting a statute. Such theories saw legislatures as assemblies of legitimately chosen representatives of the people, assembled to find and implement some shared public purposes through the use of statutes. The job of interpretation was to identify or find those purposes in order to help give them legal effect. In the 1980s, the cogency of this view came under attack from two quarters. A new and robust form of textualism, drawing some of its inspiration from public choice theory, debunked concepts of intent and purpose and argued that statutory text is the only legitimate basis for ascertaining statutory meaning. Theories of dynamic statutory interpretation, on the other hand, challenged the claims of static meaning made by both traditional and textualist theories and emphasized the ways in which statutes (legitimately) change over time to reflect changing contexts, norms, and public values.

Several of the conceptual battlegrounds for competing theories of statutory interpretation have involved alternative theories or conceptions of legislatures. Thus, the different theories of interpretation argue that their approaches make the best sense of the legislative process. The new textualists argue that their theory is most consistent with the actual operation of the legislature, which they consider chaotic and rent seeking, while dynamic theorists argue that their theory is most consistent with our best aspirations for the operation of the legislative process.

Taking a consistently beady-eyed view of the legislative process, the new textualists are harshly critical of the traditional theory's reliance on legislative history to interpret statutes, because these sources are likely to be slanted toward "extreme" and not "median voter" interpretations and (in the case of committee reports, the main focus of attack) are written by staff and not the legislators themselves. The new textualists, in turn, have been criticized by dynamic theorists for their own reliance on canons of statutory construction, which are (in the eyes of the critics) more undemocratic than committee reports, because they are created by, and sometimes manipulated by, unelected judges.

In our view, all of these legal theoretical debates involve conceptions of the legislative process that need to be articulated and discussed. For this reason, we think it worthwhile to investigate the issue of the connections between theories of statutory interpretation and theories of legislatures and to ask, in particular, whether (and how) an acceptable theory of interpretation is connected to an adequate theory of legislative behavior.

## IV. Theories of Interpretation and Legislative Behavior: A Defense of the Old Legal Process against the New Textualism

As we suggested above, an adequate theory of legislative behavior must rest on expectations of how statutes would be interpreted in agencies or courts. When legislators vote on statutes or logroll to cement statutory deals and compromises, they are assuming consequences they expect statutes to have in the world (or consequences their political party, their constituents, or relevant interest groups think the statutes will have). Because these consequences depend on how statutes are interpreted by courts and agencies, legislator assumptions involve their understanding of how courts and agencies will go about interpreting statutes. Thus, in equilibrium, if the mode of interpretation were to shift, so too would rational legislative behavior; legislators would require different assurances before signing onto deals and before casting their votes. In this regard, interpretative regimes can be seen as "causing" or "inducing" legislative behavior.

This elementary fact about the equilibrium relationship between legislation and interpretation is sometimes missed, for any of three reasons. First, analysts implicitly assume a trivial theory of interpretation. Legislators, in most models, are thought to act as though interpreted outcomes are identical to the alternatives being voted on in the legislature. But there is no theoretical reason why this should be so, and in fact it is not true empirically. Second, in thinking about interpreting statutes, analysts often contemplate shifts in interpretation that are "surprises" to the legislature. The legislature produces law x on the expectation that the interpreted outcome by the agency will be a(x), but then the agency interprets x as permitting some other outcome, y. Such unexpected outcomes obviously do not play a causal role in producing legislative behavior. We doubt that courts or agencies could consistently fool the more political branches over the medium or long term, however. Whatever these interpretive bodies do, the legislature will form more or less accurate expectations, and these will be employed when it makes choices. Third, legal analysts in particular assume that the legislature is generally not aware of how its statutes are interpreted. That assumption only reveals the rudimentary state of lawyers' understanding of the legislative process and is demonstrably false.[14]

The primary implication of this observation is that legislative action is conditioned by expectations of court behavior and cannot be comprehended independently of those expectations. What about the reverse connection? In what sense does an interpretative regime depend upon a shared conception of legislative behavior? The leading theorists of the new textualism— Judge Frank Easterbrook and Justice Antonin Scalia—constantly refer to the way things "really are" in Congress as a reason for ignoring legislative history and arguments of fairness. Easterbrook argues, for example, that much legislation really amounts to logrolls or bargains among private interests and that, while the actual letter of such laws must be enforced by the courts, there is no reason to construe such statutes broadly by using gap-filling or other interpretive methodologies.[15] Scalia, arguing against the use of legislative history in statutory construction, depicts such materials as expressions by nonrepresentative staff members or extreme supporters of the legislation. Both of these descriptions of various aspects of the legislative process are offered as "facts" about legislatures or at least about the Congress.[16] Maybe these are facts about Congress. But even if Congress is filled with venal, short-sighted people seeking lesser goals than the public good, does this license the courts to adopt a narrow interpretive theory?

Legal scholars have thus far criticized Easterbrook and Scalia by questioning their description of the legislative process[17] or by suggesting that courts must defer to the process, warts and all.[18] Our observation offers a third way of criticizing Easterbrook and Scalia: legislative action cannot be understood independently of anticipations of judicial interpretation, as they assume, but is partly induced or caused by it. We can see this by examining Scalia's complaint that legislators let their staffs write committee reports without much supervision.[19] But, in equilibrium, the degree of legislator supervision of staff-written reports will in large part be determined by legislators' anticipations about the role committee reports play in statutory interpretation. If courts are believed to place substantial weight on committee reports (as has traditionally been the case), legislators will have a powerful incentive to ensure that staff members write reports that carefully reflect their views[20] and accurately depict whatever deals have been made. There will be careful legislator supervision of staff. If, on the other hand, legislators let their staffs write committee reports in a completely unsupervised fashion, it's because they believe that courts will not treat those reports very seriously. In either case, the accuracy and informativeness of committee reports depends on the way courts use such materials in statutory construction. Thus, insofar as Scalia's textualism prevails, his claim about the relationship between reports and congressional intent becomes self-fulfilling.

Easterbrook's argument has the same characteristic. Suppose that legislators believed (truthfully) that statutes would generally be construed liberally, with courts and agencies attributing purposes to enacted laws and filling gaps in them. Facing such interpretive practices, an attempt by private interests to enact a narrowly based logroll would be seen by members of Congress as having relatively far-reaching third-party effects, and would rationally provoke a high level of congressional scrutiny. If, conversely, the courts are thought to construe such bargains narrowly, there is no reason for unaffected members of Congress to monitor such agreements closely, and such legislation will tend to move though Congress relatively easily.[21] Easterbrook's proposal is, like Scalia's, self-fulfilling, in that its adoption would provide incentives for rational legislators to adopt the form of behavior that it describes (and condemns).

Of course, that a theory is self-fulfilling is not a sufficient reason for rejecting it. Indeed, in this setting the opposite is the case: that a theory cannot be self-confirming is a decisive argument against it. But a practical yet powerful criticism of the new textualists is suggested by our analysis. There would seem to be many candidates for self-fulfilling theories of interpretation, and these alternatives need explicitly to be considered and compared. Both Easterbrook and Scalia tend to be iconoclasts acting under the aegis of democratic theory: they claim they are "returning" statutory interpretation to an approach (textualism) that better reflects what is true of the legislative process, after a long period of doctrinal error (original intent and purpose) that did not reflect the true characteristics of the legislative process. But what "truth" amounts to here is itself questionable.

Our analysis suggests not only that these theoretical claims are questionable, and therefore that they offer no unique "reality" advantage, but also that substituting their approach for the traditional approach would be positively antidemocratic, in at least two separate senses. First, since the New Deal, federal statutory interpretation has been strongly purposive. This has had the predictable effect of encouraging legislative deliberation, especially detailed and informative committee reports, in part premised upon the legislative assumption that such materials would be important in subsequent interpretation of the statutes. If in the 1980s and 1990s the Supreme Court starts interpreting all of these statutes according to the stingy approach of the new textualists, the Court is betraying the assumptions under which these statutes were written. While we agree with Easterbrook and Scalia that Congress in the future could adjust to a new interpretive approach, their methodology, if applied retroactively, would amount to an unconstitutional game of "bait and switch."[22]

Even if we assume that the new textualists' approach were only to be applied prospectively, our analysis suggests a second line of criticism: before the Court adopts such an approach, it is necessary to evaluate the kinds of outcomes such an approach would support. Both Scalia's and Easterbrook's recommendations as to how statutes should be construed would, in equilibrium, produce nondeliberative legislative processes in which the legislature would be simply a place where sufficiently powerful private interests were able from time to time to capture control of the coercive powers of the state for their own use. Such a legislative process would, on their view, be best seen as a price that we must pay in order to remain a democracy. On the views of others, though, such a legislative process is hardly the best that our country can make it.

This is a splendid insight suggested by traditional legal process theory, whose purpose-based theory of statutory interpretation was grounded upon the presumption that the statute was "the work of reasonable [legislators] pursuing reasonable purposes reasonably."[23] Although the new textualists and others criticize Hart and Sacks for making unrealistic assumptions about the legislative process, that is off the mark, since they were offering a normative and not a descriptive theory of legislatures. Our analysis in this paper is receptive to Hart and Sacks's approach, because it may induce Congress to behave in a more public-regarding way. Having made this observation, though, we must immediately qualify it.

The fact that legislators rationally anticipate agency and court behavior does not imply that just any form of legislative behavior can be supported by a suitable set of expectations about interpretation. There may be some things that legislatures—by virtue of their institutional characteristics—are simply incapable of doing. An example is be found in the collective choice literature. No matter how a legislature is conceived, as long as its members pursue goals through the use of voting strategies, it is effectively impossible for it to issue completely coherent patterns of statutes. A theory of interpretation that is based on the assumption that such coherence is possible (such as Hart and Sacks's interpretive principles) needs to show how it is that interpreted law is connected to statutes.[24]

Thus, the connection between the theory of legislatures and the theory of statutory interpretation must be subtler than anything yet found in the literature. While the theory of legislatures must rest on anticipated interpretations, the theory of interpretation may or may not be causally related to judges' expectations or beliefs about legislatures. It is not yet clear in what sense an adequate theory of statutory interpretation is constrained by a theory describing what legislatures actually do or are capable of doing. There seem to be at least two theoretical possibilities, both of which are suggested in the Hart and Sacks legal process materials and have been developed by the intellectual heirs of Hart and Sacks: (1) normativism, under which courts and agencies adopt modes of interpretation leading to normatively attractive policy, ignoring the response this will evoke from the legislature,[25] and (2) conventionalism, under which courts and agencies choose interpretive stances having the property that equilibrium legislative behavior confirms the interpretive assumptions.[26] Conventionalist interpretive theories have the feature that the legislature actually does behave as the court assumes in interpreting legislation. The conventionalist court is fundamentally bound by what we shall call the *capacities* of the legislature in that its assumptions about the legislative process have to be the kind of thing that could be true of a legislative process. A normatively oriented court seems not to be so bound: it seeks to produce the best pattern of interpretive law that it can, no matter what patterns of behavior this produces in the legislative process.[27]

## V. LIMITS OF INDUCING LEGISLATIVE BEHAVIOR THROUGH INTERPRETIVE THEORY: A CRITIQUE OF STRONG NORMATIVISM

The cautious, and largely submerged, normativism of Hart and Sacks has been the starting point for explicitly normativist theories of interpretation in the 1980s. There are two types of normativist theories. The first, which we call "weak normativism," suggests that substantive policy presumptions exert a pervasive influence on statutory interpretation.[28] We reserve analysis of weak normativism for the next section. In this section, we analyze "strong normativism," the view that statutory interpreters should always read statutes in light of overarching moral norms, to make our law the "best" that it can be.[29] Ronald Dworkin's theory of "law as integrity" is the most celebrated example of strong normativism in the literature, and our analysis will focus on his account.[30]

Dworkin argues that both courts and legislatures should treat what he calls "integrity" as a positive value of law. "Integrity demands that the public standards of the community be both made and seen, so far as this is possible, to express a single, coherent scheme of justice and fairness in the right relation."[31] Integrity requires of the legislature that it refrain from enacting piecemeal or "checkerboard" patterns of law (which include logrolling and private bargains) but attempt (where it does not conflict with other values) to produce a coherent pattern of legislation that could be construed as flowing from a single will.[32] Integrity perhaps requires even more of courts acting as interpreters of legislation. A court guided by integrity will think that litigants "are entitled, in principle, to have their acts and affairs judged in accordance with the best view of what the legal standards of the community required or permitted at the time they acted, and integrity demands that these standards be seen as coherent, as the state speaking with a single voice."[33]

For Dworkin, the attraction of integrity as the primary value guiding legislation and interpretation is normative and not descriptive. The reason why legislatures should enact coherent patterns of statutes and courts should interpret the law as coherent (even where the statutes themselves are not) is that the public life of the community is better if this way is followed. He recognizes that his counsel would have the effect of condemning checkerboard statutes and judicial interpretations that enforce them.

Our criticism of Dworkin's version (and other versions) of strong normativism is not that it is somehow wrong or misguided but, rather, that it is dangerously incomplete. This is illustrated by the dilemma Dworkin faces when interpreting legislative logrolls. Would his interpreter ("Hercules," in a bit of significant nomenclature) invalidate all legislative logrolls or would he (like Easterbrook) urge them to construe such bargains narrowly?

The former course of action (invalidation) risks conflict with democratic values, which are after all fundamental to Dworkin's "community of integrity." That is, even Dworkin admits that logrolls might be necessary for the enactment of worthy legislation. If Hercules were to invalidate all logrolls, then legislators desiring to enact needed legislation cannot credibly offer compromise provisions and logrolls to undecided or opposing legislators, because all would know that these checkerboard statutes would not be enforced. Once logrolls become unavailable as a bargaining chip, a lot of worthy legislation becomes impossible or greatly delayed, such as the civil rights and environmental statutes, all of which are filled with checkerboard rules that reflect logrolls needed to surmount opposition.

The second course (narrow interpretation) offers much less of a risk that good but imperfect legislation will be defeated but poses another sort of risk: encouraging legislative behavior that is nondeliberative, something inconsistent with Dworkin's vision of the legislature. The overall sense of his writing suggests that Dworkin would opt for the broader interpretive stance (invalidation), but if he does, much more needs to be said about what kind of consequences this would have for the kind of government we could have and the pattern of law we would have to live with.

This points to a larger problem with Dworkin's theory: while it might aspire to a global integrity in our statutory law, it can induce the legislature to produce laws that do not yield checkerboard patterns only if broadly construed. But, if broadly construed, strong normativism would seem to emasculate government by preventing the enactment of important legislation. But if weakly construed, strong normativism seems to lack the rational expectations property that we argue is a necessary condition for a theory of statutory construction to be attractive. This does not mean that some version of normativism is not viable as a theory of statutory interpretation; it only means that the strongest versions of normativism will not work.

## VI. The Canons of Statutory Construction as a
## Basis for Workable Normativist and
## Conventionalist Theories

Interpretive regimes typically employ canons to construe the meanings of words, to fill gaps, or to resolve ambiguities in statutes. This practice is often thought to be analogous to the use of such techniques in construing contracts. Because of the costs of considering them, statutes, like contracts, are inherently incomplete in that they generally do not take account of all future contingencies that could arise. For statutes, like contracts, courts have created a collection of "off-the-rack" gap-filling rules that are accessible *ex ante* to the drafters. The practice of using canons as interpretive devices is, on this account, a relatively efficient method of filling in gaps and resolving ambiguities in incompletely specified laws. Faced with the judicial practices of statutory construction, legislators, like contractors in a market, can economize on the effort to contemplate and treat each future possibility.

This view of the canons—what we might call the *contract model*—dominates traditional treatises on statutory interpretation; it might be called *purely conventionalist,* in that canons are seen as interpretive conventions that permit a more efficient policy-making process. On this view, the public adoption of conventions of interpretation permits legislators to economize on the use of their limited time and resources while permitting members (and citizens) to anticipate the effects their statutes will have.

The contract model has severe deficiencies as a model of legislation. Because statutes can be enacted by bare majorities but have application far beyond the interests of those responsible for their drafting and enactment, statutes are plagued by "third party effects" (i.e., minorities). This possibility is classically termed the problem of "majority tyranny." Unlike the case of bilateral contracts (without external effects), we cannot assume that the use of canons as interpretive devices will lead to overall efficiency gains. Canons may make it easier to write statutes, but these statutes will frequently impose harms on some people. For this reason, the evaluation of interpretive methods, including canons and other interpretive conventions, remains inherently political and must rest on an assessment of the overall effects of such methods on the quality of legislation that is produced.

Analytically, we view the choice of interpretive methods and specifically the choice of canons as a choice among alternative conventions, and recognize that alternative sets of canons may lead to distributions of welfare that cannot be compared according to an efficiency criterion. The choice and defense of interpretive conventions requires normative grounding. Because efficiency notions are evidently too weak to do the job, such grounding must be sought elsewhere in political theory. This understanding of the canons is *weakly normativist* (in the sense that normative principles are required to justify interpretive conventions) and has been the basis for the recent revival in legal academic interest in the canons as a way in which "public values" influence statutory interpretation.

Legal realists, both recent and long departed, often regard the use of canons as fundamentally deceptive and misleading. They argue that there are so many canons available to a judge and that they are in such obvious and flagrant conflict with each other that they are merely used ex post, to explain decisions reached on other grounds.[34] And they argue that at least some of the canons are based upon unrealistic assumptions about legislatures, such as omniscience about the law.[35] Realists deny that the canons can reliably constrain courts and suggest that their invocation only obscures what is really going on in adjudication (which is "really" a response to the private values of judges or to economic forces).

Like the new textualists' criticism of legislative intent or purpose, the realists' criticism of the canons rests on a misunderstanding of the value of conventions of interpretation in a well-functioning system of law. The critics mistake the canons of statutory construction for a mechanical jurisprudence that mindlessly applies rigid formulas to resolve new cases, and fails to see that canons have another function altogether in regulating the interactions of courts and legislatures. Most fundamentally, the realists, by locating their conception of "reality" outside of and independent from the operation of the legal system, fail to see the sense in which social, economic, and political reality (pick your poison) responds to judicial practice.

We argue that the canons are conventions—just as the practice of driving a car on the right-hand side of the road is a convention—and that the practice of using them can allow agents, in this case legislators, to coordinate their behavior in ways that would not be possible, or as easy, without them. A canon is *efficient* if its use permits the drafting and enacting of legislation that improves everyone's well-being relative to not using a canon. Two canons are *equivalent* if they permit the actors to attain identical levels of utility or well-being. Thus, we can now set forth our central idea about the canons: where each set of canons is efficient and all are equivalent, legislative agents should be indifferent as to which set of canons is employed in the courts as long as one of them is. This elementary idea has an analytical payoff for both the new textualist and the weak normativist theories of statutory interpretation developed in the 1980s.

Perhaps the most valuable insight of the new textualists is their insistence that the "grammar" canons (those relating to grammar, word choice, and inference from different gramatical or syntactical configurations) be taken seriously. Scalia has set forth the precise reason why they should be: "What is of paramount importance is that Congress be able to legislate against a background of clear interpretive rules, so that it may know the effect of language it adopts."[36] Much of the Supreme Court's work in the 1980s consisted of elaborating upon, and bringing Congress's attention to, its collection of grammar canons. We consider this effort to be the most worthwhile thing the Court has done in statutory interpretation, even when the grammar canons are "unrealistic."

Consider, for example, the canon *expressio unius est exclusio alterius,* which directs that if a statute contains an enumeration of individuals or categories eligible for special treatment, omitted items are rebuttably presumed not to be so eligible. This long-standing grammar canon has been acidly criticized by virtually everyone because it is logically deficient. Yet Scalia has made it a cornerstone of his interpretive lexicon, and we support his effort. Under Scalia's approach (and we should hope even before its current revival), legislative drafters seeking to implement legislative preferences through statutes know in advance that if they want to make lists in their statutes the lists should be exhaustive, and that if they have little confidence in the exhaustiveness of their lists they should either forego listing or indicate that the list is not intended to be exhaustive. Of course, one can imagine an "equivalent" canon in which the items in a list would be scrutinized to see what feature they all possess and then all items with such features would be made eligible for the special treatment in the statute. In that case legislators would be induced to use "illustrative" lists rather than exhaustive ones. In either case, the use of the interpretive canon induces a corresponding practice of drafting legislation. What is important is not which of two equivalent canons is recognized by the Court, but instead that the Court's approach be "transparent" to Congress. In short, the practice of consistently recognizing and deploying particular canons allows for a degree of coordination between the legislature and the judiciary, and reduces uncertainty in the legislative drafting and bargaining process.

Even if two coherent collections of canons are each efficient, they may not be equivalent. The use of one set of canons rather than another may affect the distribution of benefits and costs within the legislative bargaining process. This feature is most apparent in the "substantive" canons, namely, those canons that represent presumptions in favor of a certain substantive policy. For example, the rule of lenity posits that the Court will not impose a punitive sanction upon defendants unless directed to do so by clear statutory text.[37] This canon has distributive consequences, which are subject to serious normative debate. On the one hand, it makes it easier for criminal defendants to escape punishment due to a "technicality" and makes it harder for government to punish wrongdoing in a highly technical, dynamic society. On the other hand, the rule of lenity constrains prosecutorial discretion and conveys to the citizenry that we will not be prosecuted for activity that a reasonable person would not have considered criminal under relevant statutes. Weak normativists generally endorse the rule of lenity (mainly for its due process value) but question other substantive canons as unjustified in the modern regulatory state.

Certain of the substantive canons have become a battle-ground between the new textualists and the weak normativists—specifically, the presumptions and clear statement rules protecting values of sovereign immunity and federalism.[38] The Court's textualists (and their allies) have vigorously enforced clear statement canons against congressional abrogation of state and federal immunities from lawsuits and congressional invasion of state autonomy. Weak normativists object to the Court's clear statement rules to the extent that they sacrifice individual rights in exchange for hard-to-defend values associated with sovereign immunities. They also object that the Court has "changed" the federalism-based canons in ways that amount to the "bait and switch" that we criticize above.

## VII. The Use of Extrinsic Sources

Perhaps the most controversial area of statutory interpretation centers on the use of evidence surrounding the enactment and interpretation of legislation in construing its meaning: floor debates, committee reports, statements by sponsors before, during, or after legislative enactment of a statute. One common justification of the use of such sources is to permit courts or agencies to determine the intentions that the legislature, or at least important legislators, might have had in enacting the statute. We call such justifications "intentionalist" for obvious reasons.

Another, more subtle, argument is this: statements in a committee report or by a floor manager may provide evidence as to common understandings of people interacting in the area in question. Such statements may embody what is generally understood by people (potential litigants, etc.) in the area and may be employed by courts to resolve ambiguities in the statute. Such a justification might be termed "contextualist." Both of these justifications might be thought to be connected to inherent problems of making rules in a complex environment, and are in this sense similar to problems of writing contracts: because it is difficult to foresee all possible contingencies when writing statutes, such documents will generally be incomplete or even contradictory under some circumstances, forcing courts to make use of other devices to "fill gaps" or resolve ambiguities.

The new textualists are particularly scornful of the Court's traditional use of extrinsic sources to find legislative intent. There is no coherent way, it is said, to ascribe intentions to collective bodies, with the result that the "intentions" found in statutory construction exercises are either pure fiction or are the intentions of particular agents who have no greater claim than others to have their beliefs given special weight in the courts. The use of extrinsic sources to construct "intentions" or "purposes" results at best in arbitrary rulings and, at worst, in judicial interpretations that favor particular interests illegitimately. New textualists are also critical of the use of extrinsic sources to construct context: such practices endow (unelected) practitioners (and judges) with unearned legislative authority that ought to reside in the legislative process.

Yet the new textualists' use of (some of) the canons of statutory construction suggests a powerful defense of the use of extrinsic sources in statutory construction, under the analysis of this chapter. This defense is neither intentionalist nor contextualist but grounds the use of such sources in the idea of an interpretive convention. As canons do for statutes, the judicial practice of consulting extrinsic sources can affect the operation of the legislative process by giving significance to extrastatutory words and arguments employed in the legislative process. By according weight to statements made in debate and deliberation, courts can give those expressions weight within the deliberative process. If speakers and listeners all know that words spoken in the legislative process are accorded weight by courts and agencies, then members have an incentive to ensure that the record reflects his or her interpretation of the statute and that misleading or extreme interpretations do not stand unchallenged. Moreover, insofar as courts and agencies accord weight to deliberative statements, proponents of legislation are able to make credible persuasive statements, where otherwise such statements might not be possible.

For example, if courts rely on interpretations by legislative sponsors in interpreting statutes, sponsors gain the capacity to make *credible commitment* to an interpretation during legislative deliberations. The capacity to make commitments generally enlarges the scope of legislative agreements that can be reached and can be expected to affect the capacity of the legislature to produce statutes. Such justifications of the use of extrinsic sources might be termed *deliberative,* in the sense that they would seem to enhance the persuasive capacities of legislative deliberation.[39]

These ideas can be developed by considering the practice of using statements by a floor manager in interpreting a statute. The episode we examine is the Senate floor consideration of Title VII of the Civil Rights Act of 1964. It was generally known that before a vote could be taken on the House-passed bill (H.R. 7152) in the Senate, cloture would have to be imposed, in those days requiring the assent of two-thirds of those voting. Thus the Democratic floor manager, Hubert Humphrey, was faced with the task of getting the bill into a form that would be acceptable to two-thirds of the senators. As we see the political problem, Humphrey could count on the votes of most of the nonsouthern Democrats and liberal Republicans and, faced with the intransigent opposition of the southern Democrats, needed the votes of some conservative Republicans to obtain cloture against the southern filibuster. It was generally understood that, in order to avoid a conference, the House would accept any Senate amendments; hence, the floor debate in the Senate was crucial, and the pivotal voter was a conservative Republican.

As things evolved, it became clear that one of major issues of importance to conservative Republicans (and to their traditional business constituency) was in Title VII: did the language of Title VII require employers to adopt preferential quotas advantaging minorities? Senator Humphrey said in his opening speech on H.R. 7152: "Contrary to allegations of some opponents of this title, there is nothing in it that will give any power to the Commission or to any court to require hiring, firing or promotion of employees in order to meet a racial 'quota' or to achieve a certain racial balance."[40]

While there is still a lively dispute about what Humphrey's

words meant in 1964 or now, we suggest that it is useful to consider their use and meaning within his contemporary political context. In order to get the Senate to vote cloture, Humphrey had to persuade the marginal voters—led and personified by Senator Everett Dirksen, the minority leader of the Senate—that Title VII did not actually require employers to adopt quotas. While he *said,* and other supporters said, that Title VII did not require employers to use racial quotas, it was apparent that not everyone was convinced.

They were not convinced, because it was not clear how an interpreting court would use the statements by Humphrey and the other Senate sponsors in construing the meaning of Title VII. Lacking a credible commitment from the sponsors, the marginal voters wanted some kind of concrete assurance as to how courts would interpret the language of Title VII. Eventually, a bipartisan coalition (including Dirksen, Kuchel, Humphrey, and Mansfield) offered a successful amendment that, among other things, codified Humphrey's promise as section 703(j).[41]

In our view, the formal language of section 703(j) was necessary to convince marginal voters to support the legislation precisely because the legislative sponsors could not "commit" to an interpretation in the course of debate. If it had been the common practice in the interpretive regime for the courts to accord conclusive weight to nonstrategic statements of floor managers in the course of a debate on a critical vote (which in this case was the cloture vote), pivotal voters would have found such statements to be reliable guides to interpretation. In this sense, if the Court strongly signals to Congress that it will rely on such statements, their informativeness and usefulness in congressional debates would be enhanced, and Congress would become a more deliberative chamber than it would otherwise be.

Easterbrook or Scalia might suggest that it was a good thing that Dirksen proposed his amendments and got them formally agreed to by a majority vote. Indeed, they might argue that the fact that a majority was willing to vote for the amendments accords them greater democratic authority than judicial constructions would have. Insofar as we are speaking only of a specific legislative action like section 703(j), we have no quarrel with this response. The problem is that if the Court adopts the policy of ignoring sponsors' statements, *every* such agreement has to be encoded in the statute. By adopting such a policy, the Court would be effectively requiring Congress to write complete statutes, something that is impossible even if it were desirable. At the same time, such a policy impoverishes congressional debate by emptying sponsor promises (to pivotal voters) of reliable meaning.

Thus, from a conventionalist perspective, reliance on sponsor statements during floor debate prior to a critical vote would permit floor managers credibly to make commitments to those who need to be convinced, without formally amending the legislation itself. The legislative world produced by this policy would be one with simpler and more general statutes and more informative (and perhaps shorter) congressional debates.

## VII. Conclusion

The key concept we have introduced in this chapter is the idea of an interpretive regime, a notion for which we claim both positive and normative importance. Courts and the legal cultures surrounding them do in fact evolve shared and more-or-less integrated interpretive conventions that are applied to legal materials. These conventions permit coordination of judicial actions by establishing and maintaining expectations, both in courts and in the broader legal community, as to how legal texts will be read. At the same time, these conventions help to stabilize legislative expectations of judicial actions; and by establishing beliefs, they play a significant causal role in accounting for and regulating legislative activity. In this sense, by establishing an interpretive regime, courts help to establish and maintain rule of law.

That an interpretive regime can have such far-reaching consequences inevitably makes the choice among them intrinsically conflictual. At stake in the choice among regimes is not only the meaning of current statutes, but also the nature of judicial and legislative institutions and their roles in our public life. Because the stakes are so high and because they involve all of us, judges and legal commentators deserve no special deference in making this choice.

Court interpretation can affect both the kinds of statutes that are enacted and the nature of legislative deliberation. These effects are inescapably political, in the sense that they can have distributional consequences as well as implications for the nature of public life. In this sense, courts cannot avoid taking fundamental political positions, however implicitly, in deciding how to read the work of the legislature. As these issues are profoundly political, it seems especially unlikely that their resolution can turn on a set of factual claims about what it is that legislatures are "really" doing when producing a statute.

The view we have taken here is that statutes and theories of legislation are codependent. The form of this codependence suggests that certain theories of interpretation fit well with certain kinds of legislative processes. New textualist interpretation works to support a venal and small-minded Congress, filled with special pleaders, pasting together ad hoc coalitions to serve narrow interests. It produces this effect by discouraging those legislators concerned with the public weal from expending their scarce resources to prevent such narrow legislation. Alternative interpretive conceptions, on this account, can induce legislators to deliberate to more genuine consensus rather than constructing flimsy checkerboard statutes. We suggest that the best candidates for such an alternative construction are those that take seriously the reciprocal relationship between statutes and interpretation and induce legislators to adopt an expansive and responsible view of their role. We do not have a shortcut for producing such a theory: its elements will have to be debated and decided piecemeal with a view toward the pattern of law that results.

## NOTES

1. This listing of characteristics is related to those in Margaret Jane Radin, "Reconsidering the Rule of Law," *Boston University Law Review* 69 (1989): 781.

2. In the American constitutional tradition, generality may be un-

derstood as a strengthened form of the prohibition of bills of attainder. The classical theoretical expression can be found in Rousseau's *Social Contract*, in which he requires that legislative proposals be general in order to encourage or allow the sort of deliberation that would lead to a revelation of the "General Will" as opposed to the "Will of All."

3. Within the American tradition, knowability prohibits ex post facto bills.

4. See especially William Riker, *Liberalism against Populism* (New York: Freeman, 1982).

5. Though this is done at the price of increasing the influence of the inherited status quo on the legal structure.

6. Riker, *Liberalism against Populism*.

7. For explorations of the consequences of this vulnerability see Pablo Spiller and Rafael Gely, "A Rational Choice Theory of Supreme Court Statutory Decisions with Applications to the *State Farm* and *Grove City* Cases," *Journal of Law, Economics, and Organization* 6 (1990): 263, and the references cited there.

8. For an argument that courts can and should act so as to increase law's stability, and that such action can enhance democratic values, see John Ferejohn and Barry Weingast, "Limitation of Statute: Strategic Statutory Interpretation," *Georgetown Law Journal* 80 (1992): 565.

9. See Ferejohn and Weingast, "Limitation of Statute": also William N. Eskridge, Jr., "Overriding Supreme Court Statutory Interpretation Decisions," *Yale Law Journal* 101 (1992): 331.

10. Depending on how the interpretive regime is elaborated, courts may, at one extreme, maximize lawlikeness subject to a constraint of deference, or at another, maximize democratic deference subject to a coherence constraint.

11. Of course, legislators and executives are expected to enhance the stability and coherence of law as well, but it is expected that their institutional circumstances will more frequently tempt them to give too little weight to these values.

12. However, the various positive theories of legislatures provide ways to develop a theory of legislative error, pointing essentially to capture or corruption phenomena.

13. Peter C. Schanck, "The Only Game in Town: An Introduction to Interpretive Theory, Statutory Construction, and Legislative Histories," *Kansas Law Review* 38 (1990): 815.

14. Eskridge, "Overriding Supreme Court Statutory Interpretation Decisions."

15. Frank H. Easterbrook, "Statutes' Domains," *University of Chicago Law Review* 50 (1983): 533.

16. Antonin Scalia, Speech on legislative history, delivered at various law schools (1985–86).

17. Daniel J. Farber and Philip P. Frickey, *Law and Public Choice: A Critical Introduction* (Chicago: University of Chicago Press, 1991).

18. Richard A. Posner, *The Federal Courts: Crisis and Reform* (Cambridge, MA: Harvard University Press, 1985).

19. Scalia can hardly complain that the elected legislators do not do every bit of legislative work themselves. The actual words of statutes are not drafted by the legislators, but Scalia relies on the actual words because he assumes legislators pay careful attention to them and therefore monitor the words carefully (this is in fact empirically questionable, and it is quite possible that many legislators pay more careful attention to committee reports than to the statutory language). Additionally, it should be noted that most federal judges, including those on the Supreme Court, have law clerks draft their opinions. Yet judges consider the language and reasoning in the opinions to be authoritative, upon the (often quite flimsy) assumption that judges carefully monitor what their law clerks write.

20. There remains, of course, the question of whose "consensus"— the consensus of the legislature as a whole, the committee as a whole, or just the chief sponsors. In a one-dimensional model, reports might be more or less accurate depictions of what the median member of the chamber would agree to on issues, had she thought of them.

21. A good example of this might be seen in the politics of rivers and harbors legislation before the advent of environmentalism in the 1960s. Rivers and harbors bills in that period were typically made up of large collections of relatively small projects, each of interest to a small group of congressmen. Because the impact of the legislation was limited, such bills provoked little controversy, and they received relatively little attention on the chamber floors, rarely even provoking roll call votes. In effect, courts and agencies interpreted such legislation narrowly as bargains to deliver projects to specifically targeted constituencies; as long as the projects were not too costly, other members saw little reason to intervene. The environmental movement subverted this system by inducing members to consider how even small projects in remote districts should be seen as affecting their interests.

More broadly, the judicial practice of interpreting appropriations statutes narrowly encourages congressmen to treat such statutes as bargains targeting funds on specific groups, rather than as principled policy statements as to how government benefits should be distributed. Such an interpretive posture works to minimize the extent to which such legislation would be seen as having important third-party effects and should work to reduce its controversy.

22. William N. Eskridge, Jr., and John Ferejohn, "The Article I, Section 7 Game," *Georgetown Law Journal* 80 (1992): 523.

23. Henry Hart, Jr., and Albert Sacks, *The Legal Process: Basic Problems in the Making and Application of Law* (tentative edition, 1958), 1157.

24. In Hart and Sacks and in Dworkin, this is achieved by making the interpretive assumption—that legislation is thought to be purposive—into a normative assumption guiding the interpreter. Hart and Sacks ask courts to "deem" legislation as having a coherent purpose and Dworkin asks them to see legislation as written by a single hand. This assumption will, they suggest, yield better-*interpreted* law than would otherwise be produced and is therefore normatively justified even if it is not true and could not be true of any legislature.

25. Ronald Dworkin, *Law's Empire* (Cambridge: Belknap, 1986); Cass R. Sunstein, *After the Rights Revolution: Reconceiving the Regulatory State* (Cambridge, MA: Harvard University Press, 1990); William N. Eskridge, Jr., "Public Values in Statutory Interpretation," *University of Pennsylvania Law Review* 137 (1989): 1007.

26. Jonathan A. Macey, "Promoting Public-Regarding Legislation through Statutory Interpretation: An Interest-Group Model," *Columbia Law Review* 86 (1986): 223.

27. In a sense a normativist court is nonconsequentialist in its orientation to interpretation. It tries to make the best interpretation of the pattern of law it finds even if that induces behavior by others that leads to relatively bad consequences.

28. Eskridge, "Public Values in Statutory Interpretation"; *see* Sunstein, *After the Rights Revolution*.

29. T. Alexander Aleinikoff, "Updating Statutory Interpretation," *Michigan Law Review* 87 (1988): 238; Heidi M. Hurd, "Sovereignty in Silence," *Yale Law Journal* 99 (1990): 943.

30. Dworkin, *Law's Empire*.

31. Dworkin, 219.

32. Dworkin, 176.

33. Dworkin, 218.

34. Karl N. Llewellyn, "Remarks on the Theory of Appellate Decision and the Rules or Canons about How Statutes Are to Be Construed," *Vanderbilt Law Review* 3 (1950): 395.

35. Posner, *The Federal Courts: Crisis and Reform*.

36. *Finley v. United States*, 109 S. Ct. 2003, 2010 (1989).

37. James Willard Hurst, *Dealing with Statutes* (New York: Columbia University Press, 1982).

38. William N. Eskridge, Jr., and Philip P. Frickey, "Quasi-Constitutional Law: Clear Statement Rules as Constitutional Lawmaking," *Vanderbilt Law Review* 45 (1992): 593.

39. Note that increased deliberative capacities can have distributional as well as efficiency effects.

40. *Congressional Record* (1964), 110: 6549.

41. Currently codified as 42 U.S.C. § 2000e-2(j).

# PART IV

# LIMITS TO THE RULE OF LAW

# 13

# LIBERALISM AND THE SUSPECT ENTERPRISE OF POLITICAL INSTITUTIONALIZATION: THE CASE OF THE RULE OF LAW

## RICHARD FLATHMAN

Liberals who promote the ideals of individuality, plurality and freedom have sometimes been and ought always to be skeptical concerning institutionalism and wary of established political institutions.[1] As with "institutionalizing" a person, to institute an organization, arrangement, or procedure is to attempt to fix and to settle, to structure and to secure, to order and to control larger or smaller aspects of the thinking and acting of some number of human beings. It is to attempt to render uniform, constant, and predictable that which would otherwise be diverse, fluctuating, and uncertain. By adopting and enforcing the norms, rules, offices, and procedures of which institutions primarily consist, successful processes of institutionalization confine and direct the conduct of those who are subject to the arrangements that they establish.[2] As antinomians and individualist anarchists—whose thoughts haunt the best liberal thinking—constantly insist, these processes stand in a troubling and

Thanks to Bill Connolly, Sue Hemberger, and Kirstie McClure for helpful suggestions and good conversation concerning this essay.

often troubled relationship with the ideals of individuality, plurality, and freedom.

Of course liberalism as a specifically political tendency of thought cannot altogether do without institutions or entirely avoid commitment to the values forwarded by institutionalism. As an outlook that accepts (however ruefully) the all-things-considered desirability of some rule by government, liberalism is also obliged to accept the on-balance benefit of the institutionalization of some aspects of human affairs. Lacking the resolve or courage, perhaps reckless, of the antinomian and the anarchist, liberals perforce accommodate themselves to authority, power, and the fixity, structure, and control that those who possess them incessantly seek to establish.

As exemplified by prominent liberal treatments of the topic of this volume, influential liberal thinkers and much liberal practice have gone far beyond accommodating to institutionalization and institutions, have lost or suppressed awareness of the tensions between liberal ideals and the array of values and procedures that collect under the ideological rubric of institutionalism.

The minimal and least objectionable manifestation of institutionalist thinking is the view that institutionalized government can *contribute* to the realization of the ideals of individuality, plurality, and freedom. I have argued elsewhere that this is the view of that "proto-liberal" Hobbes,[3] and I maintain here that a stance akin to Hobbes's skepticism concerning institutionalism is the appropriate one for liberalism to take.

A substantially stronger manifestation of the tendency is the view, argued by Locke and Kant and dominant in liberal theory from Kant to Rawls, that institutionalized government is a *causally necessary* condition of the realization of liberal ideals. This view allows rejection of particular forms of government and sometimes includes skepticism concerning forms of institutionalization such as corporatism. But it excludes the possibility, held open by Hobbes's view, of circumstances in which commitment to the liberal ideals requires opposition to the institution of government as such. More serious, it loads the liberal argumentational and rhetorical dice against positions that seek to engender a nervous combination of grudging acceptance and pervasive suspicion of government and politics.

There are many further variations on these themes and instances of yet stronger connections between liberalism and institutionalism. Particular institutional forms—for example, representative or direct democracy, the separation of powers or cabinet government—are often viewed as strongly contributive to and even as necessary conditions of achieving liberal values and objectives. Such views inform bastard expressions like "liberal democracy" that conflate liberalism with a particular institutional form, and they are at the heart of theories of liberalism that consist in articulations of preferred institutional structures.

We have also been treated to delineations of liberal ideals, for example Montesquieu's definition of liberty as the "right of doing whatsoever the laws permit," that link those ideals *conceptually* and hence necessarily to particular institutional forms or arrangements.[4] On such views—for example, the *rechtsstaat*-cum-Hayekian view that virtually reduces "liberal society" to fidelity to the rule of law and liberalism to advocacy of such a society—there can be no conflict or tension between the ideal and the institution, not so much as the possibility of pursuing the ideal by weakening the institution. Liberalism melds into institutionalism such that the former cannot be understood or supported without reference to and support of the latter.

With the exception of the position I attributed to Hobbes, these views are hasty and otherwise ill considered. Theorists who proclaim a causally necessary or otherwise invariant relationship between an institutional form and the flourishing of liberal projects exceed the evidence on which they depend and introduce rigidity and overdetermination into liberal thinking and practice. All institutionalization necessarily disserves liberal ideals to some extent; empirically, the institutions that these positions privilege have sometimes worked largely for, have not infrequently worked importantly against, realization of them.[5]

Liberal proponents of the views to which I have alluded aim to use less dangerous forms of institutionalism to contain what they regard as at once the most necessary and most dangerous of all institutions. Convinced that government is essential to a liberal society, they seek to control what they fully expect to be persistent attempts to put its authority and power to unnecessary and otherwise unwarranted uses. They recognize that government's institutionalized standing, together with wide acceptance of the doctrine that established institutions ought to be supported, is the source of much of the danger that government poses. Accordingly, they look to institutionalization and institutionalism themselves as means of keeping government under restraint. They fight the dangerously spreading fire of institutionalized government with the fires of institutionalization. Those who, like Hobbes, depend primarily on non- or little-institutionalized means to keep government within proper bounds are regarded as favoring oppressive government, as naive, or both.

Abstractly considered, there are undeniable merits to the view that institutions and institutionalism can be potent weapons in the struggle to confine and control governmental authority and power. As intersecting and interwoven arrays of beliefs and ideas, principles and rules, offices and procedures, established institutions are concentrations of that which is regarded as authoritative, of formal authority itself, and often of expertise that gives individual persons the standing of authorities concerning certain subject matters and issues.[6] When buttressed by acceptance of the institutionalist view that the rules, procedures, and decisions of established institutions ought to be honored and obeyed, they also become formidable concentrations of power. Successful creation of a variety of institutions, within and without government, may enhance the resources of those who are disposed to restrict and control the activities of government. On the widely received assumption that authority and power can only or can best be controlled by authority and power themselves, institutionalization and institutionalism are necessary or valuable means of achieving this objective. The former propositions, and the latter plausible if risky assumption, inform the view that prudence, if not the science of government, requires intragovernmental institutional devices such as elections, federalism, and the separation of powers, as well as the proliferation of organized and well-provided extragovernmental institutions such as political parties and interest groups, corporations and unions, churches and professional associations.

Skepticism concerning this view, however, should not be confined to those whose objective is to maximize the range and the efficacy of governmental activity. The authority and power of all such institutions are exercised over those who are in their jurisdictions as well as against the activities of other institutions. If those in positions of institutional authority identify or agree with one another rather than with those who are subject to their jurisdictions—hardly a rare phenomenon—the proliferation of institutions is likely to weaken rather than advantage the positions of the latter. Whatever the merits, for our time, of Hobbes's view that it is less costly to sate the lusts of one than of many rulers, the day of optimistic eighteenth-century political mechanics has passed. We know too much about collusion and cooptation, about the oligarchic tendencies of bureaucratic and other forms of organizational behavior, about the proclivity of institutional elites to generate and effectuate hegemony over those subject to their rule.[7]

In the perspective I have outlined, the institution and form of institutionalism known as the rule of law offends several times over. Its very name doubles both the nominal and the verbal notions of imperative control. The desirability of some number of rules of the distinctively impositional type called laws is presupposed and a chief thrust of the theories that privilege the rule of law is that promulgated rules and laws ought strictly to govern the conduct of those to whom they apply. It is true that, taken abstractly or formally, the idea of the rule of law speaks primarily to the question of fidelity to law and leaves largely unresolved the issue of the proper scope and content of legal regulation.[8] Perhaps, however, because the significance of the institution they cherish would diminish to the extent that law became a negligible feature of social and political life, more likely because they prize the values of order, control, and predictability that they associate first and foremost with law, proponents of the rule of law have favored extensive use of lawmaking and law-implementing authority. And those of its advocates who have partly dissented from this recommendation have nevertheless held that "free" activities, for example those that occur in "the market," are successful only or primarily to the extent that they occur in the regularian setting established by perspicuous, general, and prospective legislation and sustained by an impartial and meticulously rule-governed bureaucracy and judiciary. Thus versions of institutionalism that strongly promote the rule of law typically accord high if not principal value to imperatival control and mandatory obedience.

It is less than obvious that this stance is favorable to individuality, plurality, and freedom. If in practice it has sometimes proven to be more favorable to those ideals than competing points of view, we have to consider whether this circumstance is itself an artifact of the too ready, the insufficiently skeptical and cautious, acceptance of the institution of government itself.[9]

# I

From Plato and Aristotle through the Roman jurists, the medieval natural law thinkers, the neo-Stoics and modern natural law theorists, Montesquieu and the American founders, the nineteenth-century advocates of the *rechtsstaat,* and up to contemporary enthusiasts such as Friedrich Hayek and John Rawls, Lon Fuller and Theodore Lowi, champions of the rule of law have assumed the desirability or at least the ineliminable reality of extensive political rule of human conduct. For the thinkers in this long and otherwise varied tradition, anarchism and antinomianism are not attractive but regrettably unrealizeable ideals; they are conditions to be disdained and feared. The dominant concern of these thinkers, accordingly, has not been with the question of whether or how much governance there should be, but rather with preventing arbitrariness and other misuses of political authority and power.

These general remarks obscure an imperfect but important distinction within rule of law thinking. In the *Laws* Plato treated a proper system of law as a poor but in all likelihood unsurpassable approximation of the ideal source of constraint, namely, fully philosophical knowledge of the good on the part of the rulers. In the *Politics,* Aristotle defined law as "reason without passion." Law suffers the limitations inherent in all practical reasoning and judging, but the laws of a well-conducted "polity" consolidate the best reasonings of its citizenry while the requirement that rule be by law diminishes the influence of the irrational passions of those "men" whose turn to rule happens to be now. On these views, as on various Roman, traditional, and modern natural law theories, and on theories of the common law as an accretion of the wisdom of experience, the idea of the rule of law includes requirements concerning the content that laws must or must not have in order that rule by them be justified. On some of these views, rules that do not satisfy such requirements are not laws at all and rule by them is not rule by law. On others, for example, those of Hobbes and his legal positivist followers, the question whether a rule is a law is decided by looking to its source, not its content, but laws that do not satisfy further criteria may not deserve obedience and rule by them may be unjustifiable.[10]

By contrast, the nineteenth- and twentieth-century thinkers who have given the idea of the rule of law its presently most influential formulations have labored to distinguish between the content of this or that law and the form or formal characteristics of law as such. Many of these thinkers are legal positivists who treat the source of law as its defining property. They argue, however, that the rule of law demands more than that all laws emanate from a jurally authoritative source. Rule by laws that lack characteristics such as clarity, generality, and prospectivity may be rule *by* law or "legality" but it does not meet the requirements of the rule *of* law. Similar requirements are imposed by antipositivist theorists of the rule of law. The theory of the rule of law leaves the content and particular purpose of this and that law to the lawmaking authorities. But it is part of the task of that theory to identify the qualities of law necessary to achieve the purposes of the institution that is the rule of law.

There is, moreover, substantial agreement among recent proponents of the rule of law that the chief such purpose is to subject human conduct to rules, thereby affording predictability in legal relationships and in the interactions that occur within the frame of law. It is also widely agreed that "arbitrariness," primarily defined as particularity and retroactivity but also as uncertainty and unpredictability (little if at all in terms of the intentions or purposes of particular lawmakers), is the single greatest antagonist of these objectives. Assessing these views, which now constitute the version of institutionalism that is the idea of the rule of law, is the present task.

## II

As is clear from the distinction between mere legality and the rule of law, the latter is a set of ideas that stands apart from law itself. The ideology provides criteria for determining the extent to which the requirements of the rule of law are satisfied by actual legal systems. Most proponents of the rule of law allow, moreover, that it is an ideal that legal systems may approach but can never entirely realize. This is true concerning those elements of the ideology that are themselves matters of more or less rather than either or, for example, stability, readiness of lay comprehension of the laws, and avoidance of conflicts among the laws.[11]

It is also true of requirements that are frequently taken to allow of complete satisfaction, such as the categorical prohibition of retroactivity and bills of attainder in criminal law. In actuality, *all* general and prospective laws, regardless of the clarity of their formulations, require interpretation in order to be applied to actions and events. For this reason, and because the ideology itself requires that criminal convictions be for actions already taken, those subject to laws can never be certain, when they act, whether their act will be adjudged legal or illegal.

The widest and deepest difficulties here reside in the two requirements most frequently associated with the rule of law, generality and prospectivity. In canvassing these difficulties I begin by attending to the fulsome formulations of Friedrich Hayek.

Often explained by contrasting laws with commands, the generality proper to law concerns the subject of laws in two senses: their addresses, that is, the persons who are subject to them; and their subject matters, that is, the actions they require or forbid. (I leave aside laws that permit or license rather than require or forbid.) The clearest case of a law that violates the requirement of generality in the first respect is a bill of attainder, a law addressed exclusively to an unambiguously identified person. Equally, the clearest case of a law that violates this requirement in the second respect is one that requires or forbids a particular action at a specified time and place. Thus, in both respects generality is defined by opposition to particularity.

As every reader of Rousseau will attest, it is far more difficult to give an affirmative account of generality. In respect to the addressees of laws, this is the vexed question of classification and of equality before the law. As Hayek concedes, classification is inevitable in law, but "[i]t must be admitted that, in spite of many ingenious attempts . . . no entirely satisfactory criterion has been found that would always tell us what kind of classification is compatible with equality before the law. To say . . . that the law must not make irrelevant distinctions or that it must not discriminate between persons for reasons which have no connection with the purpose of the law is little more than evading the issue."[12]

Matters are no easier in respect to generality in the second sense. To quote Hayek again, "Law in its ideal form might be described as a . . . command that is directed to unknown people and that is abstracted from all particular circumstances of time and place and refers only to such conditions as may occur anywhere and at any time." The notion of obedience to laws that meet these criteria of abstraction is at best elusive; subjects will have no easy time determining what conformity requires. And however perspicuous our *criteria* of generality might become, in all known legal systems the "degree of . . . abstractness ranges continuously from the order that tells a man to do a particular thing here and now to the instruction that, in such and such conditions, whatever he does will have to satisfy certain requirements." Thus "it is advisable . . . not to confuse laws and commands, . . . [but] we must recognize that laws shade gradually into commands as their content becomes more specific."[13]

The utility of conceptions related to Hayek's notion that all actions "will have to satisfy certain requirements" will concern us as we proceed. At this juncture my interest is in the discordant relation between the requirement of generality and the objective of predictability. Hayek contrasts predictability with being subject to the "whims" of those who are in positions of authority. "Arbitrary" rule makes it impossible for subjects to know what rules are in place or forthcoming and hence makes it impossible for them to plan their activities so as to avoid punishments. By contrast, in a regime that respects the rule of law, I as a subject can "know beforehand that if I place myself in a particular position, I shall be coerced." Hence I can "avoid putting myself in such a position." In this circumstance, "insofar as the rules . . . are not aimed at me personally . . . they are no different from any of the natural obstacles that affect my plans. In that they tell me what will happen *if* I do this or that, the laws of the state have the same significance for me as the laws of nature."[14] Again, "In observing such rules, we do not serve another person's end, nor can we properly be said to be subject to his will. My action can hardly be regarded as subject to the will of another . . . if I use his rules for my own purposes . . . and if that person does not know of my existence or of the particular circumstances in which the rules will apply to me. . . . [T]he law merely alters the means at my disposal and does not determine the ends I have to pursue."[15]

These passages are at war with one another. I can avoid being "coerced" and can otherwise confidently predict and plan because the law gives definite descriptions of the "this's and that's" the doing of which is required or forbidden. Calculability in this sense requires that I can know what I may, must, and must not do. Laws must have the obtrusive particularity of "natural obstacles." Pursuing this side of his ideal, Hayek favorably quotes Aristotle's prescription that "[i]t is of great moment that well drawn laws should themselves define all the points they possibly can, and leave as few as possible to the decision of the judges." Laws that satisfy this requirement leave "the judge . . . no choice in drawing the conclusions that follow from the existing body of rules and the particular facts of the case."[16]

On the other hand, laws avoid being "whims" of the lawgivers only if, by "abstracting" from the particulars of persons and circumstances, they leave "many kinds of action permissible as satisfying the conditions the law prescribes." The giver of "true laws" "cannot foresee what will be their effects on particular people or for what purposes they will use them. . . . [S]pecific ends of action, being always particulars, should not enter into general rules."[17] "In fact, that *we* do not know their concrete effect, that *we* do not know what particular ends these rules will further . . . is the most important criterion of formal rules." "It is in this sense alone that it is at all possible for the legislator to be impartial. To be impartial means to have no answer to certain questions—to the kinds of question which, if we have to decide them, we decide by tossing a coin. In a world where everything was precisely foreseen, the state could hardly do anything and remain impartial."[18]

There are numerous possibilities intermediate between entire predictability and tossing coins. Hayek's lurch from the one to the other, and his identification of rationality with the first and impartiality with the second, dramatize the Janus-faced, one might say the schizoid, character of his rule of law thinking.

But there is nothing distinctively Hayekian about the generic problem before us. Gains in the kind of predictability that rule of law theorists contrast with arbitrary rule can be achieved only by increasing the detail and specificity of laws and regulations. Gains in this respect necessarily entail losses as regards the range of actions all of which will satisfy "the conditions the law prescribes" and hence also the extent to which subjects can put laws "to their own purposes."

In this conspicuous respect it is seriously misleading to say that the rule of law is an ideal that can be approximated albeit not fully achieved. A legal system that embraces this ideal can pursue (through law and lawlike devices such as administrative regulations) particularity and predictability in this or these domains, generality and diversity of legally permissible action in that or those domains; it cannot pursue (by use of these devices) both objectives on one and the same terrain. If we make individuality, plurality, and freedom depend on specificity in law, laws that are general will disserve these values. If we associate individuality, plurality, and freedom with generality in law, laws that are definite in reference and hence afford predictability necessarily disserve the same values.[19]

## III

There have been a number of responses to these complications. Consideration of a few of the more influential proposals will underscore the discrepancies and suffice to show that none among them does more than ameliorate the difficulties to which they are addressed.

Late nineteenth- and twentieth-century proponents of the *rechtsstaat* gestured to the ideal of generality in statute law but bent their efforts to achieving definiteness, particularity, and hence predictability through the more supple means of administrative regulation. Legislatures were to adopt general policies or set broad objectives. Administrative agencies were accorded wide discretion in formulating the rules that would actually govern the conduct of citizens. The problem of arbitrariness in administrative law or regulation was addressed less by leaving subjects with numerous legally sanctioned options than by creating a cadre of officials expert concerning particular domains of social and economic life and instilled with a strong sense of discipline. Consistency and equality were to be achieved and responsibility enforced through a strictly defined hierarchy of administrative authority and power. Administrative action was to be subject to court review, but by administrative tribunals whose primary task was to insure that officials faithfully implement the directives issued by their superiors.

Rule of law thinkers who oppose the tendencies just sketched often concede that the *rechtsstaat* established effective state control over large parts of economic and social life. Some favor, some oppose such control, but from Weber and Dicey through McIlwain and Neumann and up to Oakeshott and Hayek, Fuller and Lowi,[20] they have objected that such efforts produce the antithesis of the rule of law. The administrative states they have empowered, whether or not they have consolidated and fortified the freedom-, plurality-, and individuality-destroying "iron cage" that Weber thought modernity was becoming, are pervaded by arbitrariness, are destroying the independence of the judiciary, and are in blatant conflict with the norm of equality before the law.

What, then, to do? If statutes that are general and prospective leave their addressees in debilitating uncertainty, and if the administrative state that remedies this defect substitutes the arbitrary rule of caste-serving bureaucrats (the rule of banal but often deeply evil "nobody's" as Hannah Arendt acutely characterized them), how can governance that deserves the honored name of the rule of law be achieved and sustained?

Articulating his Humean views concerning the vital role of custom and convention in human affairs, Hayek seeks to diminish the incompatibility between the ideas of generality and predictability by invoking tacit but widely shared understandings that are the background of any rule-governed activity or practice. Attempting to explain how judges (and subjects or their lawyers) can have "no choice" but to draw "the conclusions that follow from the existing body" of abstract "rules and the particular facts of the case" before them, he argues that the determined and determinate character of judicial decisions rarely results from the "explicit, written down beforehand in so many words" formulations of the rules they are following.

> There are "rules" which can never be put into explicit form. Many of these will be recognizable only because they lead to consistent . . . decisions and will be known to those whom they guide as, at most, manifestations of a "sense of justice." Psychologically, legal reasoning does not . . . consist of explicit syllogisms, and the major premises will often not be explicit. Many of the general principles on which the conclusions depend will be only implicit in the body of formulated law and will have to be discovered by the courts. This, however, is not a peculiarity of legal reasoning. Probably all generalizations that we can formulate depend on still higher generalizations which we do not explicitly know but which nevertheless govern the working of our minds. Though we will always try to discover those more general principles on which our decisions rest, this is probably by nature an unending process that can never be completed.[21]

Hayek's inconsistencies aside, there is much to agree with in these remarks and with the wider view that *all* rule following, regardless of the clarity and consistency of the rules in question, presupposes a setting of widely shared and seldom examined concepts, beliefs, and dispositions, of capacities and skills acquired early in one's involvement in an activity and thereafter taken for granted, and the like. Wittgenstein (among numerous others) has surely taught us this much.

But there are major components of the Wittgensteinian curriculum from which Hayek has either averted his glance or that he rejects without defense (he relies on Hume and Michael Polanyi in these regards). In what we might regard as the more comforting moments in his "later" thinking, Wittgenstein advances a variant of the view that we often do "know how to go on" with our language games; do nonetheless succeed in conducting our practices and in sustaining our institutions. He also promotes a version of the view that often we think of ourselves as having "no choice" but to go on in a particular manner, that our conventions, rules, training, and the like allow us one and only one action, judgment, or conclusion. Regularity, certainty, and predictability are indeed salient features of many of our practices and activities.

Contrary to Hayek, however, this steadiness and certitude is not due to the logical or rational necessities somehow resident in, the "calculations" strictly if inexplicably mandated by, our norms and rules. As with all ostensive definitions and all uses of language, rules can "be variously interpreted in every case." When we are most likely to think of ourselves as deducing or inferring rather than interpreting, we are, instead, "acting blindly." In the circumstances in which we have the strongest sense of certitude or necessity, these result from the less gratifying fact that we "cannot see" the beliefs and assumptions, the "agreements in judgment" rather than in "opinion," that subtend our thinking and that move us to our conclusions. Moreover, Wittgenstein insists on the innumerable respects in which we are enigmas to one another, in which, despite sharing a language and hence a "form of life," we cannot "find our feet" with one another.[22]

On these views, the regularity and predictability in our activities stem importantly from what Hayek's (but not Wittgenstein's) criteria would oblige us to regard as "arbitrariness" in our affairs. On the same views, the considerations Hayek summons to explain the possibility of the orderliness and calculability for which he yearns are necessary but never sufficient to produce them and are often radically inadequate to doing so.

Hayek (and Fuller, Ronald Dworkin, John Finnis, and others who make importantly comparable moves) is right to introduce these considerations into his rule of law thinking; his treatments of them are naive and his confidence in them excessive.

My larger purposes in this essay suggest a quite different characterization of and response to appeals to custom, convention, principles, laws of nature, etc., to close the "gaps" left by the letter of the law. If the subjects of a legal system *believe* that they and their judges "have no choice" but to act in a particular way, that belief might itself bring about the order and predictability that rule of law theorists ardently desire. It is the effect of the beliefs, not the logic or truth of the arguments for them, that matter. And while Wittgenstein is untroubled by the "prodigious diversity" and "open texture," the flux, indeterminacy, and opacity, of our language games, these are the very features that rule of law theorists want to lessen if not eradicate. In attempting to eradicate them by promoting firm and uniform beliefs that will produce the order and regularity they desire, they dramatize the ideological character of rule of law thinking.

To assess this anything but entirely agreeable project, I appropriate to my purposes elements of a view that is analogous to Wittgenstein's but that has a sharper critical edge.

In a lively engagement with Kafka's stunning miniature *Before the Law,* Jacques Derrida plays out by repeatedly playing on Kafka's maddening image of the countryman who is summoned before the law but who is prevented by the law's guardian from actually "reaching" it, prevented from closing the conceptual, normative, and psychological distance between himself and the law itself.

Derrida gives a twofold account of the "inaccessibility" of the law itself. One part of this account is strongly continuous with Wittgenstein's discussions of rules and rule following. From the moment when the law "begins to speak and to question the moral subject," for example, from the moment when legislators, judges, etc., attempt to theorize and promote the authority and bindingness of laws, "historicity," "narrativity," and hence "imagination" and "fiction" are introduced "into the very core of legal thought."[23] And with these features inevitably come those uncertainties and indeterminacies that Wittgenstein foregrounds. In part for this reason the subjects can never achieve "a rapport of respect" with the law.[24]

The guardians of the law, however, "interrupt" the relation between the subject and the law deliberately as well as unwittingly. Why? They do so, Derrida suggests, out of the realization that full access to the law would profane it, would deprive it of what Kant called its "categorical authority." In order for laws to have such authority there must be a "law of laws" that is "without history, genesis, or any possible derivation." If "historicity and empirical narrativity" would permit subjects of the law of laws to achieve a measure of rapport with it, they would thereby jeopardize the majesty or sanctity that it must have. Representatives of the law (Kafka's doorkeeper) are "interrupters as well as messengers"; by preventing the subjects from gaining access to the law they combat the effects of the historicity and narrativity that they themselves—sometimes inadvertently, sometimes knowingly—have introduced into it.[25]

There is no such thing as an ahistorical concept or idea—of law or anything else. But, again, what if subjects can be gotten to *believe* that there is a law of laws, a law that authorizes, sanctifies, makes binding each of the particular laws that gather under the "genre" that the law of laws regulates or constitutes? What if they believe—can be gotten to want desperately to believe—that somewhere in the forbidden recesses guarded by the uncountable doorkeepers there is a pure and perfect LAW, a LAW unsullied by the contingencies and indeterminacies that come along with historicity, narrativity, and imagination? If, as appears to be the case with Kafka's doorkeeper, the guardians believe that they are the keepers of such a LAW, they might be more unyielding and otherwise resourceful in protecting its purity. If the subjects of the law believe that there is such a LAW, as appears to be the case with Kafka's man from the country, they might be more likely to submit to the directives and punishments of the guardians—indeed, to do so "blindly." As a matter of conduct, "blind" acceptance of the *deep* convention that is the law of laws might make up the deficits left or rather created by the laws themselves and by the less determinate and more fluctuating conventions intermediate between the law of laws and the law.

Faithful to Kafka's disturbing tale, Derrida thinks that the subjects of law (and also, if with less self-awareness, the guardians?) are always and inescapably in "the terrifying double-bind" of Kafka's man from the country. They at once must and cannot know what the law is. They desperately want the assurances of a legal order and the esteem that comes with recognized fidelity to it; what they get is doubt, guilt, and shame. They are "both . . . subject[s] of the law and . . . outlaw[s]."[26] The upshot seems to be that subjects of law are fated to the despair and humiliating shrinkage of self that befalls Kafka's man from the country.

Derrida does not draw the anarchist or antinomian inference that his story would seem to mandate. As with Wittgenstein, he knows perfectly well that there are effective laws and working legal, moral, and other disciplinary systems—that in fact we often "go on" successfully with activities that bring us "before" such systems. And it seems to be his view that a law of laws, and messengers/interrupters who at once enforce and prevent access to it, is always or at least typically a feature of such institutionalized activities and practices. In this and numerous other volumes he is concerned with the "law of the genre" that purports and is widely believed to stand to "Acts of Literature" as the law of laws stands to the acts of adopting, enforcing, and obeying the laws that governments make. By engaging texts that are uncontroversially within the genre of literature and therefore taken to be "before" the purported LAW of that genre, he exposes the dissonances and paradoxes of that relationship, displays their potent effects on the activities that produce and surround Acts of Literature. The anarchist and antinomian counsel, we might say, is a counsel of despair. Alternatively, if it is our own beliefs, at once force-fed to us and desperately maintained by us, that sustain the law of laws, it is so disturbing a counsel that we will almost certainly reject it.

Let us treat the metalegal doctrine of the rule of law as the LAW of the genre consisting of the law of the state, that is, as a delineation or prescription of the criteria that do or ought to govern what law is. If we must be "before" this LAW, cannot simply deny or otherwise dispose of it, how should we think about it and our relationship to it?

At a minimum, we should follow Derrida's example and ex-

pose and contest the highest pretensions of that law of laws that
is the rule of law. We, especially we liberal theorists, should
expose the historicity and contingency of the rule of law and
thereby contest the claim that fidelity to it will banish arbitrariness and indeterminacy from the law. Doing so will not eliminate, may well deepen, the difficulties inherent in being before
the law. As Wittgenstein and Stanley Cavell say about all of our
"criteria," we cannot do without standards by which to identify
and assess laws, and in much of our thinking and acting we do
and must accept them "blindly." But if we recognize, at least in
our more self-critical moments, that they inevitably "disappoint"
us,[27] we may loosen their hold on our thinking, may prepare
ourselves to think and act against as well as with the law and its
messengers/interrupters. If so, taking this stance may help us to
stave off the diminution and despair that overtake those who,
like the man from the country, persist in the naive faith that the
law is or "should surely be accessible at all times and to
everyone."

"But is it not necessary for all literature [all law and acts
before the law] to exceed literature? . . . The work, the opus
[the thought and the act within, around, against the law] does
not belong to the field, it is the transformer of the field."[28]

## IV

By way of concluding I consider a number of views concerning
the rule of law that are at least partly in the spirit of these last
remarks. But first I examine a theory, or rather an imagining,
of the rule of law that, were it fully and durably realizable,
would recommend a less suspicious or antagonistic stance toward this institution and institutionalism.

"Taken precisely," Michael Oakeshott avers, "the expression
'the rule of law' . . . stands for a mode of moral association
[consisting "of *personae* indistinguishably and"] exclusively ["related in respect of"] . . . the recognition of the authority of
known, non-instrumental rules . . . which impose obligations to
subscribe to adverbial conditions in the performance of self-
chosen actions of all who fall within their jurisdiction."[29]

In the largest perspectives of this essay, the idea that is finally most important in Oakeshott's vision is that of a mode of human association that would be characterized and distinguished from all others not by its collective purposes or institutional structures but by the "personae" of its subscribers and the qualities that their thinking and acting do and do not have. It is the vision of an association each of the members of which have their own ends and purposes that they pursue through their self-chosen actions. Members as such *("cives")* are associated with one another not by agreement in objective or purpose but exclusively by their subscription to "adverbial" rules, rules that do not require them to do this or that but rather to do whatever they do in certain (civil) ways or manners, obligate them to avoid doing whatever they do in uncivil ways.

As is evident from Oakeshott's willingness to denominate his vision of association in terms of the "Rule of Law,"[30] a version of institutionalism is integral to it. The constitutive and distinguishing features of this vision, however, are not its institutions in what we might call their material form but rather the understandings its *personae* have of themselves, of their relationships with one another, and of the institutions to which they jointly subscribe. They think of themselves as disclosing and enacting themselves by "imagining" and pursuing various and fluctuating "substantive satisfactions" and as doing this with consideration for the adverbial requirements enunciated in law and in various other principles and rules. In short, the institutions of such an association, including the rule of law in at least some of the more familiar senses that I have been exploring, are fashioned to be consonant with the demands of that understanding or conception, not the other way around.

These features of Oakeshott's vision of the rule of law inform my thought that subscribers to such an association would adopt an affirmative stance toward it and the requirements it places on them. Quite rightly, however, Oakeshott states unequivocally that, so understood, "the rule of law cannot" be taken to characterize any "modern European state."[31] As he articulates and idealizes it, the "expression . . . 'the rule of law' stands for a mode of human relationship that has been glimpsed, sketched in practice, unreflectively and intermittently enjoyed, half understood, left indistinct."[32] Agreeing with this judgment, I postpone further discussion of the apparently more encouraging possibility to consider respects in which Oakeshott's construal of the rule of law is continuous with and departs from formulations already discussed.

Viewed as a version of institutionalism, the distinctive feature of Oakeshott's account is his insistence on the nonpurposive, noninstrumental, purely adverbial character of the rules and relationships that compose a rule of law association. But let us note respects in which the core idea in this distinction is akin to Hayek's notion that subjects put the laws to their own, not the lawmaker's, purposes and to his closely related prescription that laws specify not particular actions but "conditions" that all actions must satisfy. We should also note that Oakeshott incorporates into his conception of the rule of law a number of the requirements common to virtually all current rule of law thinking and endorses Fuller's view that these "formal" characteristics are "inherent in the notion . . . of law itself . . . and [that] in default of [them] . . . whatever purports to be a legal order" does not deserve that designation.[33]

In these respects his view of the rule of law departs from those considered earlier primarily in his refusal to make exaggerated claims concerning the certitude and predictability that they afford. The reader will have noticed the somewhat casual quality of his remarks about the features inherent in the notion of the law (the sentences quoted in note 33 are the entirety of his remarks on this topic). Yet more striking is his repeated insistence that laws "are unavoidably indeterminate," that the judicial procedures through which they are applied to particular cases are not only "an exercise in retrospective casuistry" but something of a "devious engagement," one that has no concern with the intentions of legislators, knows of no absolute rights, and looks to previous cases not for binding precedents but for "the analogical force of the distinctions they invoked."[34] Although operating with and through its own internal rules of procedure and evidence, and in part because these too are "unavoidably indeterminate," judicial deliberations "float upon the acknowledgement that the considerations in terms of which the *jus* of *lex* may be discerned are neither arbitrary, nor unchanging, nor uncontentious, and that they are the product of moral experience which is never without tensions and internal discrepancies."[35]

Association in terms of the rule of law has "no place for enthusiasm." It requires "a severe and incurious kind of faithfulness or ceremoniousness which modifies without emasculating the self-chosen character of human conduct."[36] The freedom subserved by the rule of law is a presupposition, not a consequence, of the mode of association it names[37]; the rule of law "bakes no bread, . . . is unable to distribute loaves or fishes, . . . and [what in the violent history of the modern European state has proved to be its truly fatal defect] it cannot protect itself against external assault." Nevertheless "it remains the most civilized and least burdensome conception of a state yet to be devised."[38]

In the essay to which I have been responding, Oakeshott is decidedly sparing of examples of rules that are purely adverbial in character, leaving—perhaps deliberately—that notion in a somewhat obscure or elusive condition. In the more extensive (and hence vulnerable?) discussion in *On Human Conduct,* in the course of arguing that the norms and rules of all human "practices" are of this character, he elaborates on the notion in the following terms: "A practice may be identified as a set of considerations, manners, uses, observances, customs, standards, canons, maxims, principles, rules and offices specifying useful procedures or denoting obligations or duties which relate to human actions and utterances. It is . . . an adverbial qualification of choices and performances . . . in which conduct is understood in terms of a procedure." The emblems of such considerations are concepts "such as punctually, considerately, civilly, scientifically, legally, candidly, judicially, poetically, morally, etc." These concepts "do not specify performances; they postulate performances and specify procedural conditions to be taken into account when choosing and acting."[39]

All human actions involve both substance and procedure. The former enter through the agent's choice of an "imagined and wished-for" outcome or satisfaction, the latter are given by, become available to and obligatory for agents by virtue of, practices that specify conditions in which choices are made and acted upon. A "practice is an instrument to be played upon, not a tune to be played." This is a matter of the distinctive logic and categorial character of practices, not of the preferences of their practitioners. "A rule (and *a fortiori* something less exacting, like a maxim) can never tell a performer what choice he shall make. . . . The appearance procedures and rules may have of excluding (forbidding), or more rarely enjoining, substantive choices and actions is illusive. Practices identify actions adverbially; they exclude (forbid) or enjoin them in terms of prescribed conditions." Turning to the practice in respect to which the illusion he is dispelling is most widely promoted (because most avidly desired?), he declares that "[a] criminal law . . . does not forbid killing or lighting a fire, it forbids killing 'murderously' or lighting a fire 'arsonically.' "[40]

Because one can light a fire arsonically only by lighting a fire, laws can forbid arson only by prohibiting certain classes of action. *Cives* who subscribe to such laws will therefore be under obligations to desist from actions they might otherwise take with legal impunity. Oakeshott is hardly unaware of this fact. In observed fact, proposals for new laws commonly take their origin from the purposes of their proponents; "there is, indeed, no want which may not set going a project" to change the laws. In fact, laws commonly yield substantive "benefits or advantages to . . . assignable interests"; for example, "every piece of legislation has an outcome of advantage to a legal profession."[41]

The *personae* of a rule of law association do not deny these realities. But neither do they make them the focus of their thinking and acting. In deliberating proposed changes in *lex,* their question—rather than *cui bono?*—is how the proposed law would affect the conditions under which all associates would thereafter be obligated to act. In choosing courses of conduct in the domain of *lex* they ask whether the actions they are considering could be performed in a manner consistent with their own civil characters and with the civility of associational life.

Accordingly, life in a rule of law association, particularly participation in the "politics" in which the *lex* of such an association is deliberated, requires no less than a "disciplined imagination."[42] *Cives* must cultivate their human capacities to imagine desirable outcomes and to devise ways of pursuing them. At the same time, they must subject that imagination and those pursuits to the discipline of the considerations signaled by words such as "politely," "temperately," and "fastidiously"; "resolutely," "candidly," and "forthrightly"; "morally," "legally," and "civilly." If they fail in the first of these endeavors, they deteriorate into the dull, torpid, and *ressentiment*-laden characters that Oakeshott calls the "individual manqúe" and the "anti-individual."[43] If they fail in the second task, rule of law society is gone, in all likelihood replaced by a teleocratic enterprise association the ugly insignia of which are "Purpose, Plan, Policy and Power."[44]

As we have seen, attempts at creating and sustaining rule of law association have never succeeded entirely and have rarely succeeded at all for very long. There are deep reasons for this perhaps dispiriting fact. In addition to the intricate and never fully harmonious combination of characteristics it demands of its *personae*, the deliberations such association require have to be sustained despite certain knowledge that "there always must be more than one opinion" concerning the questions that arise and hence that the engagement to deliberate them will most often be "vexatious." It "calls for so exact a focus of attention and so uncommon a self-restraint" that we cannot be "astonished to find this mode of human relationship to be as rare as it is excellent."[45]

V

Oakeshott is correct that the conception of civil or rule of law association that he has glimpsed in the theory and practice of the modern European state represents "the most civilized and least burdensome conception of *a state* yet to be devised." It is civilized in postulating individuality, plurality, and freedom; it is civilized and potentially civilizing in looking to qualities of character, understanding, and spirit rather than power-driven political mechanics to abate the difficulties inherent in political association. The (Hobbesian) demands it makes, severe as they are, would be as little burdensome for the human beings it postulates and promotes as life in a politically organized association can be.

If we also agree that the possibility of associations with these characteristics has been and remains elusive, then his reflections concerning the rule of law reinforce results reached through consideration of more widely influential thinking about this ideology-cum-institutional device. If known politically orga-nized associations (including those said by less discriminating theorists to approximate satisfaction of the requirements of the rule of law) are predominantly teleocracies, then human beings who treasure individuality, plurality, and freedom will stand in a wary, defensive, even antagonistic posture toward their laws and other institutions and institutionalisms. Oakeshott's ideal-ized rule of law association carries further the Wittgensteinian/ Derridian exposure of the institutions that, empirically, bear this name; indeed, it stands as a rebuke to those institutions.

It is therefore no difficult matter to join the company of theorists who, while respecting the rule of law as a sometimes valuable institutional idea and device, nevertheless take a less than celebratory stance toward it. It is especially easy to agree with the view of H. L. A. Hart and of proponents of civil disobedience that the fact that a rule is a law is anything but a conclusive reason for obeying it. The fundaments of this view were persuasively argued by Hobbes in respect to a state that (as Hobbes conceived it) had many of the attributes of an Oakes-hottian civil association and in any case was intended to be far less active and powerful than the juggernaut enterprise associations under the thrall of which we now live. Given the emergence and consolidation of the latter, the presence of citi-zens ready and willing to disobey law, however good its creden-tials by rule of law standards, is a necessary condition of realiz-ing the liberal ideals.

It must be emphasized that this is a decidedly political stance. Of course it is not a "participationist" or "civic republican" posi-tion, does not urge us to sacrifice our other concerns to political involvement or to look to political activity as the chief source of gratification or self-realization, of virtue, of fraternity or communal solidarity. Rather, it warns against enhancing the power of the state by adding the force of one's own thinking and acting to the politics that energize it. From Hobbes forward, however, proponents of this point of view have insisted that subjects of the state must give close attention to the activities of

government, must watch it warily and be prepared to contest
and resist laws and commands that threaten their interests and
their well-being.

From the point of view in question, life in the states we in
fact have makes demands akin to but arguably yet more difficult
to meet than Oakeshott's "exact focus of attention" and "uncommon self-restraint." Insofar as these states do act by authority, not power, insofar as they do rule by laws, not commands,
the understandings and sensibilities that Oakeshott promotes
are appropriate if not essential. In particular, subjects must
sustain the distinction between the authority and the substantive
merits of laws. Because, as Hobbes said, a body politic makes
policy rather than policy making a body politic, if this distinction is lost, "government" is supplanted by action more or less
in concert—typically the concerted action of some against and
over others.

But while these states have some of the elements of a civil
society, they are predominantly enterprise associations that use
their authority to pursue ends or goods purported to be common to all their members. This being the case, it seems that
their subjects are faced with a choice between actively involving
themselves in the politics through which highly purposive laws
are adopted or resigning the care of numerous of *their* ends and
purposes to some number of other people. In short, if the
understandings and attitudes characteristic of the *cives* of a civil
association were transferred, wholesale as it were, to states as we
know them, those understandings—particularly the understanding that they should practice a "severe and incurious faithfulness"—might have the same unwelcome implications and
consequences as do the preachments of conventional rule of
law thinkers.

Oakeshott agrees with the last of these judgments. For subjects of an enterprise association state to choose resignation or
political withdrawal is tantamount to abdicating, throughout
whatever domain of life the state elects to regulate, the activities
of self-disclosure and self-enactment. Those who make this
choice thereby become "individuals manqués" and very likely
"anti-individuals." He attempts, however, to identify a third
option that is political in a sense close to the one that emerged

in discussing Hobbes, Hart, and civil disobedience. But let us first consider views of critics of the rule of law who work primarily with the two options identified above.

If those are the options, avid participationists are not the only theorists who have disdained withdrawal and argued for forms of political involvement and activity that include but go well beyond wary attentiveness and ready disobedience. For otherwise diverse thinkers such as Franz Neumann, Judith Shklar, and members of the Critical Legal Studies movement, the withdrawal option, and the doctrines of strict obedience to law that often go with it ("legal absolutism"), is so grossly imprudent as to be beneath consideration. Highly effective in displaying tensions and pretensions within the theory and practice of the rule of law, they go on to expose the deeply ideological character of rule of law mentalities, particularly the ways in which their underdefended but vigorously promoted assumptions concerning order and predictability serve class, caste, and other partisan interests. Most important here, they argue that these assumptions are enforced by political authority and power. For this very reason, for the reason that the rule of law is a system of organized and institutionalized political authority and power, it must be contested and resisted by organized and institutionalized political means.[46]

It is impossible to reject this position altogether. There have been, are, and will continue to be circumstances in which continuous, organized, and vigorously affirmative political activity is indispensable. Once regimes such as contemporary China, Iraq, and Syria, or former Nazi Germany and the Stalinist Soviet Union, have consolidated their massive resources of power and violence, the political attitude and stance I discussed earlier, even if—as seems to have been the case in the Soviet Union— they have their effects, are often suicidal. There are also extended periods in the histories of virtually all modern states in which organized and quite possibly violent action is the only effective way to counter organized violence and cruelty. The evils of state-enforced racial segregation in the United States and South Africa were and continue to be diminished by those self-enacting and magnanimous free spirits who achieved and who sustain a distancing and resistant stance toward them. More than this was and is necessary to end these evils. If more Americans had steadily taken or would now take a skeptical and contestational stance toward government and law, atrocities such as the Vietnam "war" might not have been committed and would be less likely to recur. Once such brutal uses of state power have gained momentum, more than this was and will be necessary to end them.

The achievements of rule of law thinking and practice notwithstanding, the fires of state power burn hot and destructively among us. If it is therefore sometimes necessary to fight them with flames of equal heat and intensity, we should not forget that all combustions reconstitute—rarely for the better when the "materials" are human beings—the matter they consume.

In configuring his "ideal characters," civil and enterprise association, Oakeshott treats them as categorially distinct. But every actual political association that can claim to include the rule of law is an unstable amalgam of the characteristics of these two ideal types. More important, no human association can be tolerable without the qualities of human character and spirit that he, along with Hobbes and Constant, Emerson and Nietzsche, Mill, William James, and other lovers of individuality, plurality, and freedom, treasure and promote. All forms of collective and hence institutionalized conduct, particularly those that add the force of our thinking and acting to the power of the state, diminish those qualities. Oakeshott's third option, never entirely unavailable to those with the willfulness to choose it, is the option of maintaining a "pathos of distance" vis-à-vis such conduct and the institutions and institutionalisms—including the rule of law—that it sustains.

## NOTES

1. I articulate a version of liberalism that foregrounds these ideals in *Willful Liberalism: Voluntarism and Individuality in Political Theory and Practice* (Ithaca, N.Y.: Cornell University Press, 1992). This essay is the first of what I project as a series of attempts to examine relationships between these ideals and the institutions of the liberal state.

2. "Every institution has a controlling as well as an organizing function. For institutions, being established social forms, constitute an

inner social environment. This environment . . . reacts upon those who
are exposed to its influence, and so the relation of institutions to social
life becomes very complex. They do not merely reflect and express
social life, they modify it profoundly; they do not merely fulfil men's
purposes, they are means by which these purposes are determined"
(R. M. MacIver, "Institutions as Instruments of Social Control," *Political Quarterly* 2 [1914]: 109–10).

3. Richard E. Flathman, *Thomas Hobbes: Individuality, Skepticism,
and Chastened Politics* (Newbury Park, CA: Sage, 1992).

4. Recall Benjamin Constant's exquisitely appropriate response to
Montesquieu: "No doubt there is no liberty when people cannot do all
that the laws allow them to do; but laws could forbid so many things as
to abolish liberty altogether." Quoted in Bruno Leoni, *Freedom and the
Law,* (Indianapolis: Liberty Fund, 1991), 152.

5. For an instructive analysis of the complex, fluctuating, and
always problematic interaction between liberal ideals and institutions,
in the American case, see Samuel P. Huntington, *American Politics:
The Promise of Disharmony* (Cambridge, MA: Harvard University Press,
1981). Huntington's formula, "Ideals versus Institutions," or the "IvI
gap," expresses some of the themes I develop here. I am, however, in
disagreement with his pronounced tendency to prefer institutionalism
and the order *it* idealizes when there are conflicts between it and other
liberal values. Of course putting the matter this way problematizes the
"IvI" formula.

6. For these distinctions see Richard B. Friedman, "On the Concept of Authority in Political Philosophy," in Richard E. Flathman, ed.,
*Concepts in Social and Political Philosophy* (New York: Macmillan, 1973);
Richard E. Flathman, *The Practice of Political Authority* (Chicago: University of Chicago Press, 1980).

7. Institutionalists sometimes deliberately arrange structures and
procedures that engender competition and conflict among the several
components of the overall system of institutions. Famously, some of
the American founders favored bicameralism and the separation of
powers on the ground that these devices would make it difficult for the
federal government to act. In addition to the points made above,
however, this strategy "succeeds" only to the extent that its motivating
concern is widely shared. If there is a general desire for and expectation of vigorous and extensive use of state power, either the several
centers of authority cooperate to bring it about or dissatisfaction and
disaffection mount.

Institutions and institutional structures matter. As I argue throughout, however, they matter less than institutional*ism,* less than the beliefs

and attitudes, hopes and fears, that inform the thinking and acting of those whose institutions they are.

8. For example Lon Fuller, who treats his version of the require-ments of the rule of law as constituting law's "inner morality," allows that "over a wide range of issues" the morality internal to law "is in-different toward the substantive aims of law and is ready to serve a var-iety of such aims with equal efficacy" (*The Morality of Law* [New Haven, CT: Yale University Press, 1964], 153). This pronounced tendency in contemporary rule of law thinking is sharply and effectively crit-iqued, especially in respect to legislative law, by Bruno Leoni, op. cit.

9. Cf. the Weberian pronouncements of Franz Neumann and Bruno Leoni: "The [rule of law] doctrine clearly reveals the ambivalent position of modern man—the emphatic assertion of the autonomy of man is accompanied by the equally passionate insistence on the rule of the state" (*The Democratic and the Authoritarian State* [Glencoe, IL: Free Press, 1957], 140). "One of the paradoxes of our era is the continual retreat of traditional religious faith before the advance of science and technology, under the implied exigency of a cool and matter-of-fact attitude and dispassionate reasoning, accompanied by a *no less continual retreat from the same attitude and reasoning in regard to legal and political questions.* The mythology of our age is not religious, but political, and its chief myths seem to be 'representation' of the people, on the one hand, and the charismatic pretension of political leaders to be in pos-session of the truth and to act accordingly, on the other" (Leoni, op. cit., 23).

These remarks help us to understand how and why enormously complicated and internally conflicted institutions such as the United States government continuously produce a vast number of laws and regulations on a myriad of subjects.

10. In our time this view has been forcefully advanced by H. L. A. Hart. See, for example, *Essays in Jurisprudence and Philosophy* (Oxford: Clarendon, 1983), esp. 81–82.

11. For a concise listing of the usual components of the ideology, expanded and much ambiguated in the pages that follow the account, see Fuller, op. cit., 39–40.

12. F. A. Hayek, *The Constitution of Liberty* (Chicago: University of Chicago Press, 1960), 209.

13. Ibid., 149–50.

14. Ibid., 142. Later I comment on aspects of Hayek's indebtedness to Hume. Given Hume's insistence that the laws of nature *as we know and use them* are deeply subjective, Hayek might have asked himself whether his comparison serves his purposes.

15. Ibid., 152–53.

16. Ibid., 153–54. Franz Neumann makes meeting this requirement a condition of an independent judiciary. The law must have "a minimum of substantive content" in order that it "guarantees to the judge a minimum of independence because it does not subordinate him to the individual measures of the sovereign" (Neumann, op. cit., 30).

17. Hayek, op. cit., 152.

18. F. A. Hayek, *The Road to Serfdom* (Chicago: University of Chicago Press, 1944, 1976), 74–76; emphasis mine. I have added the emphasis to underscore what seems to be implicit in Hayek's "we," namely, that neither the authors nor the addressees of such laws can know or make reliable predictions concerning what the laws require, forbid, and permit.

19. As Leoni emphasizes, laws that are sufficiently particular to afford predictability nevertheless deprive their addressees of that advantage if they are frequently changed. "We are actually far from attaining . . . the ideal certainty of the law, in the practical sense that this ideal should have for anybody who must plan for the future and who has to know . . . what the legal consequences of his decisions will be." Given the rage to legislate and administer that is rampant in the modern state, "people can never be certain that the legislation in force today will be in force tomorrow or even tomorrow morning" (Leoni, op. cit., 9–10).

20. A. V. Dicey, *Introduction to the Study of the Law of the Constitution*, 8th ed. (Indianapolis: Liberty Classics, 1992); C. H. McIlwain, *Constitutionalism and the Changing World* (Cambridge: Cambridge University Press, 1939); T. J. Lowi, *The End of Liberalism*, 2d ed. (New York: Norton, 1979); Michael Oakeshott, "The Rule of Law," in Oakeshott, *On History and Other Essays* (Totowa, N.J.: Barnes and Noble, 1983).

21. F. A. Hayek, *The Constitution of Liberty*, 208–9.

22. I have gathered and underlined these features of Wittgenstein's thinking in chapter 1 of *Toward a Liberalism* (Ithaca, N.Y.: Cornell University Press, 1989) and in chapters 2 and 3 of *Willful Liberalism*, op. cit. Restrictions on space make it impossible to do more than advert to these discussions here. Of course these views, while in a distinctive idiom, are hardly unique to Wittgenstein. Yet more insistent and unsettling contemporary versions of them are discussed below, but it should be remembered that they are pervasive in the thinking, from Plato to Hobbes to the present, of most of those who have given critical attention to language in the wide Wittgensteinian sense.

23. Jacques Derrida, "Before the Law," in Derrida, *Acts of Literature,* ed. Derek Attridge (New York: Routledge, 1992), 190.

24. Ibid., 203.

25. Ibid., 204.

26. Ibid.

27. See Stanley Cavell, *The Claim to Reason* (Oxford: Oxford University Press, 1979), esp. part 1; *In Quest of the Ordinary* (Chicago: University of Chicago Press, 1988), 5, 38, 59, 85–87, 110–11, 132–33, 147–48; *Conditions Handsome and Unhandsome* (Chicago: University of Chicago Press, 1990), 92–100.

28. Derrida, op. cit., 215.

29. "The Rule of Law," 136. The materials interjected in brackets are from 160–61.

30. In *On Human Conduct* (London: Oxford University Press, 1975) he calls it *societas,* or civil association, and contrasts it with *universitas,* or enterprise association.

31. Ibid., 155.

32. Ibid., 120.

33. Requirements of law as such include "rules not secret or retrospective, no obligations save those imposed by law, all associates equally and without exception subject to the obligations imposed by law, no outlawry, and so on. It is only in respect of these considerations and their like that it may perhaps be said that *lex injusta non est lex*" (ibid., 140).

34. Ibid., 146–47.

35. Ibid., 143–44.

36. Ibid., 148–49.

37. Ibid., 161.

38. Ibid., 164.

39. Oakeshott, *On Human Conduct,* 55–56.

40. Ibid., 58, 58n.

41. Ibid., 169–70.

42. Ibid., 165.

43. Ibid., Third Essay.

44. "Rule of Law," 125.

45. *On Human Conduct,* 180.

46. See Neumann and Leoni, op. cit.; Judith N. Shklar, *Legalism* (Cambridge, MA: Harvard University Press, 1964, 1986). Roberto Mangabeira Unger, *The Critical Legal Studies Movement* (Cambridge, MA: Harvard University Press, 1986); Mark Kelman, *A Guide to Critical Legal Studies* (Cambridge, MA: Harvard University Press, 1987).

# 14

## PUBLIC REASON AND THE RULE OF LAW

### GERALD F. GAUS

### 1. Four Ways of Being Ruled by Law

Political and legal philosophers have identified at least four ways in which citizens and governments can be ruled by law. (1) The rule of *law* is often contrasted to the rule of *men,* that is, rule by mere will or caprice of political authorities. "In this sense," said A. V. Dicey, "the rule of law is contrasted with every system of government based on the exercise by persons in authority of wide, arbitrary, or discretionary powers of con- straint."[1] Clearly, then, a dictator who rules through fiat based on passing whims does not rule through law. However, on many interpretations this ideal of the rule of law demands more than a Hartian union of primary and secondary rules. If Rex enacts vague statutes giving his secret police sweeping discretionary powers to decide what is a crime, or if he singles out political opponents by name and enacts regulations directed to them alone, his claim to rule by *law* is dubious.[2] This understanding of the rule of law thus seems to require adhering to something very much like Lon Fuller's "internal morality of the law," that is, the defining characteristics of distinctly *legal rule* such as

I would like to thank Sterling Burnett, John Chapman, Bob Ewin, and Julian Lamont for their suggestions and criticisms.

generality, publicity, exclusion of retroactive legislation, clarity, stability, exclusion of legislation requiring the impossible, congruence of official action and declared rule, etc.[3]

(2) As Dicey pointed out, the ideal of rule by law also has a less formal and more substantive sense: the protection of personal freedom.[4] Ronald Dworkin stresses this substantive aspect of the rule of law (though expanding it beyond protection of personal freedom), which he calls the "rights conception" of the rule of law:

> It assumes that citizens have moral rights and duties with respect to one another, and political rights against the state as a whole. It insists that these moral and political rights be recognized in positive law, so that they may be enforced *upon the demand of individual citizens* through courts or other judicial institutions of the familiar type, as far as this is practicable. The rule of law on this conception is the ideal of rule by an accurate public conception of individual rights.[5]

(3) Dworkin makes clear that the ideal of the rule of law not only requires that government rule *through* laws but also that it be ruled *by* laws; courts are to enforce rights "against the state as a whole." This is one way in which the rule of law requires an independent judiciary: if citizens are to enforce their legal rights against the government, the judiciary cannot be a mere instrument of the executive or the legislature.[6] This aspect of the rule of law also points to a tie between constitutionalism and the rule of law, insofar as a constitution is viewed as articulating "fundamental law" which limits the authority of the legislature itself.[7]

(4) For governments to be ruled by law thus requires an independent judiciary and, perhaps, some form of judicial review. But what does it mean for a citizen to be *ruled* by law — should a citizen allow himself to be ruled by law even if it conflicts with his moral judgment? This is the problem of the moral obligation to obey the law: does the mere fact that the law directs us to $\phi$ in itself provide us with a moral reason to $\phi$ even if we judge $\phi$-ing to be immoral? Despite their fundamental differences on most issues, Hobbes and Kant agree that to be ruled by law is to defer to the judgment of the government as

expressed by the law, in the sense that one has conclusive moral reason to do what the sovereign commands regardless of one's own judgments of the merits of the case.[8] Today this view is generally out of favor; David Lyons is just one of many who reject any "automatic obligation to obey the law."[9] Civility, we are told, may require that we generally act as the law instructs, but it does not rule us so sternly that we are always morally obligated to obey a law that clashes with our moral convictions.[10]

These four different ways of being ruled by law present two related questions. First, are they genuine aspects of a defensible understanding of the rule of law, or are some, such as the moral obligation to obey the law, misguided and better omitted? Secondly, why are these somewhat diverse elements—formal requirements, individual substantive justice, legal regulation of political authority, and the moral obligation to obey the law— all thought to be aspects of the ideal of the rule of law? A *theory of the rule of law* would answer these questions, by showing which of these aspects are justified, and how those justified aspects are part of a coherent concept, rather than a hodgepodge of unrelated legal aspirations.[11] Moreover, as the rule of law is a central component of the liberal conception of justice,[12] we would expect a theory of the rule of law to follow closely from basic liberal commitments.

In this chapter I sketch such a theory. In section 2 I analyze the basic liberal commitment to the public justification of principles of justice; I shall argue that liberal citizens reasonably disagree on what specific interpretations of basic liberal principles are publicly justified. Section 3 maintains that because of this inconclusiveness of public reasoning, liberal citizens committed to public justification require a certain sort of political authority—an umpire—to resolve their disputes about justice. Section 4 then tries to show how the reasons that justify political authority require that the citizens and governors be ruled by law in our four ways. Finally, I conclude in section 5 with some comments about the way in which moral community is a precondition for an effective rule of law.

## 2. THE ASPIRATION TO REASON PUBLICLY

### 2.1. Private Values and Public Reasons

"The moral loadstar of liberalism is," says Stephen Macedo, "the project of public justification."[13] Moral and political principles regulating social life are justified only if each and every member of the community is provided with adequate reason to embrace and conform to them.[14] On an individual level, the liberal commitment to public justification implies a commitment on the part of each liberal citizen to making only those moral demands on others that can be justified to *them*. If, for instance, Alf wishes to justify to Betty a rule requiring that she redistribute some of her holdings to Charlie, he must advance considerations that *from Betty's perspective* are reasons for redistributing. It will be of no avail for Alf to present Betty with considerations that are reasons from his perspective but are not reasons for a perfectly rational Betty, for he would then fail in justifying his demands *to her*. Liberalism is in this way grounded on what Kant called the "public use of reason"; it requires that we "think from the standpoint of everyone else."[15]

This requirement could be met easily if Alf's perspective were universally valid, in the sense that whatever was a reason for Alf to act was also a reason for every agent to act. His standpoint and the public standpoint would then be identical. But the liberal account of values, ends, and projects precludes this easy identification. As Loren Lomasky puts it,

> An individual's projects provide him with a *personal*—an intimately personal—standard of value to choose his actions by. His central and enduring ends provide reasons for action that are recognized as his own in the sense that no one who is uncommitted to those specific ends will share the reasons for action that he possesses. Practical reason is *essentially differentiated* among project pursuers.[16]

Consequently, as Gilbert Harman points out, "we only fool ourselves if we think our values give *reasons* to others who do not accept those values."[17]

As a liberal citizen seeking to justify a moral demand on Betty, then, Alf must be able to distinguish between his idiosyncratic (or private) reasons and public reasons. The former are reasons that flow from his values, ends, and plans; though they may well be central to Alf's way of living and his character, he must acknowledge that no matter how important they are to him, they are not in themselves reasons for Betty. Public reasons, in contrast, are considerations that are verified not only from Alf's perspective but from Betty's as well. Without going into the matter in depth here, it seems as if public reasons are of two general types.[18] (1) Alf may argue that some rule or arrangement is of mutual benefit, or promotes the values of each. In this case, Alf justifies the rule to Betty, not on the grounds that it promotes his values, but, crucially, on the grounds that it promotes hers too.[19] (2) Alternatively, Alf may take a more Rawlsian tack and try to show that Betty and he share "certain fundamental intuitive ideas," and that on the basis of this "fund of shared ideas," they both have reason to embrace certain principles.[20]

## 2.2. Is Impartiality Possible?

Liberal citizens thus need to develop a theory of impartiality, allowing them to distinguish idiosyncratic from public reasons, and they must refrain from appealing to the idiosyncratic in their public justifications. And this despite the fact that the private or idiosyncratic reasons may, in their own lives, be far more salient. In his discussion of the place of religious convictions in politics, Kent Greenawalt maintains that such compartmentalization is an unattractive as it is impossible:

> To demand that many devout Catholics, Protestants, and Jews pluck out their religious convictions is to ask them how they would think about a critical moral problem if they had to start from scratch, disregarding what they presently take as basic premises of moral thought. Asking that people perform this exercise is not only unrealistic in the sense of the impossible; the implicit demand that people try to compartmentalize beliefs that constitute some kind of unity in their approach to life is positively objectionable.[21]

Greenawalt concludes "that the threads of publicly accessible reasons cannot be disentangled from religious convictions and personal bases of judgment, and that strenuous efforts to make the separation would carry psychological costs and impair people's sense of individual unity."[22]

Now I certainly do not wish to deny that many find such impartiality unattractive and so do not seek it, but in itself that only shows that many are illiberal. The deeper question is whether "compartmentalizing" one's beliefs, and recognizing that some of them (which are important to one) properly do not sway others, is as "psychologically taxing" as Greenawalt would have us believe. Two considerations suggest that, far from being impossible, such compartmentalization is common and even necessary. (1) Considerations of computational complexity indicate that compartmentalizing our beliefs is necessary to avoid computational paralysis. Because of the tremendous calculation costs involved, "an agent could never attempt to make an inference from . . . his entire belief set, or even a large portion of it."[23] Consequently, we render computational problems tractable by compartmentalizing beliefs and so ignoring "relevant" beliefs outside the compartments being operated on. To be sure, this says nothing about whether people can compartmentalize religious from moral beliefs; but it does indicate that general appeals to the "unity of personality" and the dangers of "compartmentalization" are insufficient.

(2) At this point the critic may retreat to a more specific claim: when deliberating about moral matters, people cannot abstract from considerations that are important to them; that is, in such contexts they cannot recognize that their cherished concerns do not have universal validity. But this too is, at best, greatly overgeneralized. Considerable evidence indicates that what Piaget called "decentering" is a normal human cognitive achievement.[24] Whereas the child is egocentric and so "mixes up subjective and objective facts," equating his perspective with a universally valid one (and develops universalistic proposals based on it), as a person develops through adolescence, he comes to appreciate the difference between his perspective and others', and so develops objectivity.[25] Again, while this says

nothing specifically about religious beliefs, it does indicate that distinguishing personal and important beliefs from those that can be validated from the perspectives of others is within the grasp of normal adults.

## 2.3. Defeated and Victorious Justifications

I think it reasonable to suppose that a normal adult can develop a theory of impartiality or objectivity that allows him to distinguish his personal or idiosyncratic reasons from his public reasons. The latter are to provide the basis of his public justifications of demands on others. Suppose that on the basis of his theory of impartiality, Alf offers a public justification (*p*) to Betty that she must redistribute some of her holdings to Charlie. As is fairly likely, suppose that Betty resists; she believes that Alf has erred. To support her claim she might advance several different challenges.

(1) First, she may contest Alf's theory of impartiality: what he calls a public reason, she charges, actually stems from his private concerns. The line between personal and public reasons is not clear and bright for all to see; we can and do disagree. Some claim that this shows impartiality cannot be achieved,[26] but this is surely wrong. A valid claim that *R* is a public reason is not necessarily uncontroversial or certain. Objectivity, certainty, and consensus are all distinct notions, and we must resist the Cartesian temptation to equate them. That we all accept that *R* is an impartial reason is neither necessary nor sufficient for its impartiality. We all can be mistaken in thinking a consideration to be a public reason (since any person can be mistaken about what reasons he has); and so too I may be entirely correct that *R* is a public reason despite your dissent. To be sure, disputes about the correct account of impartiality pose difficulties for liberal theory (and resolving such disputes will occupy us presently), but disputes about the demands of impartiality do not show that impartiality is a chimera. (2) Secondly, Betty may argue that Alf's purported reason just isn't a reason at all, as it is based on false beliefs, a misinterpretation of her values, etc. (3) Lastly, Betty may acknowledge that Alf has advanced a genuine public reason in support of redistribution, but she may

advance a counterreason, which she insists is stronger, against redistribution.[27]

What is Alf to do in the face of these challenges?[28] As I have said, the easy and automatic response—that Betty's dissent ipso facto shows that his public justification is not valid—won't do, for consensus is neither necessary nor sufficient for a valid public justification.[29] As a citizen committed to advancing public justifications, Alf ultimately has no choice but to evaluate the cogency of Betty's challenges. Even if he seeks to rely on the judgment of a third party whom he believes has superior wisdom, this still could only be justified if Alf has grounds for believing that the third party was better able to evaluate the cogency of Betty's challenges; and that means that Alf's response to Betty would ultimately be based on his conclusion about the merits of her challenge. In the end, Alf cannot help but rely on his own cognitive resources in deciding what constitutes a valid public justification. After all, what *other* resources *could* he rely on to make a judgment?

One judgment Alf might make is that Betty has *defeated* his proposed justification. Let us say that, characteristically, Alf's justification $p$ is defeated by Betty's response $q$ if

a. $p$ and $q$ are directly competing; $p$ and $q$ are directly competing for Alf if, given Alf's other beliefs, Alf's accepting $q$ rationally undermines his belief that $p$.[30]
b. Given Alf's beliefs, Betty's shows (1) that he has adequate reason to accept $q$ and (2) he has better reason to accept $q$ than he has to accept $p$.

A word of explanation about this second clause: it does not require that Betty be correct.[31] The point, rather, is that the argument comprising $q$ is such that, given his system of beliefs, Alf has adequate reason to accept it, better reason to accept it than he does $p$, and that acceptance rationally undermines his acceptance of $p$. For instance, in the following case Betty's response does not meet (b):

*Betty Gets Lucky:* Alf argues that justice demands that the highest marginal tax rate should be 65 percent; that, he claims, would result in a political-economic order that works to the benefit of all citizens. Betty responds that this rate is far too high; after a top marginal rate of 25 percent, economic growth slows, unemployment increases, and the least well off are disadvantaged. Rawls told her so in a dream. It just so happens that Betty is right about the relation of marginal tax rates, growth, and the advantages to the least well off.

Even though she turns out to be correct, it is not more reasonable for Alf to embrace $q$ than $p$, as her case relies on a nonpublic consideration. Thus the requirement that Betty must *show* Alf that his accepting $q$ is reasonable. Nothing much changes if the basis for Betty's conclusion is an apparently reliable but mysterious ability to guess how tax rates will affect economic growth.[32] Public justification, we must remember, is constrained by the requirement that only reasons accessible to all rational agents can be employed; esoteric sources of information thus must be excluded.

The requirement that Betty "show" that it is more reasonable for Alf to embrace $q$ than $p$ is also meant to indicate that Betty's position is strongly justified. It seems manifest that moral beliefs can be justified to varying degrees;[33] we can distinguish arguments that provide some evidence for a proposition from those that are conclusive. This is not a matter of the simple probability that the proposition is true;[34] it is better described in terms of the metaphor of the strength of the reasons for accepting a proposition. The intuitive idea here is that to claim soundly to have rationally defeated a competing proposal we must provide a strong case that the other has reason to adopt our view and abandon his challenge. "[W]e must," as Jeffrey Reiman says, "be able to *show* that the other person is mistaken if he persists in his earlier decision about how to act. For that, we must be able to show that the principle invoked is somehow valid beyond reasonable doubt."[35]

The second possibility, of course, is that Alf may conclude that his justification is *victorious* over Betty's challenge. Let us call a justification victorious if it has been open to challenges for a significant period[36] and has defeated all of them. That is, $p$ is a victorious justification if, each time it has been confronted with a challenge, Alf has replied in such a way as to defeat the challenging claim—he shows all challengers that it is more reasonable for them to embrace $p$ than their competing position. Of course, the status of the claim that $p$ is a victorious justification is provisional; it may be defeated by future challenges. But that is only to say again that justification does not imply certainty.[37]

## 2.4. Undefeated Justifications and Minimal Rationality

Carl Wellman describes this justification game as a trial by combat, one that "is usually terminated by an admission of defeat or a proclamation of victory or both."[38] Indeed, epistemologists who adopt this general approach to justification typically maintain that defeat or victory are the only two options. If one does not meet (i.e., defeat) every challenge, it is often said, one must abandon one's claim.[39] It should be clear, however, that defeat and victory do not exhaust the possibilities; claims can be *undefeated but not victorious.* Alf's justification $p$ is undefeated if no challengers have shown that it is more reasonable for Alf to accept their challenge than to continue believing $p$; but for this to occur does not imply that Alf has shown any of them, much less all of them, that it is more reasonable for them to accept $p$ than continue holding to their challenges. As Bernard Williams argues, showing your own beliefs to be reasonable is not equivalent to showing competing beliefs to be unreasonable.[40]

The widespread resistance to this idea stems, I think, from what may be called the ideal of the comprehensively rational agent. According to this ideal, Alf's belief that $p$ is a fully rational belief only if it is based on full consideration of all the relevant evidence and all his well-grounded beliefs, all his premises are true, and his deliberations leading to $p$ are logically impeccable.[41] To be sure, it is acknowledged that actual agents usually can only approximate this ideal, but that is only to say that actual agents can seldom be fully rational. However, insofar as one has done one's best, and so has concluded that $p$, one then (on this idealized view) must conclude that belief that $\sim p$ is a less reasonable belief. This does not imply that one believes one's own deliberations to be infallible, but insofar as one has concluded that *p*, one has also ipso facto concluded that others manifest a defect of reason if they believe that ~*p* even after one has defended the virtues of *p*. If all this is so, then as long as one is convinced that one's belief that *p* is warranted, one must believe that all competing positions are less reasonable. Victory or defeat then seem the only possible outcomes of epistemological combat.

The ideal of comprehensive rationality understands information gathering and computational costs as excuses for falling short of the ideal, but not as the basic conditions of human cognition. Employing computational complexity considerations from computer science, Christopher Cherniak nicely demonstrates that ideal rationality is *so ideal* "that it cannot apply in an interesting way to actual human beings."[42] In place of the comprehensive ideal, Cherniak proposes a conception of the minimally rational agent; a minimally rational agent makes some, not all, sound inferences from his belief set and he responds to some, not all, inconsistencies.[43] Indeed, that is all any human can do, as searching a belief set for all possible inferences or checking it for all possible inconsistencies is hopelessly beyond the capacity of human cognitive resources. On the other hand, checking inferences and inconsistencies that are actually brought before us (into our active memory) is much less costly, which helps explain why responding to actual challenges rather than all possible ones is fundamental to justification.[44]

Now, as a first approximation, we might say that a minimally rational agent's beliefs are reasonable. But that clearly will not do. Say that Alf is a minimally rational agent, who makes some but not all the valid inferences from his belief set, and checks it for some but not all inconsistencies. Suppose that Alf systematically ignores counterevidence to his beliefs, ignores challenges presented to him, or refuses to revise his beliefs in the light of discovered inconsistencies. All these epistemic vices would lead us to question whether Alf's beliefs are reasonable. In addition to minimal rationality, then, we need to develop a list of minimal epistemic virtues,[45] which would include some devotion to evidence gathering, a disposition to alter beliefs in the face of evident inconsistencies, a disposition to believe what he sees as more justified over that which he sees as less justified, a disposition to respond to challenges with relevant replies, a disposition to abandon defeated beliefs, etc. Having developed such a view, we could then say that the beliefs of a minimally rational agent displaying the minimal epistemic virtues are characteristically reasonable.[46]

For present purposes at any rate, the specifics of such an account are not important.[47] The relevant point here is that characterizing reasonable belief in terms of the beliefs of minimally rational agents displaying the minimal epistemic virtues will certainly lead to different people holding inconsistent reasonable beliefs. That Alf, a minimally rational and virtuous agent, believes that $p$ will not be grounds for him to conclude that Betty's belief that $\sim p$ is ipso facto unreasonable. And that being the case, the confrontation between their beliefs may result in neither defeat nor victory but an epistemological standoff.

## 3. When Public Reasoning Is Inconclusive

### 3.1. Inconclusiveness Distinguished from Indeterminacy

Because our belief systems are so complex, and so many considerations are relevant to disputes about what is publicly justified, it is often impossible to defeat another's proposed justification and proclaim victory. To be sure, it is not always impossible to do so; we must be careful not to press the point too far. Despite their popularity, explicitly religious arguments are defeated. And there is good reason to think that liberal theory has had some important victories; principles of free speech and other civil rights, some rights of private property and some redistributive (i.e., welfare) rights are, I think, elements of a publicly justified conception of justice. Yet even these important victories point to the limits of public reason; as John Gray emphasizes, as soon as we move beyond these abstract principles to their application in specific cases, "indeterminacy" arises.[48] However, talk of "indeterminacy" can easily lead us astray. Because two roots of inconclusiveness are the complexity of our belief systems and our limited ability to process all the information at our disposal, it seems to me quite misguided to claim, as does Greenawalt, that in such cases public reasons "run out," and so must be supplemented by private reasons.[49] The problem is not that public reasoning is indeterminate in the sense that there are not enough reasons to yield a conclusion; the difficulty is that there are so many relevant reasons that all cannot be adequately canvassed and weighed.

It is because our moral disputes are not typically indeterminate that it makes sense to form opinions and keep arguing about them. If the totality of reasons is really insufficient to form a conclusion, forming *any* opinion is unreasonable. If the only way to get enough reasons to form an opinion is to rely on essentially private reasons, arguing with others is generally pointless, for we know that many others, though reasonable, simply do not share these private reasons. And even if we do form our opinions on such private reasons, to impose a morality based on them is to abandon the liberal commitment to public justification. Moral debate among liberal citizens makes sense because we can and do form opinions on the basis of public reasons; it is so inconclusive because so many considerations are relevant either directly or because problems about which of two reasons is "weightier" can only be discussed by appealing to yet other, background, considerations, thus reintroducing problems of complexity.

Consider, for instance, disputes about the protection of animals. Greenawalt would have us believe that publicly accessible reasons simply are not enough to tell us what to do;[50] it is as if one who restricted himself to public reasons would be, quite literally, speechless on this issue. Greenawalt leads us to this conclusion, though, by examining the differing, but very definite and not at all uncertain, views of such philosophers as Peter Singer and Tom Regan. Now assuming that neither has achieved victory on this issue, there are two possibilities: (1) since the relevant public reasons are not sufficient to ground a conclusion, Singer and Regan can only come to their conclusions by relying on essentially private considerations, or (2) they arrive at their conclusions by relying on publicly accessible reasons, but because questions of the nature of agency, consciousness, and moral rights are so complex, they defend different positions neither of which defeats the other. Our minimalist account of reasonable belief harmonizes with the latter. Differences of opinion on such matters are apt to result from the abundance of relevant public reasons and our inability to process all of them rather than the paucity of such reasons. Moreover, the second option has the advantage over the first of making sense of the ongoing public debate on such problems.

### 3.2. Epistemological Standoff, the State of Nature, and Adjudication

Philosophers can keep arguing and publishing about these unresolved issues—indeed, *these* are just the issues that philosophers typically *do* argue and write about. However, as citizens we are in a different position. Whether animals are to be protected or income redistributed are pressing matters of practice, not just material for philosophical reflection. If, as seems likely, most of our moral disputes result in epistemological standoffs (but see section 5), what are liberal citizens committed to public justification to do right here and now?[51] If Alf has an undefeated reasonable belief that Betty's wealth should be redistributed to Charlie, but he acknowledges that he has not defeated her challenges, what should he do? He has three options: wait for victory, make moral demands based on his reasonable belief, or appeal to an umpire.

*Waiting for Victory (or Defeat).* On the face of it, there is much to be said for waiting until his view is victorious (or has been defeated). He is, after all, committed to public justification, and in a fairly obvious sense he has yet to justify his view to Betty; he has not yet shown that she has reason to adopt his view and abandon her competing position. So imposition of his view on her would seem unjustified. Moreover, it is widely argued that liberalism is based on a presumption in favor of liberty: the burden of proof, it is said, is on those who would limit the liberty of others.[52] If so, then the burden of proof would appear to lay squarely on Alf, as his moral demands aim to restrict Betty's liberty. Until his public justification of restraints is shown to be victorious, it would seem that he is committed to noninterference. Supposing that outright victory is rare, the upshot would be a regime of minimal restraints, or perhaps even some version of anarchism according to which we simply "agree to differ."[53]

Whatever attractions this option possesses depend on the twofold supposition that the specific requirements of the right to liberty can be victoriously justified and that the right to liberty is expansive enough to cover rights to bodily integrity and property. This supposition cannot be maintained. It is not at all obvious that Alf's proposal to redistribute Betty's holdings is an interference with her liberty; Rawlsians, as we all know, would insist that property rights are not generally liberty rights.[54] Betty cannot claim, then, that in the absence of a victorious justification for redistribution she has a publicly justified right to her holdings, for her right to those holdings is apt to be just as rationally contestable as is Alf's redistributive claim.[55] Indeed, quintessential liberty rights themselves are subject to reasonable dispute. As Alexander Bickel remarked about "majestic concepts" such as freedom of speech, "men may in full and equal reason and good faith hold differing views about . . . [their] proper meaning and specific application."[56] It seems that the actual consequence of waiting for victorious justifications would be a social life in which few specific moral demands could be made. At best, all that could be justified is some general right to non-interference; and if we insist that no reasonable but contentious judgments can be imposed on others, the contentiousness of concepts such as interference, coercion, and indeed freedom itself ensures that very little, if any, content could be given to this general right to non-interference. The resulting social life would approach Hobbes's state of nature, in which we can thwart or aid each other, but are unable to make any claims on each other as a matter of right.

*Imposition of One's Judgment.* Waiting for victorious justification, then, would commit us to an essentially de-moralized social life, a condition that I have elsewhere argued is simply not open to us, as we now are.[57] The alternative would seem to be to rely on one's best judgment about what is publicly justified, and take that as determining what moral demands one can make on others. For Kant, relying on one's individual judgment characterizes the state of nature:

> Although experience teaches us that men live in violence and are prone to fight one another before the advent of external compulsive legislation, it is not experience that makes public lawful coercion necessary. The necessity of public lawful coercion does not rest on a fact, but on an a priori Idea of reason, for, even if we imagine men to be ever so good natured and righteous before a public lawful state of society is established, individual men, nations and states can never be certain they are secure against violence from one another, because each will have the right to do what *seems just and good to him,* entirely independently of the opinion of others.[58]

Kant goes on to insist that justice is absent in the state of nature because each relies on his own judgment, and thus "when there is a controversy concerning rights *(jus controversum),* no competent judge can be found to render a decision having the force of law."[59] Indeed, Hobbes, Locke, and Kant all maintain that the chief inconveniences of the state of nature arise from individuals relying on their individual, controversial, judgments about natural rights and natural law.[60] The chief inconveniences are two, one moral and one practical.

The moral flaw of the state of nature ruled by individual judgment is that we act without justification. As I have already argued, to impose an undefeated but unvictorious public justification on another fails to meet the demands of public justification. To have satisfied yourself that your demands are justified is far short of showing others that your demands are justified. If public justification is the moral loadstar of liberalism, and reflects a commitment to respect for persons,[61] relying on one's individual judgment in this way manifests disrespect and is unjust. Jeffrey Reiman persuasively argues that imposing such inadequately justified principles on another is an act of *subjection:* one is supplanting the other's own judgment about what the other should do, and replacing it with one's (merely personal) judgment about what the other should do.[62]

Leaving aside its moral shortcomings, a state of nature (i.e., a regime in which people all rely on their undefeated but unvictorious judgments) would be characterized by uncertainty and conflict, undermining the basis for cooperation. Inconsistent interpretations of each other's rights and responsibilities would lead to conflict and thwart the development of settled expectations. This, of course, is a familiar theme in liberal, and especially contractualist, political philosophy: Hobbes's, Locke's, and Kant's accounts of the state of nature all aim to establish variations of it. Although on some matters we can agree to differ, disputes engendered by competing judgments will block common action and, as R. E. Ewin points out, this includes "common recognition of the limitations on individual or private action."[63]

*Appeal to an Umpire.* Relying on our undefeated but unvictorious judgments thus would lead to injustice and conflict. For Kant, if one "does not wish to renounce all concepts of justice," one must "quit the state of nature, in which everyone follows his own judgments," and subject oneself to "public lawful external coercion."[64] Hobbes, Locke, and Kant concur that an umpire or judge is required to make public determinations of our rights and duties. Says Hobbes:

> And because, though men be never [sic] so willing to observe these laws [of nature], there may nevertheless arise questions concerning a man's actions; first, whether it were done, or not done; secondly, if done, whether against the law or not against the law; the former whereof, is called a question *of fact;* the latter a question of *right,* therefore unless the parties to the question, covenant mutually to stand to the sentence of another, they are as far from peace as ever. This other to whose sentence they submit is called an ARBITRATOR. And therefore it is of the law of nature, *that they that are at controversy, submit their right to the judgment of an arbitrator.*[65]

The social contract theories of Hobbes, Locke, and Kant, first and foremost, are justifications of an "arbitrator" (Hobbes), "umpire" (Locke), or "judge" (Kant) whose task is to provide public, definitive resolutions of conflicting judgments. Moreover, although we typically conceive of social contract theory as justifying "government," Locke's phrase is far more accurate and revealing: to escape the state of nature, in which each relies on his own moral judgments, we require rule by an "Umpire, by settled standing Rules, indifferent, and the same to all Parties."[66] That is, umpiring through law. For all three philosophers, the law is the definitive voice of public reason as articulated by the umpire. "Civil Law," said Hobbes, "is to every subject, those rules, which the commonwealth hath commanded him, by word, writing, or other sufficient sign of the will, to make use of, for the distinction of right, and wrong."[67]

My claim, and I think that of traditional social contract theory, is that because individual moral judgments are inconclusive and hence highly contentious, both practical and moral reasons justify an umpire, who, through law, provides definitive public resolutions of disputes. Two arguments are needed to defend this claim. Firstly, it has to be shown that some specific umpiring procedure can be victoriously justified. Unless this can be achieved, disputes about the publicly justified umpiring procedure will be substituted for disputes about justice. This is the main concern of social contract theory; I shall not discuss this crucial problem here.[68] Secondly, though, it needs to be shown why an umpiring *through law* is required to solve the problems of the state of nature. That is, leaving aside the question of which specific umpiring method we should employ (i.e., what form of government is justified), why does the analysis of conflicts in the state of nature indicate that the set of justifiable umpiring procedures must be restricted to those that rule through law? It is to this question that I now turn.

## 4. UMPIRING THROUGH AND BY LAW

### 4.1. The Internal Morality of the Law: The Demands of Practice

To grasp the practical problems engendered by the clash of inconclusive individual judgments, imagine individuals who are only concerned with the moral-epistemological problem. That is, suppose everyone has one and only one aim: to get the best possible answer to each moral dispute. Such relentlessly philosophical agents would *not* be concerned that laws be settled, *if* this means that the umpire continues to uphold older, marginally worse judgments rather than adopt newer, marginally better, public judgments. Call *LM* the ideal liberal morality, $lm_i$ any particular set of judgments (laws) that seek to track *LM*. Purely epistemologically motivated individuals absolutely prefer $lm_1$ to $lm_2$ if $lm_1$ more closely approximates *LM* than does $lm_2$.[69] If each change from $lm_i$ to $lm_i + _1$ moved the law closer to the most justified liberal policy (as far as this could be discerned), they would not agree that "[a] law that changes everyday is worse than no law at all."[70] To be sure, if stability was itself a desideratum of *LM*, then at some point the change from $lm_i$ to $lm_i + _1$ would lead away from *LM*. But still, since purely epistemologically motivated agents have an absolute priority of enlightenment over stability (insofar as the latter is not included in the former), they would commend any change in the law that moved them closer to the ideal liberal morality. Neither would such agents have objections to retroactive laws that corrected previous mistakes if this moved them closer to *LM*. Better that than to let moral errors go uncorrected.[71] More generally, we can imagine such agents rejecting umpiring through general laws that are simple and clear enough for all to follow. As I have stressed, moral disputes are complex; perhaps only a wise judge ruling on a case-by-case basis could possibly come close to what is most justified. Of course, if agents were really purely concerned with the epistemological dispute, they would not seek an umpire at all, but the opinions of sages and philosophers.[72]

Shifting, particularistic judgments are not obviously inappropriate for purely epistemologically motivated agents. But we are not like that. Our interest in public justification is ultimately practical; we have lives to lead, and aspire to reason publicly to formulate principles regulating our dealings with each other. It is because each seeks morality as a framework for living a life that the components of Fuller's inner morality of law—stability, generality, publicity, simplicity, nonretroactivity, noncontradiction, etc.—are critical virtues. An umpire that gave shifting, particularistic, secret, overwhelmingly complex, and retroactive rulings simply would not solve the practical problems of the state of nature, no matter how wise it might be. Thus, in contrast to our purely epistemologically motivated agents, liberal citizens have reason to prefer laws that are further from the ideal liberal code, but better satisfy the demands of practice. In this sense, Fuller's theory of law coheres well with liberalism; for liberal contractualism the ideal of rule of law has a *telos*— fairly resolving conflicts and providing a framework for cooperation through decisions by an umpire—and so contains within it the criteria of its own perfection.[73]

That the *telos* is a *fair* resolution of disputes merits emphasis. A cardinal virtue of umpires is fairness or impartiality. One can be practically certain that in some cases the umpire will make decisions that, on one's own evaluation of the merits of the case, appear quite wrong. So it is a practical certainty that sometimes one will be instructed to $\phi$ on the basis of what one sees as flawed reasoning; moreover, in such cases, one's $\phi$-ing may benefit others (e.g., Betty may be instructed to redistribute some of her holdings to Charlie) at the cost of one's own interests. For adjudication to achieve its practical aim in such cases it must be manifest that the umpire is impartial. Thus Hobbes's eighteenth law of nature:

> [N]o man in any case ought to be received for arbitrator, to whom greater profit, or honour, or pleasure apparently ariseth out of the victory of one party, than the other: for he hath taken, though an unavoidable bribe, yet a bribe; and no man can be obliged to trust him. And thus also the controversy, and the condition of war remaineth, contrary to the law of nature.[74]

Hence the demand that laws be impartially applied to all citizens and be stated in general terms.

## 4.2. The External Morality of Law: The Specification of Moral Rights

Although the liberal theory of law puts great weight on the practical importance of legal rule, the ultimate task of the umpire is make public determinations of moral rights and duties. The umpire thus has a much more specific charge than simply offering general rules that allow coordination or secure peace. We have seen that there is an area of moral dispute in which undefeated public justifications confront each other, with none achieving victory. The umpire is to adjudicate *these* conflicts, and make public determinations of the rights of citizens. The rule of law on this Dworkinian view "is the ideal of rule by an accurate public conception of individual rights."[75] Note that Dworkin identifies the rule of law as rule by an *accurate* public conception of individual rights; rule by deeply flawed conceptions does not constitute rule by law. Locke thus properly stresses that the tyrant, ignoring the rights of citizens, does not act through law; regardless of the procedures employed, an umpire who tramples the rights of citizens cannot be said to rule though law.[76] The umpire, as I have argued, is to adjudicate competing undefeated but unvictorious proposals; it is *here* that we need an authority to render public determinations of our rights. However, if the umpire systematically ignores our publicly justified rights—those that *have been* victoriously justified— its rulings depart from the *telos* of law. Such an umpire seeks to "resolve" issues that have already been decided.[77]

If I am correct, then, for both the internal and external morality of law, liberal theory identifies a *telos* or purpose; proclamations by the umpire that fall far short of achieving their practical and moral purposes—and even more obviously those that run counter to those justifying purposes—thus fail *as law*. On this account, liberalism partakes of natural law theory, and so invites the standard positivistic criticism: namely, that it is a "piece of arbitrary verbal legislation" not to count some rules (e.g., unfollowable rules or tyrannical rules) as law "when they are normally counted as law."[78] This particular chestnut probably cannot be cracked here, but it shouldn't cause too much concern. Looking at any actual institution in terms of its justification, we can always say that an instance that fails to achieve its justifying purpose is defective; it constitutes a failed instance of that institution. And in a perfectly intelligible sense, an extremely defective case of $X$ is not an $X$ at all, as a car built with no wheels or engine is not really a car.[79] Of course, in some contexts, we also can intelligibly refer to such a car as a horrible car, which would imply that it is, after all, a car, albeit a lousy one. Precisely the same can be said of highly defective laws. Denying that, in light of their justifying purposes, they are really laws is no "mere piece of arbitrary verbal legislation," though its intelligibility is context dependent.

Liberal positivists will insist that such laws are perfectly genuine laws, though thoroughly unjust. And, as I have just acknowledged, in a sense they are; but then, again, in a sense they are not. Our concept of law is sufficiently complex to ensure that both locutions are sensible and informative. Much contemporary legal philosophy notwithstanding, this doesn't seem a ground much worth fighting over. It is worth emphasizing, however, that the positivist perspective obscures the connection between justice and law inherent in liberalism. It is not merely that justice is one admirable quality that good laws possess; rather, justice is the very purpose of law. Consequently, a law that does not secure justice fails to achieve its *telos* and in that sense does indeed fail as *law*.

### 4.3. On Umpires Being Ruled by Law

I have argued that both the internal and the external morality of law constrains what counts as law (in the sense of achieving the *telé* of legal rule). For the umpire—by which I mean government, and in republican and democratic theory, primarily the legislature[80]—to be ruled by law is for it to rule in accordance with these restraints. That the umpire is to be ruled *by* law thus follows from the ideal that it rule *through* law. The independence of the judiciary is critical to ensure that the umpire rules citizens through settled and general laws to which all—including state functionaries—are equally subjected. This was one of the great achievements of English law that Dicey praised:

> In England the idea of legal equality, or that of universal subjection of all classes to one law administered by the ordinary courts, has been pushed to its utmost limit. With us every official, from the Prime Minister down to the constable or a collector of taxes, is under the same legal responsibility for every act done without legal justification. The Reports abound with cases in which officials have been brought before the courts, and made, in their personal capacity, liable to punishment, or to payment of damages, for acts done in their official character but done in an unlawful manner.[81]

The principle of formal equality before the law is doubly important. Not only does it embody the ideal that state functionaries, like citizens, are subject to their own laws (and can only justifiably act through them), but it also manifests a commitment to public reason. The principle of formal equality before the law places an onus of justification on administrators, judges, and other state functionaries: citizens are to be treated equally unless relevant grounds can be demonstrated for unequal treatment.[82] This requires that the state advance public reasons for its treatment of citizens. Governments become arbitrary when their actions are based on the private or idiosyncratic concerns of officials; a government that makes no distinction between the private concerns of its officials and public reasons is the paradigm of rule by will (or men), not by law.[83] The principle of formal equality before the law thus articulates the liberal state's commitment to rule through public reasons only.

The critical role of an independent judiciary in impartially applying law to citizens and functionaries alike is, I think, fairly obvious. Much more problematic is the role of the judiciary in ensuring that the umpire abides by the external morality of law. Given that the umpire is only empowered to make determinations of rights within a restricted set of moral disputes, it undoubtedly follows that the umpire's authority to make law is limited. The social contract, specifying the purpose and limits of the umpire, is thus also a statement of fundamental law; the law that guides the umpire itself. Early American jurisprudence acknowledged this connection between fundamental law, the social contract, and (state) constitutionalism. Constitutions were understood as articulating the social contract, which was fundamental law.[84] In *Federalist 78* Hamilton was clear that he viewed the federal Constitution similarly. "A constitution is, in fact, and must be regarded by judges as, a fundamental law."[85] Constitutionalism, in the sense of a fundamental law that applies to the umpire (in this case, the legislature), is inherent in the liberal theory of law. Interestingly, however, there is no quick move from fundamental law and constitutionalism to the practice of judicial review of legislative acts. In her study of the development of judicial review in the United States, Sylvia Snowiss identifies three possibilities, corresponding to three phases in American judicial review.

(1) The first possibility, reflected in Blackstone's writings and

important in American legal thought up to *Federalist 78,* holds that while the existence of fundamental law clearly implies that the legislature is not *omnipotent,* the legislature may still be *supreme* in the sense that no body is entitled to enforce fundamental law against it. Fundamental law may be held to limit the legislature's authority by speaking to *it.* Insofar as the courts did undertake to review legislative enactments in this period, they were viewed as extraordinary political interventions, "a judicial substitute for revolution."[86]

(2) In the second phase identified by Snowiss, from *Federalist 78* to *Marbury v. Madison,* the courts regularized their role as enforcers of fundamental law, but judicial review was still understood as a political rather than a legal act. In overturning a legislative enactment the courts, on this view, were appealing directly to the fundamental law and the social contract, charging the legislature with a manifest violation of the terms of political association. The appeal in such review was not to a legalistic analysis of a written text, but to a "publicly verifiable" charge that the legislature had engaged in a "concededly unconstitutional act" violating fundamental law.[87]

(3) Lastly, Snowiss argues that under the influence of Justice Marshall the Supreme Court converted judicial review into a regular exercise of legal interpretation of a written text, relying for its authority on its status as definitive interpreter of written laws. All three theories recognize that legislatures are bound by fundamental law, and American judicial practice has in particular vacillated between proponents of versions of (2) and (3).[88] Compared to the ideas of the independence of the judiciary, fundamental law, and constitutionalism, the practice of judicial review thus appears less central to the ideal of rule by law; its justification depends on the claim that it is the preferred method to ensure that the legislature fulfills the moral and practical purposes inherent in the rule of law.[89] We certainly should reject the common view that somehow the courts, and especially the Supreme Court, are the primary forum for adjudicating the moral disputes of citizens—"translating principle into positive law"—while the legislature is the locus of expediency and clashing interests.[90] Madison is right: "Justice is the end of government."[91] And because the determination of rights

and the adjudication of moral disputes are primary functions of all government and not simply the judiciary, the courts are not the special interpreters of principle and determiners of rights.[92]

## 4.4. On Citizens Being Ruled by Law

The umpire, I have argued, is to adjudicate a certain set of moral disputes, that is, those in which competing undefeated public justifications confront each other. Call this set $\alpha$. Both practical and moral reasons impel liberal citizens committed to public justification to adjudicate these disputes. However, not all moral issues are included in $\alpha$; the basic principles of the liberal polity, I have been supposing, have been victoriously justified. The social contract, constitution, or fundamental law contains a specification of the basic freedoms or rights; as Locke argued, an umpire who acts contrary to these victoriously justified rights does not succeed in making law. We have seen what it means for the umpire to be ruled by law; what is it for citizens to be ruled by law?

The problem is clear. Restricting ourselves for the present to $\alpha$, no matter what the umpire decides, some reasonable citizens will be convinced that the decision is wrong. To be sure, this problem would not arise if liberal citizens regarded the umpire as a sage—an extremely reliable source of victorious justifications. If that were the case, when the wise umpire spoke, we would have reason not just to do as we were instructed but to *believe* what was said, for the umpire would be held to have superior access to the truth about liberalism. Such sages, though, simply are not publicly identifiable.[93] Happily, to accept Doris as an umpire does not require seeing her as a sage. Consider an umpire in a game such as baseball. The players require an umpire because they have an unresolved epistemological dispute that leads to a practical conflict (though they probably do not describe their problem in precisely that way). Alf believes that, given the facts and the rules, Charlie is safe; Betty believes that he is out. Now, while they expect Doris to take cognizance of the rules and the facts, accepting her as an umpire in no way requires that everyone believes that she has made the right decision. As we all know, on almost any controversial call—

those cases in which umpires are most needed—someone is almost certain to believe that the umpire is mistaken. That belief, though, does not in any way prevent the dissenter from accepting the umpire; to accept Doris as the umpire, Alf and Betty must do as she instructs—they must take her decision as resolving the practical dispute. They are not committed to accepting her judgment as resolving the underlying epistemological dispute.

To accept rule by an umpire, then, is to acknowledge that the umpire's decision that you should $\phi$ gives you a reason to $\phi$ even if you believe that $\phi$-ing is wrong. That is, although on your best evaluation of the merits of the case, $\sim\phi$ is the thing to do, if the umpire says that you should $\phi$, this gives you a reason to exclude acting on your own evaluation and do what the umpire says.[94] Unless one is prepared in this way to act contrary to one's own evaluation, one is not really submitting the dispute to arbitration. (Compare here a Little Leaguer who "abides" by the umpire's rulings only so long as the umpire agrees with the child. Otherwise, the child stomps off home.) And if one has a moral obligation to abide by the umpire's ruling, then one must have a moral obligation to obey the law, in the sense that one has a moral obligation to $\phi$ just because the law says to $\phi$ even though one thinks $\phi$-ing is wrong. Contrary to much current thought, it is therefore no "fetish" to accept that "illegality per se is a reason for doing what the law requires or not doing what it forbids."[95] Those who are not prepared to accept this are justly accused of the vice of arrogance—of insisting that their own unvictorious reasonable beliefs about morality are definitive.[96]

However, the liberal theory of law does lead us to reject one very strong interpretation of the moral obligation to obey the law, namely, that one has a moral obligation to obey *all* purported laws.[97] The obligation to obey the umpire holds only for disputes in $\alpha$. If a citizen judges that the umpire is making calls contrary to victorious justifications, the citizen must conclude that the umpire is seeking to enforce an unreasonable view, and is acting outside the bounds of the rule of law. It is here that Ewin's essentially Hobbesian account of the umpire goes astray. Though Ewin believes that the decisions of a procedurally unfair umpiring procedure do not bind citizens, he follows Hobbes in insisting on the inappropriateness of citizens making obedience contingent on their judgment of the substantive merits of the decision.[98] Perhaps this is so if we submit to an umpire solely because of practical problems that result from brute disagreement; in that case, *any* disagreement may be thought to be a matter for adjudication. On the more Lockean account I have defended here, however, our commitment to adjudication follows from our fundamental commitment to public justification. It is when Alf is unable to victoriously publicly justify his reasonable views about justice that he is led to arbitration; but he has no reason to submit his publicly justified principles to the umpire. He has (he believes) publicly justified them, so he cannot see how *his commitment to public justification* could give him a reason to submit them to an umpire; he has no conceptual resources that could allow him to recognize such a reason. Certainly the mere fact that others disagree cannot show that he has failed to justify his claims, any more than the dissents of creationists show that evolutionary biologists have failed to justify their views.

## 5. CONCLUSION: THE RULE OF LAW AND MORAL COMMUNITY

Although it leads to a much messier account, Locke, not Hobbes, is right: the moral obligation of citizens to obey the law depends on the substantive merits of the law. A citizen has no obligation to obey a law if the umpire is enacting defeated proposals.[99] Now no doubt many readers, whose patience have been taxed for a number of pages, will wish to insist that this overlooks the fundamental insight of Hobbes: a citizen at best *thinks* that a principle has been victoriously justified, while the umpire and other citizens obviously *think differently*. If Alf has judged that $p$ has been victoriously justified while Betty thinks that it is in $\alpha$ (the set of undefeated unvictorious proposals), doesn't this dispute need adjudication too? Aren't we back where we began?

Not from Alf's perspective, or from the perspective of any other liberal citizen. From any particular perspective, a citizen's commitment to public justification can lead him to submit to an umpire, but this very same reason will lead him to resist an umpire who, in his judgment, is seeking to impose defeated— publicly unjustified—proposals on him. Any citizen can and will distinguish what is fundamental and justified from what is reasonably disputed; that he will submit the latter to arbitration will not lead him also to submit the former. Indeed, for liberals to submit *all* moral disputes to the umpire is to allow that, if challenged by an illiberal citizen, fundamental liberal principles themselves might legitimately be overturned by the umpire.

The problem arises when Alf's judgments about what has been victoriously justified and what remains in $\alpha$ differ from Betty's. When that happens Alf and Betty disagree not simply on what is the correct outcome of political dispute; they also disagree on what should be on the political agenda. Liberal politics will be, at best, imperfect in a community so divided, for one or the other section will refuse to admit that a political resolution of some issue is morally legitimate. If the division is restricted to a small number of issues, perhaps devices such as gag rules will allow liberal politics to function by insulating it from those conflicts that cannot, from a practical point of view, be successfully adjudicated.[100] However, if the community is deeply divided in this way on a wide range of issues, the practical resolution of moral disputes through the rule of law will be precarious, for whatever the umpire decrees, some will declare that it is a violation of fundamental law.[101] In such a society the law may still usually be complied with, but most will see no obligation to obey, and a gnawing cynicism seems inevitable.

It would be happy indeed if we had access to a God's-eye perspective, which would once and for all tell us what is really and truly victoriously justified and what we merely think is justified. But no such perspective is to be had; each can only employ her own moral and cognitive resources to arrive at her own best judgments. We can, though, avoid the Scylla of supposing that it is moral to impose any reasonable conviction on others and the Charybdis of fleeing from ever standing up for our fundamental principles, compromising on every issue, or adjudicating every disagreement. Beyond these lies the liberal ideal of the rule of law.

## NOTES

1. A. V. Dicey, *Introduction to the Study of the Law of the Constitution,* 9th ed. (London: Macmillan, 1948), 188. See Geoffrey Marshall's discussion of the elements of the rule of law in his "Due Process in England," in J. Roland Pennock and John W. Chapman, eds., NOMOS XVIII: *Due Process* (New York: New York University Press, 1977), 69–88.

2. But cf. here E. C. S. Wade's introduction to Dicey's *Law of the Constitution,* xciii–xcix.

3. See Lon Fuller, *The Morality of Law,* rev. ed. (New Haven, CT: Yale University Press, 1964), ch. 2. See also John Rawls, *A Theory of Justice* (Cambridge, MA: Harvard University Press, 1971), §38.

4. Dicey, *Law of the Constitution,* 195ff, chs. 5–7. Dicey made a great deal of the distinction between Britain, where the constitution was founded *on* personal freedom (enforced through the common law) and those countries that protected freedom *through* a constitution.

5. Ronald Dworkin, "Political Judges and the Rule of Law," in his *A Matter of Principle* (Cambridge, MA: Harvard University Press, 1985), 9–32, at 11–12.

6. See J. R. Lucas, *The Principles of Politics* (Oxford: Clarendon, 1966), §25. This also relates to Madison's argument in *Federalist 47.* See Clinton Rossiter, ed., *The Federalist Papers* (New York: New American Library, 1961).

7. Hamilton, *Federalist 78.*

8. Roughly, at any rate. For Hobbes's view, see R. E. Ewin's excellent study, *Virtues and Rights: The Moral Philosophy of Thomas Hobbes* (Boulder, CO: Westview, 1991). For Kant, see *The Metaphysical Elements of Justice,* John Ladd, trans. (Indianapolis: Bobbs-Merrill, 1965), 139ff; and Kant's "On the Common Saying: 'This May Be True in Theory, but It Does Not Apply in Practice,' " in Hans Reiss, ed., *Kant's Political Writings* (Cambridge: Cambridge University Press, 1977), 61–92, at 79ff.

9. David Lyons, *Ethics and the Rule of Law* (Cambridge: Cambridge University Press, 1984), 208–9. See also A. John Simmons, *Moral Principles and Political Obligations* (Princeton, NJ: Princeton University Press, 1979). For a contemporary treatment running against the dominant view, see Hadley Arkes, *First Things: An Inquiry into the First Principles of Morals and Justice* (Princeton, NJ: Princeton University Press, 1986), esp. chs. 2, 9, 13.

10. See Leslie Green, *The Authority of the State* (Oxford: Clarendon, 1990), esp. chs. 8 and 9.

11. To be sure, it may be that they *are* simply a hodgepodge, which would be to say that the rule of law is not a coherent concept. I believe that we have reason to prefer accounts of basic practical concepts that show them to be coherent. I consider this issue in my *Value and Justification: The Foundations of Liberal Theory* (Cambridge: Cambridge University Press, 1990), 4–10.

12. See John Rawls, "The Idea of an Overlapping Consensus," *Oxford Journal of Legal Studies* 7 (1987): 1–25, at 18n.

13. Stephen Macedo, *Liberal Virtues: Citizenship, Virtue, and Community in Liberal Constitutionalism* (Oxford: Clarendon, 1991), 78.

14. I argue for this commitment more fully in my *Value and Justification*, ch. 6.

15. Kant quoted in Onora O'Neill, "The Public Use of Reason," in her *Constructions of Reason* (Cambridge: Cambridge University Press, 1989), 28–50, at 46.

16. Loren E. Lomasky, *Persons, Rights, and the Moral Community* (New York: Oxford University Press, 1987), 28.

17. Gilbert Harman, "Human Flourishing, Ethics, and Liberty," *Philosophy & Public Affairs* 12 (Fall 1983): 307–22, at 321.

18. For a more detailed account, see my "Public Justification and Democratic Adjudication," *Constitutional Political Economy* 2 (Fall 1991): 251–81, at 253–56.

19. David Gauthier's theory approximates this view. *Morals by Agreement* (Oxford: Clarendon, 1986). See also Lomasky, *Persons, Rights, and the Moral Community*, ch. 4.

20. Rawls, "The Idea of an Overlapping Consensus."

21. Kent Greenawalt, *Religious Convictions and Political Choice* (New York: Oxford University Press, 1988), 155.

22. Ibid., 176. Eric Mack essentially agrees with Greenawalt here, but charitably concedes that the position I endorse in the text is "not at all loony." "Liberalism, Neutralism, and Rights," in J. Roland Pennock and John W. Chapman, eds., NOMOS XXX: *Religion, Morality, and the Law* (New York: New York University Press, 1988), 46–70, at 57.

23. Christopher Cherniak, *Minimal Rationality* (Cambridge, MA: MIT Press, 1986), 91; see also 65ff.

24. For a survey, see Lawrence A. Kurdek, "Perspective Taking as the Cognitive Basis of Children's Moral Development: A Review of the Literature," *Merrill-Palmer Quarterly* 24 (January 1978): 3–28. See also Dennis Krebs and Janet Gillmore, "The Relationship among the First Stages of Cognitive Development, Role Taking Abilities, and Moral

Development," *Child Development* 53 (1982): 877–86; Lawrence Kohlberg argues that only those at the highest stage of moral development fully assume the viewpoint of others. See his "Justice as Reversibility: The Claim to Moral Adequacy of a Highest Stage of Moral Judgment," in his edited collection, *Essays on Moral Development.* Vol. 1, *The Philosophy of Moral Development* (New York: Harper & Row, 1981), ch. 5.

25. Bärbel Inhelder and Jean Piaget, "The Growth of Logical Thinking from Childhood to Adolescence," in Howard E. Gruber and J. Jacques Vonéche, eds., *The Essential Piaget* (London: Routledge & Kegan Paul, 1977), 403–44, at 440–41.

26. See Mack, "Liberalism, Neutralism, and Rights," 55–56. See also Marilyn Friedman, "The Impracticality of Impartiality," *Journal of Philosophy* 86 (1989): 645–56.

27. See Carl Wellman, *Challenge and Response: Justification in Ethics* (Carbondale and Edwardsville: Southern Illinois University Press, 1971), ch. 3.

28. Wellman is, I think, quite right that responding to specific challenges is fundamental to justification; considerations of computational complexity support this view. See ibid. See also Cherniak, *Minimal Rationality*, ch. 5.

29. Although in some ways this is an easy response, it also dooms the project of public justification in a community that is not solely populated by liberal agents. Macedo, I think, errs in putting too much weight on intersubjective agreement in his account of public justification. See, e.g., *Liberal Virtues*, 44ff, 69ff.

30. The idea of "rationally undermines" might be explicated as "it is less reasonable for Alf to accept $p$ on the assumption that $q$ is correct than on the assumption that $q$ is not." Cf. Keith Lehrer, *Theory of Knowledge* (Boulder, CO: Westview, 1990), 117.

31. That $q$ is correct is neither necessary nor sufficient for it to be justified. See George S. Pappas and Marshall Swain, Introduction to their edited collection, *Essays on Knowledge and Justification* (Ithaca: Cornell University Press, 1978), 11–40, at 13ff.

32. See here Lehrer, *Theory of Knowledge*, 162ff.

33. See David O. Brink, *Moral Realism and the Foundations of Ethics* (Cambridge: Cambridge University Press, 1989), 94–95. See also Douglas Odegard, "Can Justified Belief Be False?" *Canadian Journal of Philosophy* 6 (1976): 561–68.

34. See Lehrer, *Theory of Knowledge*, 127ff.

35. Jeffrey Reiman, *Justice and Modern Moral Philosophy* (New Haven, CT: Yale University Press, 1990), 1; emphasis added.

36. I shall not seek to expand on this condition here. The intuitive idea is that claims become increasingly justified as they turn back actual challenges; consequently, only claims that have been open to challenges (i.e., publicly formulated) can achieve a high level of justification. Cf. here Mill's comments on justified action in *On Liberty* in John Gray, ed., *On Liberty and Other Essays* (Oxford: Oxford University Press, 1991), 24–26 (ch. 2).

37. See Lehrer, *Theory of Knowledge*, 178ff.

38. Wellman, *Challenge and Response*, 98.

39. Ibid., 130–31. For rather different reasons, Lehrer also indicates that there are but two possibilities. *Theory of Knowledge*, 151ff.

40. Bernard Williams, *Ethics and the Limits of Philosophy* (London: Fontana Press/Collins, 1985), 85.

41. See here Kurt Baier, "Rationality, Reason, and the Good," in David Copp and David Zimmerman, eds., *Morality, Reason, and Truth: New Essays on the Foundations of Ethics* (Totowa, NJ: Rowman & Allenheld, 1984), 193–211.

42. Cherniak, *Minimal Rationality*, ch. 5. See also Stephen Stitch's *The Fragmentation of Reason* (Cambridge, MA: MIT Press, 1990). My view, however, departs from Stitch's; in the end, I am, alas, an epistemological chauvinist.

43. This is a simplification.

44. See Cherniak, *Minimal Rationality*, chs. 3, 5.

45. Alternatively, we might develop a list of epistemic defects from which the minimally rational agent must be free. See Stanley Benn, *A Theory of Freedom* (Cambridge: Cambridge University Press, 1988), 157–58.

46. My proposal differs from Cherniak's notion of normative rationality, though for both of us normative rationality is more demanding than minimal rationality. *Minimal Rationality*, 23–26. Note that I do not claim that minimally rational agents with minimum epistemic virtues always have reasonable beliefs; in some cases they may fail to display their virtues. What we can say is that if they display all their epistemic virtues, minimally rational agents have reasonable beliefs. I will not pursue this complication here.

47. If I understand him correctly, Stitch argues against the very idea of developing a conception of epistemic virtues; he would insist that this project could not be completed. *The Fragmentation of Reason*, e.g., 14. But cf. Richard Rorty, "Science as Solidarity," in his *Objectivity, Relativity, and Truth* (Cambridge: Cambridge University Press, 1991), 35–45, at 37.

48. John Gray, "Contractarian Method, Private Property, and the

Market Economy," in his *Liberalisms* (London: Routledge, 1989), 161–98, at 169ff, 186ff.

49. Greenawalt, *Religious Convictions and Political Choice*, 39ff, chs. 6–8.

50. Ibid., ch. 6.

51. Cf. Jeffrey Reiman's argument that substantive and determinate principles can be justified beyond a reasonable doubt. *Justice and Modern Moral Philosophy*. My argument supposes that Reiman's project fails, though obviously I cannot *show* that here.

52. See, e.g., Benn, *A Theory of Freedom*, chs. 5–6; Joel Feinberg, *Harm to Others* (New York: Oxford University Press, 1984), 6ff; Gaus, *Value and Justification*, 381ff.

53. Jeremy Shearmur, "Epistemological Limits of the State: Reflections on Popper's *Open Society*," *Political Studies* 38 (1990): 116–25, at 124.

54. And I believe that they are correct. See my "Property, Rights, and Liberty," *Social Philosophy & Policy* 11 (Summer 1994).

55. One might be tempted to argue that the act of taking hold of Betty's property must be seen as interfering with her liberty; this is to confuse property rights with mere possession. See my "Contractual Justification of Redistributive Capitalism," in John W. Chapman and J. Roland Pennock, eds., NOMOS XXXI: *Markets and Justice* (New York: New York University Press, 1989), 89–122, at 101–2.

56. Alexander Bickel, *The Least Dangerous Branch: The Supreme Court at the Bar of Politics*, 2d ed. (New Haven, CT: Yale University Press, 1986), 36–37. As Macedo observes, "The contours of every one of our most basic liberties remains a matter of lively disagreement." *Liberal Virtues*, 57.

57. See *Value and Justification*, 278–300.

58. Kant, *Metaphysical Elements of Justice*, §44 (p. 76).

59. Ibid.

60. For Hobbes, see Ewin, *Virtues and Rights*, 27, 43–44, 67, 125–26, 196–205; for Locke, see *The Second Treatise of Government* in *Two Treatises of Government*, Peter Laslett, ed. (Cambridge: Cambridge University Press, 1960), §§13, 87–89, 123–131.

61. See my "Does Compensation Restore Equality?" in John W. Chapman, ed., NOMOS XXXIII: *Compensatory Justice* (New York: New York University Press, 1991), 45–81, at 67ff. See also Macedo, *Liberal Virtues*, 67.

62. Reiman, *Justice and Modern Moral Philosophy*, ch. 1. "[S]ubjection is a general evil against which everyone is to be protected." Ibid., 71.

Cf. R. E. Ewin, *Liberty, Community, and Justice* (Totowa, NJ: Rowman & Littlefield, 1987), 39, 108.

63. Ewin, *Virtues and Rights*, 32. The main theme of Ewin's work is the necessity of abandoning reliance on "private" judgment to achieve cooperation. See also his *Liberty, Community, and Justice*.

64. Kant, *Metaphysical Elements of Justice*, §44.

65. Thomas Hobbes, *Leviathan*, Michael Oakeshott, ed. (Oxford: Blackwell, 1946), 102 (Ch. 15). See Ewin, *Virtues and Rights*, 34.

66. Locke, *Second Treatise*, §87.

67. Hobbes, *Leviathan*, 173 (ch. 26). See Ewin, *Virtues and Rights*, 32, 67.

68. It is the topic of "Public Justification and Democratic Adjudication," in which I argue that a democratic umpiring procedure is victoriously justified.

69. I ignore here two crucial problems. (1) What if $lm_1$ better tracks $LM$ than does $lm_2$, but $lm_1$ is a sort of evolutionary deadend; i.e., it is impossible to develop it in a way that gets any closer to $LM$, whereas $lm_2$ is rich in possibilities for such development? (2) More generally, how can we determine whether a theory tracks a goal that cannot be stated in advance? Cf. here T. H. Green, *Prolegomena to Ethics*, A. C. Bradley, ed. (Oxford: Clarendon, 1890), §353.

70. Fuller, *The Morality of Law*, 37.

71. Again, if the prohibition of retroactive laws is a part of *LM*, then epistemologically motivated agents would, of course, resist such laws.

72. This relates to the distinction between being "an authority" (i.e., an expert) and being "in authority." See Richard B. Friedman, "On the Concept of Authority in Political Philosophy," in Richard E. Flathman, ed., *Concepts in Social and Political Philosophy* (New York: Macmillan, 1973), 121–46; Green, *The Authority of the State*, 26–29.

73. See Fuller, *The Morality of Law*, chs. 3, 4.

74. Hobbes, *Leviathan*, 102 (ch. 15).

75. Dworkin, "Political Judges and the Rule of Law," 12.

76. Locke, *Second Treatise*, §§199–202.

77. This points to a contrast between Locke's genuinely liberal view and Hobbes's. In contrast to Locke, Hobbes wants to leave behind questions about what is right and focus purely on the practical matter of, "What are we to do?" Given that Hobbes wishes to focus exclusively on the practical problems engendered by reliance on individual judgment, he does his best to avoid any substantive limits on what the umpire can legally accomplish. The sovereign's task is simply to resolve any and all disputes between individuals, and thus in a sense he cannot

go beyond his charge. For even if all the citizens disagree with the umpire, there is still the clash between his judgment and theirs, which he resolves in his own favor. See Ewin, *Virtues and Rights,* 38.

78. See Lyons, *Ethics and the Rule of Law,* 76.

79. What, though, if it is only a wee bit defective—isn't it then still a car? Positivist friends have pressed this upon me as an obviously decisive point. I confess being unmoved by it; though the sets "defective cases of *X,* but still good enough to be genuine *X*'s" and "pseudocases of *X* so defective as to not count as *X*'s at all" have fuzzy boundaries, they are nevertheless distinct.

80. I defend this view of adjudication in "Public Justification and Democratic Adjudication."

81. Dicey, *Law of the Constitution,* 193. Cf. F. A. Hayek, *The Constitution of Liberty* (London: Routledge, 1960), ch. 14. Compare also Dicey's concerns about administrative law to Hayek's comments in *The Constitution of Liberty,* ch. 13. See also Alice Erh-Soon Tay and Eugene Kamenka, "Public Law—Private Law," in S. I. Benn and G. F. Gaus, eds., *Public and Private in Social Life* (New York: St. Martin's 1983), 67–92; Paul Finn, "Public Function—Private Action: A Common Law Dilemma," in Benn and Gaus, *Public and Private in Social Life,* 93–111.

82. I have considered this principle in more depth in "Does Compensation Restore Equality?" 48–54.

83. Because Hobbes only recognizes a clash of private judgments, his proposal that the sovereign's judgments determine law is ultimately a form of the rule of man—the sovereign. See Ewin, *Virtues and Rights,* 163. Locke explicitly denies that the "magistrate" has any right to impose laws that reflect merely his private views. *A Letter Concerning Toleration* (Indianapolis: Bobbs-Merrill, 1955), 49.

84. Sylvia Snowiss, *Judicial Review and the Law of the Constitution* (New Haven, CT: Yale University Press, 1990), 29.

85. Hamilton, *Federalist 78,* 467.

86. Snowiss, *Judicial Review and the Law of the Constitution,* 2.

87. Ibid., 50ff.

88. A famous latter-day proponent of the second position is James B. Thayer, "The Origins and Scope of the American Doctrine of Constitutional Law," *Harvard Law Review* 7 (October 1893): 129–56.

89. What Stephen Macedo calls "principled judicial activism" is thus, at best, contingently part of the liberal conception of the rule of law. It nevertheless may be justified and important, but it is not a fundamental dispute of principle between liberalism and other (e.g., "New Right") political theories. Cf. Macedo's *The New Right versus the Constitution* (Washington, DC: Cato Institute, 1987).

90. Bickel, *The Least Dangerous Branch*, 24–26, 40, 188ff. See also Bruce A. Ackerman, "Neo-federalism?" in Jon Elster and Rune Slagstad, eds., *Constitutionalism and Democracy* (Cambridge: Cambridge University Press, 1988), 153–93.

91. *Federalist 51*, 324.

92. "[W]hat are many of the most important acts of legislation but so many judicial determinations, not indeed concerning the rights of single persons, but concerning the rights of large bodies of citizens?" Madison, *Federalist 10*, 79. Note, though, that Madison says this in the context of explaining the rise of factions in the legislature. Cf. Macedo, *Liberal Virtues*, 127ff.

93. As I have argued in "Public Justification and Democratic Adjudication."

94. This is to say (roughly) that the umpire is in authority, providing citizens with second-order exclusionary reasons to act. See Joseph Raz, *Practical Reason and Norms* (London: Hutchinson, 1975), esp. 35–48; Green, *The Authority of the State*, ch. 2.

95. For the charge of "fetishism" see Michael J. Perry, *Morality, Politics, and the Law* (New York: Oxford University Press, 1988), 110.

96. Ewin, *Liberty, Community, and Justice*, 42–43. This also suggests that the place of the ideal of autonomy in liberal theory is rather more complex than is usually thought.

97. See Perry, *Morality, Politics, and Law*, 110; Green, *The Authority of the State*, 228ff.

98. Ewin, *Liberty, Community, and Justice*, 113–14. See also his *Virtues and Rights*, 32, 49–50, ch. 8.

99. Cf. Ewin, *Virtues and Rights*, 166. Of course, citizen Alf may well conclude that for reasons such as civility, keeping the peace, or upholding a nearly just institution, he will comply even though he is not morally obligated.

100. For a fascinating analysis, see Stephen Holmes, "Gag Rules or the Politics of Omission," in Elster and Slagstad, eds., *Constitutionalism and Democracy* (Cambridge: Cambridge University Press, 1988), 19–58.

101. Needless to say, many involved in the dispute over abortion rights perceive the conflict in precisely this way. This strikes me as quite wrong.

# INDEX